WITHDRAWN

Brownsville, Brooklyn

HISTORICAL STUDIES OF URBAN AMERICA

Edited by Kathleen Conzen, Timothy Gilfoyle, and James Grossman

Also in the series:

Brownsville, Brooklyn

Blacks, Jews, and the Changing
Face of the Ghetto

Wendell Pritchett

The University of Chicago Press
Chicago and London

The University of Chicago Press, Chicago 60637
The University of Chicago Press, Ltd., London
© 2002 by The University of Chicago
All rights reserved. Published 2002
Printed in the United States of America

11 10 09 08 07 06 05 04 03 02   1 2 3 4 5
ISBN: 0-226-68446-6 (cloth)

Library of Congress Cataloging-in-Publication Data
Pritchett, Wendell E.
    Brownsville, Brooklyn : Blacks, Jews, and the changing face
of the ghetto / Wendell Pritchett.
    p. cm.— (Historical studies of urban America)
    Includes bibliographical references and index.
    ISBN 0-226-68446-6 (cloth : alk. paper)
    1. Brownsville (New York, N.Y.)—Race relations. 2.
Brownsville (New York, N.Y.)—Social conditions. 3. New
York (N.Y.)—Race relations. 4. New York (N.Y.)—Social
conditions. 5. Minorities—New York (State)—New York—
Social conditions. 6. Inner cities—New York (State)—New
York—History. 7. Community organization—New York
(State)—New York—History. 8. African Americans—New
York (State)—New York—Social conditions. 9. Jews—New
York (State)—New York—Social conditions. 10. Public
housing—New York (State)—New York—History.
I. Series.

F129.B7 P75 2002
306'.09747'23—dc21
                                                    2001001399

Contents

Illustrations

Acknowledgments

This book is dedicated to my parents, Wendell and Carolyn Pritchett, who have provided me more love and support than any child could ever desire. They are models for me in their high standards of intellectual rigor and social commitment. As educators, they have had a positive influence on thousands of people, and I am awestruck by their contributions to society and to our family. My "other parents," Jerry and Mary Kringel, have seen this project from beginning to end, and they too have been wonderfully supportive. I am grateful to them.

This study began as a doctoral dissertation at the University of Pennsylvania, where I was fortunate to have Walter Licht as my adviser. Walter is a first-rate scholar whose dedication to retrieving the past of America's working class motivated me to tell this story.

I am proud to be a part of the Historical Studies of Urban America series. Series editor Tim Gilfoyle pushed me to critically analyze every argument and assumption upon which my dissertation was based. This is a much better book because of his involvement. Robert Devens and Doug Mitchell of the University of Chicago Press have made the editorial process productive and enjoyable.

My research was aided by several archivists and librarians, and I am grateful to them all. I would like to thank two in particular: Ken Cobb of the New York City Municipal Archives, and Judy Walsh of the Brooklyn Collection of the Brooklyn Public Library. Ken and Judy both run vibrant institutions dedicated to preserving New York's past and providing support to those of us interested in studying the city. Their devotion to public history is unmatched, and they are under-appreciated treasures to the city.

Several former and current Brownsville residents kindly shared with me their personal histories and thoughts on the neighborhood. This book would not have been possible without their insights. Irving Levine and Paul Chandler, two former Brownsville residents, spent countless hours discussing Brownsville with me and connecting me to other useful informants, and I thank them.

During my research, I was fortunate to meet filmmaker Richard Broadman, who was making a documentary on Brownsville. My collaboration with him was extremely productive, and the film, *Brownsville Black and White*, is something that I am very proud of. Richard passed away much too young, and I am saddened he will not get to see the book that he played such an important role in producing.

Several colleagues helped me think through different aspects of this project, and I want to thank all those who read and commented on parts of this book: Adina Back, Martha Biondi, Tom Jackson, Michael Katz, John Mollenkopf, Joel Schwartz, and Clarence Taylor. Steve Conn has been a wonderful friend since our graduate school days. I thank him for his sharp insights and constant support.

During the five years of this project, I was sustained by my New York "family": Paula Pritchett, Karen Kringel, Lisa Kringel, Jeff Hoeh (who also took many wonderful pictures for the book), Mark Lien, Judd and Debbie Harner, and Pam Bierman. All of them made my research trips enjoyable even when the archives were unproductive. Special thanks to Rob Halpern, my friend of more than thirty years, who always had a couch for me to sleep on.

At Baruch College, I have found an atmosphere that combines scholarly pursuit with a commitment to public education. I am thankful to all my colleagues, but I am especially grateful to Carol Berkin, Jane Bond, and Myrna Chase for the overwhelming support they have given me. Fred Liebowitz provided research assistance and an energetic interest in this project. My research was assisted by two grants from the Professional Staff Congress–City University of New York Research Foundation. An earlier version of chapter 6 appeared in the journal *Labor's Heritage*. Portions of chapters 3 and 4 appeared in "Race and Community in Postwar Brooklyn: The Brownsville Neighborhood Council and the Politics of Urban Renewal," in the *Journal of Urban History* 27 (May 2001). I thank both *Labor's Heritage* and Sage Publications for permission to reproduce these works.

Anne Kringel has shaped this book in more ways than she knows. Anne was its primary editor, its toughest critic, and its biggest supporter. But she was also the person who motivated me to be efficient in my research and organized in my writing so that I could return to my primary purpose in this world: to be with her. For ten years, Anne has been my best friend, my partner, my passion. Our relationship is a constant source of wonder and amazement, and I consider myself blessed by her presence. Ellie entered the world as I was finishing my dissertation. Her generous heart and intellectual curiosity have been my inspiration. Clara came along just as I was finishing this book. Her brilliant smile has been a constant reminder of the miracle of life.

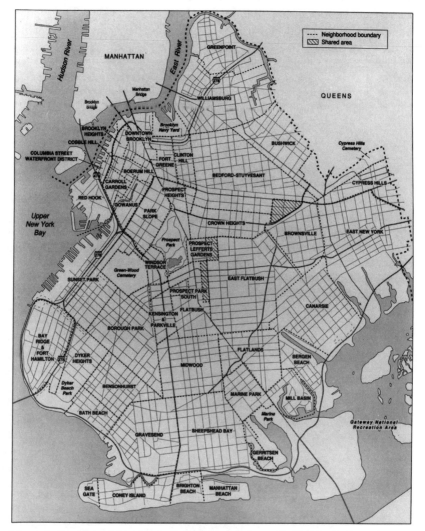

Figure 1. Brooklyn neighborhoods. From Kenneth Jackson, ed., *The Neighborhoods of Brooklyn* (New Haven, Conn.: Yale University Press, 1998).

Introduction

People journey to cities for many reasons: to find fame, fortune, a mate. Over the past two centuries, millions of people arrived in American cities seeking something. Poor individuals and their families were particularly drawn to urban areas, where they hoped to discover economic opportunities and social interaction. In cities across the country, immigrants and migrants obtained jobs and education; created communal institutions, labor organizations, and benevolent associations; and achieved a foothold in society. City neighborhoods, some squalid, others with more amenities, were the places that nurtured the hopes of these working-class voyagers.[1]

This is the story of one such area, and the people, policies, and perceptions that shaped and reshaped it for more than a century. In 1940, Brownsville, a section of eastern Brooklyn, was a white, predominantly Jewish, working-class neighborhood of approximately 100,000 residents. By 1970, Brownsville had lost almost 30,000 residents; those that remained were poorer and many lived in the largest concentration of public housing projects in Brooklyn. In addition, Brownsville's population was transformed from 85 percent white to 75 percent black and 20 percent Puerto Rican. Through a study of neighborhood activists, government institutions, and private organizations, this book examines the varying responses to the fiscal and social changes of postwar New York City. This story demonstrates the importance of Brooklyn, a borough that has received scant attention relative to its significance in New York and United States history.[2]

Brownsville for more than a century served as an early step on the ladder of upward mobility for New York residents. In the early 1900s, builders constructed cheap tenements there, which were quickly gobbled up by working-class families desperate for shelter. Because of the speculative nature of the area's development, conditions fluctuated between bad and barely satisfactory. The neighborhood's high population density taxed the inferior infrastructure, making neighborhood maintenance a constant problem. As a result, Brownsville's population changed frequently, as residents left for more luxurious accommodations. Because of its accessibility to the city's poor, Brownsville played (and continues to play) an important role in urban policy. It was both a willing and reluctant participant in numerous public policy experiments—public housing, urban renewal, the War on Poverty among others—and the initiatives of public and private institutions were instrumental forces in Brownsville's transformation. During the decades following World War II, Brownsville was a laboratory for several efforts to revitalize New York City neighborhoods.

Perceptions also shaped Brownsville's history. Before Brooklyn expanded to its eastern border, the Brownsville area was a ragged, unattractive section used for waste disposal and other noxious activities. Despite the neighborhood's dramatic growth at the beginning of the twentieth century, the city's better classes looked upon the area as a backwater, inhabited by ignorant and dirty people. The stigma that attached to Brownsville influenced the area's growth in many ways. Public and private elites frequently neglected the neighborhood when allocating scarce resources. Brownsville thus suffered from a lack of recreational and educational facilities, and social services were inadequate for the population. Brownsville citizens struggled to maintain adequate sanitation standards, and health and crime indices were consistently among the worst in the city.

As American society's opinion of cities deteriorated in the second half of the twentieth century, Brownsville was frequently pointed to as an example of urban decline. The arrival of poor blacks and Latinos served to further marginalize the area in the eyes of city elites, and Brownsville became a focal point for concerns over the negative impact of minorities on postwar New York. Many city leaders blamed the newcomers for the neighborhood's demise, but the roots of Brownsville's deterioration lay in the speculative nature of its development and the failure of public and private institutions to allow blacks and Latinos to move freely within New York society.

Brownsville natives themselves had complicated relationships with the neighborhood. Most moved out of Brownsville as soon as they had the economic wherewithal, but they looked back on Brownsville with a combination of nostalgia and disappointment in its perceived changes. Other residents saw in Brownsville the possibility of a pluralist society worth developing, and they created organizations to revitalize the area. While these groups achieved some successes, they were unable to develop the multiracial, multiclass community they sought. In recent years, while outsiders continued to believe that Brownsville offered the worst aspects of American cities, many residents, like their predecessors, saw the neighborhood as a point of entry into society.

Brownsville, along with its neighbor, Ocean Hill, is best known as the epicenter of the tumultuous 1968 New York Teachers' Strike, which pitted the predominantly white and Jewish United Federation of Teachers against the largely black and Latino Brownsville community board that took control of the local public schools. This extremely bitter conflict, in which charges of racism and anti-Semitism abounded, is often identified as emblematic of the deterioration in New York race relations and of postwar urban decline in general. The teachers' strike revealed the competing interests of white, black, and Latino New Yorkers in a period of political and economic turmoil. The story of Brownsville, however, is rooted in a much more complex history, a tale of mutual struggle and frustrated cooperation among these groups. From the 1940s through the 1960s, a diverse collection of white, black, and Latino activists worked to secure the resources to support a racially and economically diverse community. These efforts were hindered by national, citywide, and neighborhood-level obstacles.[3]

On the national stage, economic restructuring, the development of suburban areas, and the redistribution of the country's population shaped modern Brownsville. Many Americans, including Brownsville's second-generation immigrants, benefited from the postwar economic expansion, and they participated in the transformation of New York's economy from industrial to service-based businesses by taking professional jobs. When they attained new positions, many whites left Brownsville for better accommodations both within the city and in newly developing areas of Westchester, Long Island, and New Jersey.[4]

Black and Latino Americans also experienced significant changes during the 1940s and 1950s. Uprooted from the declining agricultural economy of the South and Puerto Rico, half a million of them moved to New York in the decade after World War II. New York's newest residents, denied employment in many occupations because of racism, struggled to secure a foothold in the economy. At the same time these new migrants entered the economic mainstream, low-skilled positions in the industrial sector dwindled, further restricting their economic opportunities. Discrimination in housing also excluded blacks and Latinos from many neighborhoods, and they crowded into declining areas of Manhattan, the Bronx, and Brooklyn.[5]

City leaders were slow to respond to societal changes in the post–World War II years. The political corruption of the Democratic machine combined with the inertia of public and private institutions to limit programs to deal with urban problems. The initiatives that civic leaders did develop in the 1940s and 1950s frequently had perverse effects on city populations. Public housing and urban renewal are the best known responses to urban decline in the postwar years. Meant to create a modern city, these programs achieved a mixed record at best. Public housing advocates during the 1930s and 1940s hoped that the effort would provide badly needed affordable housing to the city's working poor. Other civic leaders looked at public housing as a means to eliminate New York's decrepit slums. The New York City Housing Authority (NYCHA) was among the earliest developers of public housing, and the agency remains New York's largest housing provider to this day. The NYCHA's buildings furnish housing physically superior to the tenements and shacks that they replaced, but since the 1950s, the public housing program has faced constant criticism. New York's publicly supported projects, for more than six decades, provided desperately needed housing to the working poor. But critics deemed the initiative a failure because it did not achieve the goal of eliminating the slum. Many public housing projects occupied racial and economic ghettos worse than those they replaced.[6]

Within Brownsville at the end of the twentieth century, the NYCHA owned and operated more than one-third of the housing units. NYCHA buildings provided adequate shelter, but racial segregation, crime, poverty, and other social problems continued to trouble the area. Like others across the country, these projects became housing for New York's minority poor, emblematic of the racial polarization of American cities. City planners bore much responsibility for this segregation, because they sited projects exclusively in minority areas. But other factors were also important in shaping the black and Latino ghettos of today. Most influential was the private market, which denied blacks and Latinos access to housing in many parts of the city. The public sector contributed to this segregation by failing to enact, and then not enforcing, laws against housing discrimination. Civic leaders, public and private, also reinforced segregation through another innovation: urban renewal.[7]

During the 1950s, declining housing in many neighborhoods combined with increasing numbers of blacks and Latinos to raise concerns among New York elites over the future of the city. In response to these changes, public administrators and private developers undertook the revitalization of "slum areas" in Manhattan and other boroughs. As Robert Caro so eloquently demonstrates in *The Power Broker: Robert Moses and the Fall of New York*, residents of many of these areas did not perceive them as slums. Many of these neighborhoods provided adequate, affordable housing and served as useful points of entry for New York's new populations. During the 1940s and 1950s, however, urban renewal came to be known as "Negro removal," because the areas most frequently chosen for clearance were populated by New York's minority poor. Public officials and private developers pushed clearance of slum areas, built an inadequate supply of affordable housing, and at the same time failed to open housing in other New York neighborhoods to minority residents. As a result, large numbers of the city's poor were pushed into areas like Brownsville, where upwardly mobile whites vacated deteriorating housing that provided shelter to desperate urban renewal refugees.[8]

Brownsville natives themselves were important actors in the forging of the neighborhood. High population turnover inhibited the formation of strong neighborhood associations. The area's political marginalization prevented the development of neighborhood influence and denied the Brownsville population the ability to secure government and private investment. Throughout the 1920s, new sections of Brooklyn opened to development, but Brownsville stagnated. During the Great Depression, the neighborhood's infrastructure deteriorated further, and Brownsville received none of the public projects that rebuilt other sections of the city. By 1940, Brownsville was a community in decline.

Despite these disadvantages, in the post–World War II years many residents joined together to demand better services in their neighborhood. Brownsville citizens created organizations that planned neighborhood improvements and lobbied for new government resources. The names of these organizations and their participants changed over the decades, but their goals remained consistent. Brownsville groups rejoiced in the optimism created by victory in World War II. Activists believed that they could create a modern, diverse community that nurtured the aspirations of working-class Americans. In this context, they pushed for publicly supported housing, schools, recreation, and other services that would make their neighborhood attractive to returning veterans, and they succeeded in securing several projects.

Neighborhood-based organizations in Brownsville also made flawed but sincere efforts to incorporate new residents. Unlike those who responded violently to the arrival of blacks in their neighborhoods, Brownsville activists held progressive attitudes on race relations. At the same time they lobbied government for better services, Brownsville leaders worked to create unity between whites and the growing black and Latino population. However, social and political barriers inhibited racial cooperation, and these associations never became truly integrated. Several short-lived coalitions of blacks, whites, and Latinos won specific battles over housing and other public resources, but they were unable to prevent the neighborhood's racial metamorphosis. The efforts of Brownsville activists to create a racially and economically diverse community were also inhibited by the indifference of established citywide liberal institutions—labor unions, charitable organizations, and advocacy groups—that rejected their pleas for financial and political assistance.

By the early 1960s, Brownsville was a black and Latino ghetto. Despite the area's stigma as one of New York's poorest districts, residents continued to work for neighborhood development. Brownsville groups were influential participants in the War on Poverty, and activists created one of the nation's most successful antipoverty organizations. The coalition they forged awakened Brownsville residents to the possibility of working-class empowerment and supported the movement for community control that culminated in the 1968 battle over New York's public schools.

But the activism of the 1960s failed to halt the decades-long decline of the neighborhood. In the 1970s, when many American cities endured a prolonged economic and social crisis, Brownsville became synonymous with urban devastation. Reporters from across the country journeyed to the neighborhood to describe the devastation wrought by housing abandonment, arson, unemployment, crime, drug abuse, and other social problems. Journalists compared the area to a war zone, and the decade was devastating for Brownsville residents. At the twentieth century's end, however, Brownsville was dramatically similar to the neighborhood that emerged one hundred years prior: a working-class district with all the problems and promise typical of such areas.

Brownsville plays an important role in the debate over the responsibilities of American society to the poor. Critics of tax-supported efforts at urban revitalization argue that government efforts to revive urban areas are doomed to failure, and they point to the continuing poverty in American cities to support their position. A superficial analysis of Brownsville's history supports this assertion, but a more careful examination reveals the complexities of urban change. Critics maintain that government programs are responsible for the deterioration of neighborhoods like Brownsville, but their evidence is at best anecdotal, because little work has been done to study the process of urban change during the past century, or to assess the specific factors that contribute to neighborhood decline. By closely scrutinizing the actions of Brownsville residents and the responses of New York's political and institutional elites, this book will illuminate the complicated process of neighborhood transformation.[9]

Studies of postwar urban decline in America often describe the process with an aura of inevitability, suggesting that the combination of declining industry, expanding suburbs, and massive migration of poor people made the urban crisis predestined. The power of these nationwide social and economic forces in shaping America's cities cannot be disputed. However, the response of local communities and public and private institutions to these changes deserves analysis, because the actions of these groups have defined the contours of neighborhood change. Residents of American cities were not passive witnesses to urban upheaval. Rather, neighborhood activists, politicians, and elites all attempted to respond to urban problems. Modern cities are in part the product of the conflicts among these groups. Studying the process of urban transformation furthers our understanding of the current problems facing American cities, while revealing the limitations of American economic and political institutions in addressing the problems of the poor.

Figure 2. Brownsville in the early 1900s. In less than twenty years, Brownsville went from a rural area to a densely populated tenement district. Courtesy Municipal Archives, Department of Records and Information Services, City of New York.

1

Building an Immigrant Mecca: Brownsville, 1880–1940

Samuel Tenenbaum and William Poster both grew up in Brownsville during its early years—Tenenbaum in the 1910s and Poster in the 1920s. While both moved up to more affluent New York neighborhoods, each had a dramatically different recollection about Brownsville's role in their growth. For Tenenbaum the neighborhood was a cauldron of intellectual ferment where school "represented a glorious future that would rescue [a person] from want, deprivation and ugliness." Poster remembered a brutal, violent place that was "one huge cesspool of illiteracy and hoodlumism." The stories of Poster and Tenenbaum—both of them truthful—highlight the contradictions of the working-class section of Brooklyn named Brownsville. Brownsville was a vibrant community with communal and religious institutions, a shtetl-like feeling, and opportunities for advancement. It was also a dangerous, dirty slum looked upon with disdain by the "better classes" of Brooklyn and the rest of New York City.[1]

In a period of fifty years—from its founding in the late 1800s to the beginning of World War II—Brownsville changed from a community of small
farms to a dense neighborhood of tenements holding the largest concentration of Jews in the United States. Brownsville's development demonstrates
the impact of immigration on American cities and shows the complex relationship of housing development, commerce, ethnicity, culture, and politics
in creating urban communities during a period of dramatic city growth.
Destined as a working-class area from its inception because of its poor geography, Brownsville was marked by lack of planning, shoddy building,
poor city services, and weak provision for parks and recreation. Individual
decisions by hundreds of builders shaped the community, and these men developed a neighborhood where people struggled to maintain minimum
standards of health and sanitation.

Despite its problems, in the early 1900s Brownsville was a dynamic,
working-class Jewish community. The affinity fostered by close contact of
peoples of common heritage attracted recent immigrants, many of them
traveling directly from Ellis Island to Brownsville. Communal societies,
religious institutions, political organizations, and specialized commercial
stores all added to the area's desirability. While shabby from inception,
Brownsville offered much more than the Lower East Side; larger tenements, open (though ramshackle) spaces for play, and cheaper rents. The
speculative nature of the neighborhood, however, created long-term
problems for Brownsville residents. Housing stock declined quickly, and
community institutions could not adapt to the changing needs of the residents. The early decades of the 1900s brought fantastic growth to
Brownsville, but by the 1920s the area was outdated, and its population
began to decline.

Brownsville played an important role in the acculturation of Jewish immigrants to the United States, serving as a way station for tens of thousands
of Jews. While many looked back on their old neighborhood with nostalgia
for the community and the opportunities it provided, most area residents
shared the view of the writer Alfred Kazin, who once called Brownsville "a
place that measured all success by our skill in getting away from it." And the
outside world looked at Brownsville with contempt. William Poster remembered that in the 1920s, "every New York Jew could feel certain about
one thing; he was superior to anybody living in Brownsville." As many Jews
achieved economic stability in the 1920s, they no longer believed that
Brownsville's image reflected their success, and they moved to more genteel
neighborhoods.[2]

A Working-Class Suburb

Before the 1880s, the area of eastern Brooklyn that was to become Brownsville was known as New Lots. This territory was primarily farmland, but it was also the location of the city's largest waste dump, as well as the site of several facilities that supplied stone and other building materials. In its early history, New Lots had a diverse population. English and Irish settlers, Jewish immigrants, and a small number of African-Americans farmed the land. Many of the area's families had only recently immigrated to the United States but, unlike the majority of their compatriots, they rejected the industrial lifestyle of the Lower East Side. Others were attracted to the area by the open space and relatively fresh air it provided. Middle-class Jews and gentiles often summered in the area.³

In 1858, William Suydam, who owned a large farm in the northeast section of New Lots, subdivided his property into small lots and built several small single-family houses that he hoped to sell to working-class New Yorkers. Whereas most of Brooklyn in the nineteenth century was built for the middle class, geography and industrial development discouraged more upscale development in Brownsville. The area was full of low-lying marshes, prone to flooding, and had few of the aesthetic attractions of other parts of Brooklyn. When the wind blew, residents frequently smelled the bone-boiling plants from Jamaica Bay. Brownsville was built for the workers, and Suydam constructed what were little more than two- to four-room shacks for prospective purchasers. Shoddy from the beginning, Brownsville offered relief to the working classes from the congestion of the Lower East Side, and that was how he marketed the development. However, Suydam's subdivision plan failed to attract sufficient interest, and he went bankrupt. In 1861 real estate speculator Charles Brown purchased the remaining lots at foreclosure, renamed the area Brownsville, and set out to market it to Jews from Manhattan. By 1883 there were 250 frame houses in the village.⁴

Early settlers in Brownsville were attracted to the open spaces that seemed far removed from the congestion of Manhattan. However, they could not avoid the economic expansion of New York, and industrialization soon came to Brownsville. Workers typically followed industry in American cities, but in Brownsville the reverse occurred. By the mid-1880s, many Brownsville residents who bought or rented Brown's shacks commuted by trolley to Manhattan to work in the factories, and several manufacturers in the garment trades saw in the neighborhood an opportunity to expand their operations and secure relief from the congestion of Manhattan's industrial

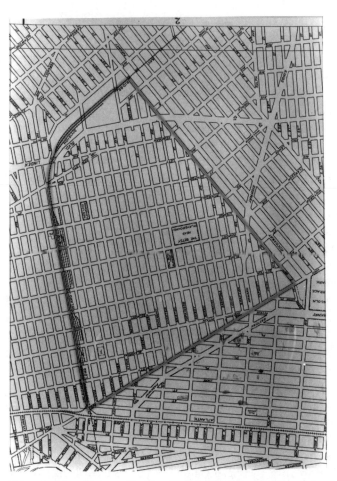

Figure 3. Map of Brownsville. Plate 17 of the City Planning Commission 1940 New York Survey. Used with permission of the New York City Department of Planning. © 1940 New York City Department of Planning. All rights reserved. Photo courtesy Map Division, The New York Public Library, Astor, Lenox, and Tilden Foundations.

districts. Among the first manufacturers to do so was Elias Kaplan, a garment producer who built a factory employing 100 workers on Watkins Avenue in the 1880s. Businessmen like Kaplan hoped that by leaving the Lower East Side, where labor organizations were flourishing, they would disconnect their workers from the union organizers and other "agitators" seeking to increase the power of the working class. Kaplan also had paternalistic intentions. In Brownsville he built housing for workers, rented it at a profit, and located the area's first synagogue, Ohev Sholom, in his factory.

Other manufacturers involved in low-technology production, in particular food processing, furniture production, and metal working, followed during the 1890s. These businesses accelerated the development of new housing, and more workers moved to the area. Multifamily houses were built around these factories, and the workplaces also served as centers for worship and entertainment.[5]

Most of the housing development in early Brownsville was done by the manufacturers themselves, who saw home building as an adjunct to their main business. Almost all the housing was rented. Brownsville's working class, many of them recent immigrants, could not afford to buy, and Jewish businessmen who achieved success on the Lower East Side saw in Brownsville the opportunity to increase their wealth through real estate. Tenancy also provided employers greater control over their workers. By 1900 almost twenty-five thousand people lived in Brownsville, most occupying wooden frame, "double-decker" houses designed for two families. When demand increased, owners subdivided many of these houses, and, with a partially finished basement, a home built for two families now accommodated eight. Most buildings had only one bathroom, and only a few had hot running water. Predictably, these houses were fire hazards and frequently burned to the ground.[6]

From its origins at Watkins and Thatford Avenues, the community grew during the 1890s to encompass what became the northeast section of Brownsville, from Dumont Avenue on the south to Liberty Avenue on the north; Rockaway Avenue on the west to Junius Street on the east. The recently completed elevated railway served as the southern border, and the Long Island Railroad provided a "natural" eastern limit to the neighborhood. Residences shared streets with factories, workshops, and stores. In 1890, there were seven tailor shops along Pitkin Avenue between Sackman and Thatford, and another five along Blake Avenue between Christopher and Thatford. While developers continued to build residences in the spaces between the shops, much of this area remained undeveloped. The *Brooklyn Eagle* reported that in the 1890s residents walking at night in the area frequently fell into unfinished cellars, and that the lack of paved streets resulted in puddles "large enough to drown a horse." Street paving, sewers, and other government services followed several years after settlement and were not completed until early in the 1900s.[7]

As Suydham had done years before, several developers constructed cheap, small buildings to accommodate this wave, but with increasing demand larger apartments became the norm. While even the Lower East Side was once an area of single-family houses, Brownsville was "born" a tenement community. High land costs, created by speculation and immigration, necessitated higher densities to ensure profit for developers. The construction of the elevated railway caused a dramatic escalation in land prices in the late 1890s. Lots that sold for $500 to $1,000 in 1890 traded for $4,000 to $5,000 by 1900. By 1890 the majority of new buildings were multifamily, and by 1895 the tenement, typically comprising five units, was the predominant building type.[8]

Ethnic tensions also shaped the community. To the west and east of Brownsville were, respectively, the villages of East Flatbush and East New York. Both areas, home to English and Irish residents, responded violently to the increasing Jewish population, and many Protestant landowners in these areas refused to sell to Jewish developers. In 1890, Brownsville residents created the "Hebrew Protection League" in response to several attacks on local Jews. The need for collective security, coupled with discrimination, pushed Brownsville's development upward instead of outward.[9]

Between 1900 and 1920 Brownsville boomed, growing from a small hamlet to a teeming ghetto. The population of 37,934 in 1905 doubled to 77,936 five years later. By 1920, 100,854 people called Brownsville home. Many of the residents came from the Lower East Side, which lost 60 percent of its population between 1905 and 1915. The construction of the Williamsburg Bridge in 1903 and the Manhattan Bridge in 1909 spurred Brownsville's growth by uprooting thousands of residents on the Lower East Side and in Williamsburg. The expansion of the subway system through Brooklyn also supported the growth of the Brownsville area, both by dislocating people living near the subway construction and by providing a convenient means of transportation to the neighborhood.[10]

But dislocation was only one cause of the dispersal of Manhattan's population. The main reason former immigrants departed the Lower East Side was upward mobility. Economic growth at the turn of the century, coupled with increases in immigrant education, enabled thousands of New Yorkers to establish better lives for their families. The most successful immigrants moved to northern Manhattan or the Bronx. Those with a more tenuous hold on economic success moved to areas like Brownsville, which offered fresher air and comparably better accommodations. Immigrants also continued to settle in Brownsville throughout the period from 1900 to 1920. Many of them, particularly those from Russia, heard about the difficulty of life on the Lower East Side, and they chose to come directly to Brooklyn. Others quickly moved to Brownsville, after a short stay in Manhattan, when they discovered that they could get more for their money in Brooklyn. By 1910, 65 percent of Brownsville's males had resided in the country less than ten years, 43 percent less than five years. In 1910, two-thirds of Brownsville residents were first-generation immigrants, and 85 percent of these residents were from Russia. While not as desirable as the new communities on the Upper West Side or in the Bronx, many viewed Brownsville as an improvement. In Henry Roth's novel *Call It Sleep*, the Schearl family is forced by economic circumstances to move from Brownsville back to the Lower East Side, and David, the main character, experiences the terror of poverty for the first time. In contrast to their new neighborhood, Brownsville was idyllic.[11]

During the 1900s, Brownsville experienced a building boom as thousands of tenements were constructed, and the community expanded to the south and the west. Established residents occupied these newer buildings, while more recent immigrants, as well as a small number of African-Americans, took their places in the older structures. The new accommodations were made of brick and stone, had indoor plumbing, and were comparatively modern, but they were still cheaply built and lacked hot running water. In a decade of dramatic expansion, Brownsville's developers re-created the surroundings of the Lower East Side, erecting cramped, high-density, multifamily tenements on narrow blocks. The streets were congested, and there was little greenery. One former resident described the area as "rows and rows of tenements and jerry-built, identical private houses, all railroad flats, so that light and sun were . . . precious." The architecture of the community had very little rationale or plan. "The dwellings were of every variety and looked as though they had been dropped chaotically from the sky," said another former resident.[12]

The tenement was an unavoidable part of Brownsville life. In 1904, 88 percent of the dwelling units in the area were in tenements. By 1907 this percentage rose to 96 percent. Most dwellings were three- or four-story structures housing four of five families apiece. Generally some type of commercial activity occupied the first floor. Immigration at the end of the century's first decade caused another speculative boom in Brownsville, and the price of vacant land again rose dramatically. Lots that sold for $50 in 1907 were flipped for $3,000 in 1909. Boom and bust cycles were compressed in Brownsville's development. Because of the speculative nature of development, builders earned good returns one year only to declare bankruptcy the next. Most of these developers were small, operated on tight profit margins, and relied on locally acquired capital that often dried up. Sixty-four percent of the builders in the area produced fewer than five houses. A few developers like Ira and Jacob Goell created stable, large-scale operations, but most builders did not achieve lasting success. Financially insecure and opportunistic developers built for quick profit, not for long-term occupancy, which contributed to the low quality of housing in Brownsville.[13]

In 1908, the *Brooklyn Eagle* celebrated Brownsville as a "Modern Tenement City." While most of Manhattan developed through the natural expansion of the city north and east from its Wall Street origins, Brownsville emerged seemingly in the middle of nowhere, surrounded by the farmland that became East Flatbush, Canarsie, and other Brooklyn neighborhoods. Throughout the nineteenth century, working-class residents of New York settled in areas that were abandoned by those who had become better off. In Brownsville, working-class people moved into apartments especially constructed for them. However, Brownsville's new residents soon learned that new construction did not necessarily mean better quality. The overwhelming majority of the apartments were cheaply built and did not withstand the elements or the use of their tenants, and in 1906 the Brooklyn borough president charged the area's developers with constructing "flimsy buildings." By 1930 much of Brownsville's housing was in disrepair.[14]

Brownsville's construction boom took place under laissez-faire conditions. In the late 1800s and early 1900s, New York government played little role in the regulation of housing. The famous Tenement Law of 1901, which passed despite much opposition, required windows in each room in larger buildings and larger open areas. But these basic provisions were inapplicable to many Brownsville tenements, which were too small to be regulated. In addition, since zoning codes were almost nonexistent, the speculative nature of development in Brownsville resulted in an unplanned, sprawling community. Commercial districts and residential blocks intermingled with industrial facilities throughout the neighborhood. Few areas could be identified as middle class, because all of Brownsville's residents lived in similar multi-use surroundings. The new buildings were brick, but Brownsville's older frame houses were tinderboxes that frequently erupted. In 1908, the local fire superintendent said that fifty fires in a month was common in Brownsville and that the oldest section witnessed at least one fire every day. Because of the instability of the housing stock, many companies refused to insure in the area.[15]

Despite the high population densities in the established parts of the neighborhood, large areas remained undeveloped well into the 1920s. Alfred Kazin, in his classic memoir, *A Walker in the City*, described Brownsville as part ghetto and part wasteland. Writing in the 1950s, Kazin remembered the "raw patches of unused city land all around us filled with monument works where they cut and stored tombstones," as well as the remnants of farmhouses where "chickens came squealing into our punchball games." Kazin described these areas as "dead land, neither city nor country." Much of Brownsville in the 1900s remained what it was in the 1800s, a dumping ground for the city's refuse and for the operations that other neighborhoods would not allow. While the large undeveloped spaces attracted youths and provided opportunities for exploration, high land prices and lack of planning also resulted in a shortage of safe places for recreation. The only park in the neighborhood during the first half of the century was Betsy Head Park, finished in 1914, which was overcrowded the day it opened. Schools had little open space, as they "were erected on little more land than the buildings required," according to one observer. There were very few playgrounds, even fewer than in similarly situated neighborhoods on the Lower East Side, and most children used the streets for recreation.[16]

Haphazard, locally controlled development raised problems for Brownsville residents, but the community's separation from the city also enhanced its autonomy. Brownsville had its own institutions, its own economy, its own social structure. The commercial area around Pitkin Avenue and the open-air pushcart market on Belmont Avenue offered a significant amount of choice in consumer goods and thus a degree of self-sufficiency. Brownsville's independence increased as it became recognized as a Jewish community by 1910 and a destination for thousands of New York Jews, as well as those emigrating from Europe. These new residents brought with them kosher groceries, synagogues, and religious organizations called

Figure 4. Belmont Avenue, Brownsville, 1930s. Most Brownsville tenements also housed commercial operations. Courtesy Brooklyn Collection, Brooklyn Public Library.

Landsmanshaftn to support the burgeoning community. Local business owners reinvested their profits in the area, increasing job and housing opportunities and contributing to philanthropic and religious causes.[17]

Although there were non-Jewish residents in the area, and a small number of blacks, no one living in or visiting Brownsville thought of it as anything but overwhelmingly Jewish. In 1910, 85 percent of Brownsville residents were Jewish, and in 1920 the percentage was close to 80. Even more important to local residents than the raw numbers, Brownsville "felt" Jewish. As William Poster recollected: "A Brownsville child scarcely saw any members of other groups except for teachers and policemen, and never really felt that Jews were anything but an overpowering majority of the human race." So while most people in New York disparaged Brownsville and considered it a very poor slum, residents of the neighborhood felt at ease in their community.[18]

The Social, Cultural, and Religious Life of Brownsville

As is true of many locales, the lost culture of "Old Brownsville" is subject to dispute. Separating fact from myth, reality from nostalgia, is difficult. Was Brownsville a lively, pleasant community, or was it a disease-infected slum whose residents' deepest desire was for escape? Were Brownsville's residents upward-striving immigrants, bent on success, or was there a "culture of poverty" that limited their opportunities? Was Brownsville a community steeped in religion, or did Judaism play a marginal role in the neighborhood's development? Brownsville was all of these things.

Separated geographically and psychologically from the more assimilated Jews of Manhattan, Brownsville residents developed a distinct culture that maintained many Old World aspects. First- and second-generation immigrants shaped Brownsville society without much influence from those Jews who had come to America earlier. "Brownsville was left largely to itself," remembered neighborhood leader Rabbi Alter Landesman. Unlike the Lower East Side, where wealthy Jews established settlement houses, religious schools, and other institutions to help recent immigrants, Brownsville residents were left to create their own communal structures from insufficient resources. An inventory of neighborhood institutions in 1920 revealed few social agencies or recreational programs, and the community's religious institutions were small and underfunded. Brownsville, where more than 100,000 people lived by this time, had one significant hospital, one park, no high school, and only two notable community centers. At the same time, local civic associations proliferated. Often they had narrow goals and disbanded upon achieving them, but Brownsville residents used these associations to fight for better services and to counter the negative perceptions of their neighbors.[19]

Religion was the center of much of Brownsville life, particularly in the 1900s and 1910s. Judaism permeated the community to such a great extent that in the early part of the century, many named the area the "Jerusalem of America." The oldest synagogues in the community were Ohev Sholom, founded in Elias Kaplan's workshop in 1882, and Eitz Chaim Machzikei Horov, founded in 1883. Both congregations drew members exclusively from the recently built factories in the area, but soon other independent congregations were formed. The oldest of these were Beth Hamedrash Hagodol, founded in 1889, and Thilim Kesher Israel, founded in 1891. These original synagogues were still functioning in the 1950s, but most local congregations had a short life span. Most of Brownsville's synagogues were Landsmanshaftn, religious organizations comprised of members who immigrated from the same European community. These groups fostered ties among neighbors and kept alive European traditions. According to Irving Howe, Landsmanshaftn were "probably the most spontaneous in character" of all Jewish institutions, and they represented the "fierce affections for the little places they had lived in." Most were small, poor organizations that provided a place for worship, social interaction, and economic support for struggling immigrants. They operated in private homes or in rented quarters, including basements, halls, or lofts. Few Brownsville congregations had the funds to employ full-time rabbis, and they often hired a cantor specifically for holiday services. During the rest of the year they relied on lay members to conduct services. Membership was limited to men, ranging in age from eighteen to forty-five. Because Orthodox law decreed that only men were allowed to worship in the synagogue, several congregations provided separate spaces for female family members to worship.[20]

Throughout Brownsville's early history, congregations formed and closed rapidly. Synagogues required little capital investment in structures or religious articles, and the Landsmanshaft community was extremely dynamic. While most groups were based on "Landsleit" (people of the same town), as the community grew, congregations coalesced for different reasons. Many congregants often left their synagogues in personal or doctrinal disputes and formed new institutions. Other congregations supported the ambitions of a particular rabbi or layperson. Congregations also formed around labor organizations and to serve financial needs in specific times of trouble. Yet others brought together members of common philosophical or ideological positions. Although they differed with respect to doctrine, ideology, and background of their members, almost all of these congregations

Figure 5. Early Brownsville synagogue. Brownsville synagogues were small and cheaply built. Courtesy Municipal Archives, Department of Records and Information Services, City of New York.

were "mutual benefit societies," providing assistance to congregants in times of sickness and death. The majority bought plots at local cemeteries for use by members. In immigrant society, death was a frequent and traumatic event, and a Jewish burial was extremely important even to nonreligious Jews. Landsmanshaftn provided assistance in times of crisis.[21]

The organizational documents of Congregation Thilim Kesser Israel are typical of Brownsville Landsmanshaftn. The stated purpose of the group was to "unify all members so that they may live in harmony and in a spirit of friendship and brotherhood," to "support each brother in times when he has fallen on bad days," and to provide burial "according to the Jewish laws and customs at our cemetery." The congregation provided the following support to its members: (1) a sick benefit up to $1.50 per day, (2) immediate relief up to fifteen dollars, (3) a shiva benefit of five dollars, (4) funeral expenses including payment for a hearse, (5) payment of up to twenty dollars for a tombstone, and (6) a death benefit based on a contribution of one dollar from each member.[22]

In 1920, forty-seven congregations operated in Brownsville. The largest was Thilim Kesher Israel, which reported 470 members, but the average local congregation had only 50 members. The rented storefronts or converted residences many used for worship were bare-bones facilities, with no special religious decorations. They also lacked heat or ventilation. Doc Baroff, who grew up in Brownsville during the 1920s and 1930s, remembered that his father always sought to get a window seat at services. "There," Baroff said, "at least he could breathe during the long ceremony." The exceptions to this rule were the oldest, most established groups, like Thilim Kesher, which built a four-story brick structure, faced with limestone, in 1910. The synagogue had Florentine glass and religious symbols carved into the windows. Only Beth Hamidrash Hagodol and a few other congregations enjoyed similar structures. Beth Hamidrash's building, completed in 1901, had a grand outdoor staircase leading to the second floor synagogue. It also had a special balcony for use by female worshipers. But into the late 1930s, only half of the Brownsville congregations employed a full-time rabbi, and even fewer worshiped in a building constructed as a synagogue. Most groups at this time occupied converted buildings—typically they were modified two-family residences.[23]

Although religious institutions were central to the lives of many recent immigrants, their long-term influence on Brownsville residents, particularly local youths, is a matter of debate. While one former resident argued that the "vast majority of boys received at least a rudimentary Jewish education," one contemporary observer stated that synagogues "do not play so active a part in the lives of residents as the leaders wish or as a comparable number of churches would in most other American communities." A 1927 community study found that only 8 percent of neighborhood men attended synagogue regularly and that the large majority of these men were over fifty. Unlike the priests in working-class Catholic neighborhoods, who were connected to the Democratic machine and the business community, rabbis did not take positions of leadership in social or political institutions. Rather, they devoted their attentions to the interpretation of the Talmud and the religious needs of area Jews, without attempting to influence public policies toward the neighborhoods they served.[24]

Brownsville synagogues had difficulty attracting worshipers because they competed with so many other avenues for social interaction and entertainment in Brooklyn and New York City. On Saturdays, Brownsville residents could travel to Coney Island or to Central Park; they could take a ferry to Staten Island or the Bronx; or they could attend movies or theater in the borough. Brownsville residents were not wealthy, but many had enough disposable income to enjoy some type of entertainment, often during the time that synagogue was in session. The desire of religious Jews to maintain conservative religious traditions also caused problems for many synagogues and their members. Orthodox Judaism required a great deal of commitment from its adherents and imposed significant restrictions on diet, social relations, and work that many Brownsville residents were unable or unwilling to uphold. A 1916 study of thirty-four congregations found that all of them barred people who violated Jewish law by working on Saturdays. In times when jobs were scarce, meeting such a requirement was very difficult for many working-class Jews.[25]

Brownsville's religious institutions generally did not attempt to make themselves more "user-friendly" to Americanized Jews. Most of the synagogues were designed to meet the religious and social needs of older, first-generation immigrants but not those of their assimilated children. Few synagogues opened Sabbath schools, nor did they sponsor social or recreational programs for children or young adults. One of the few area congregations to depart from this tradition was Temple Petach Tikva, which sponsored both men's and children's clubs and other social programs. This modern Orthodox temple, founded in 1914, was located on the western border of the community, and many of its members had moved from Brownsville to the new middle-class developments in East Flatbush. These successful congregants, many of whom were former members of Ohev Sholom, wanted a more Americanized synagogue than was available in old Brownsville. Congregations in newly developed, "second-generation" neighborhoods like Flatbush created "synagogue centers" designed to make religion the focus of Jewish social life. They provided religious instruction, organized community activities, participated in civic affairs, and actively sought to make the synagogue the focal point of the neighborhood. Brownsville synagogues never developed into such institutions. As a result, a 1959 Yeshiva University Dissertation on Brownsville Jews concluded that "none of the synagogues nor any of the rabbis made any special contribution to the community of Brownsville worthy of note."[26]

Second-generation Jewish immigrants, like other migrants, experienced conflicted feelings of attachment and estrangement from their religious culture. As immigrants and their children assimilated into American society, tensions with traditional culture increased. Much of orthodox Judaism did not resonate with the daily experiences of American Jews. Alfred Kazin described his conflicted feelings about his Brownsville synagogue: "Secretly, I thought the synagogue a mean place, and went only because I was expected to." However, Kazin, like many Jews, realized that religion was an essential part of his identity. Second-generation Jews may not have adhered strictly to orthodox tradition, but synagogues were well attended on holidays, and Jewish fraternal organizations were popular throughout the community. So while synagogues may not have received many Brownsville residents on days other than the most holy, Jewish newspapers, Jewish grocers, Jewish labor organizations, and other institutions in Brownsville all reinforced the religious connection of community residents.[27]

Although synagogues were insular and apolitical, Brownsville did not lack for community organization in its early years. A 1908 *Brooklyn Eagle* article reported that the neighborhood teemed with activity and described the efforts of several groups to improve the area—including the Daughters of Israel, who provided food and medical aid to poor residents; the Melbish Arum Society, a group of women who collected clothing for local children; the Gemilath Chesed Burial Society, with an annual budget of four thousand dollars; and the Brownsville Taxpayers Association, an organization of property owners who lobbied for neighborhood improvements. Brownsville women also created the Hebrew Ladies Day Nursery to provide child care and training to working mothers. In 1912 the group built a three-story facility "fitted up with every convenience for the care of children," which continued to serve area youths for decades. Business groups such as the Brownsville Civic League also pushed for better government services, particularly the development of better transit lines to the area. Some of these organizations received support from wealthy Jews in other parts of Brooklyn, but almost all Brownsville institutions were created and managed by local residents. By the 1910s, Brownsville had a small but active elite of its own—families that had successfully developed local businesses or made money in real estate—and they served as the leadership for local organizations. Brownsville's upper class, however, was small and volatile: businesses failed frequently and successful persons quickly left the neighborhood. As a result, many organizations had a short life span.[28]

On the Lower East Side, second- and third-generation German Jews created many institutions to serve the new class of Eastern European immigrants, but Brooklyn's Jewish elites were neither as wealthy nor as active as their brethren across the East River. They did, however, try to respond to the immigration wave that hit Brooklyn in the 1890s. One of the few Brownsville institutions created primarily by Brooklyn elites was the Hebrew Educational Society (HES). Founded in 1899 with the support of the Baron de Hirsch fund, the HES was a paradigmatic settlement house, serving as an "educational center for the adjustment of the Jewish immigrant to the New World."[29]

Most of the HES's founders were second-generation Jews who achieved success as merchants or professionals. These Americanized Jews were very concerned about the image projected by the poor immigrants who were arriving by the tens of thousands from Eastern Europe during the last decades of the nineteenth century. Gentile papers like the *Brooklyn Eagle* frequently portrayed Brownsville Jews as dirty and backward. Elites worried that the rawness of immigrant society reflected poorly on them, and they worked to acculturate new arrivals quickly. In 1909, the HES Annual Report argued that "if we do not take care of these unfortunate immigrants, if we do not try to uplift them, then as sure as fate our own children, or children's children, will pay the penalty."[30]

The HES building, dedicated in 1914, included an auditorium, a gymnasium, a club, classrooms, and music rooms. With this new facility, HES became a community center, focusing on educational and cultural programs within the organization while providing leadership to the whole community. HES opened the first library and reading room in the neighborhood, the first kindergarten, the first penny savings bank, a summer vacation school, a country camp, and an "old age" club. In addition to its own activities, the HES offered its facilities and staff assistance to other important Brownsville organizations such as the Workmen's Circle, local labor unions, political societies, and the local chapter of the National Council of Jewish Women. According to Rabbi Alter Landesman, the director of HES for over thirty years, the organization "became in a real sense the Bet Am, the cultural and recreational center for the entire locality, from which flowed the cultural life within and outside the neighborhood." HES was for many years Brownsville's dominant neighborhood advocate, lobbying for the creation of Betsy Head Park, and pushing for improved streets, better sanitation, more schools, and other facilities. However, while it was a significant institution, the HES could not meet the needs of the changing community. During a typical year in the 1920s, the organization served 2,500 residents, but its 1922 budget was only $25,000. And Brownsville at this time had more than 120,000 residents living within one mile of the HES building.[31]

Outside of the synagogue and other local institutions, the primary centers of social activity in Old Brownsville were the front stoop, the fire escape, and the street corner. Gerry Lenowitz, a former resident, remembered that "when you stepped out of your house there were always forty or fifty kids on a corner." Grocery stores and soda fountains were also important places for congregation. Gerald Sorin, who interviewed dozens of boys who grew up in Brownsville during the 1930s, said that there was a "relatively independent street culture" in the community. One of Sorin's sources remembered that "the streets were our salvation and sometimes our primary home." Another recalled the "amazing camaraderie among those of us who grew up on the streets," and a third "couldn't wait to finish eating and get out of the house into the street." Life on the streets was exciting but dangerous, and Brownsville youths suffered a disproportionate number of injuries through automobile accidents.[32]

In most areas Brownsville was neglected, but in the development of libraries the neighborhood received more attention than most Brooklyn communities. Two were built during the early years of the neighborhood. The first, completed in 1908 with funds from the Carnegie Endowment, was located at Glenmore and Watkins Streets, in the heart of the immigrant community. The library had signs in Yiddish, English books translated into Yiddish, and dozens of guides providing "immigrant training" and advice on American culture and mores. When the building opened it was immediately filled to capacity. In 1909 the annual circulation was 330,000—the largest of any library in Brooklyn, an honor the branch would retain until 1940. The administration had to hire security officers to maintain order in the reception area, and residents often waited hours in lines outside the building just to gain access to its holdings. After-school hours were the most crowded. Many Brownsville mothers worked outside of the house, and local youths were directed to the library as a place to learn and to keep out of trouble.[33]

To decrease the demands on the facility, the library administration proposed an additional "children's branch" in the community, the first erected in New York City. Completed in 1914, the children's branch was open to all Brownsville residents under eighteen. In addition to its role in the education of Brownsville youths, the library was one of the few architecturally significant buildings in the community. Writer Arthur Granit called the library a "Tudor-styled brick building [that] would have been more at home in the English Midlands; instead it squatted here, although with great dignity among a vast sea of tenements and an endless array of clotheslines." Located on Stone Avenue, the library was designed in Gothic style, had nine shades of brick, and was trimmed with limestone. The library cornice was decorated with carvings representing themes in children's literature and important historical events, the reading rooms had specially designed and carved furniture, and the interior was designed to accommodate long lines of Brownsville patrons. One former resident called it "a 'spiritual island' in a neighborhood marked with physical deterioration."[34]

While a small number of local children attended full-time religious schools, the overwhelming majority were students at public schools. Brownsville parents hoped that these institutions would provide social and economic mobility for their children. In the first two decades of the twentieth century, most public school teachers were Christian, because Jews were excluded from the political process of teacher selection. After World War I, when the number of public schools increased dramatically, New York's Jewish community fought for and gained new standards for teacher hiring, eliminating much of the patronage system. As their power within the Democratic Party increased, Jewish communities also commanded a greater role in the school system. By 1930, Jews made up 44 percent of the new teachers in the public school system, and more than 30 percent of the teachers in Brownsville schools were Jewish. Although the basic curriculum remained the same, these teachers changed the classroom dynamics in predominantly Jewish schools by providing role models for Jewish children. These changes coincided with one of the largest expansions of a school system in this century. Between 1924 and 1929, the New York City Board of Education oversaw the construction of 130 new school buildings to ease overcrowding and enable all students to attend a full-day program for the first time. In concert with the increasing political power of New York Jews, which lifted ethnic barriers within the teaching profession, expansion created many opportunities for second-generation Jews.[35]

The impact of the educational system on Brownsville's children has been another subject of debate among historians of the neighborhood. Several memoirs describe the desire of Brownsville residents to improve themselves; Alter Landesman's history, for example, was in large part a list of the hundreds of successful people who grew up in Brownsville. But other reminiscences depicted a community of young people more interested in fighting that in reading. This attitude, according to these authors, was encouraged by an educational system that did not foster academic success. "We were all on a special Board of Education blacklist," said William Poster, who attended local schools in the 1920s. "I don't think I ever heard anyone express a longing to be any kind of professional or even go to college." Poster estimated that out of the hundred boys he knew, only ten had the opportunity to go to college. According to Poster, "many sons of fairly affluent parents never got past grade school, the lure of punchball, movies and 'workin' proving stronger than parental authority or desire."[36]

When Thomas Jefferson High School, located in East New York, opened in 1924, educational opportunities expanded for many Brownsville youths. However, Brownsville continued to battle the perception that it was a slum. Throughout the early decades of the twentieth century, the *Brooklyn Eagle* reported on the squalid conditions in the area and the frequency of "mob violence" in Brownsville. To the *Eagle's* readership, Brownsville was a world apart, and a place to be avoided.[37]

Economic Life in Old Brownsville

Since Brownsville began as an outpost removed from Manhattan and much of the rest of Brooklyn, a relatively autonomous economy grew in the neighborhood during the early decades of the twentieth century. As the population of Brooklyn expanded across the borough, Brownsville became more connected to the regional economy, but Brownsville's local commercial life continued. Brownsville residents were usually employed, although much of the work was sporadic and all of it was underpaid.

The majority of Brownsville residents worked in blue-collar occupations. Like Jews in all of New York's working-class neighborhoods, most of Brownsville's first-generation immigrants toiled in the sweatshops of the garment trades. Jews owned a large percentage of New York garment shops, and they were a natural point of introduction to the American economy for Jewish immigrants. Many European Jews already had experience in garment production before they arrived in the United States, and the expansion of the "ready-made" clothing industry after the Civil War was directly related to the massive waves of immigration in the late eighteenth and early nineteenth centuries. The booming garment industry drew tens of thousands of people from eastern and southern Europe to New York, Philadelphia, and Chicago, and these new immigrants spurred urban economic development. In 1909, 340,000 New Yorkers toiled in the garment trades, and 40 percent of them were foreign-born Jews. The sweatshop was attractive to recent immigrants who spoke no English and lacked preparation for the industrial economy. There, unlike other workplaces, the boss spoke Yiddish and coworkers were often from the same town. Jewish owners were more flexible about the religious needs of their workers and scheduled operations so that employees would worship on the Sabbath. Garment work also provided opportunities for women, who were a majority of the workers in the production of ladies' clothing. Women received lower pay than men, but the garment industry provided independence and an introduction to the American economy for many Jewish women.[38]

The early entrepreneurs in the field were German Jews, but by the 1880s, many Russian and Polish immigrants also founded their own businesses. Unlike other industries, where there were clear distinctions in wealth between owners and operators, many garment shops provided only marginal improvement in the economic and social status of the proprietor. A prosperous firm was one worth between twenty-five and fifty thousand dollars, but most shops were valued at much less. "Contracting" was vital to the system of production in the garment industry. In 1913 more than three-quarters of all firms employed five or fewer workers. These shops employed family members, Landsleit (people from the same European town), and neighbors, and they often, according to historian Susan Glenn, "consisted of no more than a few tables, chairs and sewing machines squeezed into a tenement apartment." Contractors provided a surplus pool of workers when demand for clothes was high, and they took on work that the large shops could not produce quickly. Because of the cyclical nature of the industry, contracting shops were the first to suffer the inevitable recessions, and workers at these small operations were the lowest paid in the industry. Shops competed with one another by cutting their rates, and workers suffered from this race to the bottom. In 1914, garment workers in New York City made between seven and fourteen dollars per week and few worked a full year. An annual income of four hundred dollars was typical.[39]

The United States did not classify occupations by census district until 1940, so local statistics are sparse for Brownsville's early years, but a 1905 employment survey found that of 459 families questioned, 57 percent worked in the apparel trades. Most of Brownsville's residents worked for Manhattan contractors, but the number of local shops grew early in the century. In 1900, there were approximately twenty local garment shops. A 1912, *Trow's Brooklyn Business Directory* listed sixty-two producers of women's clothing and eighty men's garment companies in Brownsville. The number of local shops continued to grow throughout the decade. In 1922 the *Regional Plan of New York* located 145 operations involved in the production of men's clothing in Brownsville and 150 producing women's clothing. Sixty percent of New York's garment factories employed five or fewer workers—and the typical Brownsville shop was smaller than those in Manhattan or Williamsburg. Most of the factories were poorly capitalized and changed hands often, but a few garment makers grew their businesses into substantial operations. Among this small number were New Lots Clothing, Sidmar Clothing, and A. Werman and Sons, each of which employed more than one hundred workers.[40]

The predominance of working-class occupations changed little over the next thirty-five years. Second-generation residents seldom remained in these sweatshops, but many of them continued to work in some part of the clothing industry. A large number of Brownsville workers moved into larger factories that offered better pay and more consistent employment, and several opened their own shops. In a 1925 study of thirty-six hundred Brownsville residents based on the 1920 census, 59 percent of those studied worked in the "crafts and operators" category, 21 percent in clerical and sales, and 17 percent in professional and managerial positions. A 1940 study, also based on census data, noted that "a high proportion of the working population is engaged in seasonal trades like the needle trades, furs, and building and construction." Brownsville was also the home to a large number of small, low-tech businesses in other fields, including food processing (including Schechter Poultry, famous for the Supreme Court decision that invalidated the National Recovery Administration during the New Deal), metal processing, and packaging. But all of these occupations offered inconsistent employment at low pay.[41]

Most Brownsville residents not engaged in the garment industry worked in some aspect of construction. Although such work was often difficult and dangerous, the opportunities in this field were significant in New York during the first three decades of the century. Before the Great Depression, housing and office construction expanded dramatically in the city, and large numbers of Brownsville men secured employment as carpenters, bricklayers, plasterers, roofers, and painters. A 1939 WPA survey found four thousand carpenters who were members of Local 2027 of the Carpenters Union, and another three thousand painters and paper hangers. Brownsville residents occasionally were able to find stable employment with a large contractor, but the majority of Brownsville's tradesmen worked intermittently, on a job-to-job basis.[42]

The factories in which Brownsville's residents worked may have seemed somewhat more spacious than the cramped locations of the Lower East Side, but they were sweatshops just the same. Many manufacturers opened these plants hoping to avoid unionization and the increasing government inspection encouraged by reformers on the Lower East Side. While the location of these plants made visits from the Labor Bureau less frequent, union organizations were more active in Brownsville than in many parts of New York, and by 1920 Brownsville had a long history of labor agitation. The Knights of Labor organized a local branch of garment workers as early as 1885, and several significant strikes erupted in the area during the 1880s and 1890s. In 1908, more than eight hundred workers struck local garment factories, and police arrested dozens of operators who attempted to stop strikebreakers from taking their places. In 1910, the United Hebrew Trades and the International Ladies Garment Workers Union carried out a series of major strikes across the city that impacted Brownsville's shops. By 1917, Brownsville's ILGWU local comprised more than twenty-five hundred members, and the United Brotherhood of Tailors local more than one thousand members.[43]

"Working-class" describes not only the economic situation of Brownsville, but the culture of the community as well. Brownsville families endured a daily struggle to make ends meet, particularly those who worked in occupations with significant seasonal unemployment. Alfred Kazin recollected his confusion upon reading in college that Jews were shrewd people and among the richest in the country. "All the Jews I knew had managed to be an exception to the rule," he remembered. "I grew up with the belief that the natural condition of a Jew was to be a propertyless worker like my painter father and my dressmaker mother." Many Brownsville residents attempted to deal with irregular employment by starting their own businesses. Most of these were small, undercapitalized shops that sold groceries, candy, or homemade goods. Delicatessens and bakeries were common family enterprises. Other neighborhood occupations included real estate management and home maintenance, the sale of fruits and vegetables by pushcart, and wholesaling. The neighborhood also supported a small number of professionals, primarily doctors and attorneys, but even these businesses were fragile because Brownsville residents were often unable to pay for the services they needed.[44]

A few pushcart operators and peddlers built thriving businesses during the economic boom of the 1920s. "While selling vegetables from a pushcart may not have looked very elegant, it was sometimes amazingly lucrative: one peddler was reputed to have three cellars and a fleet of four trucks, devoted solely to stocking his cart," William Poster argued. But only a minority of the more fortunate and hardworking entrepreneurs were able to develop their businesses into successful enterprises. The most significant of these operations were located on Pitkin Avenue, the area's largest commercial avenue, called the "Fifth Avenue of Brooklyn" by Brownsville residents. This street was the social and economic center of the community as well as one of the most active business avenues in Brooklyn. Memoirs of Brownsville describe Pitkin Avenue as the pride of the neighborhood, the place where people dressed up when they had business to conduct.[45]

The crown jewel of the strip was the Loew's Pitkin Theater. Designed by Thomas W. Lamb, renowned at the time as the country's premier theater architect, the Loew's Pitkin opened in 1929, one month after the stock market crash, at the corner of East New York and Pitkin Avenues. While not comparable to big theaters in Manhattan, the Loew's Pitkin was typical of the lavish style of movie theater in the new age of sound motion pictures. The facade was a Mayan–Art Deco design of terra-cotta. The interior, dubbed "hispano-moresque" by Loew's publicity department, featured a blue polychromed ceiling, peacock-blue carpet, and embroidered draperies. The grand stair to the mezzanine was lined with Spanish-style furniture, paintings, and tapestries. The auditorium walls were accentuated with

Figure 6. Pitkin Avenue, 1930s. Pitkin Avenue was Brownsville's main commercial thoroughfare, and one of the largest in Brooklyn. Courtesy WPA Collection, Municipal Archives, Department of Records and Information Services, City of New York.

a variety of sculptures, towers, and carved balconies, and the stage was surrounded by a polychrome mantel in the baroque style. The theater, which also supported Yiddish theater and Jewish performers, seated thirty-six hundred people.[46]

Pitkin Avenue was a commercial center supplying most of the needs of Brownsville residents, as well as the location of more expensive specialty stores that attracted other Brooklynites and even customers from Manhattan. In 1942, according to the Pitkin Avenue Merchant's Association, 372 stores—including eight banks and forty-three men's clothing stores—on Pitkin from Stone Avenue to Ralph Avenue did an annual business of ninety million dollars and employed one thousand people. At that time, Brownsville's commercial area, which was centered on Pitkin but extended two blocks south and two blocks north, was the largest in Brooklyn. According to a 1936 Brooklyn Edison survey, the area had the largest concentration (200 total) of furniture and household appliances stores in Brooklyn, the largest concentration of apparel stores (393 total), and the most non-food service stores (782).[47]

Brownsville became a commercial center because the neighborhood's merchant class was aggressive in pursuing business opportunities. Several Brownsville stores, like Fortunoff's Jewelry and Boxer's Clothing, grew from small shops to large stores that served all of Brooklyn. Pitkin Avenue continued to flourish despite Brownsville's fluctuating population because it was close enough to the neighborhoods of East Flatbush and Eastern Parkway to serve these residents. And because newer middle-class areas had zoning restrictions that limited commercial operations, Brownsville businesses served most of the borough well into the 1960s. While most shops sold bargain goods, many of the stores sold expensive products, like appliances, out of the reach of the average Brownsville resident: the Brooklyn Edison survey found that fewer than 5 percent of local residents could afford a refrigerator.

While most of these retail operations were run by family members, these stores provided hundreds of jobs to local residents. Retail employment was an important Brownsville occupation. The luxurious apartments of Eastern Parkway became a favored location of Brownsville's business elite, who often reinvested their profits in real estate or other ventures within Brownsville, and during the 1920s, Brownsville also developed a small industrial base of modern factories located primarily in the northeast corner of the neighborhood along the eastern border of the Long Island Railroad. There, the Imperial Paper Box Company, the Perkins Marine Lamp and Hardware Company, the Imperial Crown and Toy Company, the Ideal Rubber Company, and Hardy Plastic each employed more than two hundred workers.[48]

But few Brownsville families achieved middle-class status. A 1933 New York City study found the median income of a Brownsville family to be $2,490, significantly lower than the recently developed middle-class areas of Brooklyn ($4,320) and the Bronx ($3,750) but much higher than the $1,360 median family income on the Lower East Side. While few residents achieved financial security, the fact that so many Brownsville residents owned businesses mitigated the impact of unemployment. Also, food was relatively cheap and accessible, especially compared to Manhattan, and rents were lower in Brownsville. Brownsville's second-generation did better than their parents, but only by a little. Carol Bell Ford, in her ethnography of Brownsville women, found that a large percentage of their fathers were industrial workers during the 1930s and 1940s. The men in Ford's sample worked as fabric cutters, jewelry makers, printers, carpenters, roofers, and painters. A few had higher-skilled occupations, including railway operator and plumber, but none held white-collar positions.[49]

Since the majority of its workers toiled in the garment industry or in construction, the Great Depression hit Brownsville especially hard. Thousands of people lost their jobs as the garment industry collapsed and shops were forced to close. Brownsville carpenters and tradesmen benefited from the building boom of the 1920s, but they suffered accordingly during the building bust of the 1930s. By 1940, one-quarter of all Brownsville residents in the workforce reported to the Census Bureau that they were looking for work. As many as 2,243 local workers depended on employment from the Works Progress Administration. To save money, many Brownsville residents, according to Ford, moved "repeatedly back and forth between Brownsville and East New York, taking advantage of 'concessions,' that is, two or three months of free rent offered by desperate landlords."[50]

According to the 1940 census, Brownsville remained an overwhelmingly working-class community. Slightly more than 2 percent of Brownsville residents in the labor force were categorized as "professional workers." In the oldest sections of the neighborhood, two-thirds of the residents toiled in blue-collar occupations. In the newer sections to the west and south, more residents held lower-level white-collar positions, particularly clerical and sales. But the census categories did not completely capture the economic difficulties facing even these Brownsville residents. The Census Bureau classified peddlers and pushcart operators as "proprietors," a white-collar category, but they were far from middle class. Even those residents who owned their own stores, most of them corner groceries or candy stores, barely scraped together enough to meet their monthly expenses. Furthermore, many people in sales worked on commission and therefore depended on the economy for their survival. A working-class community from the beginning, Brownsville residents only rarely achieved economic success.[51]

Radicalism and Liberalism in Brownsville

On October 16, 1916, Margaret Sanger opened the nation's first birth-control clinic on Amboy Street in Brownsville. Sanger selected Brownsville for her experiment because she knew from her conversations with residents that the clinic would have the neighborhood's support. "Here in this Jewish community I need have no misgivings over breaking of windows or hurling of insults," Sanger recalled. But even Sanger was surprised by the warm welcome she received from Brownsville, and she was "scarcely prepared for the friendliness offered from that day on." Sanger's clinic served 140 women on the first day of operation. Each paid ten cents to receive information and counseling on contraceptive options. Such information was in great demand in Brownsville, where large families struggled to care for their children. Desperate for help, the women arrived in droves, and "at seven in the evening, they were still coming," Sanger remembered. Over the next two weeks, hundreds of women came to the clinic—from Brownsville, from the other boroughs, and, according to Sanger, from as far away as Massachusetts. Local merchants and community leaders also dropped in to offer greetings and food. But nine days after the facility opened, the Brooklyn District Attorney's Office shut the clinic, holding it in violation of state law that barred the dissemination of information on birth control. And although Sanger, with help from Brownsville women, reopened the storefront, the authorities closed it for good in 1917. Nevertheless, Sanger's groundbreaking efforts were nurtured by an atmosphere of progressive experimentation that infused Brownsville.[52]

Financial difficulty contributed to the growth of a large radical faction in Brownsville. As in the Lower East Side, living conditions spurred many recent immigrants to form organizations opposing commercial interests that discriminated against the working class. Radicalism came naturally to those first-generation Jewish immigrants who had participated in leftist organizations in Eastern Europe. And their exclusion from New York's political patronage system gave them the freedom to focus on community issues that often conflicted with the goals of the Tammany machine. These factors contributed to the flourishing of socialist causes in the 1910s and the continued activity of leftist organizations well into the 1920s and 1930s.[53]

These groups' efforts were not viewed favorably by the city's better classes. In the early 1900s, the *Brooklyn Eagle* frequently reported on the activities of local "anarchists" and "socialists" and highlighted the efforts of "right-minded citizens" to respond to these un-American activities. One 1909 report praised the efforts of a local policeman who arrested a resident named Goldberg for carrying "the red flag of anarchy in a street parade." According to the article, in spite of the fact that two thousand paraded behind Goldberg, the officer was able to wrest the flag from him and take him into custody. However, the *Eagle* bemoaned the quick release of the man (he had committed no crime) and stated that "it seemed like bedlam had broken loose when the crowd discovered that the red flag had been returned." Another report described a riot that occurred when three men criticized socialism at a Brownsville tavern. The men were badly beaten when hundreds of local residents joined in the conflict. The paper noted that "little things like that happen about fourteen times a week in Brownsville when 'outsiders' take a notion to pry into the affairs of the ghetto folks." While the *Eagle*'s editors considered neighborhood residents ignorant, within Brownsville, socialism drew wide support because it resonated with the experiences of poor immigrants.[54]

The center of socialist activity in Brownsville was the Brownsville Labor Lyceum. Taken over by the United Hebrew Trades (a union coalition) around the turn of the century, the Lyceum was the Socialist Party's headquarters throughout this period. The building served as the headquarters for most of the area's labor organizations and workers' societies (such as the Workmen's Circle) and provided a meeting place for strike organization, rallies, political protests, and other events. In addition, during the years that Sol Hurok, later to become the nation's leading concert producer, managed the Lyceum, it was the cultural center of Brownsville, providing music and theater as well as international expositions. Hurok himself remembered that "there was never any lack for audience." In other parts of New York, music was not a big business, "but music thrived in Brownsville."[55]

Rebuilt in 1917 after a fire, the Lyceum featured a library, bowling alleys, a pool, billiard and recreation rooms, and a large auditorium. In addition to serving the needs of labor organizations, the Lyceum was the focus of Brownsville intellectual life, and residents filled the auditorium for weekly lectures. The neighborhood's desire for learning drew famous speakers from throughout the country. The Lyceum lecture program for January 1923 is revealing: in just that month, Lyceum members heard socialist leader Norman Thomas lecture on the impact of World War I, labor activist A. Philip Randolph examine "The Negro Problem in America," and academic Michael Cohen discuss the importance of the Russian Revolution to American society. Dudley Gaffin, who grew up in the neighborhood, remembered "a ferment of social and political activity" there. A resident could participate in street corner debates, go to the Lyceum, or "to Nanny Goat Park (a local field) on any Saturday and see hundreds of guys talking politics, talking religion, talking philosophy."[56]

The Lyceum was also the home of the Brownsville Socialist Sunday School, started in 1912 to "foster understanding of and allegiance to working-class interests and basic socialist tenets" and to "counteract the overly individualistic, competitive, nationalistic, militaristic and anti-working-class themes that seemed to be prevalent in public schools and other aspects of capitalist culture." The Brownsville branch of the Socialist Sunday Schools was one of the most active in the country. Throughout the 1910s, more than one thousand young people regularly attended classes, where

they were educated in politics, social problems, and community organization. Brownsville's school also provided instruction in "singing, elocution,
drawing and dramatics." Socialist schools declined in the face of the Red
Scare repression following World War I, but their teachings shaped the political understanding of a generation of Brownsville youths.[57]

The Sunday Schools were just one part of a complex web of organiza-
tions created by the Socialist Party, the most active radical organization in
Brownsville during the early twentieth century. Between 1915 to 1920 New
Yorkers elected eleven socialist candidates to the state assembly and the
New York Board of Aldermen. Several of these candidates were from
Brownsville, most importantly Abraham Shiplacoff. Born in Russia, Shiplacoff immigrated to the United States in 1891 and worked in the garment
trades. After several years of night school, Shiplacoff completed his degree
and became at teacher at Public School 84 in Brownsville. Throughout
these years, Shiplacoff became increasingly active in New York's Socialist
Party, rising to top leadership positions. In 1915, he was the first socialist
elected to the New York state assembly. After resigning that post in 1918,
Shiplacoff also served as the principal of Brownsville's Socialist Sunday
School, as labor editor of the *Jewish Daily Forward*, on the Board of Aldermen, and as an executive with the Amalgamated Clothing Workers union.
Up until his death in 1934, Shiplacoff was a leader of the Brownsville com-
munity.[58]

The Socialist Party was successful in working-class neighborhoods like
Brownsville because its leaders came from the sweatshops and understood
the struggles facing their constituents. Socialism was a grassroots movement in New York City, based on immigrant culture, and party leaders won
the support of residents by arguing their cause from soapboxes on street
corners and in neighborhood taverns and barber shops. Socialist parades
and pageants drew community members to protest discrimination and support their striking neighbors, but they also provided entertainment to poor
residents who could not afford the theater or cinema. While critics often
claimed the socialists were controlled from abroad, support for the party
was deeply ingrained in the lives of New York immigrants.[59]

Within Brownsville, Shiplacoff and his associates supported striking
workers, assisted residents in battles against landlords and city agencies, and
provided a structure through which Brownsville residents could voice their
concerns. The Socialist Party also promoted cooperative enterprises: they
established a bakery, a bank, a consumers league to buy wholesale groceries,
and two tenants unions—the Brownsville Tenants League and the Brook-

lyn Tenants Union—to protect against rent increases during World War I. In the fall of 1919, the socialists organized several strikes to protest increased rents. For more than two months, tenants and landlords battled. Landlords or their henchmen beat several tenant leaders, had others arrested, and evicted several families. So although the conflicts secured rent reductions in many buildings, many Brownsville residents lost their homes in the process.[60]

During the late 1910s, socialists gained support because of their opposition to World War I, a position that a large number of Brownsville residents shared. In reaction, the Democratic Party sought to weaken the Socialist Party and take control of neighborhood politics. Brownsville resident Hymie Schorenstein, the first Jewish Democratic District leader in Brooklyn, led this effort. Schorenstein immigrated to the United States from Poland in the late 1800s and slowly rose through the party ranks, becoming one of the most powerful politicians in Brooklyn. Though he could neither read nor write, Schorenstein held many governmental positions and was a friend of Governors Alfred E. Smith and Herbert Lehman. Within Brownsville, Schorenstein solidified his power by distributing patronage jobs to his formerly excluded constituents and by exploiting second-generation Jews' desire for assimilation through casting socialism as un-American. By questioning the patriotism of Brownsville socialists, Schorenstein drew many residents into the Democratic orbit.[61]

After World War I, Brownsville was an important target of the nationwide effort to suppress radical movements. On April 28, 1919, the Brooklyn District Attorney's Office, supported by New York Governor Al Smith and United States Attorney General Mitchell Palmer, raided the Brownsville Labor Lyceum, arrested several members of the Socialist Party for violation of the Sedition Acts and other laws banning criticism of the government, and confiscated their records. The pretext for the raid was a meeting held several days before in which speakers advocated a general strike in sympathy with Eugene Debs, then imprisoned for sedition. The organizers of the meeting also, according to the *Eagle*, praised their "valiant comrades in Russia and Germany who are leading the proletarian revolution." Although the district attorney determined that none of the speakers broke the law, the goal of this action was to weaken the party and frighten its supporters. But despite the efforts of the Democratic power structure, voters reelected five socialists, including one from Brownsville, to the state assembly in the fall of 1919. In March 1920, however, the legislature removed them from office. When New Yorkers sent most of them back to the legislature in special elections, the assembly immediately ousted them once again. Despite much protest from local and national leaders, the court of appeals confirmed the expulsion.[62]

Schorenstein then gerrymandered Brownsville into three separate assembly districts to weaken the power of the socialists. He also collaborated with the Republicans in the area, creating "fusion" candidacies that were difficult for socialists to overcome. After 1920, the Socialist Party never regained its power, and the Democratic Party dominated Brownsville politics for the remainder of the century. Schorenstein's maneuvering had a significant long-term impact on the neighborhood. By dividing Brownsville into three districts that shared representation with other neighborhoods, Schorenstein contributed to the marginalization of the community. An area with few institutional resources, Brownsville had to compete for the attention of its representatives with the more prosperous areas of East Flatbush and East New York.[63]

Even though Democratic candidates consistently won a majority of votes in local elections after 1920, leftist movements remained active in Brownsville. In 1929, socialist Norman Thomas, running for mayor, received 23 percent of Brownsville's votes. Another socialist, Morris Hillquit, garnered 26 percent of Brownsville's votes in the 1932 mayoral contest. During the depression, the American Labor Party (ALP) was extremely active in Brownsville, providing a vehicle for Brownsville leftists to support President Roosevelt without having to vote for Tammany Hall. Although support for FDR was the founding purpose of the ALP, in communities like Brownsville the party took on a life of its own, organizing protests and other activities. Among its most significant activities was its support for tenants against landlords. In October 1937, two Brownsville ALP activists chained themselves to a building to prevent the eviction of local residents who were on a rent strike against the landlord. Ironically, the rise of the ALP sped the decline of the Socialist Party and led to the further incorporation of Brownsville Jews into the Democratic Party. During the 1930s, many second-generation Jews transformed their parents' radicalism into the urban liberalism that supported the New Deal order. In doing so, Jews rejected ethnic solidarity in support of a multiethnic urban coalition committed to social change and government regulation. This was certainly true in Brownsville, where Franklin and Eleanor Roosevelt's pictures graced the mantelpieces of many neighborhood homes.[64]

Not all Brownsville residents moved easily into the liberal fold. During the depression, Communist Party members were active in Brownsville and gained a large following in activities like rent strikes and demands for employment. As the construction industry collapsed, many Brownsville residents had no means for survival. From the early 1930s, Alfred Kazin remembered, "my father could never be sure in advance of a week's work." The needle trades did not fare much better, and the overwhelming majority of Brownsville families were eligible for relief. As a result, protest in Brownsville occurred frequently in the 1930s, and Communists were often in the forefront of these efforts.[65]

George Aronov was one of the activists working in Brownsville, and he helped organize several "sit-down" strikes at local welfare offices. With the support of the Unemployed Council, residents took over the area branch of the New York City Relief Bureau and demanded an increase in assistance. Each night of the strike, Aronov would take to a soapbox on Hopkinson Avenue and collect money and food for the protesters. Because all Brownsville residents struggled against poverty, neighborhood demonstrations received wide support. (Police, for fear of inciting riots, were often reluctant to intervene.) Brownsville's radicalism extended to international affairs. The neighborhood sent at least ten volunteers to Spain to serve in the Abraham Lincoln Brigade that fought the Fascists in the Spanish Civil War. Socialist affiliations remained strong in Brownsville after World War II and influenced the efforts of neighborhood organizations to redevelop the area. Leftist ideology also shaped the response of Brownsville residents to the increasing number of African-Americans who moved into the community in the 1930s.[66]

A Separate World: Blacks in Early Brownsville

During the colonial era and the early 1800s, New York had the largest black population of any northern city. But from the Civil War through the 1890s, New York's black population grew very slowly. Aware of the extreme violence to which the city's blacks were subjected during the Draft Riot of 1863, many black migrants chose to live in other cities during the second half of the century. That changed after 1890. In 1900, 66,000 blacks lived in the city, with the majority in Manhattan, where they occupied several areas along the West Side between Twenty-third and Sixty-fifth Streets. By 1910, the city's black population grew to 90,000 as migrants from Virginia, North Carolina, and other southern states came in search of greater opportunities. Most of these migrants settled in Manhattan, whose black population increased by more than 24,000 during the decade. Brooklyn's black population increased by only 4,000 during the same period. Between 1910 and

1930 New York's black population exploded, increasing by 66 percent between 1910 and 1920 (to 152,467) and by another 115 percent (to 327,706) in the following decade. The majority of these blacks were drawn to Harlem, which became the center of black life during the 1920s, but other areas expanded at the same time.[67]

A small number of blacks had lived in Eastern Brooklyn since the early 1800s, many as slaves. According to the *Brooklyn Eagle*, the first black man to own property in the area was Tom Willets, a veteran of the Union army who settled in the area after the Civil War. But few other blacks joined the Willets family. As Brownsville developed after the 1880s, Jewish merchants drew their employees from their existing workforce on the Lower East Side, and they did not need or desire black workers. However, by 1920, the area's cheap housing drew a small number of blacks to Brownsville.[68]

Throughout the city, landlords forced blacks to pay high rents for the worst housing available. In their 1919 annual report, the Brooklyn Urban League argued that "the houses in which the great bulk of colored people are forced to live are totally unsatisfactory as houses in which to bring up healthy, moral families." Most of the accommodations rented to blacks were ancient frame tenements located in the older areas of the borough. Despite the decrepit conditions, Brooklyn blacks were better off than their Manhattan counterparts in at least one way—rents in these buildings were more than 30 percent less than comparable units across the East River. In the 1910s, Brownsville expanded to the west and the south, and many residents relocated to buildings in the newer neighborhoods. As the area's original buildings aged, more of them filled with blacks desperate for housing in the segregated New York market. Local landlords, unable to rent these dilapidated buildings (many of them fire hazards and lacking heat or indoor plumbing) to anyone else, offered them to housing-starved blacks.[69]

In other areas where vacancies were high, active recruitment of blacks caused dramatic changes in neighborhoods. Because of the changing demographics of the city, Harlem and Bedford-Stuyvesant became the focal points for African-American New Yorkers. In both cases, black middle-class residents were the first to settle in these areas, but poorer blacks quickly followed. Brownsville, close geographically to Bedford-Stuyvesant, was another place to which working-class blacks were drawn. In 1920 only 253 blacks lived in Brownsville—less than 0.5 percent of its population—but that number increased dramatically as the area became a viable option for working-class blacks.[70]

The 1920 census provides a glimpse of life for these pioneers. Brownsville's black residents were typical of the black working-class of the period.

Before World War I, blacks were almost completely excluded from New York's industrial economy, and in 1910, well over half of the city's blacks were employed in domestic or other personal service occupations. World War I, however, opened up opportunities for many blacks, and by 1920 nearly a quarter of black men worked in industrial occupations, many of them on the docks. But blacks remained excluded from many trades, and opportunities for advancement within New York factories were few. Black industrial workers almost always occupied the least-skilled and lowest-paid positions. A 1929 Brooklyn Urban League survey of black industrial workers found that 80 percent were classified as "unskilled." The average weekly wage for Brooklyn industrial workers was $19.72, an annual income of $1,025 provided that they were able to secure full-time employment.[71]

At the same time, the census shows that many of Brownsville's black families eked out a relatively stable existence: the men worked full-time, the women were homemakers, and their children attended school. Typical was the Bailey family, who lived at 348 Rockaway Avenue. William was a laborer at the Brooklyn shipyard. His wife maintained the house. Just down the street were the Trebleams, whose patriarch, George, worked at a brass foundry. Two doors away from them lived the Jacksons and the Higginses. William Jackson and Walter Higgins both worked along the docks as long-shoremen. The Baileys, Trebleams, Jacksons, and Higginses each lived in the typical two- to four-room shacks of the original community. Black families often shared these buildings with whites. For example, longshoreman Charles Weber, his wife, and their four children shared their rented duplex with Phillip Cudler, his wife, and their six children. Samuel Stone, a meat-packer, his wife, and their four children lived at 444 Rockaway with six white families, and Ella Freeman, a linen presser, and her sister lived at 492 Rockaway in a tenement with ten other white families.[72]

Ella Freeman and her sister were exceptional in another way in that they were among only a few nonmarried households. Of twenty-five black households on the blocks of Watkins, Osborne, Thatford, and Rockaway, twenty-three had complete nuclear families. None of the wives in these households had outside employment, which suggests that their husbands made enough money to support their families. The working women in the survey held the occupations available to them—two were laundresses and three did housework. The occupations of the males in the area were also typical of those available to blacks at that time. Seven men worked at the docks, six were drivers of some sort, two were auto mechanics, and three were building laborers. Five men worked in factories—one as a meatpacker and two as metalworkers. Tom Willets, grandson of the original black family in Brownsville, and one other resident worked as porters, a prestigious, well-paying job for blacks at that time. All of the men above the age of sixteen worked, but no one younger listed an occupation.[73]

Between 1920 and 1930 Brooklyn's black population doubled from 31,912 to 68,921. Before this time, blacks lived along the commercial avenues of Fulton and Atlantic in many neighborhoods, in housing nearest to the elevated trains and the factories on these streets. During the 1920s and 1930s, however, the neighborhood that became known as Bedford-Stuyvesant emerged as the center of black Brooklyn. Thousands of whites moved out of this area, whose housing stock was substantial but declining, during the 1920s. At the same time, subway projects and other renewal efforts in the borough uprooted many blacks. High vacancies in Bedford-Stuyvesant combined with increased demand for housing among New York blacks, and segregation within the borough intensified.[74]

As the area became recognized as a black neighborhood, it developed institutions and a social life of its own. Although not as vibrant as Harlem, "Bed-Stuy" was certainly active. In addition to several large churches and community organizations, Bedford-Stuyvesant had several movie houses that catered to black audiences—showing, for example, films directed by black directors like Oscar Micheaux. The grandest of these theaters was the Brevoort, whose twenty-five hundred seats and facilities rivaled Manhattan's opulent cinemas. Fulton Street also had many bars, restaurants, and clubs; some, including the Kingston Lounge, the Bedford Lounge, and the Pleasant Lounge, attracted clientele from as far away as Harlem.[75]

By 1930, Brownsville's own black population had swelled from 253 to 5,062. In the oldest sections of the neighborhood, blacks constituted more than 10 percent of the population. Bedford-Stuyvesant, second only to Harlem in the concentration of blacks, had filled to capacity, and many blacks looked elsewhere for housing. Rents in Brownsville were lower and space became available as white residents left the crumbling buildings built forty years before. During the 1920s, the population in the oldest section of Brownsville dropped dramatically. The dwellings in this area were among the most decrepit buildings in all of Brooklyn, but, as Doc Baroff remembered, the blacks "lived there because no one else wanted to."[76]

Black Brownsville had no significant institutions of its own before the 1930s, and black residents traveled to Bedford-Stuyvesant to worship and socialize. Slowly, however, the neighborhood built its own small community. During the 1920s, the number of black churches, the majority of them Baptist, in Brooklyn more than doubled from twenty to forty-nine. The first black church in Brownsville was St. Paul's Baptist Church. Founded in

1927 by fifteen men and women in the living room of one of the parishioners, the church grew to forty members within two years and opened a storefront facility. Long-standing members of the church remember that the windows were thin and the furnace weak—worshipers often kept their coats on during the service. Reverend Henry Milerson founded another parish in 1932; its original twenty members met in the living room of his mother but eventually moved to a storefront in the late 1930s. The chosen name for the congregation was Mount Olive Baptist Church, but the bureaucrats in the state corporation department made a mistake in filing the group's papers, and the church has been Mount Ollie ever since. The Universal Baptist Church, founded by thirteen Brownsville blacks in 1933, met at the Brownsville Community Center, a storefront established by Reverend W. B. M. Scott to serve as a meeting place for local blacks. Scott became pastor of Universal, which bought their building on Thatford Avenue for $10,000 in 1940.[77]

If whites tolerated blacks in Brownsville, they did not welcome them. Alfred Kazin, who grew up on Sutter Avenue, remembered that "We just didn't think about them. They were the people three and four blocks away you passed coming home from the subway." But Kazin also noted his parents' reaction when "another block of the earliest wooden shacks on Livonia Avenue near the subway's power station filled up with Negroes: some strange, embarrassed resentment would come out. . . . They were moving nearer and nearer. They were invading our neighborhood." Despite the resentments felt by many local whites, blacks lived in Brownsville without incident. Unlike other New York neighborhoods, there were no threats or attacks upon black families. The peace with which blacks were received drew additional families to the area over the decades to follow.[78]

Brownsville in Middle Age

Abe Reles was born on the Lower East Side, but his family moved to Brownsville when he was in seventh grade. Reles soon found the life of petty crime more attractive than school, and by the age of thirteen, he spent his time gambling, stealing from pushcarts, and extorting money from local children. He joined an emerging group of small-time criminals, including Martin "Mugsy" Goldstein, and Harry "Pittsburgh Phil" Strauss, who became his partners for life. Reles's first arrest was in 1921, when he was picked up for breaking a vending machine. Over the next twenty years, police arrested Reles at least forty-three times, and his crimes escalated from petty larceny to grand larceny, burglary, robbery, assault, and murder. Though charged five times with homicide, Reles escaped serious jail time until 1940, when he became the focal point of a criminal syndicate that local papers dubbed "Murder, Inc."[79]

In the 1910s and 1920s, employers often used gangs to prevent union organizing by threatening and beating labor leaders and workers. These syndicates grew in strength over the years, and by the 1920s they controlled much of the garment industry through intimidation of employers and infiltration of union locals. They expanded their operations to other illicit activities, including gambling, prostitution, narcotics, and loan-sharking. During Prohibition, these organizations flourished through the control of the bootlegging industry. Brooklyn's gangs, however, were never as wealthy or as powerful as the organizations that ran Manhattan speakeasies, and they never developed the hierarchical structure that enabled gangsters like Al Capone and Bugsy Seigel to become millionaires. Within Brownsville, mobsters subsisted on petty extortion, small-time money-lending, prostitution, and control of local taverns. Upwardly aspiring gangsters either made it to the "big leagues" when they were asked to join the Manhattan syndicates, or they were removed by the same mobsters for attempting to expand into already-claimed territories.[80]

Throughout the 1920s, Reles and his friends survived as low-level members of the local mob, but in the early 1930s, they won a bloody battle

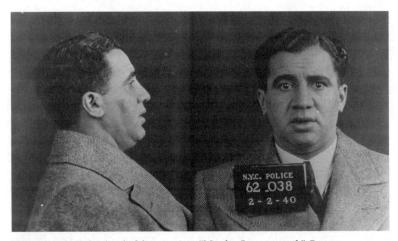

Figure 7. Abe Reles, head of the notorious "Murder, Incorporated." Courtesy Municipal Archives, Department of Records and Information Services, City of New York.

with the Shapiros, the most powerful family in Brownsville. After Reles's gang killed all three Shapiro brothers, they turned on their own partners, the Ambergs, and eliminated them. By the mid-1930s, Reles's group controlled Brownsville crime. Expanding their portfolio, Reles's group emerged as the elite of the city's hit men. Between 1936 and 1939, they worked to obstruct Attorney General Thomas Dewey in his investigation of the New York City mob. Contracted by the big mobsters, Reles, Goldstein, Strauss, and their associates killed several suspected informants. They were known for their extreme brutality, setting one man on fire, burying another alive, and hacking a third to death. In September 1936, the men killed Brownsville merchant Joseph Rosen in his candy store. Six months later, they strangled another Brownsville man in a local garage. Paid $100 to $250 a week for their work, Reles and his associates, according to historian Albert Fried, "swaggered through Brownsville or East New York streets with their vassals and hangers-on, wore the best, or the loudest clothes, and had the girls and cars of their dreams." Reles and his friends were famous men, reviled by most, but admired by others.[81]

Their success did not last. An intense effort initiated by Brooklyn District Attorney William O'Dwyer broke the mob's stranglehold. The syndicate began to fall apart in 1940 when O'Dwyer began a sweep in several high-crime areas, focusing on Brownsville in particular. Using a recently approved vagrancy law, police picked up hundreds of suspected criminals and closed local pool rooms, candy stores, and taverns. Several low-level criminals began to implicate the more powerful mobsters, enabling O'Dwyer to arrest Reles and several others. Reles himself became a prosecution witness, confessing to six murders and implicating several others in dozens of crimes. The district attorney's show trials revealed the depravity of New York mobs, leading to the conviction and execution of several mobsters, including Reles's associates Strauss and Goldstein. The crusade occupied the front pages of New York's papers for more than a year, catapulting O'Dwyer into citywide celebrity that culminated in his election as mayor. While Reles escaped the death penalty by testifying against his friends, he did not avoid the retribution of the mob: he was found hanged in his cell.[82]

The scandal brought much unwanted attention to Brownsville, and reporters from national papers and journals came to chronicle the seamy side of the neighborhood. O'Dwyer himself credited Brownsville with the distinction of "spawning more gangsters and criminals than any other section in the city." Crime statistics supported his assertion. As a result primarily of gang activities, Brownsville was the site of twenty murders in 1939. Novelist Arthur Granit, describing these years, said that in Brownsville "it was nothing unusual to have a body shot up and thrown in some side alleyway." A study of Brooklyn's high-crime areas cited Brownsville's northeast quadrant as the worst in the borough. The area had the highest rates of assaults, robberies, and total crime in Brooklyn.[83]

Many Brownsville youths were attracted to the glamour of the mob, and local gangsters worked to gain the trust of their prospective recruits. "We used to play cops and robbers with them," remembered Doc Baroff. "They were the cops and we were the robbers." Gang activities contributed to the area's high juvenile delinquency rate, which in 1939 was 25 percent higher than Brooklyn as a whole. Residents complained that it was not possible to walk down Rockaway Avenue from the train station at night, because they were beaten and robbed by local youths. The situation was severe enough that several organizations, led by the Jewish Board of Guardians, organized a special program to deal with juvenile delinquents in Brownsville.[84]

Several memoirs of Brownsville youths describe a significant level of violence in the area. As William Poster recalled: "we were content with being what everyone else reviled, and ardently desired to be even rougher, tougher, dirtier, more ill-mannered, more uncompromisingly opposed to every kind of law, order and authority." Although there were many neighborhoods in New York where youths were unruly, Poster argued, "in Brownsville, somehow we worked at it full time." Like most immigrant neighborhoods, Brownsville had long provided a great deal of freedom, and opportunities for trouble, to its young. Many recent immigrants possessed neither the language ability nor the understanding of American culture to combat the vices evident in the community. Often it was the children who interpreted American rules for their less educated parents. As a result, parental authority was undermined, and children were free to develop without mature guidance. Brownsville was a rough community, and Brownsville boys quickly developed the swagger and attitude necessary to survive. "The weak were simply despoiled of all rights and privileges and every shred of self-respect. Pity, charity, remorse were nearly non-existent emotions among Brownsville male juveniles," remembered Poster.[85]

Violence is a constant theme of novels set in Brownsville, including Henry Roth's *Call It Sleep*, Arthur Granit's *In the Time of Peaches*, and Irving Shulman's *Amboy Dukes*. Although set in different periods, each work devotes much attention to the chaotic life of the streets and constant confrontations between local youths. These novels describe the streets as the major influence on Brownsville boys, with their parents mostly helpless by contrast. Shulman in particular poignantly depicts the inner struggle of Brownsville youths as they try to be good, law-abiding citizens but often succumb to the attractions offered by the camaraderie of the gang. Most teenagers avoided a life of crime, but all Brownsville youths in these stories were affected by the underside of Brownsville society. These novels revealed the tensions facing working-class youths as they navigate the path to adulthood, a journey that some never completed. All of the boys in these Brownsville-based novels had limited options in their economically and socially isolated neighborhood. Most Brownsville teens followed the rules, but, these novels argue, Brownsville's ghetto status restricted their options.[86]

Crime and delinquency were only two of Brownsville's woes. Built quickly and cheaply, housing declined rapidly in the neighborhood, and high-density apartment buildings resulted in serious sanitation and health problems. The area's deterioration coincided with the growth of outer Brooklyn, and developers constructed more than 118,000 residential units in the borough during the 1920s. Most of these homes were built in sparsely populated areas in the southern half of Brooklyn, including Bay Ridge, Bensonhurst, Sheepshead Bay, Flatbush, and Canarsie, and they drew on an upwardly aspiring class of Brooklynites. Realtors stressed the privacy and quiet provided by these new homes. They also touted the "modern interiors" and new appliances, things in scarce supply in Brownsville. Many successful Brownsville residents moved to these new areas during the 1920s, and their departure weakened neighborhood institutions. Brownsville's population peaked in 1925 at 108,097; the number of area residents declined by almost 5,000 in 1930. In reality, many more people left Brownsville during the 1920s. The continued arrival of new European immigrants in the first half of the decade eased the departure of successful residents. Eighty-four thousand Polish and Russian Jews immigrated to New York City in the 1920s, and large numbers of them settled in Brownsville. In the long run, however, these immigrants were not enough to stem the decline in Brownsville's population. Between 1925 and 1940, the number of people in the neighborhood decreased by more than 9,000 at the same time the number of people in the borough increased by more than half a million.[87]

To prevent further deterioration, local leaders pushed for new services and investment in the area. In 1935, the Brownsville League for New Housing held a mass meeting to demand the clearance of deteriorated buildings and the construction of "model tenements," like those being built on the Lower East Side. Brownsville business and political leaders protested the city's neglect of the area and its failure to provide playgrounds, parks, and other facilities. "Every section has improved in the years," stated

Brownsville activist Isaac Siegmeister, "but Brownsville has not. Throughout the land the demand has gone up for public improvements. Federal and
state governments must rebuild and again improve. Unless we in Brownsville make our demands felt we will continue to be neglected." Another
Brownsville patron, attorney Irving Feinberg, argued that Brownsville had
not changed a bit since he graduated from high school twenty-seven years
before. "It's about time that money was appropriated to clear away these old
buildings," he concluded. And a third activist said, "our children have
moved away as soon as they could. Let us rebuild our old homes and make
places for them to bring them back."[88]

But the task in front of these politicians and businessmen was immense.
In 1934, the city of New York conducted the Real Property Inventory of all
the boroughs, in part to help the city decide which areas to designate for
clearance and renewal, and planners quickly focused on the oldest section of
Brownsville. The City Planning Commission designated a "slum area"
bounded by Rockaway, Livonia, Sutter, and Stone, comprising 222 buildings. The survey classified 30 percent of the buildings as "poor" and another
60 percent as "fair." Only 8 of the 222 buildings were less than fifteen years
old; 49 were more than thirty-five years old. Two-thirds of the homes had
frame structures, a style that had violated building standards for decades.
Sixty percent of the buildings in the slum area lacked heat and 46 percent
had no hot running water. Tellingly, in a year in which families searched
desperately for affordable housing, 15 percent of this area's apartments
were vacant. A report by the Home Owners' Loan Corporation described
Brownsville as "a very old and congested neighborhood, the character of
which has shown no improvement and little change over a period of many
years." According to the HOLC investigator, the area had "poor upkeep,
lack of pride," and a "communistic type of people who agitated rent strikes
some time ago." The area was not a good place for investment, the description concluded.[89]

In several ways Brownsville in 1940 was not very different from
Brownsville in 1910. The majority of the residents were Jewish and working-class, and full of hardworking people hoping for a better future. Despite
devoting a 1939 report to the significant problems facing the community,
one social worker noted that the "crowded parks, playgrounds and recreation centers, the great number of churches and synagogues, of clubs and
other organizations, indicate the desire as well as some ability to achieve
communal life on a limited scale." The main difference between the
Brownsville of 1910 and that of 1940 was its apparent age. The years had
taken their toll on the neighborhood; the housing stock was deteriorated,

the schools were crumbling, the community facilities were overextended, and the infrastructure was in crisis. During the boom years before the Great Depression these deficits appeared to be surmountable, but by 1940 problems such as haphazard development, social and political marginalization, and economic instability severely weakened the community. All these factors had a big impact on post–World War II Brownsville and shaped the efforts of area residents to revitalize their neighborhood.[90]

Figure 8. The Brownsville Neighborhood Council, Sanitation Campaign, 1948. Brownsville community groups frequently included children in their activities. Courtesy Brooklyn Collection, Brooklyn Public Library.

2

The Optimistic Years:
Brownsville in the Forties

Rae Glauber grew up in Brownsville during the 1930s and
1940s and continued to live there until her death in the
late 1960s. She was an activist throughout her adult
years—an organizer for the Brownsville Community
Congress of Industrial Organizations, a board member of
the Brownsville Neighborhood Council, and later an antipoverty worker in the 1960s—and her work touched almost every organization in the community. Glauber's
memoir, *All Neighborhoods Change: A History of Brownsville
Brooklyn* (1963), paints a lively picture of the neighborhood and is particularly useful for understanding the
role women played in Brownsville during the 1940s
and 1950s. Women had a long tradition of activism in
Brownsville, and the war years saw their heavy involvement in supporting the men overseas. Brownsville women
formed "Victory Clubs" to sell war bonds, ran knitting circles, sent letters to soldiers, gathered scrap metal for bul-
lets, and organized parties honoring fallen soldiers. They
also organized Russian relief groups to provide food and
financial assistance to starving families, and they operated
the civilian defense organizations that prepared local resi-

dents for war. Brownsville women were also active in political affairs, although the Democratic Party club was closed to them. Several groups, most significantly the Brownsville Women's Non-Partisan Committee for Registration, pushed Brownsville residents to get involved in politics to secure badly needed government services. In September 1944, First Lady Eleanor Roosevelt spoke to thirty-five hundred Brownsville women at a rally sponsored by the group.[1]

Domestically, the war brought the nation out of the depression by putting millions to work in war industries. The war transformed migration patterns, drawing many people to cities and to the developing West Coast. More than two million blacks left the South in search of better opportunities. Thousands of them came to New York and settled in Brownsville. The war also had a dramatic impact on American society, drawing people closer together in pursuit of a common goal. This was especially true of immigrant Americans, many of whom did not feel completely accepted in American society until this period. These immigrants, particularly Jews, worked actively to support the war effort. Hitler's destruction of Jewish society in Eastern Europe certainly was an important factor in the involvement of American Jews, but the war also presented an opportunity to prove their patriotism. Second-generation immigrants aided the war mobilization more directly by volunteering to serve in the armed forces. These servicemen not only testified to their own commitment but also to the patriotism of their families and their communities.[2]

In prewar Brownsville, residents were generally isolated, relying primarily on their families, their neighborhoods, and their congregations; most Brownsville organizations were small and focused on specific issues. In the 1940s, however, the residents started to look more broadly to the city and the nation, and several communitywide groups emerged that sought to unify the neighborhood and struggle for area improvements. The most significant of these groups were the Brownsville Neighborhood Council (BNC), the Brownsville Boys Club (BBC), and the Brownsville Community Congress of Industrial Organizations (Brownsville CIO). Although they represented different constituencies and espoused different ideologies, each of these groups worked to make government agencies more responsive to the needs of Brownsville residents. The founders of the BNC, BBC, and Brownsville CIO believed that through organization Brownsville residents could create a better neighborhood and increase opportunities for the most unfortunate residents.

In the short term, the war mobilization brought increased activism to Brownsville, and these groups racked up several achievements during the optimistic forties. They secured new housing, new parks, and other community facilities, and they forced government and private institutions to be more accountable in protecting the poor from the housing, health, and other social problems that plagued the neighborhood. In the long run, however, the economic and social changes brought on by the war had negative effects on Brownsville. In the late 1940s and early 1950s, thousands of second-generation residents took advantage of the GI Bill and economic expansion and moved to newer areas. The departure of young men and women, many of them activists, weakened the community by removing many of the people with the energy, ability, and financial resources to keep the neighborhood viable.[3]

But the impact of these demographic changes was not readily apparent in the late 1940s. Most Brownsville residents assumed that the neighborhood would continue to serve the function it had for more than forty years—the slow acculturation of Jewish immigrants. The organizations that Brownsville activists created sought to improve life for neighborhood residents, but they were not prepared to deal with the dramatic shifts that the community witnessed in the 1950s.

Brownsville in the War Years

Hundreds of Brownsville residents served in the military, and those who remained at home bought war bonds, donated blood, and supplied materials needed to support the troops. Brownsville community organizations actively assisted both the European Jews fleeing the holocaust and the Allied effort to win the war. Since most Brownsville residents traced their ancestry to Russia, they were also excited by the short-lived detente between the United States and the Soviet Union. America's alliance with the Soviets allowed Brownsville Jews for a short time to proudly proclaim their heritage. Many congregations organized Russian relief efforts and several rallies were held in area halls to welcome Russian leaders. "No other section of Brooklyn so heralded the new (second) front," remembered one resident. On Victory in Europe Day, Brownsville residents turned out in droves at a rally and march to celebrate the end of the conflict.[4]

Brownsville women and men also created organizations that responded to changes in American society brought on by the conflict. Wartime inflation was a major concern to the working-class residents of the area, and Rae Glauber and other activists worked with the Office of Price Administration to combat price gouging. Throughout the country, the government established local boards known as "little OPA's" to enforce price regulations, and Brownsville's female activists became frontline inspectors. Three hundred thousand volunteers, mostly women, served across the country, many as "price panel assistants" who regularly compared prices at local grocery stores to the OPA guidelines. In Brownsville, the women also exposed corrupt inspectors who took bribes from local grocers. Within the neighborhood, Glauber and others organized meat strikes against exploitive local butchers and rent strikes against local landlords. Sometimes these battles got violent, Glauber remembered. "A woman passed the picket line and entered the butcher shop. When she emerged, she got hit on the head with a chicken by a picket. Soon there was a battle. The police wagons came out and arrested some of the leaders." Brownsville women were in the forefront of these movements.[5]

Labor organizations provided much of the infrastructure for the OPA effort and for local activism in general. The war effort increased the influence of labor unions across the country, in particular the fledgling Congress of Industrial Organizations. Throughout the industrial areas of the nation, CIO locals flourished in this short-lived period of labor-corporate cooperation. Brownsville, long a center for union organizing, was a leader in this movement. Unlike the competing American Federation of Labor (AFL), the CIO actively sought to develop grassroots support for labor organizations by creating Industrial Union Councils (IUCs) in working-class neighborhoods. The main purpose of the IUCs was to bring together representatives of local unions to coordinate support for local strikes, organizing campaigns, and political elections. In many cities, IUCs took on a larger mandate, fighting against price gouging in consumer goods and rents, organizing campaigns for civil rights and social justice, and assuming the mantle of community leadership. The Brownsville Community CIO was an active member of New York's citywide CIO Council. In addition to its work on consumer protection, the Brownsville CIO organized neighborhood groups and block clubs and brought together civic and institutional leaders to fight for neighborhood improvements.[6]

Most IUCs did not play an important role in their communities. The difficulties faced by working people did not ease quickly with the wartime mobilization, and food and housing shortages were severe. CIO councils were not equipped to respond to such concerns, and as a result they received little support from residents. Although the Brownsville CIO could not solve the problems created by wartime inflation, it did encourage residents to seek solutions. At the Brownsville Labor Lyceum, large groups of neighborhood residents met to organize protests against local landlords and grocers who violated wartime price controls. The Brownsville CIO also produced a community resource guide that provided information on government and privately run programs to aid residents in need of assistance, and it gave guidance to tenants regarding their rights in rent-controlled apartments. The group focused both on local concerns, such as removing an anti-Semitic policeman, and national concerns, such as fighting for the passage of the Fair Employment Practices Act. To strengthen ties within the neighborhood, the Brownsville CIO organized goodwill dinners and holiday parties that sought to improve relations between blacks and whites and keep union members abreast of the activities of the CIO's affiliates.[7]

Throughout the 1940s, housing demand in New York was high and landlords dramatically increased rents in many buildings, making thousands of families unable to afford shelter. During the war the OPA attempted to impose rent restrictions, but it was often unable to enforce these guidelines. The "Temporary State Rent Commission," created through pressure from New York's labor organizations, was also charged with the responsibility of protecting residents from price gouging, but it too was ineffective. The Brownsville Tenants Council was thus created by CIO activists to prevent local landlords from exploiting residents. The group distributed circulars to inform tenants of their rights and supported local tenants' organizations. Brownsville's housing stock was in serious disrepair, and rats, refuse, crumbling walls, and rusted pipes were a constant problem, as were fires and gas explosions. Through the Brownsville Tenants Council, residents pressed the State Rent Commission to investigate and fine local landlords. According to Glauber, the council had five thousand members during the war, one-third of them black. "Tenant Council headquarters became a haven for refugees of landlord terror. . . . the faithful helped raise money, run functions, sweep—in short, to them it was a kind of union hall." Council volunteers helped local residents make complaints, organized presentations at local meetings, and pursued major violators in court.[8]

It is difficult to determine how many Brownsville residents participated in the programs of the Brownsville CIO. Leftist organizers were unquestionably the leaders of the organization, and often other groups declined to work with CIO activists because of their Communist connections. In 1943, Rae Glauber attempted to organize a protest against the reinstatement of a local policeman accused of anti-Semitism. Several Jewish advocacy organizations, including the American Jewish Committee, the American Jewish

Congress, and the Brooklyn Jewish Community Council (BJCC), attended the meetings, but they squelched the protest rally. The BJCC representative concluded that the protest "was influenced by a number of Communist Front elements which were present, and that because of the make-up of the group, it would be unadvisable for our office to participate in any of its activities." Established groups like the American Jewish Congress and the American Jewish Committee were generally opposed to grassroots organization, choosing rather to use connections and private pressure to secure changes. In the case of the anti-Semitic police officer, these organizations preferred to organize "a group of leading citizens to try to arrange an appointment to meet with Commissioner of Police Valentine." Their efforts failed, and the commissioner placed the officer back on the beat.[9]

The leadership of elite advocacy organizations did not live in Brownsville, and they did not bear the brunt of discrimination. They resided in more genteel communities and looked at such matters in abstract terms. Brownsville residents were used to protest and believed that it was often the only productive means for achieving a goal. While the CIO Councils were less successful elsewhere, the Brownsville CIO provided a forum for liberal and leftist political activism in the neighborhood. As in most parts of the borough, the Democratic Party in Brownsville was controlled by professionals who used the party apparatus for their own benefit. Most local politicians were unresponsive to the needs of the area, and the Brownsville CIO Council provided organization and influence to residents lacking political clout. These groups created communitywide unity in an area that was otherwise divided by race and gradations of class. Glauber remembered that the CIO Council created "consensus among ministers, CIO, rabbis, councilmen, police captains, legislators, [community] leaders, [and] political, Jewish, [and] parent leaders." Throughout the war years, the Brownsville CIO served as a clearinghouse for Brownsville organizations, providing them information and logistical support.[10]

The Brownsville Boys Club

Children were the focus of much activity in these years. Political leaders, during the war and the anticommunist crusade that followed, were particularly concerned with securing the patriotism of American youths. Activism for youth took all forms during the 1940s, from the mundane Parent-Teachers Associations to the exotic "Pied Pipers." The Schools Council of Brownsville and East New York, led by Reverend Homer McEwen, the black minister of Congregational Church on Watkins Avenue, established "Telephone Tuesday," where each week parent leaders called all the other parents to discuss important issues at local schools. Another mechanism designed to educate children was the "Pied Piper" program, which organized entertainment spectacles that included patriotic education. In 1941, eight hundred area youths paraded through the neighborhood to Public School 64 to hear about plans for civil defense. At the event, local rabbis and black ministers stressed the need to overcome "racial, religious and political differences" in the battle against Hitler. In 1944, Brownsville children attended the "Good Will Youth Festival" at the Loew's Pitkin Theater. There they took an "Oath of Good Will" written by Judge Joseph Proskauer that committed them to "the advancement of the highest ideal—dignity of mankind, human equality, fellowship and brotherhood." In changing neighborhoods like Brownsville, local leaders gave additional attention to race relations among youths. On February 16, 1947, local groups organized another goodwill event, the "Know Your Neighbor Interracial Youth Festival," featuring lightweight champion boxer Henry Armstrong. Organizers weighed in against both anti-Semitism and racism at these unity events. Like their black neighbors, many Jews were subject to employment and housing discrimination in the 1940s, and many were denied jobs at Manhattan firms like Metropolitan Life Insurance. Injustice was not an abstract idea to Brownsville residents.[11]

Brownsville's teenagers took these lessons of goodwill to heart and many participated in local organizations during the war years. The Brownsville Boys Club (BBC), like other groups in the area, emerged out of the residents' belief that Brownsville was not receiving the resources it needed. Other than Betsy Head Park, a recreation area too small to serve the densely populated neighborhood, there were almost no places for local children to play. Private institutions like the YMCA and YMHA served other Brooklyn communities, but they did not have a major presence in Brownsville. According to a 1940 study of recreational facilities, Brownsville fell far below acceptable levels in every category, from playgrounds to fields to park areas. Parks Department head Robert Moses himself acknowledged that Brownsville's need in this area would be great even after planned facilities were completed, noting that "[t]he small space set aside in the [Brownsville Houses] project for playground use will not meet the entire demands of the residents of the new houses. Even at the present time, Betsy Head Park is hardly large enough to meet the needs of the neighborhood." Another study found, not surprisingly, that blacks' access to recreational facilities was even more limited. The shortage of recreational areas resulted in an intense competition for those that did exist.[12]

In 1940, after a number of cars parked near the PS 184 (the local elementary school) fields were damaged, a the school board decided to restrict the use of the fields to those younger than thirteen. In response to their exclusion, a group of boys led by Jacob "Doc" Baroff organized a campaign to get the Board of Education to allow them to use the fields. Even though they secured over one thousand signatures, city officials rejected the boys' petition without consideration. This rebuff motivated the boys to organize a larger group of petitioners, and with the support of neighborhood adults, they regained access to the field. The success served as a rallying force for the creation of the BBC, enabling the boys to unite in their efforts to improve their situation in the neighborhood.[13]

While many boys played important roles in the creation of the BBC, Doc Baroff was the founding father. Baroff's parents came to Brownsville from Russia early in the century. Like many residents, they worked in the garment trades originally, and Baroff's father also worked on the construction of the subway system. After a few years, the Baroffs turned to peddling, and they eventually opened a small secondhand shop in Williamsburg. "We were very poor," remembered Baroff, "but we were rich in tradition." Baroff's extended family included many notable rabbis and scholars, and they passed their love of learning on to him. Just a teenager, Doc Baroff was the responsible person to whom adults turned when they had problems with Brownsville juveniles. Over time, he gained such respect that local police called on him to take supervision of first-time juvenile offenders. Before he reached his twenties, Baroff was a substitute father to many of the boys in the neighborhood.[14]

During the depression and after, many Brownsville boys suffered from economic and social neglect, and a large number had no fathers at home. Because there were few jobs in New York, male heads frequently left their families to find work in other parts of the country. Under New York's public assistance program, a family became eligible for aid if the father died, and many local men disappeared so that their families could qualify for financial support. "Many men who I thought were dead I later found out had just left," remembered Dudley Gaffin, a former BBC member. But in fact, during the 1930s and 1940s, many young fathers did die, often as a result of occupational hazards—for example, the inhalation of lead paint and other noxious fumes by those in the construction trades. "In my first group of youth, more than half had no fathers," remembered Baroff. Through the BBC, Baroff and the others increased the number of facilities and the amount of resources devoted to Brownsville children. In addition, the group provided a mechanism for peaceful interaction between different groups of young people.[15]

After winning the right to use the fields at PS 184, the BBC set its sights on other facilities. Through the cooperation of Parks Department officials, who were impressed by their organization, the BBC was able to achieve almost open access to the neighborhood recreational facilities, including the right to regulate the use of the parks and their equipment. Almost two thousand boys were BBC members by 1945. During its first five years, the BBC developed strong relationships with several organizations, including the Police Athletic League, the YMHA, and the Brooklyn Council for Social Planning. With the support of these groups and others, the BBC was able to secure funds for equipment and the rental of a clubhouse. Baroff, Izzy Lesovoy, and Norman Goroff were active recruiters of local boys, through their clubs and gangs, and they created an organizational infrastructure envied by many established social work organizations. They published a newsletter written by the members, organized trips to museums and to sporting events (to see the beloved Dodgers), and sent several hundred poor youths to camp for the first time.[15]

The BBC provided not only recreational opportunities but also a training ground for Brownsville males. The group charged dues of one penny a month to all members and had detailed operating guidelines. It had its own "penal code," which punished members by denying them athletic privileges, and each constituent club had voting rights in the BBC assembly in accordance with the number of people in its group. The officers, with the approval of the "board of directors," allocated the BBC revenues to specific programs and arranged for competitions among the groups. Baroff and the other BBC leaders also organized all-star clubs in basketball, baseball, and other sports to compete in borough and citywide competitions. "We had Friday night meetings in the library. We met there for seven years without an adult," remembered Baroff. By providing a safe, supportive atmosphere for local boys, the BBC filled a great need in Brownsville during the 1940s. Juvenile delinquency, long a problem in the area, had increased during the war. The problem was so severe that when the Brooklyn Council for Social Planning (BSCP) launched a pilot program against delinquency in 1944, the council selected a site at the heart of Brownsville. After World War II, when delinquency intensified, the BBC was one of the major institutions in

Brownsville working to solve this problem. From its beginning as an athletic club, the BBC thus developed into a resource for many of Brownsville's youths, while serving as a mediator between the young people and several adult institutions.[17]

The Brownsville Neighborhood Council

Brownsville's working-class activists operated in many forums during the 1940s—as tenants' advocates, union organizers, and political leaders. Local institutional and business leaders were also energized by the war effort, and they too increased their community participation. The focal point of their efforts was the Brownsville Neighborhood Council (BNC), founded in 1938 as a coalition of more than twenty local civic associations, leaders of community institutions, and owners of area businesses. The forces behind the creation of the BNC were attorney Milton Goell, Rabbi Alter Landesman, director of the Hebrew Educational Society, and local businessman Thomas Atkins. The primary goals of the BNC, as stated in its charter, were (1) to stimulate more active and effective participation by the citizens of the community; (2) to secure neighborhood improvements; and (3) to cooperate with governmental and private agencies in matters affecting community welfare. The organization was active in the neighborhood for more than two decades.[18]

In its early years neighborhood elites controlled the BNC. While the group eventually became more representative of the whole Brownsville community, most of its early board members were established businessmen, or their wives, and institutional leaders. For Thomas Atkins, the BNC provided a means to "give back to the community" that had helped him grow his business into a flourishing operation. Local politicians, such as Democratic district leader and state assemblyman Jacob Gralla and Alfred Lama, also a state assemblyman, were also board members. As the board expanded in the mid-1940s, black ministers were also elected to executive positions, notably Reverend Homer McEwen of Congregational Church and Reverend Boise Dent of Tabernacle Baptist Church. Leaders of boroughwide organizations such as the Jewish Board of Guardians and the board of education also participated. Women too became active BNC members. Dorothy Montgomery, the head librarian at the Brownsville branch of the Brooklyn Library, was a board member, as was Sarah Fox, a local teacher. While men held a majority of official positions, the organizational work of the group was often done by the women, particularly Montgomery and Fox, as well as political activists Mildred Wickson and Sue Hein. Several BNC members who had moved from Brownsville to Eastern Parkway looked upon their BNC involvement as an obligation to those less fortunate.[19]

The public faces of the group were Alter Landesman and Milton Goell. Landesman ran the Hebrew Educational Society (HES), the most important Jewish organization in the community. The BNC enabled Landesman to maintain the HES as a center for community activism and to connect local residents to their religious heritage, and the BNC held meetings most frequently at the HES headquarters. After four years as the first president of the group, Landesman turned his title over to Goell in 1942. Goell's interest in the BNC was shaped by his family's success in getting out of the area. His father was one of Brownsville's main builders, but the Goell family moved out of the neighborhood in the 1920s. Goell's upbringing was dramatically different from the typical Brownsville youth: he graduated from Harvard in 1925, received a law degree from St. John's University, and later received a Ph.D. from Yeshiva University. Goell's law practice was located in downtown Brooklyn, but he also owned property within Brownsville. He wrote at least seven books, novels and memoirs, including *Tramping through Palestine, To All You Ladies, America—The Fourth Decade*, and *The Wall That Is My Skin*, and he also published several poems.[20]

Despite or perhaps because of his comfortable economic situation, Goell was active in many leftist causes. He was a friend of Eleanor Roosevelt, was active in political parties that opposed the Tammany machine, and was nominated by the American Labor Party to the city council in 1945. Each of the pamphlets produced by the BNC in the 1940s was written by Goell, and he used each not only to advocate for resources in Brownsville but also as a political platform to promote the themes of government responsibility for the poor and equal rights. The involvement of men like Goell gave the BNC entry into many of the corridors of power in New York City and provided the BNC with the resources necessary to publicize its activities. In addition, a publicity campaign preceded each BNC publication to ensure that it received attention from media and government officials.[21]

Under the bylaws of the BNC, all organizations of fifty or more persons "in good standing and interested in the civic affairs of Brownsville, without regard to creed, race, sex or political party," were eligible for membership. Each member organization was allowed to elect two delegates to the BNC. Despite these democratic provisions, in its first decade the BNC was hardly a grassroots organization. It claimed in 1940 that its twenty-eight constituent groups represented more than five thousand people, but these residents rarely participated in the group's deliberations. They were only called upon when the BNC wanted a large crowd at one of its rallies. Local elites ran the BNC and pushed their own agenda, and the primary concern of the group was to bring new government and private resources to Brownsville. During these years the BNC lobbied for slum clearance, public housing, health and recreational buildings, and other programs that they thought would make Brownsville more attractive. All of these programs would certainly improve life for Brownsville's poor, but they would also, BNC leaders hoped, keep residents in the neighborhood, maintain or increase property values, and support local businesses and institutions like the HES. Thus the first major activity of the BNC was its effort to secure slum clearance and public housing in the neighborhood.[22]

The Case for Public Housing in Brownsville

New York was a pioneer in the development of affordable housing, with innovations such as cooperative housing and not-for-profit housing corporations that promoters hoped would solve the housing crisis for the city's working class. Although many of these projects were successful, housing advocates realized that without government support they would never be able to meet the enormous demand for affordable housing, and they pushed for expanded federal housing programs during the New Deal. New York's liberals were behind the funding of the Public Works Administration (PWA) Housing Program in 1933 and the creation of the U.S. Housing Authority in 1937. The first units completed by the New York City Housing Authority (NYCHA), the First Houses, were built on Manhattan's Lower East Side in 1935. Over the next six years, nearly thirteen thousand units of public housing were under construction or completed.[23]

From the commencement of the New York public housing program, Brownsville leaders worked to secure a project for their own neighborhood. City officials selected the oldest section of Brownsville as a future site for public housing in 1934, along with Williamsburg and Red Hook, but by the end of the decade, Brownsville alone lacked plans for such a project. This neglect brought protests from many area leaders, and State Senator Jacob Schwartzwald complained to the USHA that Brownsville was "sorely in need of slum clearance projects" and requested that the situation be rectified. Representatives of the businesses in the area also pushed for the clearance of Brownsville's worst slums, arguing that "it is disgraceful to permit human beings to inhabit them, for they are breeders of disease and should be forthwith demolished."[24]

Although NYCHA officials acknowledged the need in Brownsville, the amount of money allocated for public housing was small, and the eligible areas were numerous. The lack of funds, Assistant Director George Brown argued, "makes it incumbent upon us to attempt to alleviate the worst conditions throughout the City." He told the BNC's attorney that because Brooklyn already had two projects, one in Williamsburg, and the other under construction in Red Hook, "you can readily see that attention must also be given to other sections of the City which up to now have received no consideration." For the short-term, at least, Brownsville had to wait for public housing. In the spring of 1940 the Brownsville Neighborhood Council, with the support of other local groups, increased the pressure on local government through a well-organized campaign for public housing. The group commissioned drawings of buildings, held community meetings to describe the housing program and solicit support for it, and met with city officials to lobby for selection. The most important facet of this campaign was the publication of "Brownsville Must Have Public Housing," a pamphlet written by Milton Goell.[25]

In cities like Chicago and Detroit, and even in certain parts of New York, white working-class neighborhoods responded violently to the development of public housing during the 1940s. Even in its early years, many whites identified public housing as housing for blacks, and they believed that the development of these projects would result in the "invasion" of their neighborhoods. By contrast, Brownsville lobbied hard for public housing. Such activism fit comfortably within the ideology of Brownsville residents, because, unlike other working-class groups that opposed any type of "socialistic programs," Brownsville Jews believed that government should intervene when the market failed. Many Brownsville business leaders looked upon public housing as a way to stabilize the community and maintain a substantial white population in the neighborhood. Upwardly mobile residents had been leaving Brownsville for two decades, and even though the depression slowed this process, local leaders were justifiably worried about the future of their neighborhood. Housing advocates did not have the financial wherewithal to develop a private project, so they looked to the government to clear the dilapidated area.[26]

Slum clearance was just as attractive to Brownsville activists like Goell, Landesman, and Atkins as were new projects. Liberals all, they philosophically supported the program, but they also knew that the projects had to be better than the rotted buildings they would replace. One-third of the residents of the slum clearance area were black, and race certainly played a role in the considerations of BNC leaders. But the racial motivations of the BNC leaders were more complicated than those of their counterparts in other communities. BNC leaders believed strongly, and stated frequently, that all people deserved a decent home, regardless of color. They also knew that the area's black residents lived in the worst housing in the neighborhood. Goell and other BNC leaders expected blacks and whites to live together in the new projects, functioning as models for interracial living. Most practically, unlike other neighborhoods where projects might bring the introduction of new races, blacks were already in Brownsville. They occupied housing "that no one else wanted." Public housing could serve as a savior to both blacks and whites in the area and prevent the expansion of blacks into the surrounding neighborhood. The slum clearance area had the highest crime rate in the neighborhood, and if BNC leaders did not imply that blacks were the cause of the problem, they certainly believed that blacks were partially responsible. Progressive philosophy held that "environmental problems" created crime, delinquency, and health problems. New housing could cure these problems and prevent them from spreading into other areas (that is, those areas inhabited by whites).[27]

The purpose of "Brownsville Must Have Public Housing" was to rally the population to increase pressure on city officials and to use government statistics to make the case for urban renewal. Like other areas that received public housing, the pamphlet argued, much of Brownsville fit the definition of a slum. The clearance area—the northeast section of the neighborhood—abounded "in shacks and hovels which were flimsy, ill-designed, and badly equipped to start with, and have grown tenfold worse with age, neglect, and poor management." According to Goell, homes lacked adequate light, air, sunshine, space, water, heat, safety, and sanitary facilities, and the Brownsville slum area was filled with "dirty, bad-smelling, germ-ridden structures, abutting upon crowded, ugly, barren streets." These areas deteriorated even more quickly during the depression. Most of Brownsville's landlords, Goell noted, were working-class or middle-class people who owned only a few properties and were forced to abandon them or see them foreclosed when they could not meet their mortgage payments. The lucky ones able to hold onto their buildings were unable to afford the necessary maintenance or improvements. As a result, much of Brownsville's housing stock was uninhabitable.[28]

The majority of the clearance area's housing stock was more than twenty-five years old. These apartments were built with low-quality materials, and "construction originally was in large part slap-together, speculative, jerry-built." Many of the buildings had long since deteriorated, held together only by the "meanest kind of tinkering and fixing." According to the 1934 Real Property Inventory, twenty-five thousand Brownsville residents lived in improperly heated units, more than fifteen thousand lived in apartments that lacked running hot water, more than thirty-seven hundred had no bathing facilities, and almost two thousand people had to use outdoor toilet facilities. The worst conditions were in the designated slum area. Goell showed that 56 percent of the buildings were more than thirty-five years old, and that 87 percent were in fair to poor condition. Approximately four hundred units in the slum area were vacant. The fact that such substandard housing was the only shelter affordable to so many people, especially black families, supported the argument that the private market could not provide housing to Brownsville's poor. "The hard fact remains that, in general, neither the white people nor the Negroes dwelling in the housing zone can afford to pay for adequate private housing," argued Goell. Private enterprise, according to the BNC, could not provide for these people, and it was "the duty of our democratic society to help provide housing for those in the lowest income brackets."[29]

Goell argued that the new buildings would create a better environment for local residents. "It has long been common knowledge among social and health workers that this section has been spawning anti-social elements entirely out of proportion to its population. The history of the community, its economy and social complexity, and its deplorable housing facilities, have all made for a concentration of anti-social factors which our society must now obliterate without hesitancy or delay, in self-defense, and for the physical, moral and economic health of our city." Brownsville activists looked to slum clearance and public housing development not only to improve the housing stock of the area but also to revitalize the social fabric of the community. They expected the same neighborhood transformation that they believed developments in Williamsburg and First Houses had caused. In its research, the BNC found that the Williamsburg Houses experienced only one case of delinquency among the 1,622 families. Public housing, Goell argued, would provide not only adequate shelter but also "a new life" to its residents, giving them "cheery, comfortable, healthful homes which will have a tonic effect upon their bodies, their minds, their souls. ... The playgrounds, municipal health centers, domestic science classes, musical organizations, cultural clubs, forums, and classes, which would no doubt be found in a public housing project in Brownsville, would bring physical, social, and intellectual improvements to a larger part of Brownsville," said Goell.[30]

According to Goell, public housing would assist the whole community by eliminating crime, disease, and "other evils of the slums" and thus increasing property values. Real estate prices had so declined, he argued, "that it is almost impossible to get fresh mortgage money here." Most important to the businessmen who made up much of the BNC, the project would "pep up" local commerce, which was hurt not only by the depression but also by the decline of the area in general. Goell complained that "those inhabitants of Brownsville who can possibly do so, forsake this region as soon as they can, to find better homes and better environment for their children and for themselves."[31]

Public officials acknowledged the concerted effort of BNC leaders, but in reality, housing planners were well aware of Brownsville's problems. Scarcity of funding, not lack of interest, delayed the approval of a public housing project for the area. In the fall of 1940, the federal government al-

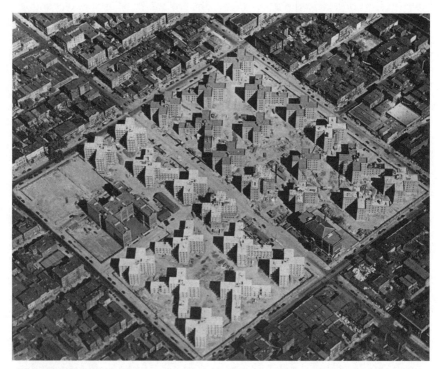

Figure 9. The Brownsville Houses. Courtesy Municipal Archives, Department of Records and Information Services, City of New York.

located additional funds, and the New York City Housing Authority announced that Brownsville would be the next area cleared. The war delayed the project for several years, but the Brownsville Houses, the first of several projects to be built in the neighborhood, opened in 1948.[32]

In addition to its efforts to secure public housing for Brownsville, the BNC worked to provide other resources for the neighborhood. In 1942, the organization published its second pamphlet, "For Better Health in Brownsville," which described the BNC's plan to improve the health problems that had plagued the community for decades. In this pamphlet, the group made its case to local government for a new, state-of-the-art health facility to replace the small existing center that could not possibly meet the demands of the residents. Illness rates among Brownsville residents exceeded the district average in several categories, with incidents of tuberculosis, gonorrhea, and infant mortality almost double the borough average. To secure a new facility, the BNC launched a well-organized lobbying campaign that included press releases to local media, several large rallies in the area, a letter-writing campaign to local politicians, and increased pressure on city health officials. All these efforts emphasized the findings in the pamphlet "For Better Health in Brownsville" and argued that the area deserved increased attention. As a result of this campaign, the New York City Health Department approved the Brownsville Health Center in 1945. Goell described it as a "modern, well-equipped building close to the heart of its [Brownsville's] worst slum area" that would become a "health mecca."[33]

Like the BNC's battle for public housing, its efforts on behalf of a health facility were useful but not vital. The New York City Health Department had planned a health center in Brownsville for several years, and when the city's budgetary restraints loosened, they moved ahead with the project. BNC leaders and Brownsville residents, however, believed that they were responsible for securing these facilities. Regardless, the health center, coupled with the public housing project, greatly increased community optimism and motivated BNC members to work for other neighborhood resources. Unfortunately, after World War II, as demands on city agencies from other neighborhoods increased, the BNC's ability to secure needed facilities declined.

The Shaping of a Postwar Community

Victory in World War II nurtured a feeling of optimism in a majority of Americans. The overwhelming sacrifices made by millions of citizens that enabled the United States to defeat its enemies convinced Americans that the nation could overcome any obstacle. Americans returned from the war confident that they could confront and conquer domestic concerns such as poverty and racism just as they had defeated Japan and Germany. In Brownsville, activists feverishly prepared their plans for a time when resources could be devoted to local concerns. However, although many individuals benefited from the economic expansion that began in the years after the war, Brownsville residents quickly learned that the neighborhood problems they hoped to cure remained intractable. Throughout the late 1940s and early 1950s, Brownsville organizations demanded city services to fight neighborhood problems such as juvenile delinquency, poor sanitation, and deteriorating schools. In each of these areas, government and private institutions ignored the requests or made only superficial attempts to solve them.[34]

During World War II, government officials at all levels took the opportunity to think about, and plan for, postwar America. Much of the planning was promoted by economists such as Alvin Hansen, who worried that the end of the war would bring the return of the depression. Keynesians argued that "public works" projects were needed to employ returning servicemen and prevent economic collapse. Yet other leaders looked upon the war as a turning point in the organization of American society. The success of the government-regulated and privately operated war mobilization convinced them that America had accepted the need for long-range planning. Across the country, cities, chambers of commerce, and other institutions prepared "master plans" for the future. In New York City, progressive elites promoted the "Regional Plan of New York and Its Environs," a broad proposal for new highways, bridges, public works, and a reshaping of the city's industrial network. Mayor La Guardia released his own "Post-War Public Works Plan," a program designed by Robert Moses to continue the redevelopment of the city. The "postwar plan" had little of the grand scope of the New York regional plan but rather focused on basic needs in city neighborhoods, offering new schools, parks, and street improvements. Neither of these proposals envisioned much new development in Brownsville.[35]

Not content to be left out of the postwar planning, in 1944 the Brownsville Neighborhood Council presented "A Post-War Plan for Brownsville," a grand scheme for the redevelopment of the neighborhood. The BNC program included demands for a nursery school, an indoor produce market, a new post office, transit improvements, the covering of the Long Island Railroad trench, public housing in eastern Brownsville, development of the shore in nearby Canarsie, zoning restrictions on development, middle-income housing, new playgrounds, a new recreation center, and a casework center. The postwar plan was a well-thought-out wish list of facilities needed in Brownsville and a request for clearance of decrepit housing and warehouses. Most of the requests expressed reasonable desires for additional facilities that had long been needed in the densely crowded neighborhood. Taken together, however, the proposals would have required tens of millions of dollars for a relatively small section of a huge city. Through the pamphlet and the accompanying campaign, the BNC aimed to ensure that Brownsville received adequate consideration in the city government's postwar plans. "Brownsville does not wish to be one of the parts where nothing, or not much, will be done. The purpose of this brochure is to set forth what Brownsville lacks, and to propose improvements which would make this world a better place in which to live, in the part of which is closest to the people of Brownsville," the introduction stated. Brownsville's postwar plan, if adopted, would dramatically reshape the neighborhood, but it received little attention outside the community.[36]

In the postwar plan, BNC leaders focused in particular on services to the poor. To complement the recently approved health facility, they argued that a social service center was needed. Brownsville had only one center providing welfare assistance, the Hebrew Educational Society, and its programs were oversubscribed. The new social service center, according to the pamphlet, would provide casework services to individuals and families and would serve as "one stop shopping" for all the social service needs of Brownsville's poor. Such a center would "facilitate the organization of a joint referral service, where people in need could be expedited—across the hall instead of across the city—to the agency best able to handle their problem." As a result, the large number of problem families in the Brownsville community would receive intervention early enough to provide the most benefit.[37]

BNC leaders also lobbied for redevelopment projects to complement the approved public housing. To provide more space for recreation, the plan proposed that the Long Island Railroad trench be enclosed and a park constructed above it. The tracks were a particular trouble spot for Brownsville youths, many of whom were injured or killed while playing along them. Five children were electrocuted in a six-month period during 1946. One Brownsville resident stated that during the seventeen years she lived in the neighborhood, at least one child was killed every summer. This proposal would eliminate a major blight on the community and erase a significant barrier between Brownsville and the more middle-class East New York. BNC leaders hoped that the park would also enhance real estate values in the surrounding area by causing the demolition of several unsightly factories and warehouses. This area could then become residential. Understanding that urban renewal required the razing of substantial parts of the neighborhood, the BNC also advocated the rehabilitation of other areas. Not all of Brownsville was a slum, Goell argued: "There are many happy memories, there are many valuable institutions, there is much worth saving." Using the medical language typical of the period, he said, "Let us cut out the cancer, let us scrape away the disease, so that the healthy tissues may live, and the bad be succeeded by good." Already cognizant of the attractions and problems of planned communities then going up on Long Island and in other parts of the borough, Goell concluded, "Let us not, in other words, make a brand-new, restless, canned community."[38]

Activists hoped that public resources would attract private dollars. Specifically, they envisioned programs to keep homeowners and landlords investing in their properties. "It is hardly economically sound," said Goell, "for an individual owner to improve his house . . . when the rest of the neighborhood remains blighted." The BNC proposed allowing owners to pool their resources and, with the support of local banks and insurance companies, to rehabilitate whole blocks at a time. The postwar plan hoped New York's recently passed Redevelopment Act would create cooperative housing out of blocks of tenements. Government would finance rehabilitation of the buildings and the landscaping of their backyards into gardens and play space. Public assistance, Goell argued, would give "enlightened property owners the chance to carry along obstructionist owners, even against their will." These efforts were important, BNC leaders believed, because Brownsville would play an important role in the housing of returning war veterans. "There are no available good dwelling units to be had in New York City," the pamphlet asserted, and nowhere for servicemen and women to go "if they want to start anew." With government support, Brownsville's tenements could be rehabilitated to provide much-needed housing. Combined with new public improvements outlined by the BNC, "it would pay private enterprise to erect new buildings, because in an improved area the owners could obtain a fair return on their investments." The pamphlet proposed the redevelopment of several blocks that "could be developed into fine thoroughfares with spacious medium-rent apartment houses, the same as in other good residential areas."[39]

The overarching goal of the postwar plan was to modernize Brownsville and make it attractive enough to hold onto its existing population while also drawing newcomers to the area. Perceptions of the neighborhood were extremely important to these leaders, and they responded to every disparaging remark made by local papers or city leaders. The businessmen on Pitkin Avenue were also concerned about the images projected by two remnants of the early community—the open food market on Belmont Avenue just to the south and the pushcart peddlers who patrolled the neighborhood. Both the market and the pushcarts contributed greatly to the unsanitary conditions in the area. Brownsville merchants wanted their area to remain competitive with other commercial strips and felt that modernization was vital to this goal. To eliminate these "blights" on the community, the plan proposed an enclosed market, on Belmont Avenue, similar to those constructed on the Lower East Side and in other communities during the 1920s and 1930s. At this market, Belmont Avenue merchants and peddlers would rent space from the public authority that owned the building. Such a plan, argued Goell, would "make Brownsville streets more fit for what they are, thoroughfares, not open air stores." The market would not, the pamphlet asserted, put peddlers out of business but would instead "give them facilities to conduct business in a clean and orderly way." At the same time, the market would increase property values "for pushcarts do not lend desirability or attractiveness to the buildings in front of which they park." And, of, course, it would help established businesses, "for storekeepers find it hard to keep up with competitors who have no rent to pay." BNC leaders seemed more concerned with the appearance of the open-air market and the competition provided by vendors than with the provision of inexpensive food or the livelihood of the vendors themselves.[40]

At the end of the postwar plan, Goell quickly listed many other facilities requested by the community, including parking facilities for Pitkin Avenue, improved sanitation, and upgraded schools, police stations, and fire stations. The pamphlet made no estimate of the cost of these improvements, but instead argued that it would be more expensive not to make them. "It is generally recognized now that slums are fertile breeding places for crime, delinquency, immorality, disease and premature death, and that they are destructive of public safety and virtue," Goell asserted. Poverty, of course, Goell argued, was responsible for the slums, "but till we remove that ultimate cause by giving slum dwellers the opportunity to acquire competencies, let us endeavor to remove the vicious conditions which may be the immediate cause of the evils." In addition, the proposed improvements would increase property values, business prospects, and therefore tax revenues. Most importantly, "people and their money [would] remain in or come to Brownsville, instead of going away from it, as they have been doing for decades."[41]

The postwar plan was a nuanced attempt to create a modern Brownsville while giving consideration to the needs of the old. The proposal received a ringing endorsement from the editors of the *Brooklyn Eagle*, which called the plan "inspiring" and noted that Brownsville was "entitled to more such recognition than it has received in the past." The BNC leaders wanted to attract middle-class residents, but they sought at the same time to provide for the poor. Local activists did not see a contradiction in these goals. The proposal revealed a sincere concern for the welfare of the poor, but it was certainly cognizant of the needs of businesses and landlords for profit. In many ways the document represents the high point of American optimism. The United States could defeat Hitler, and it could defeat poverty at home. With organization, Americans could provide housing, recreation, and services for the poor, and build middle-class housing at the same time. This optimism was short-lived. For the next ten years, BNC leaders would refer to the "Post-War Plan" in their contacts with government officials, but none of the proposals made in the plan came to fruition. Throughout the 1940s and 1950s, Brownsville residents would battle government intransigence in pursuit of their goals of community revitalization.[42]

Brownsville in the Postwar Years

After devoting so much of their energies to the war effort, many Americans turned away from public affairs in the postwar years. Within Brownsville, many residents celebrated the return of family members, and they welcomed the opportunity to take advantage of the recently passed GI Bill. Many local veterans used government funding to become the first in their families to attend college, and hundreds of residents took advantage of VA loans to purchase new houses. These programs provided significant benefits to Brownsville families, but they did not help the community as a whole, because most participants did not remain in the neighborhood. In the late 1940s, many people, including Doc Baroff, moved to new developments in areas like Sheepshead Bay and Canarsie. Many bought houses while others rented, but all dramatically improved their living conditions. Like many activists, Baroff continued to work in Brownsville after he moved out, but activists' ties to the neighborhood began to weaken as opportunities became available to them elsewhere.[43]

The BNC continued to be active after the war, but its focus shifted from lobbying for significant new investments in the area to promoting the maintenance of existing institutions. After producing three significant pamphlets between 1940 and 1945 on the needs of Brownsville, the BNC published nothing in the fifteen years to follow. Some of its leaders remained on the BNC board but shifted their focus outside of the neighborhood. Board member Abe Stark, for example, who later led the Brownsville Boys Club through a significant expansion, began a political ascent that would lead him to the borough presidency in the 1950s. Milton Goell, who lost a race for city council in 1945, became increasingly active in citywide leftist politics. Staffers of the Brooklyn Council for Social Planning had been hopeful that the BNC would provide a model for organization in a working-class community, but by 1947 BCSP secretary Flora Davidson "felt that they had not been entirely successful" with the group and argued that the BNC had "become more and more concerned with political matters and less with social welfare." But the organization did not disappear. In fact, the BNC experienced a significant increase in activity during the early 1950s. However, the years immediately following the war were a transitional period when the original leadership pulled away and a new cadre of leaders was yet to emerge. Consequently, much of the energy generated by the group's early successes was lost.[44]

Other local organizations did not survive the postwar retrenchment. The Brownsville CIO Council was an early casualty of the fight against Communism. In New York, Communist-run organizations—including the Transport Workers Union, the Fur and Leather Workers, and the Clothing Workers—were leading forces in Industrial Union Councils. These organizations provided a powerful political forum for Communist leaders, and the activities of local Communists raised concerns within the CIO's national leadership. In the midst of the anticommunist hysteria of the late 1940s, national CIO leaders purged Communists from their leadership, and local IUCs were often battlegrounds for these intra-union conflicts. In 1946, the CIO convention adopted rules for IUCs that directed them to follow the policy positions handed down from CIO national offices in Washington. These rules also prohibited local CIO councils from associating with organizations (such as the Negro Labor Council) that were not approved by the CIO. In 1948, New York's IUCs and other leftist IUCs battled with the national organization over such issues as support for the Marshall Plan and for presidential candidate Henry Wallace. In response, anticommunist factions in the New York Council charged Communist leaders with numerous rules infractions, and many were expelled. The result of these battles was that many IUCs lost their leaders and began to decline. By 1950, Brownsville's CIO Council was no longer active, and Brownsville's connection to the labor movement declined.[45]

The demise of the Brownsville CIO also accelerated the decline of other advocacy groups, particularly the Brownsville Tenants Council. The tenants' movement was in some ways a victim of its success. After World War II, a dramatic increase in New York City housing costs brought about protest from voters, and city politicians were forced to pass one of the nation's most comprehensive rent-control laws. These new laws, which protected tenants from exorbitant rent increases, combined with the slow easing of housing shortages for middle-income persons and weakened support for tenants organizations. Many tenants groups ceased their grassroots efforts and became part of the public/private rental system, serving as mediators between tenants and housing providers rather than as agitators. While thousands of residents continued to need assistance in securing and maintaining affordable housing, many community members who were active in tenants unions found new accommodations in newly developed areas of Brooklyn and in public housing projects. The Brownsville Tenants Council lasted longer than most organizations, but it failed to address the problems of the new, predominantly black residents. The decline of local organizations left Brownsville without the strong infrastructure necessary to demand government resources. After World War II, as many neighborhoods battled for the attention of city agencies, Brownsville was a low priority.[46]

Receiving increasing attention, however, was Brownsville's rising rate of juvenile delinquency. During World War II, concerns about "wayward youth" intensified across the country. Many civic leaders worried that, with their fathers abroad and their mothers at work in the factories, thousands of teens were wandering the streets without oversight. Social workers talked forebodingly about the lack of control exhibited by such youths, and this resulted in increasing police attention to American teenagers. Within Brownsville, juvenile delinquency had long been a concern, but anxiety escalated during and after the war. In 1942, the Brooklyn Federation of Jewish Charities announced the opening of a new recreation center focusing on local teens and "calculated to save youth from the dislocating effects the war has had upon the day-to-day life around them." And in 1944, the Brooklyn Council for Social Planning decided that its pilot project to combat delinquency would be located in the Brownsville–East New York area. Brownsville leaders gave mixed responses to outside involvement in Brownsville affairs. While leaders like Goell frequently noted that juvenile delinquency, caused by bad housing and lack of recreation, was a serious problem, others like Abe Stark worried about the image of the neighborhood. In response to the announcement of the pilot project, Stark complained that Brownsville was being "singled-out for finger pointing."

Brownsville, he stated, was not "a setting for 'Green Pastures,' but neither is it a place out of Dante's Inferno." Stigmatizing the neighborhood was unfair, he continued, to the area's "good and honest people to be asked to suffer the indignities that have been heaped upon them by thoughtless people." Officials from the BCSP argued that Brownsville was chosen because it was racially and ethnically diverse and therefore a good test case, not because it was worse than other areas. Brownsville's juvenile delinquency rate was, however, among the highest in the borough.[47]

After the war, gang violence and juvenile arrests in the area increased, and Brownsville became a major focus of the newly created New York Youth Board, the city agency given the responsibility to commence a "War on Juvenile Delinquency" across the city. In 1949, the accidental shooting of a fifteen-year-old local boy named Stanley Fox brought additional attention to the area. Fox, a member of the "Black Hats," was killed by a gun that discharged while his group prepared to "rumble" with the rival "Bristol Street Boys." Fox's family and teachers at Public School 156 argued that the group was more a social club than a gang, but the newspaper articles that followed the shooting noted that the Black Hats had a significant arsenal, typical of the dramatic rise in gun possession among the local youths. A Brooklyn assistant district attorney stated that many weapons were sold in comic books, while others noted that the boys used weapons brought home by their veteran fathers and brothers.[48]

Stark and Goell responded to the shooting by insisting that Brownsville was "a nice place with a fine community spirit and with thousands of fine upstanding boys and girls." Whatever juvenile problems existed were caused by the deterioration of local housing and the failure of the city to provide recreation opportunities. Stark further asserted that the bad name given to the neighborhood by local papers was responsible for the juvenile problem. According to Stark, area youths "were developing various types of complexes because this neighborhood has a reputation . . . as a breeding ground for crime." Milton Goell added that neighborhood improvements would solve the delinquency problem. "Incidents occur in all communities," Goell argued, and would occur in any area "where families are crowded together and youngsters are deprived of proper facilities for wholesome recreation." Brownsville leaders were justifiably concerned about the impact of outsider perceptions on the neighborhood. In the spring of 1948, the *Brooklyn Eagle* reported that most insurance firms had "blackballed" Brownsville, refusing to issue new policies to local businesses and apartment owners. One company flatly stated that it was "staying out of the Brownsville area." Another company admitted avoiding Brownsville because "petty crimes are on the rampage." Insurers further argued that Brownsville residents were "claims conscious" and that the number of small claims filed made the area a bad investment.[49]

Local leaders and public officials struggled to address youth problems. The New York City Youth Board initiated a program that sent young adults to work with gangs in their neighborhoods, and it created a referral service for concerned schoolteachers. However, in general, most leaders relied on the traditional philosophy that recreation would cure delinquency. The Youth Board provided workers and equipment for four summer play streets, which were blocked to traffic. Local activists called for a more "integrated program" of social work, recreation, and better housing. Mildred Wickson, head of the Brownsville Tenants Union, argued that "delinquent landlords and delinquent national state and city agencies should take their share of blame for juvenile delinquency," but politicians ignored broader plans like those proposed by the BNC.[50]

Many people put their hopes in the expanding program of the Brownsville Boys Club (BBC). As an agency successfully working with youth, the BBC received increasing support from social welfare organizations like the BSCP in the last years of the 1940s. In 1946, local businessman and politician Abe Stark began to support the group, and he persuaded the boys to incorporate. By 1947, the BBC was affiliated with the Boys Clubs of America and had a new board of directors made up of local businessmen and politicians. Through the political connections of Stark, Governor Thomas Dewey, Mayor William O'Dwyer, Borough President John Cashmore, and dozens of other city leaders became BBC sponsors. Funds raised by the board enabled the BBC to purchase new equipment and transformed the organization from a volunteer institution to one with staff and offices. The change, however, was not completely smooth. Since its founding, the BBC had prided itself on the philosophy of "No Adult Control," and the bylaws of the organization specified that no one older than twenty-one could be a member. The changes in the structure of the organization were not welcomed by all BBC members, but the new board did not interfere in the group's daily operations. Despite their greater dependence on adult financiers in the late 1940s, the BBC continued to be run by the teenage members. Three alumni members were elected by a representative council to sit on the board of directors, and they fought to protect the prerogatives of the teenagers. And Doc Baroff, then in college, became a BBC "professional group worker," at a salary of $110 per month.[51]

The late 1940s brought not only a growth of the organization's budget but also a change in its orientation. Many of the founders, who were in their twenties by this time, returned from the war with a desire to remake their community. In 1947, BBC founder Norman Goroff wrote that the goal of the club was "not to keep the boys off the streets, but to make the streets attractive and safe." These young social workers felt that it was necessary to move away from sports as the focus of the BBC's attention, and to place more emphasis on the educational, social, and economic needs of the boys. This change in philosophy helped the BBC attract greater support and acclaim from other welfare organizations.[52]

Irving Levine was one of this group of socially minded BBC leaders. He joined the club in 1941 at the age of eleven. One of Baroff's protégés, Levine became the president of the club's Junior Division. By 1947, he was in charge of the BBC recreation program, and the members elected him president in 1950. When he entered Brooklyn College in 1947, Levine was more interested in working at the BBC than in his studies. "The Brownsville Boys Club for me was all-consuming," he remembered. While Levine was originally attracted to the sports programs the club offered, over time he came to see that the BBC could be a means to a better life for Brownsville's poor. Levine, who graduated from New York University, became a paid worker in 1950 and went on to a long career in race relations. Although Levine and other BBC members believed that good jobs and housing were as important, if not more important, than recreational opportunities to the development of Brownsville's youth, Abe Stark and other members of the BBC board continued to endorse a traditional "juvenile program" of recreation and tutoring. In response to several gang-related killings in the neighborhood, Stark insisted that "the way to fight 'boy gangsterism' was for the city to finance new recreational facilities." The BBC board did not share the loftier goals of its staff, and in the early 1950s conflict between the groups escalated.[53]

While increasing juvenile delinquency and declining infrastructure concerned many Brownsville activists, for most residents the neighborhood had changed little over the decade. Many Brownsville institutions continued to function without concern for future neighborhood transformations, but Brownsville synagogues continued the numerical decline that would accelerate in the 1950s. The 1939 WPA Survey tallied seventy-three Brownsville synagogues; in 1951, the BNC counted fifty-one in the area. Several of the area's oldest congregations, including Thilim Kesher Israel, saw their buildings condemned to make way for the development of the Brownsville Houses. The congregants of Thilim Kesher, still several hundred strong, merged with Brownsville's other aging synagogue, Ohev Sholom. Other congregations did not continue services, choosing instead to disband. Many of their members had already left the neighborhood, and those remaining found other synagogues.[54]

The Hebrew Educational Society, however, maintained its large program of activities. In 1940, the HES celebrated its fiftieth year of operation, and it created a new program, in a separate facility, called the Young People's Fellowship to serve the area's young adults. HES staff were concerned about the increasing number of "Cellar Clubs" in the area. The clubhouse of the fictional "Amboy Dukes" in Irving Shulman's novel was more organized and sinister than most real clubs, but these informal associations of teens and young adults did often introduce members to alcohol and drugs, and incidences of sexual assault were common. The Fellowship program employed young social workers who sought to direct Brownsville youths toward more productive avenues. In 1948, approximately one thousand young people participated in weekly programs that included dance, theater, and arts and crafts, as well as socials, films, and dances planned specifically for them. Members of the Fellowship produced a monthly journal and governed themselves through an executive council that reported to the HES board. In their annual report to the board, Fellowship staff bragged that the program had provided opportunities to gain "knowledge and respect for American Jewish ideals and culture . . . a larger community perspective . . . development of leadership potentialities . . . and a permissive atmosphere to meet the young adult's needs for exclusiveness apart from other age groups." Also concerned about the expanding aged community in Brownsville, the HES staff in 1946 created the "Golden Age Club," which provided fellowship and activities for seniors. Like the Young People's Fellowship, the Golden Age Club sought to keep area seniors engaged in the community in which they had spent their lives. Members paid yearly dues of one dollar to participate in daily activities that included films, dances, and theater. More than four hundred people took part in 1948.[55]

Other groups focused on the broader political needs of Brownsville residents. Jews continued to face racism and discrimination in the 1940s, and the rise of Hitler abroad was not the only concern of New York's Jewish community. Within the United States, Father Charles Coughlin and other anti-Semitic clerics proselytized against Jews, and synagogue vandalism occurred all too frequently. Even in an insular community like Brownsville, where Jews were the majority, anti-Semitism was a fact of life. In response to the continued discrimination, Brooklyn Jewish activists organized the Brooklyn Jewish Community Council (BJCC). The purpose of the group were to combat the "false stereotypes concerning different racial, religious and nationality groups" by "creating better intergroup understanding," and to nurture Jewish traditions through education. In addition, the BJCC sought to "help member organizations with their cultural programs, and thus stimulate and enrich the cultural and organizational life of the community." With funding from the United Jewish Appeal and other national organizations, the BJCC provided organizational support and literature to local groups for special events, and acted as a clearinghouse for Brooklyn's Jewish community. BJCC also investigated incidents of anti-Semitism, and filed fifty-three reports on attacks against Jews between September 1946 and June 1947.[56]

The BJCC also sponsored local councils to coordinate its activities. The first groups were located in Williamsburg and Flatbush, but in 1943 BJCC leaders met with Alter Landesman, Milton Goell, and other local activists to create the Brownsville–East New York Jewish Community Council. During 1946–47, the Brownsville–East New York branch created a Sunday School program for unaffiliated adults, organized special events at the Children's Library to celebrate Jewish Book Month, and held a concert at the HES for Jewish Music Month. The local branch also sponsored a "Brotherhood in Action" rally to support pending state antidiscrimination legislation, and participated in the reorganization of the Brownsville Boys Club. A 1948 BJCC evaluation concluded that, unlike many areas where the local affiliate was unresponsive to the guidance of the council leadership, the Brownsville–East New York council had been very active. The BJCC executive director asserted that under his guidance, Brownsville Jewish organizations had "become more willing to submerge their individual differences in favor of over-all planning for the welfare of the total community." Throughout the 1950s, the BJCC and its Brownsville affiliate continued to support the needs of the Jewish community.[57]

Brownsville at midcentury suffered from a variety of problems, including decrepit housing, deteriorating schools, persistent juvenile delinquency, and troubling indices of disease. But residents were not lacking in hope, and Brownsville activists continued to work to better conditions within the neighborhood. The leaders of Brownsville's diverse and vibrant advocacy community, in particular the Brownsville Neighborhood Council, the Brownsville Boys Club, the Brownsville CIO, the Hebrew Educational Society, and the Brooklyn Jewish Community Council, all believed that postwar Brownsville would continue to serve the working-class Jewish population that had occupied the neighborhood for half a century. None of them were prepared to deal with the significant changes that the neighborhood would experience in the decade to follow.

Figure 10. Children on Brownsville street corner, 1940s. Courtesy Brooklyn Collection, Brooklyn Public Library.

3

Blacks and Whites in the Optimistic Years

Reverend Boise Dent was born in Virginia but moved to Brooklyn in 1936 to become pastor of the First Baptist Church of Brownsville. Unlike many black ministers of the time, Dent was more interested in the practical concerns of his parishioners than their spiritual needs. "He takes his religion to the people, avoiding formalized dogma and creeds," wrote one *New York Amsterdam News* reporter. While the church grew under his leadership, Dent left First Baptist in a conflict with some members of the congregation. The deacons, according to Dent, were worried that he was spending too much time with the troubled youths of Brooklyn, and they fired him. Dent then established Tabernacle Baptist Church, and during the 1940s, he was a leader of Brooklyn's black community and extremely active in Brooklyn politics. From 1948 until his death in 1951, Dent served on the board of the BNC (and was chair of the Recreation Committee), as well as on the board of the Brownsville Boys Club. Dent was also a spokesperson for the BNC's efforts to improve sanitation in the neighborhood, and he organized several congregations for this effort. His main focus, however, was helping children through recreational and educational activities. Dent created the Brownsville Neighborhood Interracial Community Center, a storefront operation on Livonia Avenue, and worked to expand the BBC program. As a leading minister, Dent was often called upon to intercede for youths who had been arrested, and he had many Brownsville youngsters released into his custody. According to the *New York Amsterdam News*, there was "scarcely a judge in Brooklyn that he doesn't know." Dent worked frequently with white leaders in the area, particularly Milton Goell and Judge Daniel Gutman.[1]

Like other ministers, Dent's position made him valuable to local politicians, and he developed close ties to businessman and political aspirant Abe Stark. "Anytime there was an important event involving Stark, Reverend Dent was there," remembered his friend and former Brownsville resident Reverend Harold Burton. Stark appointed Dent the chair of his election committee for the city council presidency in 1949 and frequently called upon him to campaign in the black community. Because of his commitment and political connections, both of which extended past Brownsville, Dent became a leading figure in black Brooklyn. In 1947, Brooklyn readers of the *New York Amsterdam News* placed him second on the list of the most important blacks in the borough, behind the director of the Carlton Avenue branch of the YMCA and ahead of the leaders of Brooklyn's largest churches. In 1949, voters made Dent the unofficial "mayor" of Brooklyn in the annual poll. However, while Dent was increasing his political power, Tabernacle Baptist struggled to survive. "We could have had a good church if he had fought for the church. A man with his stature, they would have given him a church," argued Burton. Instead, the congregation moved from storefront to storefront. While Dent's church established several youth programs during the late 1940s, each failed because of lack of funding and staff. While many in the community praised his leadership, one critic argued that Dent "had little training" and was "autocratic and jealous of his own prestige."[2]

Dent's efforts were emblematic of the struggles facing Brownsville activists seeking to achieve integration in the postwar years. The Brownsville Neighborhood Council, the Brownsville Boys Club, the Brownsville CIO Council, and other neighborhood groups held firmly to the liberal values—equal opportunity and respect for individual rights—that were imparted by Jewish culture and reinforced by the war effort. Each made efforts, some more significant than others, to respect, if not embrace, the increasing number of black residents in the neighborhood. In comparison to other New York neighborhoods, and those in other cities, Brownsville was a beacon of racial harmony. Many white and black activists struggled to bridge the gaps between the groups, and they were successful in fostering interracial acceptance. Race riots were a common occurrence in 1940s America, but in Brownsville blacks and whites, for the most part, "got along." Despite significant achievements, however, the efforts of these activists were limited by the long-standing barriers between blacks and whites. While black and white youths frequently played together, interaction between adults was less common. Blacks and whites did not often meet as equals in Brownsville organizations, and blacks did not participate in many neighborhood programs.

Black-led institutions in Brownsville were limited. Only a few blacks achieved a modicum of influence, and more established groups such as the NAACP and the Urban League were not prominent in the neighborhood. Brownsville was not an integrated community, but rather two communities resolved to avoid conflict. During the 1940s, when the percentage of blacks was small, such a strategy was possible. However, this posture could not survive the demographic, political, and social changes of the postwar years. In the late 1940s, Brownsville's black population expanded, and white residents' concerns about the neighborhood, particularly crime and juvenile delinquency, increased. Black Brownsville residents also had worries, specifically discrimination in local businesses, housing problems, and police brutality. The racial aspects of neighborhood issues, however, were frequently ignored by activists.

While Brownsville civic leaders pushed for community improvements, many whites took advantage of economic growth and found better housing in new neighborhoods. The exodus began just as Robert Moses commenced his efforts to redevelop the city, a plan that resulted in the construction of four thousand units of public housing in Brownsville. Although activists had lobbied for such developments, they were unaware that New York's postwar development would reshape the city's racial geography and direct thousands of blacks and Latinos to the neighborhood. Government policies would accelerate the transformation of Brownsville.

The Emergence of Black Brownsville

While the "Great Migration" of the late 1910s and 1920s holds the title, the second wave of African-Americans which hit northern and western cities during the 1940s was significantly larger than the first. Almost two million African-Americans moved north during the decade, and 221,000 settled in New York. Brooklyn's African-American population grew to 108,623 in 1940, and it exploded in size throughout that decade. Dislocation in the South's agricultural economy and the attractions of the booming industrial sector of the North and West both shaped the migration. In New York, while many defense industries discriminated against blacks, they were able to move into many other industrial and white-collar jobs previously closed to them. Many black women moved out of domestic service and into the factories (particularly the garment trades), and they also made inroads in the clerical, communications, and sales sectors. Black men were hired for skilled positions, were promoted to foremen in some factories, and also secured jobs as trolley and train operators. But economic advancement did not mean the end to discrimination in housing and other sectors. Blacks remained excluded from many New York neighborhoods and were forced to crowd into existing black areas in Bedford-Stuyvesant and Brownsville.[3]

Brownsville was home to 7,842 African-Americans in 1940 (up from 5,062 in 1930), just over 6 percent of the population. The overwhelming majority of blacks lived in the oldest section of the neighborhood. In a few places, most noticeably the area's two oldest public schools, blacks were prominent. PS 125 was 60 percent black in 1940, up from 33 percent in 1933. PS 84 went from 9 percent black to 28 percent black during the same period, and PS 178 experienced a similar increase. No other local school, however, was more than 12 percent black. Much would change in the 1940s, when the black population increased dramatically. As tens of thousands of African-Americans left the South during the war, Brooklyn's black population doubled to 208,478, and several thousand of these migrants settled in Brownsville. By 1950, the black population of Brownsville had almost doubled to 14,209. According to a 1948 Brooklyn Urban League report, many blacks were lured into Brownsville by landlords "hoping to cut cost and increase profit."[4]

As they had in previous decades, blacks lived in some of the area's most decrepit housing. On Osborne Street, the wood frame houses were "roach and rat infested," according to the *New York Amsterdam News*, and had lost most of the plaster on the walls and ceilings. Mothers in the buildings reported that their children frequently received treatment for rodent bites. The dwellings built for two families were subdivided to house up to six families, and one building had almost fifty residents. Yet the tenants in these buildings paid $55 a month—almost twice the $30 average for the area—and were forced to undertake repairs themselves without reimbursement. The problems in the area were so severe that they raised the ire of the normally reticent editors of the *New York Amsterdam News*, which noted that

Figure 11. Mother and child in front of typical Brownsville tenement, 1940s. Black residents lived in the oldest and worst housing in the neighborhood. Courtesy Brooklyn Collection, Brooklyn Public Library.

"Brownsville does not have a reputation of being a good place to live," and asked the city to investigate the situation. Fires were also frequent in these dilapidated structures. In one typical incident, a mother and her three children perished in a fire that destroyed their building on Thatford Avenue.[5]

Other than Baptist churches, black institutions failed to grow commensurate to the population. Several new churches opened during the decade, and the existing congregations continued to be the focal point of the black community. St. Paul's Baptist Church grew steadily during the decade thanks to the efforts of Adolphus Smith. Chosen to lead the congregation in 1938, a position he held until his death in 1967, Smith expanded the church's membership and facilities. By 1944, the church had several hundred congregants and its small storefront building was bursting at the seams. As the oldest church in Brownsville, St. Paul's membership included many of the black community's elite. According to Samuel Freedman, "St. Paul prided itself on its middle-class members, the teachers, lawyers, principals and police." St. Paul's congregation was a proper one where "no one would dare worship without shined shoes and a choked-up tie; women wore stockings, the seams had to be straight." The success of the church and its members enabled them to expand their operations, and in 1944, despite the limited building supplies available during the war, Reverend Smith announced a plan for a new facility. After two years of fund-raising through a weekly collection (men fifty cents and women twenty-five cents), chicken dinners, bake sales, and raffles, the church gathered $60,000, enough to buy a lot on Osborne Street and construct a proper brick church with stained-glass windows.[6]

Mount Ollie's congregation was not as genteel as St. Paul's, but it was proud of its successful members, and of its pastor, Reverend R. D. Brown. Appointed in 1939 (he would serve for forty-six years), Brown too led his church on a fund-raising drive soon after his arrival. The congregation's efforts resulted in the construction of its new building on St. Mark's Avenue in 1943. Mount Ollie quickly became the leading institution in the working-class community that occupied the houses surrounding the warehouses and factories along Brownsville's northern border. Mount Ollie's members were primarily factory workers, dockworkers, or in the construction field, and a large number of the church's female congregants worked as domestics for families in Flatbush, Brooklyn Heights, and other wealthy communities. Many of these women lived in with their employers and were free only on Thursdays and Sunday mornings. For decades, the Mount Ollie Ladies Club met on Thursday evening so that everyone could attend.[7]

Universal Baptist Church, which purchased its own building in 1940, developed more slowly than the other congregations. Its founder, Reverend Scott, grew increasingly ill and was forced to retire in 1945. The church's second pastor, Reverend J. I. C. Montgomery, came from the prestigious Cornerstone Baptist Church in Bedford-Stuyvesant, and several members were added during his term, but he only served a short time. Lacking strong leadership, Universal did not attract large members of Brownsville blacks until the 1950s. Other Brownsville churches opened during the decade, including Pilgrim Baptist Church, Tabernacle Baptist Church, and First Baptist Church. Each of these congregations used storefronts to hold their services, but they quickly expanded to accommodate the hundreds of new members drawn to the community. First Baptist Church, founded in 1941, grew from fifty members to four hundred by 1952. Like the other churches, Pilgrim originally occupied a storefront, but the congregation built a church at Stone and Watkins Avenues in the late 1940s.[8]

Black Baptist congregations in Brooklyn were relatively volatile. They organized and disbanded frequently, and the personality of a church was frequently established by the minister. Throughout the 1930s and 1940s, Baptist churches bloomed in Brooklyn, particularly in the growing Bedford-Stuyvesant area. Several of these churches, most notably Concord Baptist and Cornerstone Baptist, had more than a thousand members by 1940. Because of their influence over large numbers of parishioners, Baptist ministers were seen as community leaders—a role not all of them embraced. Historian Clarence Taylor criticized Brooklyn's black clergy for failing to respond to social and economic problems in their communities during the 1940s and 1950s: "Brooklyn's black led churches should have organized themselves into a much more cohesive group. . . . The ministers could have organized thousands of people inside and outside the churches and put pressure on city, state and federal officials to do something about the dire conditions of Bedford-Stuyvesant and other poor black communities," Taylor argued.[9]

But the black ministers in Brownsville were not militants, nor were they interested in grassroots organizing or protest. Among the most highly educated people in the black community (several, like Reverend Gardner Taylor, had graduated from elite seminary schools such as Oberlin), most black clergy were moderates by nature, and many had long-standing family ties to the Republican Party. Yet some black clergy were involved in Brooklyn politics, and they were courted by white politicians for their influence over registered voters. Reverend Benjamin Lowery of Zion Baptist Church headed the "Ministers and Citizens Committee to Re-elect Governor Thomas Dewey" in 1950, and Reverend Gardner Taylor of Concord Baptist Church developed close ties to Mayor Robert Wagner, who appointed him to serve on the New York City Board of Education. Black ministers sought to increase their influence within the Democratic and Republican Parties, and they often succeeded in creating relationships with powerful politicians. But these connections seldom resulted in practical advancements in black areas.[10]

While Brownsville ministers did not organize their congregations to protest discrimination or lobby for resources, they often worked together to support the interests of Brooklyn blacks. Reverends Dent, Smith, and Brown were leaders of the effort to get the Long Island Railroad to erect more secure fencing around the tracks, where many black youths were electrocuted. They also responded quickly to incidents of police brutality, which occurred frequently in the late 1940s. All these ministers achieved recognition for their activities, and their efforts produced some practical results. "Reverend Brown saved many young black men from jail," remembered Reverend Spurgeon Crayton, current minister of Mount Ollie. Dent was an important part of the growth of the BBC. However, the clergy's successes were limited by the marginal role of Brownsville blacks in Brooklyn.[11]

Most of Brownsville's black residents were poor, and black organizations like the NAACP or the Urban League were inactive. In 1947, Lillian Lampkin, supervisor of the Urban League's Group Work Department, conducted an informal study of the needs of Brownsville's black youths. After interviewing several black and white leaders in the area, Lampkin recommended that the Urban League initiate a program of social services in Brownsville to provide recreational and educational opportunities to local teenagers and young adults, and "actively involve indigenous community leadership in planning and executing this program." Lampkin's proposal was never adopted, and the Urban League's Group Work Department was closed in the early 1950s. Based in Bedford-Stuyvesant like the Urban League, the Brooklyn branch of the NAACP was not a participant in the Brownsville community during the 1940s. The NAACP was controlled by the borough's black elite and did not focus on grassroots organization. Its activities were generally nonconfrontational, taking the form of voter registration drives, political lobbying, and campaigns against police brutality. Although the NAACP expressed an interest in working with Brownsville organizations, the local branch avoided movements supporting the interests of working-class blacks. During the 1940s, several groups agitated for an end to employment discrimination and other forms of racism, but, according to one critic, the local chapter was "distinctly aloof on these matters." For example, the Brooklyn NAACP did not participate in a 1940s program, led by the National Negro Congress and the Harlem Labor Committee, to end employment discrimination in New York's transit system.[12]

Rather than worshiping at the storefront congregations prevalent in Brownsville, the majority of Brooklyn's NAACP members belonged to the borough's most prestigious churches, including Bethany Baptist and Concord Memorial Baptist (home of Reverend Gardner Taylor, chairman of the National Council of Baptist Churches). The gap in perceived social status between Brooklyn's middle-class and poor black communities was much wider than it would be in the 1960s, and, as a result, the Brooklyn NAACP was reluctant to reach out to Brownsville blacks. Neither the Urban League nor the NAACP, both of which had credentials recognized by whites, seemed interested in helping to bridge the gap between the black and old white residents in Brownsville.[13]

Many Bedford-Stuyvesant residents perceived black Brownsville as low-class, and criminal incidents did nothing to decrease these prejudices. The *New York Amsterdam News* reported frequently on violent crime in Brownsville during the late 1940s. In May 1946, police arrested one Brownsville man for shooting a bartender at a saloon on Christopher Avenue during an attempted robbery, and a Livonia Avenue woman was slain that same year. Intruders killed the caretaker of a local social club for blacks on Bristol Street in August 1947, and prosecutors charged another man with homicide in the beating death of a man on Livonia Avenue in October 1948. Police also reported a significant number of thefts and burglaries in the area during the later years of the decade. Violent confrontations between husbands and wives, which often ended in death, were a staple of the *Amsterdam News* crime reports of the neighborhood. Black crime in Brownsville was almost exclusively intraracial, but crimes by blacks against whites also occurred. In July 1947, two black men were arrested for burglarizing the synagogue of the Congregation of the People of the City of Bobriusk, where they stole religious articles worth $250.[14]

The New York Police Department destroyed the precinct-level crime statistics for the years prior to 1970, so it is impossible to assess the extent to which these incidents represented an increase in area crime, but several reporters noted an expansion of black gang activity in Brownsville. The two most significant black Brownsville gangs were the "Saints" and the "Socialists Gents," and they frequently battled in the area between Rockaway and Stone Avenues, where many blacks lived. In November 1949, eighteen gang members were arrested after a police sweep initiated by a shoot-out in which three teenagers were injured. The gangs were small according to local police—each had fewer than twenty members—and most of the gang members were between the ages of fifteen and twenty. While these groups usually did not engage in other criminal activities, many local residents were caught in the middle of gang battles, and Brownsville citizens told the police that they were afraid to walk the streets at night. Reverends Dent, Smith, and Brown and others saw the problem as serious enough to request additional police presence in the area. They particularly wanted more black police officers to deal with the gangs and to work with the black community.[15]

Brownsville's black population wanted protection from criminals, but police actions were aimed not just at violators of the law but at all area blacks. As Brownsville's African-American population increased, police brutality did as well. Harlem activist Algernon Black reported that in Brownsville it was "impossible for men to be walking the streets at night . . . without being stopped for questioning or being searched." In his citywide investigations of police abuse, Black found that police frequently beat Brownsville residents in custody with baseball bats and rubber hoses. The problem intensified for black Brooklynites after a report on Bedford-Stuyvesant by a 1943 Kings County grand jury. The report, released after interviews with more than one hundred residents, most of them white, concluded that "gangs of hoodlums" had taken over the area, attacking, robbing, and murdering the inhabitants. The grand jury recommended a dramatic increase in police in the area to suppress the criminal element. While the Kings County District Attorney adamantly argued that race played no factor in the area's problems or in the deliberations of the jury, many Brooklyn blacks believed that white civic leaders blamed the increasing crime rate on recent migrants to Bed-Stuy. Concern about black crime coincided with fears of juvenile delinquency and resulted in increased police activity in Brooklyn neighborhoods where blacks lived.[16]

In July 1945, one Brownsville policeman attacked five area teens, sending them to the hospital for treatment. According to reporters, the police officer was coming out of a bar when he spotted the boys carrying window shades and accused them of theft. When the boys denied the charge (they were asked to return the shades to the store by one of the boys' mothers), he beat them with his nightstick. In another serious case of brutality, two officers hit a twenty-two-year-old black man with a rubber hose, blackjacks, and their fists, all with the aim of securing a confession from him that he had stolen a car and committed several other robberies in the area. The *New York Amsterdam News*, which frequently praised the police for their swift response to Brooklyn's criminal element, criticized the police in this instance, stating, "respect cannot be demanded if it is not practiced." In 1948, local police attacked two black couples, one of which included a pregnant woman, when they were loading their car to go on vacation. The police accused them of stealing the articles, and when one of the men protested, they beat him unconscious. Another officer pushed the pregnant woman to the ground when she tried to help her husband. The incident created such a fury in the neighborhood that the normally reticent black clergy, including Ministers Smith, Brown, and Dent, organized a mass rally at Mount Ollie Baptist Church to protest the attacks on law-abiding citizens. Conflicts between black residents and local police were a consistent problem that most whites chose to ignore. Many argued that the incidents did not represent the views of most Brownsville citizens; and, despite evidence to the contrary, both black and white residents remembered the 1940s and 1950s as a time of racial harmony. Former residents argued that, for the most part, there was seldom any racial conflict in Brownsville. [17]

Blacks and Whites in the Optimistic Years

The Craytons moved to Brownsville in 1929. Spurgeon, who would later become pastor of Mount Ollie, and his brother Leroy were born in the neighborhood in the late 1930s. They lived on Dumont Avenue and then moved to Stone Avenue during the early 1940s. Spurgeon and Leroy's father worked as a garment cutter in Manhattan, and when the industry declined during the depression, he found employment with the Works Progress Administration. One of the small number of blacks to secure construction jobs through the WPA, Crayton worked on several highway projects, including the Interborough Parkway. The Craytons were among the first members of Mount Ollie, and the family members remained leaders of the congregation for decades. On their block, Spurgeon and Leroy Crayton had many white friends. "Race relations were very good," said Spurgeon. "We remember growing up with them in our neighborhood." Blacks and whites played together and went to school together without conflict. The community was, Leroy remembered, "very provincial. We seldom left our street, and we only went to Pitkin Avenue on special occasions," such as a birthdays or holidays. While individual relationships were often successful, informal segregation certainly existed in Brownsville. The Craytons, however, were too young and too poor to be aware of it at the time. "We didn't even know that the Concord Restaurant was closed to us, because we didn't have the money to go anyway," said Leroy. Blacks were relatively comfortable in the small areas of the community in which they lived, but in many parts of Brownsville, blacks were less than welcome. The Loew's Pitkin often refused admittance to blacks, who instead frequented the Stone Avenue Theater.[18]

Some older blacks were more forceful in demanding access to community facilities. Harold Burton moved to Brownsville in 1948, after serving in the army during World War II. In Brownsville, he lived with his brother, who had migrated several years before and secured employment at a garment factory on Linden Boulevard in the southern tip of the neighborhood. By the time Harold arrived, his brother was a foreman of the shop, and Harold began to work for him. A young man who had seen much of Europe and the United States, Harold Burton did not accept the informal exclusion of blacks from certain facilities. "You weren't really welcome in Betsy Head Park or the Ambassador Theater on Hopkinson Avenue," he remembered. Many of the restaurants on Pitkin Avenue also refused to serve blacks. "I went to the Pitkin Theater, and I made them let me in," Burton said. Living on Bristol Street, Burton also remembered having many white friends, but most of them left during the 1950s. Despite evidence of discrimination, other former residents recalled a close-knit society in the mixed-race community. According to Danny Culley, "On Jewish holidays everything in this town closed down . . . everything. We used to have to go and help them light the stoves, and they couldn't touch money. And it was things that were just accepted. It wasn't done demeaningly. I guess at that time everybody was poor and they just got along." Contact often occurred at commercial institutions shared by poor whites and blacks. Dudley Gaffin's father bought a bar on Rockaway Avenue in 1940. Gaffin remembered spending time with many black customers.[19]

But fifty years of experience can easily cloud the memory, and at least some aspects of Brownsville race relations were less positive. Many Brownsville whites ignored the increasing black population, just as they had done in Alfred Kazin's time a decade earlier. Police and merchants were among those whites who had the most consistent contact with blacks, and their relations were not always amicable. While it cannot be determined whether the police involved in the aforementioned brutality cases were Brownsville residents, the efforts of local cops to control the movements of blacks was clearly one response to the increasing number of residents of color. In addition, while stories of interracial cooperation were more typical in the pages of the *New York Amsterdam News* and the *Brooklyn Eagle* than stories of conflict, the *Amsterdam News* published several accounts of racial hostilities during the summer of 1946. In June the paper reported a "riot" that began when a "Jewish merchant struck and used abusive language" on two black women who had come into his store to make a purchase. The women asked to buy some stockings, but were told none were available. When a white woman subsequently bought stockings the black women protested and the conflict quickly escalated into violence. Several area blacks gathered outside the store, and police called in Reverend Dent to moderate the dispute.[20]

Later that summer, a fistfight between black and white gangs escalated when the whites returned with guns. They shot two bystanders, a black man and an eight-year-old black boy, who were not involved in the conflict. Reporters of the story noted that "tension between the races had been holding away for quite some time." In response to the gang violence, local police raided the Bombay Café, a saloon owned and frequented by Brownsville blacks, later that week and arrested sixty-six people for disorderly conduct, all but one of them black. According to the reports, "women and men were tossed about like cattle, and the area went into an uproar and just fell short of a riot." Police said they were trying to get information on the gang battle, but in reality they arrested blacks indiscriminately and let whites go about their business. Despite this serious conflict, according to former residents, gang violence between blacks and whites was infrequent. "You go into their area and they chase you back," remembered Arthur Lawrence, a black youth at the time. Brooklyn papers reported no similar events in the years following. Lawrence's memory, however, points out the reality of race relations in 1940s Brownsville—for the most part whites and blacks lived separate lives.[21]

Despite the isolated nature of the two groups, Brownsville's white activists made constant reference to their "darker populations." In every publication produced by the Brownsville Neighborhood Council in that decade, the situation of African-Americans was featured prominently. Activists described their black neighbors as the "poorest of the poor," those most in need of government assistance. The fact that Brownsville residents welcomed them and acknowledged the needs of the black community was proof, to BNC leaders, of Brownsville's goodwill. The BNC pamphlet "For Better Health in Brownsville" noted that "Negroes did not come to dwell here from choice: they came here because they were poor. There are other hovels in New York, but not even the hovels of New York are all available to Negro poor people." Before the civil rights movement emerged as a national cause, Brownsville residents were aware of the severe problems that racial discrimination caused for blacks. Brownsville activists vocally protested racism in the South, holding rallies against "Jim Crow" laws and other discriminatory practices there. In the fall of 1943, dozens of local leaders—including Rae Glauber, Milton Goell, Councilman Peter Cacchione, and Reverend Boise Dent—held a dinner at the Parkway Restaurant on Pitkin Avenue at which they signed a petition to Congress demanding that it outlaw poll taxes. More than 150 people attended the event. BNC leaders were organizers of local unity rallies, and the BNC held its own annual "Goodwill Dinner," which it hoped would cement "unity and friendship among Negroes and white churches and synagogues and political, social and fraternal groups." White activists, however, neglected to address more practical concerns of local blacks, including police brutality and discrimination, and they failed to confront the fact that several restaurants on Pitkin Avenue refused to serve blacks.[22]

Brownsville leaders emphasized their progressive politics when they demanded consideration of their requests for communitywide resources like housing, recreation, and schools. They argued that Brownsville, unlike other New York neighborhoods, welcomed blacks, and that the city should support their liberal attitudes in this regard. The BNC prided itself on racial understanding and never missed an opportunity to preach on the subject. "Our people must learn to live with one another," argued one BNC press release, "to work with, and for one another, to fight side by side against ignorance and darkness and for knowledge and betterment." The stated goal of the BNC was a society of equal rights for all. "There must be a place for all in work, play, government and culture—for all Americans, regardless of race, color or creed," declared the group's organizing principles. The BNC put actions behind its words, requesting facilities for the areas of Brownsville where blacks lived. Realizing that many black mothers worked, the BNC also fought for nursery facilities in the black areas of Brownsville.[23]

Often, however, the BNC's statements reflected the conflicting feelings of some whites toward their new neighbors. In its "Post-War Plan for Brownsville," the BNC lobbied for recreational facilities for African-Americans, and argued that with a building in the black area of Brownsville, "they [blacks] would not be admitted by sufferance—they would be admitted because the building belonged to them as citizens." This request was either a sincere effort to secure better facilities for black children or a cynical attempt to keep blacks away from the parks and playgrounds frequented by whites by providing separate-but-equal facilities. Undoubtedly both motives were present in the minds of Brownsville residents. In general, however, through their words and deeds, BNC leaders promoted integration in housing, schools, and other activities. In private, Brownsville residents may have lamented the migration of blacks and Latinos to their neighborhood, but in public, through their community organizations, they did not voice such views.[24]

Brownsville ministers participated in neighborhood unity events, but their congregations were not active in BNC functions. A staff member of the Brooklyn Council for Social Planning, speaking for a black minister, noted that the BNC appeared "to have only spasmodic and limited support from the Negro population." The staffer argued that blacks, "because of educational and other social handicaps, have not felt able to compete with the white leadership," and therefore "tended to withdraw from activities sponsored and initiated by the white leaders rather than play a secondary and somewhat inactive role." He additionally concluded that blacks were skeptical about the success of the BNC's efforts, because blacks did not play a major role in the formulation of BNC policy. The BNC solicited the advice of black leaders like Reverend Dent and relied on ministers to convey information to Brownsville's black population, but black and white residents did not meet frequently to discuss issues of common concern.[25]

Black and white youths, by contrast, had intimate daily contact. During the 1940s, the Brownsville Boys Club emerged as the most important organization dealing with race relations among Brownsville youths. Unlike the BNC, the BBC was by definition a grassroots organization and faced racial questions every day in the operation of its program. By 1947, blacks were a significant component of BBC membership, and BBC staff members called the BBC headquarters a place of interracial cooperation where young people reached "better understanding through working and playing together." Remembered Irving Levine, "This was a very idealistic organization," and "the idea of racial integration was one of the great ideals." The BBC clubhouse on Christopher Avenue became a haven for many black youths. "It was a rescue operation for them," Levine said. Two black children who became very active in the group were Raymond and Arthur Lawrence. "Hooker Levine, he came and recruited us more so than we going down to them. They came on the block and asked our parents did the kids want to join the boys club," said Raymond Lawrence. The Lawrence brothers practically lived at the clubhouse. "You'd go down to the BBC, stay down there all day, all night. Because at that time you knew when you got out of school, you had some place to go," remembered Raymond.[26]

While segregation was typical for Brownsville adults, the BBC sought integration among its members, and BBC leaders worked to calm racial tensions within the neighborhood. "Once they came into the boys club, they were members of the same group. Now it was no longer that they were outsiders, they were insiders," said Levine. In 1947, Reverend Boise Dent joined the BBC Board of Directors and a black program director, Vincent Tibbs, was hired to work out of the BBC office on Christopher Avenue. The BBC also helped organize communitywide events, like a Halloween youth dance at the newly opened Brownsville Houses, attended by black and white teenagers.[27]

Although the headquarters and the staff of the BBC were integrated, most of the sports teams, social clubs, and other groups that made up the organization were organized along racial lines. BBC leaders argued that while teams were frequently segregated, club meetings were open to representatives of all teams and block clubs. In addition, the BBC teams that competed in citywide tournaments were integrated. This created problems for black and white members, who felt hostility directed at them from outside. "The

Figure 12. Brownsville Boys Club softball team. The BBC was one of the most integrated organizations in the neighborhood. Courtesy BBC Alumni Association.

hate was extraordinary," remembered Irving Levine. "It came from the stands, it came from the teams." The animosity against the boys brought them together. "There was a fusion of blacks and Jews—we were both very conscious that when we went out of the neighborhood we were together targets," Levine argued. BBC staff themselves were often active in civil rights causes, and they encouraged BBC members to participate. The BBC worked with the Brownsville Neighborhood Council in its pursuit of interracial cooperation, and organized discussion groups of BBC members on what they called the "Race Question." As the BBC grew, it opened its facilities to younger groups of children; and many black children, who had working mothers and few recreational opportunities, participated.[28]

Efforts to integrate the BBC were not viewed favorably by some Jewish institutions. Since 1946, the East New York YMHA had provided assistance to the group in recognition of the YMHA's failure to serve the predominantly Jewish community of Brownsville. When BBC leaders asked YMHA leaders to donate funds toward their new building, the charity rebuffed them, citing the diversity of the BBC's membership. YMHA leaders wanted the BBC to develop a more narrow program that supported Jewish cultural preservation. When BBC leaders declined, the contact between the organizations decreased. The Federation of Jewish Philanthropies also denied the BBC's request for support. According to Gerald Sorin, the Federation stated that "Brownsville's declining Jewish population made that neighborhood a low priority for them." Despite the skepticism of New York's charitable organizations, throughout the late 1940s and early 1950s, BBC leaders worked to bring black and white youths together. The efforts of BBC leaders, however, were exceptional, and most Brownsville organizations ended the decade ill-equipped to deal with the racial transformation to come in the 1950s.[29]

Public Housing Comes to Brownsville

Most requests by Brownsville residents received little consideration from city politicians during the 1940s. The demands from more powerful communities superseded the needs of the politically weak Brownsville area. The only city agency that did give attention to Brownsville was the New York City Housing Authority. After World War II, Robert Moses and his associates saw Brownsville as an area where the program could serve both its mandates: clearing slums and providing needed housing to the poor. The Brownsville Houses opened in 1948. The project contained ten three-story buildings and seventeen six-story buildings, and its configuration was an early example of the compromises necessary to make public housing economically viable. Community groups and housing advocates had asked for buildings no larger than three stories, to fit with existing neighborhood structures, but NYCHA planners determined that the project would not be economically feasible without the larger, denser buildings that would produce more income. Housing developers also wanted to replace the number of units demolished, so as not to diminish the total number of apartments in housing-starved New York. Housing advocates argued that one of the purposes of slum clearance was to lower population densities in areas such as Brownsville, but NYCHA officials were more concerned with building as many units as was efficiently possible. Even though the project that opened in 1948 was different than that proposed eight years before, it was celebrated by the whole community and was viewed as a significant improvement in the housing of Brownsville residents. According to the *New York Times*, the NYCHA received more than sixteen thousand applications for the thirteen hundred apartments.[30]

At their opening in 1948, the ratio of whites to blacks in the Brownsville Houses was 52 percent to 48 percent, and, as a racially integrated project, the Brownsville Houses were an exception for public housing in New York. Like public projects in other cities, NYCHA housing during this era was strictly segregated—projects in black neighborhoods (as determined by the NYCHA) accepted only black tenants, and projects in predominantly white neighborhoods accepted only whites. According to historian Joel Schwartz, Robert Moses "regarded talk of dispersing black ghettos as quixotic blather" and did not believe that public housing should be used to advance social goals. From its inception in 1934, civil rights leaders complained about the need for additional housing for blacks; the NAACP's Walter White protested "the barring, or at least the non-admission of Negroes to any of the existing housing projects in Brooklyn." NYCHA leaders argued that they did not discriminate; they only gave preference "to applicants having lived on the site so as to avoid, as far as possible, the dangers inherent in disturbing an established community pattern." Since the early Brooklyn housing projects at Red Hook and Williamsburg were in predominantly white neighborhoods, argued the NYCHA officials, they obviously should have a predominantly white tenancy. In fact, less than 1 percent of the tenants in both these projects were black, a smaller percentage than that of either neighborhood.[31]

Despite their protestations of color blindness, the NYCHA's own correspondence and internal memoranda revealed that all projects were defined by the projected race of the tenant body. According to Joel Schwartz, "these agglomerations were defined by race. . . . Moses would casually [refer to] the Rockaway [Queens] colored project or the Bronx colored project." In his 1942 response to Walter White, NYCHA Chairman Rheinstein acknowledged the same: "We are planning a housing project in a colored slum district in Brooklyn. The location of this project cannot now be made public as approval has not as yet been given thereto by the U.S. Housing Authority." The "colored project" to which Rheinstein alluded happened to be in Brownsville. In 1939, Moses recommended Brownsville to the NYCHA for a "colored project," but NYCHA staff, in an internal memo titled "Report on Survey for Brooklyn Negro Project," rejected the recommendation. Staffers felt that the Brownsville site should "be eliminated for future study because of low Negro population," which was less than 20 percent in the clearance area. Despite the staff's concern about the placement of a project for blacks in a predominantly white neighborhood, the NYCHA executives selected the site. The correspondence among Moses, his staff, and the housing authority staff did not reveal the specific reasons behind their decision to place a "colored" project in Brownsville, but the fact that Brownsville's Jews were less likely to protest the inclusion of blacks than the Italians and Irish in other Brooklyn neighborhoods also probably affected their decision making. Moses, fearing a political backlash, soon thereafter decided against projects in the mostly Italian Bushwick and Greenpoint sections of Brooklyn. The BNC advocated for integrated housing as early as 1940, and housing planners did not have to fear a violent response to Brownsville's selection.[32]

After World War II, the U.S. Housing Authority eased its "neighborhood composition" rules, and statistics on NYCHA projects built after World War II reveal a changing policy on racial matters. Before 1948, only two out of eleven projects (Kingsborough and South Jamaica) were integrated. However, between 1948 and 1954, the NYCHA opened forty subsidized housing projects, and thirty of them were integrated (no less than 20 percent and no more than 80 percent white). The move to a more "enlightened" policy was made possible by new rules for public housing site selection. After World War II, almost all of the NYCHA projects were located in either black majority neighborhoods like Harlem, or in "changing" neighborhoods such as Brownsville, Fort Greene, and the South Bronx. These areas were chosen to relieve the pressure from other neighborhoods fighting black incursion. Moses and his staff viewed places like Brownsville as the most likely location for future expansion of the black ghetto. Demand for housing was extremely high in Bedford-Stuyvesant and few New York politicians supported the passage and enforcement of fair housing legislation, so new, segregated areas for blacks were required. To the north of Bedford-Stuyvesant lay the Italian working-class section of Bushwick, and to the south were the middle-class neighborhoods of Crown Heights and Flatbush. Blacks were excluded from all these areas by racism and economics. To the east was Brownsville, a relatively open-minded community with a somewhat upwardly mobile population and a large stock of deteriorating housing that no one wanted. Considering all the alternatives, Brownsville certainly presented the least contentious area for expansion of Brooklyn's black ghetto.[33]

After visiting several possible sites in 1945, Moses's assistants Arthur

Hodgkiss and George Spargo designated Brownsville and nearby East New York as the worst sections they had seen. They wholeheartedly recommended additional public housing developments there, and argued that the area "will not lend itself to satisfactory development." In 1945, Brownsville still had no public housing, but it did have in the works not only the 1,300 units of the Brownsville Houses, but also a massive $18.5 million "Brownsville Houses Extension," later renamed Van Dyke Houses. The extension included twenty-two high-rise buildings with 1,603 units constructed on two master blocks. In addition to the Van Dyke project, conversion of the Howard Houses, a military housing project in the northeast edge of the neighborhood, was transferred from the Department of Defense to NYCHA ownership; its rehabilitation in 1951 added ten more buildings and 815 more apartments to northern Brownsville.[34]

Like Moses' proposals on the Lower East Side, the Brownsville extension resulted in a higher concentration of public housing than many housing advocates considered acceptable. Many questioned the need for such large developments and raised concerns about concentrating public housing in a few areas. Moses brushed these criticisms aside, stating that projects in Lower Manhattan existed side by side without any problems. Regarding the huge Brownsville development, Moses conceded that the density was high, but he rejected arguments for combining them with middle-income housing. He responded, "here again we have a neighborhood which needs to be cleared and apparently can be rehabilitated in no other way." Mayor La Guardia echoed Moses in stating that all the projects "are in undesirable areas where there is not the slightest possibility of rehabilitation through private enterprise."[35]

Brownsville at Midcentury

On March 27, 1948, the BNC, with the assistance of the BBC and several other organizations, held an "Easter/Purim Festival" at the newly opened Brownsville Houses. The purpose of the party was to celebrate the opening of the project, welcome residents to the community, and acknowledge the "brotherhood of man." BNC leaders hoped that the party would stimulate the interest of the new tenants in the BNC and therefore increase the membership of the group. A planning meeting several days prior to the festival had attracted more than two hundred residents to discuss the "intercultural aspects" of the housing project. BNC staffer David Suher felt that "the tenant's council co-chairmen will be good leaders" and hoped for an "excellent relationship between the tenant's council and the neighborhood council." During the spring of 1948, BNC leaders also focused on developing recreational programs for the project's youths, and they were successful in creating several small summer programs in the Brownsville Houses and the surrounding neighborhood. However, these programs were discontinued because of lack of funding. Glauber, Goell, and other activists also stepped up their efforts to replace public schools in the area, arguing that Junior High Schools 66, 84, 109 and Public School 125 were all too decrepit to be used. According to the *Brooklyn Eagle*, nearly one thousand people attended a March 1948 rally to protest conditions at local schools. The protesters also called for the appointment of an African-American to the New York City Board of Education, and for greater resources to fight juvenile delinquency.[36]

The year 1948 was, in many ways, the high point of optimism regarding American race relations. For the first time in the twentieth century, a major political party, the Democrats, made equal rights a significant part of its platform. Prodded by Clark Clifford and other policymakers, President Truman promoted antidiscrimination legislation on the basis of race, and he campaigned for the votes of black Americans. This effort was the result of several years of advocacy by liberal groups like the American Jewish Congress and the NAACP. In 1946, the American Jewish Congress created the Commission on Law and Social Action (CLSA) to promote equal rights among all Americans. The CLSA worked to protect the rights of all citizens, but it focused on fighting bigotry against Jews and blacks. While African-Americans suffered severely from job, housing, and other types of discrimination, Jews in the 1940s were also frequently denied their civil rights. Forty-three percent of complaints to the New York Fair Employment Practices Commission were filed by Jews, many of whom were excluded from white-collar jobs and professional opportunities in health care and law. The struggle against discrimination was not an abstract issue for second-generation immigrant Jews, and the comity of interest between Jewish and black advocacy groups formed the basis of the civil rights coalition that would last for several decades.[37]

Brownsville residents, white and black, celebrated the Brownsville Houses for what they represented: the possibility of integrated neighborhoods and the support of government for the housing and social needs of all Americans. However, economic and social trends constrained these ideals. Working-class whites, and Jews in particular, benefited from the economic expansion of the postwar years. Second- and third-generation Jews broke down barriers in education and the professions and secured positions in the expanding service economy. When Brownsville's youths achieved success, they, like their predecessors in prior decades, left the neighborhood to find better housing and surroundings. The departure of upwardly mobile whites opened desperately needed accommodations to New York's expanding black population. African-Americans, while they too benefited from post-war growth, continued to be excluded from many occupations and re-stricted to certain New York neighborhoods. In 1950, more than a quarter of the buildings in Brownsville's oldest section (the area surrounding the Brownsville Houses) were dilapidated, according to census takers (only 8 percent of buildings boroughwide were in similar condition). These units were among the least desirable in the city, but they were taken by blacks, who had few other options. The northeast section of Brownsville became increasingly black and Latino in the early 1950s, as did the Brownsville Houses, and this racial transformation doomed the hopes of Brownsville ac tivists.[38]

The response of Brownsville activists to neighborhood decline and racial change differed greatly from other, similarly situated neighborhoods. Robert Fisher, a historian of community organizations in America, recog-nized the era 1946–60 as one of "conservative neighborhood organizing." In this period, Fisher argued, "radical organizing weakened under intense pressure," and "conservative efforts at building support for the Cold War and 'protecting' middle- and upper-class communities became the domi-nant forms of neighborhood organizing." Tom Sugrue, similarly, in his study of postwar Detroit, located at least 192 neighborhood organizations operating during the 1940s and 1950s to "protect" their communities from the "invasion" of blacks. "The threat of a black influx became the raison d'être of community groups" in the 1940s, Sugrue argued. One such group stated in their history, "originally we organized in 1941 to promote better civic affairs, but now we are banded together just to protect our homes." These organizations used the language of "rights" in protesting change in their neighborhoods. Detroit homeowners believed that they had a right to segregated neighborhoods, and they fought all perceived attempts to in-fringe upon this prerogative. Whites in Chicago responded to blacks in sim-ilar fashion. Blacks and whites in the city's South Side engaged in dozens of skirmishes along the area's changing racial borders. Often blacks won these battles, and whites receded farther south. However, in the most publicized incidents, such as the conflict at the Chicago Housing Authority's Airport Homes, white violence drove blacks out of the area. Opened in 1946, the Airport Homes admitted just a few black families to the small bungalows at Chicago's southern border as an experiment in integration. The male heads of these households were veterans of World War II, but this made no differ-ence to the whites who pelted them with eggs, stones, and bricks. After sev-eral death threats and gunshots, the black families moved out.[39]

Extreme cases of violence such as those in Detroit and Chicago hap-pened in every northern city in the postwar years, but within Brownsville blacks and whites coexisted relatively peacefully. Activists from the Brownsville CIO, the Brownsville Boys Club, the Brownsville Neighbor-hood Council, and other groups worked to foster understanding and coop-eration among residents, and in doing so they provided a positive contrast to other neighborhoods. However, local organizations could not combat the broader economic and social changes sweeping New York City in the postwar years. In the 1950s, these changes were exacerbated by the policies of New York City government, and this brought about a swift racial trans-formation in Brownsville.

Figure 13. Brownsville street scene at midcentury. Trash was a constant problem on Brownsville's high-density streets. Courtesy Brooklyn Collection, Brooklyn Public Library.

4

Activism and Change:
Brownsville, 1950–1957

Henry Fields, a married black man with four children, was a longtime resident of Brownsville. On May 26, 1951, Fields was driving down Osborne Street in Brownsville when he lost control of his automobile and ran into a parked car. Fields got out of his car, but, finding no damage to the other vehicle, he drove away. A police officer named Sam Applebaum witnessed the incident, and he chased Fields down in his police cruiser. When Fields again got out of his car, Applebaum shot the unarmed man in the head, killing him. Several Brownsville residents witnessed the unprovoked shooting and protested the case of clear brutality. Reverend Boise Dent, called immediately to the scene, counseled residents against the "sort of mob violence [that] would not solve nor tend to prove any injustice." Dent and NAACP leaders were extremely concerned about "leftist influences" in the community, and they bragged that their swift action had "wrested the case away from the Communists."[1]

But many residents, including the Fields family, were not satisfied with the response of Brownsville's conservative leadership. With the support of the Brooklyn American Labor Party, they organized the Brownsville Citizen's Committee for Justice in the Case of Henry Fields, Jr., led by Bishop Reginald Barrows of Christ Church Cathedral on Watkins Street. They called a mass rally to protest the shooting. Dent and the Brooklyn NAACP refused to work with the group, citing its Communist affiliations, and asked Brownsville residents to "exercise caution" and allow the legal process to investigate the matter. Fear of association with Communists, combined with fear of a race riot, also limited the participation of white organizations in protests against police abuse. American Labor Party leaders solicited the support of the Brownsville Neighborhood Council (BNC), the American Jewish Congress, and the Brooklyn Jewish Community Council (BJCC), but they were rebuffed. While these groups expressed their concern about police brutality and the intransigence of the department, they refused to participate in the mass protest. Local police attempted to undermine the protest by raiding meetings of the Brownsville Citizen's Committee and recording the names of participants.[2]

Though Mayor Vincent Impelliteri personally promised Dent that the case would be fully investigated, police officials stalled for more than two months, blaming all community protest on "Communist agitation." Despite the testimony of several eyewitnesses, two grand juries failed to indict the officer, and anger within the community increased. In protest of the judicial system's failure, the Brownsville Citizen's Committee held its own "Community Public Trial," which indicted Applebaum for the "wanton killing." The committee criticized city officials whose "indifference to the most recent instance of police murder of an innocent Negro has been emphasized by . . . inertia." In response, the Brooklyn NAACP attempted to organize a rally to protest the continuing brutality against the borough's black citizens. NAACP officials only took this stand after it was clear that the obstruction of political leaders was providing the ALP and other groups a platform for agitation. The leaders of the American Jewish Congress and the Brooklyn Jewish Community Council supported continued legal action but refused to participate in the rally. Despite several months of demonstrations, no charges were filed against the officer. The Fields family struggled for more than a decade in legal battles before receiving a $30,000 settlement for the murder.[3]

The Fields case was just one example of many in which the politically charged climate of the 1950s inhibited the activities of civil rights organizations in responding to institutional racism. Throughout the decade, racism and anticommunism shaped the failure of New York's political and institutional leadership to respond to neighborhood change. The inability of New York's liberal groups to support Brownsville activists inhibited the efforts of neighborhood organizations to secure badly needed resources and accelerated the departure of upwardly mobile white residents.

To New York's planners and politicians, Brownsville's racial transformation was accepted as fact. For that reason few had any misgivings about selecting the neighborhood as one of the city's major sites for dumping the poor and dislocated. Brownsville activists had a different perspective on the future of their community, and throughout the 1950s these residents advocated positive changes, focusing in particular on the development of middle-income housing and new schools, social services, and recreational opportunities that would make the neighborhood more attractive to young New Yorkers. However, Brownsville activists failed to convince city leaders and private institutions to support their efforts. Public housing projects were funded without difficulty—new schools were another matter.

The Fields case also reveals the difficulties of interracial cooperation in the 1950s. Brownsville's activists were liberals, and they prided themselves on their progressive attitudes toward minorities. But the BNC and most Brownsville organizations continued to be overwhelmingly white even as the neighborhood's population changed. Other than the Baptist churches, which continued to flourish, black and Latino residents did not have their own institutions. The BNC was open to them, but few white activists made significant attempts to incorporate these new residents. Although Brownsville groups were often successful in limiting racial conflict in this period of change, most never became truly integrated because they focused on abstract, global issues of race relations while ignoring the specific concerns of local residents. A few black ministers participated in local organizations, but their role was limited by their focus on the growth of their churches and their desire to avoid connection with leftist groups. As a result, areawide, interracial actions were infrequent, and serious issues like police brutality failed to receive the attention they deserved. Brownsville in the 1950s comprised two communities: one white, older, and declining; the other black and Latino and growing.

Robert Moses's efforts to revitalize Manhattan during the decade resulted in the dislocation of hundreds of thousands of people, the majority of whom were black or Latino. Many of the uprooted settled in Brownsville's declining tenements. Civil rights leaders were successful in achieving the passage of a New York City fair housing law in 1957, but the enforcement of the statute was sporadic at best. As a result, blacks and Latinos were severely limited in their housing options. Brownsville, adjacent to Bedford-Stuyvesant, became part of an expanding ghetto, the largest in the United States according to some observers.

Through action and inaction, New York's municipal government played a major role in the transformation of Brownsville. Public housing and urban renewal became the battlegrounds for complaints about racial change that were really caused by a complex set of factors. Brownsville's public projects, like many across New York City and other cities, became increasingly black and Latino, and they were the focal point for complaints as these neighborhoods became darker. Urban renewal received deserved blame for uprooting people and pushing them to declining areas, but the program was only part of the problem. With housing shortages extreme and racial barriers high, blacks and Latinos found shelter where they could. Most often these dwellings were in public housing or in other parts of "changing neighborhoods" like Brownsville. Activists blamed the city for sending blacks and Latinos to the area, and policymakers were culpable in the creation of this new ghetto. But government officials faltered in a much broader sense. By failing to open housing across the city to blacks and Latinos and by reinforcing segregation in the selection of sites for upper-class Title I housing, middle-class cooperatives, and low-income public housing, New York City's leaders further entrenched the racism of the private market and sealed the fate of transitional neighborhoods such as Brownsville.

In 1950, Brownsville's black population was 14,177, 22 percent of the total population. By 1957, the total number of residents had declined by almost 12,000 (to 87,936) while the number of blacks increased to 21,584. Brownsville also became an area of settlement for New York's Puerto Rican population. According to the Community Council of Greater New York, in 1950 only 732 persons of Puerto Rican origin lived in Brownsville, but the council estimated that there were 12,000 Puerto Rican residents in Brownsville by 1958. The council based its estimate on the number of Puerto Rican youths in local public schools. The school numbers were not taken from an actual census but rather from the estimates of school principals, and for this reason, these numbers are somewhat suspect. Many Puerto Ricans uprooted by urban renewal in Manhattan did move to Brownsville during the decade. The neighborhood's racial transformation limited the ability of Brownsville activists to secure new resources. The area's inevitable racial change, in the minds of city leaders, lessened or eliminated the need for new community facilities. Spending scarce funds on new schools and services for Brownsville was seen by the city's bureaucrats as a waste—all the worthy poor were leaving anyway.[4]

Americans' great optimism following World War II infused the activities of community groups like the BNC. But the dramatic economic and social changes of the postwar years created a severe financial crisis for cities in the United States. Neighborhoods across New York required aid in repairing and rebuilding their infrastructures. At the same time, the manufacturing base contracted and city tax revenues stagnated. In the most favorable political atmosphere, Brownsville activists faced a difficult task in revitalizing their community. But the particular racial and ideological climate of the 1950s placed additional burdens on Brownsville community organizations and contributed greatly to neighborhood decline. Other areas in New York received government and private assistance to create modern communities, but the support Brownsville received paled in comparison to the community's needs.[5]

The Rise and Fall of the Brownsville Boys Club

Abe Stark's was a paradigmatic "rags to riches" story. Born in 1894 on the Lower East Side, Stark's parents were poor like most Jewish immigrants, and he received only an elementary school education. Forced to work at age eleven, Stark became a helper at a Brooklyn clothing store. A decade later, Stark and two associates opened up a store on Pitkin Avenue. A year later Stark founded his own business, and over the next thirty years it grew to be one of the most profitable operations in Brownsville. Stark became known for his flamboyant advertising, and his most famous sign was on the outfield wall of Brooklyn's Ebbets Field, home of the Dodgers: "Hit Sign, Win Suit." As a wealthy businessman, Stark became a confidant and major contributor to many Brooklyn politicians, and in 1945 he managed William O'Dwyer's successful mayoral campaign. Appointed commissioner of commerce in 1946, Stark told many that he planned to be mayor of New York.[6]

"Abe Stark was a driven man," remembered BBC member Dudley Gaffin, who worked with Stark on several campaigns. "He really thought he would be the next mayor, after O'Dwyer." Stark ran on the Republican-Liberal-Fusion ticket for borough president in 1949, but he lost to Democratic incumbent John Cashmore. Stark's political base lay in the Brownsville area, particularly its business and civic leaders. During the late 1940s, he increasingly focused on youth programs as a way to draw media attention and political support, and the Brownsville Boys Club became an extension of Stark's political club. Stark installed his affiliates on the BBC board and used the successful program to shrewdly position himself as a man concerned about the average New Yorker. Recreational programs in the 1950s helped needy teenagers while reassuring New York adults concerned about increasing rates of juvenile delinquency. His success in developing the BBC supported Stark's political aspirations, which were achieved in 1953 when he was elected city council president. Running mate of reform-minded, Democratic mayoral candidate Robert F. Wagner, Stark was selected because he brought the support of both the Jewish and the Brooklyn voting populations.[7]

When Stark was elected BBC president in the late 1940s, he embarked on an ambitious campaign that allowed the BBC to raise hundreds of thousands of dollars, greatly expand its facilities, and hire a professional staff of recreational and social workers. With the support of other local business leaders and government officials, as well as the New York Federation of Jewish Philanthropies and the Charles Hayden Foundation, the BBC purchased a summer camp in Queens and created other programs. But Stark's main goal was to build a state-of-the-art recreational facility for local boys. Brownsville had only one significant play area, and Stark believed that a major program was necessary to cure the juvenile delinquency problem. To further these ends, the BBC bought a property on Linden Avenue at the southern extreme of Brownsville and adjacent to the growing white community of Canarsie. For this site, they planned a building with a complete gymnasium, pool, and classrooms. Stark's connections in the business and political worlds made such a development possible, and with the Hayden Foundation as its primary benefactor, Stark's efforts culminated in the opening of a new $1.5 million recreational facility in October 1953. The new building enabled the BBC to expand its program even further, making it the leading youth program in eastern Brooklyn.[8]

But these developments were not completely positive. The fund-raising activities of Stark and the board caused changes in the operation of the BBC, many of which were not welcomed by the membership. Support from large foundations required greater reliance on professional social workers, most of them from outside the community. A grant from the Hayden Foundation required the BBC to turn over all management of the organization to the social workers and board members; teenagers could participate only as advisers. But the success of the BBC, according to its founders, was very much due to the fact that it was run by its members, who were teenagers. Irving Levine remembered the BBC as "a kind of confederation of boys with very little adult leadership. Matter of fact, we're anti-adult—the adults pushed us out of the community centers." The boys and staff members felt that the reason the BBC could attract so many "problem juveniles" was because it empowered these teenagers to control their own organization. By giving members the responsibility over policymaking and operations, the BBC presented a unique model, one that BBC founders worried was being diluted by outsiders.[9]

As Stark gained influence in setting BBC policy, conflicts with Baroff, Levine, and the other BBC founders increased. And no sooner was the new facility complete than the organization began experiencing financial difficulties. Because the new BBC clubhouse was larger, the operating costs increased dramatically. In 1951, the BBC budget was $35,000; it had escalated to $185,000 by 1954. Since the BBC received funds from so many organizations to build the clubhouse, it was difficult to raise the money necessary to manage the facility. Citing these financial problems, in March 1954, six months after the new building opened, the BBC board voted to lay off five staff members, including BBC alumni Irving Levine and Lenny Dryansky, and to curtail many of the group's programs. Stark, who by then had been elected city council president, described the retrenchment as "a step in rounding out the program of activities at the clubhouse."[10]

In reality, the financial difficulties provided an opportunity for Stark to redirect the program away from the more radical ideas of the staff members. "The new professionals with their quest to educate the whole boy," argued Gerald Sorin, the BBC's historian, "and with their aggressive integrationist direction and involvement in community organizing, were going well beyond 'keeping kids out of trouble.'" Stark felt that he was losing control of the program, and during this era of heightened concern over leftist activities, he was worried about being tarred with accusations of Communism that could ruin his political career. Although it is true that the majority of the BBC staff were leftists and at least a few were socialists, staff claimed that they never used the clubhouse to advance political ideas. Although none of the BBC staff were Communists, their activities clearly worried BBC directors. Stark and the board were particularly concerned that the new facility would increase opportunities for interracial interaction among boys and girls. According to Sorin, BBC staff planned coed, interracial activities such as dances and swim parties. "Fear over the reaction to 'mixing the races' was intensified by fear over the consequences of 'mixing the sexes,'" argued Sorin. In the context of the times, an integrated facility was radical in and of itself.[11]

The staff did not accept dismissal without a fight. BBC workers had significant relationships within the neighborhood, not only with the boys but also with the adult leaders of Brownsville. Baroff, Levine, and the others went public with their allegations and were joined by Brownsville residents who picketed Stark's office. Protesters argued that the BBC center had become an armed camp, as the fired workers were replaced not with other professionals but with plainclothes policemen directed to maintain order. The staff further alleged that the layoffs violated their employment contracts, and they demanded due process in their dismissal. As a result of community protest, the board rehired all the professional staff. Ultimately, however, each of them was released within the next year, as soon as their individual contracts expired. Though the activists defeated Stark in the first skirmish, Stark won the war. In 1954, the board voted to turn over the BBC clubhouse to the New York City Department of Recreation. With city control, the board no longer had to worry about fund-raising to keep the facility open. In addition, with the Department of Recreation in charge, Stark no longer had to be concerned about radical, interracial programs. With the building complete, the BBC's political value to Stark declined, and he moved on to other causes.[12]

Even after the facility was transferred to the city, the BBC did not disband. The founders created the BBC Alumni Association, which continued to give financial support to the center and was responsible for several additions to the building. However, after 1955, the center's new employees were hired by the Recreation Department, and the program was drastically curtailed. The center continued to provide recreation programs for Brownsville youths, but the decline of the BBC damaged Brownsville in many ways. As an organization working to improve race relations and offer opportunities for Brownsville youths, the BBC was irreplaceable. The BBC represented the possibility of community empowerment and interracial cooperation. The facility that Stark and the board built was a modern asset to the neighborhood, but it was not as significant as the psychological uplift that the BBC had provided Brownsville. Furthermore, unlike the Recreation Department, which had a very narrow mandate, the BBC had been serving many youths with emotional problems and was working to prevent juvenile delinquency. These youths were not served by the Recreation Department, which did not hire social workers at that time.[13]

In addition, the city takeover of the BBC center caused a net loss in recreational resources for Brownsville in that it replaced a planned rehabilitation of the facilities at Betsy Head Park. In the early 1950s, the Parks Department began to design a new facility that was to contain a refurbished swimming pool, gymnasium, game rooms, and classrooms for domestic science, vocational training, and arts and crafts. This project had been demanded by Brownsville residents since the 1930s, and the BBC had coordinated with the Parks Department to ensure that the facilities planned for the rehabilitation of Betsy Head Park were not duplicated at the BBC's center. However, the Parks Department's plans to enhance Betsy Head Park were shelved when the BBC transferred its facility to the city. In accepting the BBC clubhouse, Mayor Wagner stated that the facility would result in "substantial saving to the city." As a result of Stark's decision, Brownsville, which had never had enough facilities for its youths, remained underserved.[14]

The transfer of the facility also accelerated the departure of young activists from Brownsville. Men like Doc Baroff, Irving Levine, Dudley Gaffin, and others, represented a generation of educated and committed leaders sorely lacking in working-class Brownsville. In reality, these men were moving on before they lost the BBC. Baroff, Levine, and Gaffin went on to receive professional degrees in the mid-1950s (Baroff and Levine in social work, Gaffin in law) that took them out of the neighborhood. Professional ties drew them away from Brownsville, and there were no family ties to bring them back. Baroff's family moved to Sheepshead Bay in the late forties, and in the 1950s Levine's and Gaffin's families moved out—Levine's family to East Flatbush and Gaffin's to Canarsie. Economic and professional opportunities provided these men and thousands of others the chance to find better living conditions, and they took advantage of them as had previous generations. All three men continued to support the Boys Club, but their careers left them little time to spend in Brownsville.[15]

Sociologist Gerald Sorin celebrated the commitment and intellectual capacity of the BBC founders. These young men saw a problem and developed a program that met the needs of hundreds of Brownsville teenagers. Sorin traced the roots of this success to the cultural milieu in which the BBC founders were raised, and argued that BBC leaders were "powerfully influenced by Jewish religious culture and by 'the secret treasures of family and Jewish togetherness.'" While the young men who created the BBC were in many ways unique, the BBC was also made possible by the particular political and economic atmosphere in which it evolved. World War II and the postwar economic expansion created unprecedented opportunities for young, white Americans, and many second-generation immigrants took advantage of them. But these new possibilities also weakened attachments to old communities. Thousands of whites moved out of Brownsville in the postwar years. The young adults were the first to do so. The BBC was an engine of upward mobility for its predominantly white clientele, and it had fulfilled that function by the mid-1950s. Blacks and Latinos were excluded from many of the same opportunities, and when they moved to Brownsville, the few institutions that could have helped them in creating a community were either gone—like the BBC—or, as in the case of the Brownsville Neighborhood Council, unable to adapt to neighborhood change.[16]

Public Housing and the Brownsville Community

Residents rejoiced at the opening of the Brownsville Houses and celebrated the groundbreaking of the extension in 1952. Within two years, however, they became increasingly concerned about the negative impact of public housing on their neighborhood. Activists worried in particular about changes in the racial composition of local developments. According to BNC leaders, approximately ten thousand African-Americans moved into the area after 1950, most entering Brownsville's projects or crowding into the tenements surrounding them. Residents attributed an increase in crime to these new neighbors. In 1951, citizens were disturbed to hear that several heroin rings operated in the area. One drug racket was on Saint Mark's Avenue, where ten black teenagers and young adults were arrested for manufacturing and distributing the drug at a local tailor shop. A second heroin ring was located on Stone Avenue, and a third market operated out of a candy store on Legion Street, where a white seventeen-year-old known as "Yankee" sold to area teens. Police arrested a fourth distributor, a white man nicknamed "Husky," for selling drugs to area youths out of his store on Christopher Avenue. Robberies and burglaries of local stores were also a common occurrence in the early 1950s. In one six-month period during 1951, the *Brooklyn Eagle* reported more than twenty-five robberies of local stores. Two men were responsible for at least twenty of them, and they hit several appliance stores along Rockaway and East New York Avenues. In the fall of that year, the New York Police Department initiated a special program to combat the crime wave, flooding the area with rookie cops.[17]

Gang violence also increased in the 1950s. One 1950 gang fight on Chester Street resulted in the stabbing of a sixteen-year-old white youth who had gone out to get a newspaper for his father. "Gang wars broke out often in our midst," remembered Bernard Lewin, a former resident of the Howard Houses. "We would scurry for cover in the midst of zip gun fire, and hurtling bricks and chains between the warring factions. There was mayhem, blood, screams and tears, but rarely did anyone die." Because of gang violence, juvenile arrests doubled in the eastern half of Brownsville between 1953 and 1957.[18]

In the early 1940s, Brownsville residents hoped that public housing

Figure 14. Brownsville gangs at Seventy-third Precinct. Courtesy Brooklyn Collection, Brooklyn Public Library.

would save the neighborhood, but in the 1950s they blamed the projects for the decline of the area. The major problem with the existing projects, as community members saw it, was that they were quickly becoming overwhelmingly black. In June 1955, BNC President Irving Tabb wrote NYCHA Chair Philip Cruise to complain that "It has become widely known, recognized and discussed, that the percentage of white and Negro tenants in the Brownsville and Van Dyke Projects is about 10-90." Tabb's numbers were incorrect, but in the mid-1950s the tenant body in Brownsville public housing did change significantly. The population of the Brownsville Houses was 52 percent white when the project opened in 1948, but by 1955 the number of white families had shrunk from 701 to 402, constituting only 30 percent of the 1,337 units. The newly completed Van Dyke Houses were immediately affected by changes in public housing's racial composition. When the first phase of the project opened in the spring of 1954, there were 300 white families (31 percent), 503 black families (57 percent), and 79 Puerto Rican families (9 percent) in the 882 units. The second phase of the project, opened just one year later, had just 182 white families (25 percent), 367 black families (51 percent), and 170 Puerto Rican families (24 percent).[19]

The BNC's research had determined that the ratio of whites to blacks was "substantially higher" in other Brooklyn projects, particularly the Breucklen, Albany, and Kingsborough Houses. In fact, only one of these projects, Breucklen, had a white majority, and the population at Albany and Kingsborough was similar to Brownsville's public developments. Brownsville projects were not the only ones to change during the 1950s. Across the city, public housing was becoming increasingly black. Two-thirds of the New York public housing tenants in the 1940s were white; that number dropped to one-half in 1955 and one-quarter by the end of the decade. The changing racial makeup of public housing was the result of several factors. During the 1930s and 1940s, the NYCHA maintained strict racial guidelines for its projects, but in the late 1940s, the authority relaxed these rules.[20]

Furthermore, the projects developed in the late 1940s and early 1950s were more likely to be in racially changing areas in Brooklyn and the Bronx. Upwardly mobile whites were already leaving these neighborhoods, and NYCHA planning exacerbated the changes these communities experienced. For example, when Brownsville whites were dislocated for the development of public housing in the 1940s and 1950s, many chose to leave the neighborhood even though they had first priority in the new projects. Whites across the city and in Brownsville were also more quick to leave public housing as their incomes increased because they had greater options. Because some whites found housing in the private market, the percentage of whites applying for NYCHA units declined. Over time, as public housing became more identified as minority housing, this became a self-reinforcing process.

The racial makeup of many New York projects changed, but Brownsville residents' concerns increased when they were told that blacks and Latinos were steered toward local projects. An officer of the Urban League who investigated the matter told them that prospective housing officials informed black and Latino tenants that there were waits of a year or longer at projects in white areas but that they could move into Van Dyke Houses immediately. Unaware of the broader changes in public housing, BNC leaders asked that the NYCHA initiate programs to maintain diversity in local developments, arguing that segregation was "un-American, and is harmful to the entire community." They demanded swift action to rectify the situation, asserting that to ignore the problem would "only serve the purpose of those who oppose public housing." BNC members additionally questioned whether the Brownsville projects were receiving their fair share of attention by maintenance employees, because the projects had shown a "marked deterioration." While BNC leaders continued to demand that the NYCHA integrate public housing across the city, authority officials blandly responded that they had no control over the racial composition of projects.[21]

Historians of public housing argue that the program strayed from its original intentions during the postwar years. Early public housing was lavish by working-class standards. The First Houses, the Lower East Side precursor to the federal public housing program, was small compared to those that followed and combined the rehabilitation of existing tenements with new construction. Unlike later projects, early developments were carefully planned to fit into existing neighborhoods, often copying the architectural styles of the surrounding buildings. In the 1940s, as a result of funding cuts and increased costs, the height and density of public housing grew dramatically. The NYCHA attempted to house more people for less money, and projects like Brownsville's suffered accordingly. The Brownsville Houses, at six stories, did not blend in with the community, but the project was much less disruptive than the Van Dyke or Howard developments, in which the majority of the buildings exceeded fifteen stories. These immense projects drastically changed the character of the neighborhood. Architectural critics like Catherine Bauer argued that the new developments were sterile and foreboding, and that they cast a pall over the surrounding neighborhoods.[22]

The Van Dyke and the Howard Houses were more dense and less luxurious than the Brownsville Houses, but they marked a dramatic improvement in the area's housing stock, and the demand greatly exceeded the supply. New Yorkers, particularly working-class and middle-class blacks and Latinos, did not look upon public housing with disdain. Rather, they clamored for it. There were over 10,000 applicants for the 1,603 units at Van Dyke, and several thousand applied for the 881 apartments at the Howard Houses. These applicants were not the poorest of the poor. The majority of the residents in these new buildings were employed persons in two-parent families. For example, 74 percent of the initial occupants of Van Dyke (in 1955) were families comprising a husband, wife, and children. Another 9 percent were married couples without children. Almost 40 percent of the families were headed by a veteran of World War II. These residents were members of New York's massive industrial class. Only 20 percent had professional, sales, or skilled occupations—the remainder were classified as semiskilled, unskilled, or service workers. But few of them relied on government assistance to pay their bills, and only 13 percent were considered "broken families."[23]

According to several histories of public housing, during the 1950s, as a result of growing industrial wages, many public housing tenants exceeded the maximum allowable income, and they were forced to leave. Those evicted were often replaced by very poor families, many of whom were refugees from slum clearance areas. The departure of working families, the argument goes, had a negative impact on projects, because those who left were often community leaders, responsible for organizing tenant councils, pushing for repairs and maintenance, and providing an atmosphere of stability. These people set the standards to which others aspired. Those they left behind faced much more entrenched poverty and were less capable of providing the tenant leadership necessary to the success of the public housing program.[24]

In reality, while many projects did change in the 1950s, the impact of the eviction policies on the operation of public housing is ambiguous at best. In 1954, 683 families were evicted from NYCHA units. This number included all families removed involuntarily (for example, for criminal activity or for providing false information to the NYCHA), but most of these people were pushed out for exceeding income limits, which varied between $3,000 and $6,000, depending on family size and type of project. While these evictions certainly affected the families forced to move, they represented less than 3 percent of 25,775 units in the NYCHA portfolio. Throughout the 1950s, total turnover in the projects, voluntary and involuntary, was relatively low—varying between 7 and 9 percent—while turnover in private housing often exceeded 10 percent. The changes within the projects were much less significant than in New York's private market, where thousands of people moved annually from the city to the burgeoning suburbs of Westchester, Long Island, and New Jersey.[25]

Eviction was a significant hardship for many families, and income limits certainly caused the eviction of some tenant leaders (and at least one in Brownsville). And one reason for the demise of tenants organizations during the 1950s was the departure of activists due to income limits, but several other factors decreased their viability. The rise in anticommunist agitation in the late 1940s also placed many tenant advocates on the defensive. As these activists were investigated and blacklisted, they lost their ability to organize New York apartment dwellers. In the late 1940s and early 1950s, the NYCHA worked aggressively to cut contact with tenants unions and even accused some tenant organizers of Communism. The authority also curtailed support for indigenous groups for fear that they would affiliate with citywide groups. While NYCHA administrators publicly bemoaned the loss of tenant leaders, they had no desire to support residents demanding better services and greater management accountability.[26]

Despite assertions to the contrary, NYCHA statistics showed that eviction was not a significant problem. In 1958, 452 families (out of almost 40,000) were forced to leave because their income exceeded the acceptable limit. The concern over income limits masked the real fear of NYCHA officials: that public housing was becoming minority housing. The changing racial composition of public housing, however, had less to do with income limits and more with the dynamics of the city's housing market. While New Yorkers still faced a housing shortage in the 1950s, a variety of options were available to whites during these years. With savings and increasing wages, a white Brownsville family could afford some of the new developments in places like Sheepshead Bay and Canarsie. Blacks and Latinos saw their wages go up too (though not as much), but these areas remained closed to them because of racial discrimination. Between 1946 and 1955, private developers completed 200,000 units of housing in Brooklyn. Only 900 of these units were sold to nonwhites. As a result, a greater percentage of minorities applied for and were admitted into public housing, and the racial balance of the projects began to change. This transformation was a nationwide phenomenon. In 1952, 38 percent of public housing tenants across the country were nonwhites. By 1961, the percentage was 46; by 1965, nonwhites constituted more than half of the nation's public housing population.[27]

The economic status of public housing tenants changed much more slowly than the racial makeup of city projects. Popular critiques of public housing conclude that urban renewal caused a significant increase in the number of very poor people in public projects, but the percentage of poor tenants did not rise dramatically during the decade. In 1948, 10 percent of the residents in subsidized projects were on welfare. By 1962 that percentage was only 15. Only 24 Van Dyke tenants (out of 1,603) were on welfare in 1956. In fact, few urban renewal dislocatees found themselves in public housing, often because the rent was too high. While Robert Moses frequently stated that uprooted New Yorkers would receive preference in public housing, only those uprooted by public housing projects were guaranteed a preference at NYCHA sites. Those affected by Title I projects like Lincoln Center did not get much assistance. By 1956, with the urban renewal program in full swing, many blacks and Latinos who were uprooted had moved into Brownsville tenements, but they did not move into area projects. Seventy-four percent of the initial tenants at Van Dyke came from

Brooklyn, and most were from Brownsville. They were not, on the whole, Title I refugees.[28]

Although the projects received a great deal of attention from Brownsville residents, they were much better managed than the crumbling tenements that surrounded them. Arthur Lewin and his family moved to Brownsville in 1955. They had shared an apartment with Arthur's grandmother in Harlem, but they were drawn to the Howard Houses, situated in the extreme northern section of Brownsville, by the prospect of modern facilities and more space for their expanding family. "We used to call [the nearby tenements] 'The Stand,'" remembered Arthur, "because they were like Custer's Last Stand." Most of the people in the Howard Houses were employed, and they lived in modern facilities. Those in the tenements lived in little more than shells that provided only marginal protection from nature. In many cities these tenements would have been abandoned as unsafe. But in New York during the 1950s they served as desperately needed housing for the city's black and Latino poor, thousands of whom were dislocated by Robert Moses's urban renewal "machine."[29]

The renewal of New York began slowly in the 1930s with a few small housing projects on the Lower East Side and in Brooklyn. By the 1940s, the program expanded to middle-income housing in Stuyvesant Town and in Harlem, and by the 1950s, upper-middle-income dwellings like those surrounding Lincoln Center were also a part of the plan. Progressive housing developers, tenants rights advocates, and union supporters all downplayed the extent of dislocation and supported the efforts of the New York City Housing Authority to revitalize slums. However, the extent of Moses's postwar plan made the relocation issue unavoidable, and caused some liberals, particularly those representing African-Americans (by 1950 already a disproportionate percentage of relocatees) to protest the lack of planning in this area. Moses responded that dislocated persons would be eligible for the public housing that was under construction at the time, and this soothed the fears of liberals enough that the issue declined in importance.[30]

Despite public protestations of concern, Moses looked at relocation as an administrative problem to be handled by the private sector. He had no sympathy about the impact of his program on the dislocated and faced little pressure from the organizations that typically would have considered the problem. The unions, the tenants organizations, and a wide spectrum of liberal groups, including the American Jewish Committee and the Urban League, all agreed that New York had to be renewed, and dislocated tenants were left to fend for themselves. The expansion of the urban renewal program exacerbated the relocation problem, and across the city, from the

Lower East Side to Harlem to central Brooklyn, New Yorkers were being uprooted by redevelopment. In 1954, City Planning Commission staffers estimated that 170,000 people had been dislocated between 1946 and 1953, and forecasted an additional 150,000 dislocations between 1954 and 1957. Those evicted were disproportionately from minority groups. Thirty-seven percent of those evicted were black or Puerto Rican, even though these groups constituted only 12 percent of New York's population at the time.[31]

Many of these dislocatees, according to Planning Commission staffer Walter Fried, were "dumped by the hundreds into vacant tenements in a section of Brooklyn called Brownsville." Moses in fact had planned for the dislocated to move to Brownsville. In responding to questions about relocation, he frequently referred to areas such as Brownsville when asked where clearance-area residents were going to settle. When he unveiled his plans for the Brooklyn Navy Yard, Moses' staff prepared "elaborate charts showing the flow of site refugees" to the neighborhood. Brownsville's crumbling tenements had been losing their white residents for years, and they were a readily available source of housing for the city's poor. New York City had a severe housing shortage in the 1950s, estimated by city planners to be 430,000 units in 1950—and tens of thousands of African-Americans and Latinos migrated to the city throughout the decade. So nine years later, despite all of the housing built, New York's housing shortage was unchanged. Because there was nowhere else for them to go, slum renewal continued to force poor residents into other declining neighborhoods, accelerating their demise. "Soft" communities like Brownsville, where vacancy rates were higher than most parts of New York, were expected to absorb urban renewal refugees. Thousands of these relocatees replaced the old residents in Brownsville's crumbling tenements. As a result, the neighborhood in the late 1950s underwent an ethnic transformation, from a white majority to predominantly black and Puerto Rican residents.[32]

Brownsville Demands Middle-Income Housing

Brownsville responded to the changing racial composition of its public housing in several ways. Many white residents requested transfers from Brownsville projects to those in other parts of Brooklyn, particularly the nearby areas of East New York and Canarsie. The white residents who lived in the tenements surrounding the projects quickly moved farther south in Brownsville or to neighborhoods like Canarsie, and northern Brownsville rapidly became part of the Bedford-Stuyvesant ghetto that adjoined the neighborhood. Within the Brownsville Neighborhood Council, members were divided over how best to approach the issue. A minority of the membership thought the organization should continue to fight to integrate the Brownsville public housing projects. But the majority of the group decided that racial change in Brownsville projects was inevitable, and the best way to maintain the economic and racial diversity of the community was to push for the development of new middle-income housing that would provide an incentive for white residents to remain in the area. "We do not want economic ghettos in our community, and we are in danger of having Brownsville become such a ghetto," argued Tabb. "There is a great need in our neighborhood for middle-income projects," he continued. In addition to writing to the NYCHA, the BNC organized a special subcommittee that sought to rally the community behind a middle-income project. The group lobbied insurance companies, labor unions, state and federal officials, and foundations like the United Housing Foundation to support the development.[33]

In an open letter to progressive labor unions around the city, the BNC wrote that "thousands of labor union members live in our area. They face a grievous problem, one which is faced by the community as a whole as well— that of adequate housing." Noting that several unions, among them the Garment Workers, Butchers, and Electrical Workers, had sponsored projects that "have brought good housing to their members and others too," the BNC asked the unions to consider such activity in the Brownsville area. "Thousands of our citizens are ineligible for low-cost housing. They live in crowded, inadequate apartments of 3–4 rooms paying high rentals when their needs require 5, 6, 7 rooms," the letter continued.[34]

Private investors did not jump at the opportunity to invest in New York's postwar redevelopment. In fact, Moses had to beg, plead, and cajole major banks, insurance companies, and other private institutions to support his program. Stuyvesant Town, the city's first major middle-income project, was an unqualified success for the Metropolitan Life Insurance Company, but Moses struggled for years to secure the private funding necessary to build it. Many investors were convinced that New York City could not be revitalized, and several had a policy against supporting any urban development. Developers argued that profitability required lower land costs and higher rents than the city program allowed. Institutional investors like Metropolitan Life also opposed mixing upper-income buildings with low-income projects, and they often refused government support because city funding required that admissions be nondiscriminatory. Securing private investment for housing anywhere in New York City was difficult in the 1950s. Brownsville residents, living in a poor, dilapidated, and racially diverse neighborhood, faced almost insurmountable obstacles to their plans.[35]

New York's labor unions were not much more receptive to Brownsville's plight than the city's insurance companies. While several unions, most notably the Amalgamated Clothing Workers, built successful projects on the Lower East Side, in the Bronx, and in Queens for their workers, labor unions—like private companies—rested their development decisions on "sound business principles." Brownsville was not attractive to most union investors, because the housing they produced was too expensive for most of the neighborhood's residents. Racial concerns also limited the interest of labor unions. While most of the Brownsville residents eligible for middle-class housing were white, blacks and Latinos also would have clamored for the opportunity to secure modern accommodations in a relatively accepting neighborhood. Like other investors, unions were not inclined to undertake the headaches that came with the then still radical idea of racial integration. Accordingly, they determined that the risk was too high. Despite continued rejection, council members persevered in their efforts to secure middle-income housing in Brownsville, and went so far as to choose the most appropriate location. "We favor this site: former car barn at Rockaway and New Lots Avenues. The property is owned by the city; it requires no relocation of tenants."[36]

In both Greenwich Village and the Upper West Side, liberal groups pushed for slum clearance that had the additional "benefit" of decreasing the area's minority population. Community associations often used the term "racial balance" to conceal efforts to reduce the number of blacks and Latinos in their neighborhood. Like their counterparts in areas such as Hyde Park in Chicago, liberal leaders argued that open housing laws would allow blacks and Latinos to disperse throughout the five boroughs, and that this would be better for everyone involved. Planners often proposed to build low-cost housing only after middle-income projects were completed. Typically the public projects were never realized. Liberals on the Upper West Side and in other urban renewal areas were often active in the American Jewish Committee, and that organization involved itself in renewal efforts. The American Jewish Committee's history as a longtime advocate for civil rights often muted criticisms about relocation. While many clearance advocates were sincere in their efforts for open housing, the immediate impact of urban renewal efforts was the dislocation of yet more blacks and Latinos.[37]

Undoubtedly, many Brownsville residents wished to halt the migration of minorities to the area, and any middle-income housing they could secure would likely be predominantly white. On the other hand, for a decade the BNC counseled interracial understanding and bragged that blacks and whites lived peacefully in the neighborhood. Like the liberal communities of the Upper West Side, the BNC actively supported civil rights causes, including fair housing and school integration. Although the majority of the BNC leadership was white, the board also included several black members, distinguishing the organization from neighborhood groups hostile to integration. BNC leaders did not address the issue of racial balance directly, but their choice of location for the proposed middle-income project reveals the complicated role of race in neighborhood development. The selection of an industrial site, which would not require the relocation of Brownsville residents, suggests that BNC leaders were sympathetic to the plight of newly arrived refugees. At the same time, the recommended site was in the extreme southern section of Brownsville, still overwhelmingly white, next to the white neighborhood of Canarsie and as far as possible from Brownsville's public projects. BNC leaders were clearly aware that a middle-income project would be more likely to succeed in an area where the majority of the residents were white. They were also concerned with maintaining the stability of the southern half of the neighborhood. In the end, BNC leaders advocated for a middle-income project that, while still in Brownsville, actually increased segregation within the neighborhood.[38]

Notwithstanding the significant obstacles, the BNC's campaign was successful. In March 1956, Abe Stark announced that the Amalgamated Meat Butchers had agreed to build a cooperative middle-income housing project in southern Brownsville at Linden Boulevard and Rockaway Avenue. The BNC's press release stated that this project was "only the beginning of more of the same type, so that the community can develop into a fully integrated one, both socially and economically, as advocated by the Council for so many years." Unfortunately, that was not to be the case. The Jimmerson Houses, as they were later renamed, were one of only two middle-income projects ultimately built in Brownsville. BNC leaders celebrated their victory, but they were saddened by the fact that press releases announced that the project was located in East Flatbush, not Brownsville. "In the interests of upgrading our area, we would like all concerned to know that the project is strictly one in the Brownsville area," the BNC release stated.[39]

Even after their victory in obtaining middle-income housing, BNC members continued to be concerned about the changing atmosphere within the area's public housing projects. They were particularly worried about plans for an additional public housing project, called Brownsville Houses South (later renamed Tilden Houses), which the NYCHA in 1954 decided would be for low-income residents (contrary to what it had originally told Brownsville activists). Later that year, BNC members requested that the housing authority reconsider the middle-income project. The Citizens' Housing and Planning Council (CHPC), a housing advocacy group, was also concerned about the concentration of public housing in Brownsville. The organization had supported the original plan of the housing authority for the Brownsville Houses South to be developed as a middle-income project, because they were pleased the "proposed new project would result in a wide range of incomes among the tenants in the various projects in the area." In May 1955, however, a CHPC staff member talked to BNC board member Clara Tabb, wife of BNC president Irving Tabb, to solicit the group's opinion on the project. Tabb said that the BNC had changed its position, petitioning the housing authority to make Tilden a low-income project because the BNC agreed that the "families on site would not be able to afford such [middle-income] rentals and that the area was so bad as not to attract middle-income families." Another CHPC representative visited the site several days later and declared it "as bad a slum as he has ever seen," and agreed that a middle-income project was unlikely to succeed there.[40]

CHPC executive director Ira Robbins, however, objected to the development of Tilden as a low-income project because it would result in a total of 3,791 low-income families in the area. On May 16 Robbins wrote to the City Planning Commission to argue that the project would result in "an undesirable concentration of low income families in one area." Robbins recommended that the housing authority redesignate this project as a middle-income development and attempt, "over a period of time, to increase the rents substantially in the present Brownsville Houses, in order to provide for some variation in the income groups."[41]

The next month, the BNC, or at least some of its members, changed its mind again. On June 7, 1955, BNC president Irving Tabb told the housing authority that "in view of the fact that there are no middle-income projects in Brownsville and no others proposed . . . we ask that the original plans be restored." Tabb argued that because Brownsville already had "three large low-income projects," the BNC, "together with the business and community leaders of our area, feel that middle-income projects should be built together with low-income projects to make for a healthy, diversified community, one that would truly reflect the various groups in our area." BNC members were obviously conflicted regarding racial change in their neighborhood. Between 1954 and 1956, BNC leaders argued among themselves about whether they wanted a low-income or middle-income project on the site; many asserted that a middle-income project could not succeed next to predominantly minority public housing. While it is unlikely that a united organization would have been able to influence the NYCHA, the ambivalence of BNC members over the viability of a middle-income project so close to the concentration of public housing resulted in their exclusion from the decision-making process.[42]

BNC members were concerned with both the changing racial composition of local projects and specifically the impact that the concentration of public housing had on perceptions of the neighborhood. Later in 1955, Rae Glauber, chair of the BNC's housing committee, wrote to the housing authority requesting that Tilden be changed to a state-funded project with income limits of $14 per room per month. Such a project would house families with incomes somewhere between the $9 average in public housing and the $20 average in middle-income projects. She also asked if it would be possible "to eliminate from the signs erected, the words, 'low-cost' as these words, in our opinion, do not coincide with a $4,500 income level." What many BNC leaders really wanted was a project accessible to people with relatively low incomes but without the stigma of a "low-income" project. Irving Tabb argued also that the term "low-income" should be eliminated from all project signs, since "with rents and income varying constantly, these words do not fit the situation." As activists interested in keeping whites in the neighborhood, BNC leaders were acutely aware of the impact that public housing had on the success for their efforts. Closely identified with blacks and Latinos, public housing was considered a negative development by many whites. Even though the criticisms were often unfair, many blamed the projects for increasing crime and creating other problems. Fifteen years earlier, in the context of the New Deal, the BNC demanded publicly funded projects, but in the changed climate of the mid-1950s, such developments were considered a community liability.[43]

The black members of the BNC were not actively involved in the debates over the Tilden project. In 1955, there were three black members of the board of directors: Reverend U. B. Whitfield of the Friendship Baptist Church, Reverend R.D. Brown of Mount Ollie Baptist Church, and Reverend Carter Pope of Universal Baptist Church. None of these men served on the housing committee. All three ministers represented changing congregations that drew their attentions away from the BNC. Universal Baptist Church would soon move to Bedford-Stuyvesant with its upwardly mobile, middle-class congregants, and Friendship Baptist Church was already located closer to Bedford-Stuyvesant (at Howard and Fulton) than it was to the heart of Brownsville. These ministers represented upwardly mobile congregations, and they most likely supported the BNC's demands for the development of middle-income housing. Many of Brownsville's oldest black residents also benefited from the economic expansion of the 1950s. They remained excluded from other parts of Brooklyn, and new middle-income housing within Brownsville was as attractive to them as it was to whites.[44]

Tabb and other leaders continued to demand the project be changed to middle-income status. In pursuit of their goal, Tabb, Assemblyman Alfred Lama, and several businessmen from Pitkin Avenue met with NYCHA staff to voice their concerns over the impact of low-income projects on the neighborhood. The group "expressed its fears that the building of another low-rent public housing project in the area would accelerate the already noticeable trend of bringing families of low economic status into the area." Area businessmen were primarily concerned about the decline in white customers, and they blamed the projects for their negative impact on the business climate. The members of the Pitkin Avenue Merchants Association worried about "losing old customers" and felt that the "newcomers, particularly the Puerto Ricans, did not buy quality merchandise or patronize the general shopping areas of the district." The group stated that they wanted a "thoroughly integrated neighborhood," and they pointed out that "there had been a number of Negro families who had been in the area for many, many years." Housing officials informed the group that, as the project had already received all the city and federal approvals, it was too late to redesignate the Tilden Houses.[45]

After meeting with housing authority officials, Tabb and the businessmen undertook another campaign to reclassify the project. According to Tabb, "the response in support of middle-income housing was amazing," and they had secured hundreds of signatures on petitions supporting the position that "many residents of Brownsville were anxious for better and larger quarters in the price range of $20.00 to $24.00 per room. . . . Literally hundreds of small and medium businesses were questioned regarding the reclassification and the response was practically unanimous." These efforts were to no avail. On January 16, 1960, the Samuel J. Tilden Houses opened. Combined with the Brownsville and Van Dyke houses, the complex was the largest in the city. The project housed 998 families in eight sixteen-story buildings adjoining the already occupied Brownsville Houses and Van Dyck Houses. Together, this complex provided a contiguous community of 3,939 apartments, with approximately 17,500 residents. Tilden Houses' ini-

Figure 15. Brooklyn public housing complex. The Tilden Houses are in the foreground, the Brownsville Houses in the middle, and the Howard Houses are in the background. Courtesy Jeffrey D. Hoeh.

tial rentals averaged from $12 to $14 per room monthly. These rentals were near the level requested by the BNC, and they were higher than rentals in some other public housing projects. The NYCHA did this in the hope that the Tilden Houses would be more integrated than its other projects, and in the early years of its operation this was true. However, in the face of the neighborhood's transformation, slightly higher rents were not enough. Like Brownsville's other projects, Tilden's residents would soon be overwhelmingly black and Puerto Rican.[46]

Brownsville Demands New Schools

Housing and schools, more than any other components, influence perceptions of a neighborhood. New schools and housing signify positive growth; dilapidated buildings represent decline. As they had advocated for public and private housing, Brownsville residents worked to secure government resources for new schools. All of Brownsville's schools were at least thirty years old by 1950, and several were much older. Unlike residents in working-class Irish and Italian neighborhoods who could send their children to parochial schools, public schools were the only option for

Brownsville Jews. Local activists realized that many parents would leave the neighborhood if significant improvements were not made to Brownsville schools. Throughout the 1950s, Brownsville residents fought for new facilities to educate their children, viewing the existing junior high schools as the most serious problems. Young parents, they believed, were satisfied with the area's elementary schools, but the junior high schools were so decrepit that many families left Brownsville when their children reached those years.[47]

In the early 1950s, officials at the City Planning Commission and the board of education informed Brownsville residents that new school facilities were not needed because the neighborhood was losing people. Neighborhood leaders countered that while Brownsville's overall population was declining, large numbers of new residents had settled in the area's public housing and neighboring tenements. These inhabitants were on average younger than those who had departed, and their children increased the enrollments at many of the area's elementary and junior high schools. Overcrowded schools were a citywide problem—the last serious wave of school construction had occurred more than thirty years before, and communities across the city were lobbying for new buildings. The increasing demands placed on the board of education by more politically connected neighborhoods, coupled with the bureaucrats' lack of concern for poor whites and blacks in Brownsville, resulted in the neighborhood's designation as number 168 on the priority list for new construction.[48]

Brownsville whites were a majority in all but one local school, but race shaped the response of the board of education to community demands. Most white New Yorkers compared their racial climate favorably to that in the South, especially in light of the convulsions that region was experiencing in the aftermath of the *Brown* decision. But New York's schools were almost as segregated as those in the South. In addition, black schools were consistently neglected in the distribution of resources, making them the worst and most crowded of the city's schools. A 1955 report found that almost all the elementary schools in predominantly black neighborhoods were full or exceeded capacity, while eighty thousand seats were vacant in predominantly white schools. However, the school board refused to enroll black students in schools in white neighborhoods, choosing instead to move students among overcrowded schools. Bureaucrats also relieved overcrowding by increasing enrollments in fringe areas, such as Brownsville, that bordered on black ghettos. Despite constant pleas that it draft a plan to balance the disparities within the district, throughout the 1950s the school board delayed action by continuing to study programs for integration. Unlike parents in several other neighborhoods, Brownsville whites did not organize to oppose the enrollment of blacks in local schools. Many Brownsville residents, including Rae Glauber, were active in the efforts to integrate Brooklyn's public schools, and they argued that Brownsville's mixed population was tailor-made for such efforts. New schools in Brownsville, they argued, would help a needy population while at the same time furthering other societal goals by providing a positive atmosphere for interracial education. However, racism and bureaucratic inertia within the board of education undermined these efforts.[49]

To secure the needed facilities, activists gathered data and organized school PTA's, teachers, and other Brownsville organizations to lobby school officials. In meeting after meeting with education bureaucrats, BBC director Ruben Bennett, BNC board member Blanche Gittlitz, and other residents showed that Brownsville schools were filled to capacity and were crumbling. The inventory of Brownsville schools revealed obvious deficiencies. At PS 125 (the school with the highest percentage of black students in the neighborhood) the lavatory facilities were unsanitary and the lunchroom was so inadequate that "dishes and floor mops are washed in the same tubs." PS 125 was built to accommodate six hundred children, but in 1950 its enrollment topped one thousand. As a result, small children were rotated throughout the day to the auditorium to allow their rooms to be used by other classes. Children always carried their belongings with them because desks and closets were overflowing. At PS 66, the teachers' lounge was part of a partitioned bathroom and maintenance area, forcing teachers to prepare for their classes in a foul-smelling space. Originally built as an elementary school, PS 66 had been converted into a junior high school, where more than 750 adolescents shared twenty-four classrooms built for young children.[50]

Junior High School 84, which had the second highest percentage of blacks in Brownsville's schools, was the worst of all the facilities. The principal of the school, the teachers, and the PTA all agreed in 1954 that it should be demolished. Of the building's sixty-eight rooms, only thirty-two were usable; the others were closed as imminently dangerous. Committee members reported that broken and peeling ceilings and walls were "a continuous hazard to children and teachers." The three wings of the school were built at different times and were not evenly aligned, forcing children to walk down and then up several flights of stairs to reach rooms technically on the same floor. The lunchroom in the basement was next to a "stinking, reeking, inadequate lavatory," and the students ate in triple shifts. The school had no cafeteria, no gym, and an enrollment of 1,200. An additional

500 students were expected to enroll when the Van Dyke Houses project was completed.[51]

The major reason for overcrowding at these schools was the opening of the area's first public housing project, the Brownsville Houses. As a result of the new public housing tenants, each school had enrollments far in excess of capacity, and children were often shifted from one school to another during the year to achieve a semblance of balance. Brownsville residents argued to city planners and local politicians that the imminent openings of the Van Dyke and Howard Houses would increase the burdens on local schools and that new structures were desperately needed. In 1953 the school committee sponsored a concert, supported by liberal organizations across Brooklyn, to raise funds for a new school. Congressman Emmanuel Celler, who once taught at PS 84, also provided assistance, recommending to Mayor Vincent Impelliteri that PS 84 be demolished and a new junior high school be funded. Several hundred people turned out at the concert to demand more classrooms.[52]

Race shaped the way that activists lobbied for resources. To gain support for their plans, community members pointed out that the influx of new, mostly minority, residents had placed extra burdens on the Brownsville community. BNC President Landesman argued that Brownsville was "a high tension area and now a veritable melting pot of many nationalities." According to Landesman, Brownsville could be a place where children of different faiths and backgrounds "learn to live with each other," but at present its "rate of juvenile delinquency is on the upsurge." Brownsville leaders publicly worried that discrimination by the board of education against Brownsville blacks and whites would exacerbate tensions within the changing neighborhood.[53]

In 1954, the efforts of neighborhood leaders were rewarded with the opening of the David Marcus Junior High School, a three-story building with thirty-four classrooms, ten workshops, an auditorium, and a gymnasium. But because it replaced another school, the new junior high did little to alleviate overcrowding, and the school population continued to grow as more public housing units were occupied. In 1955, PS 156 had 1,823 pupils, 500 over its limit; PS 184 housed 1,300 with an expected increase to 1,700 by September 1955. In addition, the Brownsville Neighborhood Council reported that more than 600 non-English-speaking children in these schools were not being served by programs necessary for their success. Council members worried publicly that because of overcrowding, Brownsville schools were losing their best teachers in addition to many local families. In 1956, despite all their efforts, Brownsville activists found themselves demanding a new junior high school and a new elementary school, just as they had been doing since 1950. Without additional facilities, the BNC leaders argued, "this seriously aggravated area will progressively deteriorate into the worst spot in the city." But Brownsville continued to suffer neglect from the board of education, and Brownsville's schools remained overcrowded and underfunded throughout the 1950s and for decades to come. Like the efforts of Brownsville activists in other areas, the fight for better schools saw Brownsville take one step forward and several steps back.[54]

Blacks, Whites, and Latinos in 1950s Brownsville

During the 1950s, as they had in the past, the majority of Brownsville's new residents moved into the northeast quadrant of the neighborhood, some to the newly opened Howard and Van Dyke Houses but most to the tenements that surrounded them. As the oldest sections of Brownsville became completely black and Latino, the predominantly white areas south of Livonia Avenue and west of Rockaway Avenue started to lose their white populations; blacks and Latinos then moved into these areas as well. Uprooted by the urban renewal program, or desperately seeking relief from the crowded ghettos of Manhattan, blacks and Latinos took advantage of Brownsville's relatively high vacancy rate.

Black and Latino organizations did not grow commensurately with the new population. Local churches expanded, and the Carlton Avenue branch of the YMCA opened a small extension in the area, but resources for Brownsville blacks remained limited. Brownsville's existing churches responded in different ways to the expansion of the black community. Some, like Mount Ollie, increased their programs, and Reverend R. D. Brown worked with the BNC and BBC to provide recreational opportunities for local youths. But most of the local congregations remained insular and focused on their internal development. Class differences also affected relationships within Brownsville's black population. While blacks continued to suffer discrimination in spite of much civil rights activism, during the 1950s a significant number of blacks benefited from the booming economy and new fields opened to them. Black lawyers, teachers, and a few doctors were able to move into the mainstream of their professions, and working-class blacks also saw their opportunities expanded. The majority of blacks continued to suffer exclusion from middle- and upper-level management, but lower-level white collar positions became attainable for an educated minor-

ity. Work in the growing service sector, particularly health care, provided
new types of stable, better-paying jobs. Many Brownsville blacks who completed their education during the 1940s were hired for these positions, and,
like their white neighbors, they aspired to better surroundings. Reverend
Spurgeon Crayton remembered that several members of Mount Ollie's
congregation moved out to Long Island and Queens during these years.[55]

The members of Universal Baptist Church saw their congregation expand during the 1950s, growing from fewer than fifty members to more
than one hundred. In 1951, the church welcomed a young, energetic pastor,
Carter N. Pope, who had apprenticed at Mount Lebanon Baptist Church in
Bedford-Stuyvesant. Over the next six years he would become a leader in
the Brownsville community. According to Alice Book, one of Universal's
founders, "Reverend Pope knew everyone in the black community, and he
always remembered where you came from. He would say 'here's brother
so and so from Richmond, Virginia.'" Born in Northumberland County,
Virginia, Pope migrated to Brooklyn with his family. He attended Julius
Rosenwald High School, and received his training from Shelter College in
New York City. In Brownsville, the minister supported the BNC and served
on its board of directors, but he was not an active member, and his efforts
were focused primarily on building his church and congregation. A member
of the Eastern Baptist Association, the NAACP, and several other organizations, Pope did not have time to devote to the BNC's neighborhood revitalization efforts.[56]

Maintaining Universal's growing congregation was a full-time job in itself. From 1952 to 1956, Pope led Universal on a fund-raising campaign to
purchase a building to replace its outmoded facility on Thatford Avenue. In
1956, with the support of several other congregations, Universal bought a
former synagogue on Jefferson Street in Bedford-Stuyvesant for $65,000.
The minister chose to move the congregation for several reasons. First of
all, the building was available, and there were not any comparable buildings
on the market in Brownsville. Second, the area in which the building was located had recently become a black middle-class neighborhood, but it had
few churches of its own. Pope realized that this building would enable him
to expand Universal's membership and reach out to an underserviced community. Third, many of Universal's members were also leaving Brownsville
at this time. The *Souvenir Journal* commemorating the church's new facility
reveals the changes in the congregation and in Brownsville's black community. Of the forty-four families that advertised in the journal, twenty-six
lived in Bedford-Stuyvesant. Only fourteen lived in Brownsville. One family had moved to Queens, another to New Jersey, and a third to the suburbs

on Long Island. The economic expansion that benefited white Americans also supported the dreams of a significant number of black New Yorkers. As had churches and synagogues for decades, Universal moved to support its upwardly mobile clientele. By 1960, the church had over two hundred members. A large number of Universal's members continued to live in Brownsville, and, as the church was less than two miles away, it served them easily. But Universal was no longer an important institution in Brownsville, and Reverend Pope resigned from the BNC board in 1956.[57]

Saint Paul's Church also underwent changes during the 1950s. In 1953 the church that the congregation had struggled for a decade to build was bought and demolished by the city as part of the construction of the Van Dyke Houses. The financial settlement allowed the church to purchase and renovate a building on Prospect Place just north of Brownsville in the Ocean Hill section, but it also removed the church physically from the heart of the community. Saint Paul's pastor, Adolphus Smith, was also a leader in Brooklyn's black Baptist organizations, and he supported Universal and many other local congregations. But he was not active in Brownsville community organizations. In Bedford-Stuyvesant, an increasing number of churches supported recreational and educational programs for youths and adults, but church resources and facilities were limited in Brownsville.[58]

Puerto Rican institutions were even smaller and had fewer resources. According to the Protestant Council of New York, in 1960 twelve Protestant churches served less than seven hundred Puerto Ricans. Most Puerto Rican residents were Catholic, and area congregations, including Our Lady of Loreto in East New York, experienced significant increases in their Latino population. None of these institutions provided leadership or organization to the neighborhood's new black and Latino residents; only Saint Luke's Congregational Church participated in community affairs. Citywide Puerto Rican organizations were not active in Brownsville.[59]

As was evident in the Fields case, anticommunism also inhibited the activities of black organizations within Brooklyn and Brownsville. In 1950 the national NAACP undertook a purge of all Communists and Communist sympathizers from the organization. W. E. B. Du Bois and Paul Robeson were only the most famous African-Americans blacklisted as a result of this crusade. The hunt for "reds" within the organization narrowed its focus and weakened the organization's ability to create coalitions between working-class and middle-class blacks. It also isolated the organization from other civil rights groups. The Brooklyn NAACP, like the national organization, was obsessed with uprooting Communists within its ranks. The group often refused to participate in local protests because of the political orientation of the organizers. According to one historian, the Brooklyn NAACP was "a militantly anti-communist organization, suspicious of its leftist members." In 1955, Reverend R. D. Brown and the BNC worked successfully to create a Brownsville branch of the NAACP. However, it received little support from the Brooklyn branch and as a result did little to organize area blacks. "Brownsville teemed with people and troubles," argued Rae Glauber, "such troubles as outside of New York would bring NAACP running with help." But in Brownsville the group did very little and "much resentment was felt and voiced by Negroes" against the organization.[60]

New York City government was constrained by both a political and a fiscal crisis in the1950s. The death of Fiorello La Guardia left a void in the city's political landscape, and the Tammany Hall machine, which deteriorated significantly during La Guardia's term, no longer had the ability to play broker to the diverse interests of New York's residents, businesses, and institutions. At the same time, declining federal support after World War II, coupled with deindustrialization, resulted in severe pressures on city finances. In this context, a poor, politically marginal community like Brownsville was ignored by city leaders. Political and fiscal turmoil provided the background for community neglect, but no issue shaped relations between Brownsville residents and greater New York more than race. The migration of blacks and Latinos influenced the shape and scope of the assistance that Brownsville received from government and private institutions, and limited the effectiveness of Brownsville organizations to combat the transformation of the neighborhood. Racial issues also strongly influenced the tactics of Brownsville activists, shaping the language of their appeals for support to politicians and elites as well as their statements to Brownsville residents. Brownsville liberals prided themselves on their progressive attitudes towards blacks and Latinos, and Brownsville community organizations boasted of their efforts at "intergroup relations." The efforts of white activists to incorporate new minority residents were sincere but flawed. Neither Brownsville nor its organizations ever became truly integrated.

In December 1950, the Brooklyn readers of the *New York Amsterdam News* elected Reverend Boise Dent the unofficial "mayor" of Brooklyn. This annual poll measured the popularity and commitment of Brooklyn's black leaders, and Dent's selection—over people such as Brooklyn's first black assemblyman, Bertram Baker, Reverend Gardner Taylor, and several other nationally known figures—was a testament to Dent's work in the borough. As one of the few Brownsville blacks involved in the BNC, and the only Brownsville black with any claim to political power, Dent served an important role as a liaison between Brownsville's white community and the area's new residents. However, several months after his election, Dent died of a heart attack at age fifty-six. His death severely hampered the ability of the BNC to reach out to Brownsville's new population, leaving it especially ill-equipped to deal with racial change in Brownsville projects and the area surrounding them.[61]

Although the presence of black leaders in the BNC increased somewhat during the 1950s, black residents remained less likely to participate in the organization than whites. There were almost no Puerto Ricans in the BNC, and none on the board of directors. Rae Glauber found that blacks were active in local unions at much higher levels than they were in the BNC. Glauber credited this lack of participation to the fact that most blacks were relative newcomers to the community, and their struggle to acclimate themselves left them with little time for group meetings. She further concluded that several other factors contributed to the low turnout of black residents at community meetings: for example, unlike many white Brownsville women who were active in community groups, most black women worked during the day and tended to household duties in the evening. Nor could many black families attend meetings held at night, because they were caring for very young children or they lived in the projects and felt uncomfortable leaving that area after dark.[62]

The executive committee of the BNC in 1956 was certainly more community-based than the BNC of the 1940s. Three of the four vice presidents, both of the secretaries, and the treasurer were women living in Brownsville and active in local PTA's. The fourth vice president, a white male doctor, was a strong proponent of civil rights. But although local politicians continued to serve on the board, Brownsville blacks (except for two black ministers) were conspicuously absent. The racial composition of the neighborhood changed dramatically during the 1950s, but this had little influence on the organizational structure of the BNC. Nor did the ministers who served on the BNC board. "Baptist ministers in the 1950s were primarily concerned with the advancement of religion," said Universal Baptist Church minister James Green. "Unlike today, they were not involved in social programs." Reverend Carter Pope, according to Green, saw community organizations like the BNC as a way to protect and promote his church, but he did not include himself in the daily activities of the group. The ministers of First Baptist Church, Pilgrim Baptist Church, and Saint Paul's Baptist Church, the largest churches in the center of the neighborhood, did not participate in the BNC at all.[63]

Black ministers and white activists came to the BNC with different goals, and they often failed to connect. "The relation of white leaders to the Negro ministers was patronizing though brotherly," Glauber argued. "Each had motives—the intellectual whites, to be their brother's keeper, and to do something about the poverty all around; the Negro leaders out of concern for the issue, out of desire to gain advantages for their churches." The average black person was not invited into the BNC coterie, and the lack of formal organizations among blacks weakened their position in the group. "The ministers were leaders, and they were very good people," said Irving Levine, "but they were not organized. Brownsville lacked a viable black leadership in the 1950s." In reality, Brownsville ministers were very organized and active in their own associations. Reverends Pope, Brown, Smith, and Whitfield were all leaders in the Eastern Baptist Association, a coalition of Brooklyn, Queens, and Long Island Baptist churches, and that is where they concentrated their efforts. Through this organization, they frequently protested discrimination in employment and in housing, and they participated in other civil rights activities. But their focus was on the broader interests of Brooklyn's blacks, not on the needs of Brownsville.[64]

The BNC was liberal in ideology, but the organization's structure was not particularly amenable to the incorporation of new residents. The BNC made only sporadic attempts at grassroots organization, relying instead on its member groups to marshal community support for their efforts. Blacks were less likely to participate in other neighborhood organizations, so they were not as active in the BNC. Like many communities, Brownsville had a fairly well delineated leadership hierarchy. Businessmen, politicians, and institutional leaders were at the top, and these men and women served on neighborhood boards and committees. Professionals, particularly social workers and teachers, made up the activist core of these groups, administering the organizations and running local programs. Black residents, however, were unlikely to be professionals or to hold positions of leadership in the community; as a result, their participation in groups like the BNC was limited.

Like liberals in other communities, Brownsville whites often looked at racial concerns as a regional or national problem rather than a local issue, and this may have contributed to the failure of these neighborhood organizations to attract black residents. In 1950 the BNC boasted that the group had sent representatives to the National Fair Employment Practices Conference in Washington, D.C., had contributed to the American Civil Liberties Union, and had supported the campaign of the New York City Schools Council for interracial camps. A 1955 report of the BNC Community Relations Committee cited several of the group's activities regarding legislation at the city, state, and federal levels—particularly regarding Fair Employment Practices—but few programs addressing issues within Brownsville. BNC members also supported the work of the NAACP, in particular its efforts to desegregate schools in the South. Community residents took part in several BNC-organized civil rights campaigns—for example, protesting the murder of Emmett Till and backing the Powell-Diggs Congressional Resolution to refuse to seat representatives elected in states that denied voting rights to blacks. Yet the BNC frequently ignored issues such as police brutality and delinquent landlords that directly affected Brownsville blacks.[65]

In 1954, the BNC organized a "Brotherhood Meeting" that included representatives from the Brownsville Parent-Teacher Association, the American Jewish Committee, the Jewish War Veterans, the Brownsville Fair Employment Practices Committee, the American Labor Party, and several leaders of black Brooklyn churches. The purpose of the meeting was to discuss race relations in the community. In the end, this meeting focused more on issues of citywide and national importance, in particular the issue of employment discrimination. The BNC membership resolved that "by discriminating against any group of our citizenry the well-being of all people is endangered. By relegating the Negro people to a position of second-class citizenship, we were undermining our democratic way of life." The BNC board resolved unanimously "that the state law against discrimination because of race, color or creed or national origin, must be changed and strengthened." There was little recorded discussion on the daily concerns of Brownsville blacks or relations between neighborhood blacks and whites. The group dealt instead with relatively distant cases and activists could feel good about their support without making substantial personal sacrifices.[66]

In the mid-1950s, when black and Puerto Rican migration to Brownsville increased, the BNC organized several meetings to foster interracial cooperation. In 1956, the BNC invited representatives from citywide Puerto Rican organizations to discuss issues of Puerto Rican history and culture and to describe the problems facing Puerto Ricans in New York. A second meeting that year, titled "Integration in Our Schools and Housing: What Does This Mean for Brownsville?" focused on efforts of Brooklyn activists to support racial integration in New York. The advertisement for the meeting stated that "this is one of the most important problems on the American scene" and that the "development and extension of civil rights will depend upon the resolution of this problem." However, these actions to support interracial dialogue were among the last significant programs undertaken by the BNC. By 1957, the organization was almost defunct in Brownsville. BNC President Irving Tabb had moved to East Flatbush by this time, and other activists had also left the community. They left Brownsville at the beginning of the great exodus that would, by 1963, create a wholly black and Latino neighborhood. The BNC's efforts to foster interracial understanding softened the impact of racial change in Brownsville but did little to reverse the trends.[67]

As in the 1940s, while children of different colors often played together, black, white, and Puerto Rican adults did not mix. "Brownsville whites were proud that they were liberal on race," remembered Irving Levine, "but most were not liberal on interpersonal relations. Most whites did not hang out with blacks." Bernard Lewin recalled that most of the white families in the Howard Houses moved out "within two or three years of our arrival," and the remaining whites were elderly. Lewin remembered playing with white children when they were young, but those families left when their children grew older. Brownsville activists of all colors struggled to deal with the migration of blacks and Latinos into the neighborhood. Compared to other areas where racial violence was the norm, Brownsville groups were extremely successful in alleviating tensions between residents of different races. However, Brownsville during the 1950s never achieved the level of integration among the different groups that local activists advocated. Despite the efforts of Brownsville organizations, social, cultural, and economic barriers continued to separate whites, blacks, and Latinos.[68]

While Brownsville's black churches expanded, Brownsville synagogues continued to dwindle during the 1950s as their congregants passed on or moved out. Second-generation Jews were much less likely to join a synagogue, and most congregations lacked a full-time rabbi to solicit membership. A 1950 survey listed 51 congregations, 22 fewer than in 1939 (although many of the synagogues in the survey existed in name only; they did not have regular services). Urban renewal also disrupted Brownsville's religious life. The NYCHA demolished two of the neighborhood's largest and most venerable synagogues, Beth Hamedrash Hagodol and Thilim Kesher Israel, to make way for public housing projects. Thilim Kesher's four-story building on Thatford Avenue was torn down in 1946 for the Brownsville Houses, and Beth Hamedrash lost its limestone synagogue on Sackman Street to the Van Dyke project. Like other Orthodox congregations, these synagogues were not active in community affairs, but they provided anchors for the Jewish community, and when they closed they left one less reason for the Jews who belonged to them to stay in the area.[69]

The Brooklyn Jewish Community Council (BJCC) was unique in that during the 1950s it became increasingly concerned with civil rights activities while also involving itself in domestic issues, including religious persecution, promotion of religious education, and fostering "understanding and mutual respect between Christians, Jews, Negroes and whites." The BJCC was active in several coalitions that advocated for fair employment, fair housing laws, and integrated education. In addition, the group sought to alleviate racial tensions and strove, in its words, to "achieve a community free from race hatred, fear, suspicion and prejudice." The BJCC was one of the leading forces—with the American Jewish Congress, American Jewish Committee, and the Anti-Defamation League (but not the NAACP or the Urban League)—that brought about the creation of the New York City Human Rights Commission, and it was involved in statewide and national legislative efforts to pass antidiscrimination laws. To further racial and ethnic harmony, the BJCC worked with churches, civic organizations, and public agencies "to develop intercultural and intergroup programs, initiate adult education programs in new housing centers, establish more non-sectarian community centers, secure greater recreational facilities and summer playgrounds," and curb juvenile delinquency.[70]

Operated primarily on a boroughwide basis, the BJCC also had several local branches, including the Brownsville JCC. Although it is likely that the Brownsville JCC members shared the liberal ideals of their Brooklyn brethren, the group became increasingly concerned with protecting Jewish residents from the violence they believed was increasing as more blacks and Puerto Ricans moved into their neighborhood. In 1954, the Brownsville JCC reported that it was working on the following "local problems": "a) Brownsville interracial housing project in predominantly Negro neighborhood. Negroes organize gangs and launch attacks on residents in projects; b) influx of Negroes into area—their resentment against Jewish businesses highlighted by Field's case and exploited by Communists; c) Talmud Torahs must be consolidated with increasing Negro migration in and Jews moving out." The organization viewed Brownsville as a neighborhood in transition and was working to see this change occur as peacefully as possible.[71]

Throughout the 1950s, the Hebrew Educational Society ran a vibrant and extensive program of social, recreational, and educational activities for all age groups. The society's weekly program listed all the following children's activities: a playschool, an after-school game room, a library, a gym, a cooking class, an art class, a social dance group, ballet classes, a crafts group, Sunday day camp, and scout activities. Among HES's teen programs were a community service league and events such as weekly dances and competitive sports leagues. Activities for adults included art programs, dance lessons, literary discussions, drama, and religious discussion groups. The seniors in the HES "Golden Age Club" participated in bingo, crafts, sewing, dancing, and music programs. In addition to all these activities, members could participate in the HES Hebrew School, the HES Sunday School, the HES Music School, the HES Day Camp, Camp HES, and the Young People's Fellowship.[72]

Despite changes in the neighborhood after World War II, the HES continued to play a vital role in the Brownsville community, as a partner in the Brownsville Neighborhood Council, as a participant in the School Council and the City Youth Board, and as a community representative to the board of education and the Parks Department. HES staff and board members insisted that the organization was needed by the community to help develop "well integrated personalities who will find pride in their Jewish heritage, while contributing to the preservation and expansion of the finest of American principles." However, outside financial supporters began to question the utility of the HES to Brownsville. In 1948, the Brooklyn Jewish Federation, HES's main contributor, merged with Jewish organizations in the other boroughs to form the Federation of Jewish Philanthropies of New York/United Jewish Appeal (UJA). Over the next fifteen years, UJA administrators consistently doubted the viability of the HES program and pushed HES staff to relocate from Brownsville.[73]

In the early 1950s, UJA representatives began to question HES staff about the impact of urban renewal and public housing on the society's operations. At this time, the population of the Brownsville Houses was approximately 50 percent Jewish, and HES members believed that the completion of the new project would "stabilize the number of Jews in the area." While they remained tentatively confident about the Brownsville Jewish community, as early as 1954 changes in the neighborhood affected the HES program. The Young People's Fellowship, a program for Jews in their late teens and twenties, was started in the early 1940s amid concerns that men and women were straying from their Jewish roots. Many of the people who participated in this program had moved out of the immediate area after World War II and therefore commuted to Fellowship activities. In 1954, HES staff decided to find a new facility to house the program because many of its members, particularly the women, would not venture through the neighborhood surrounding the building on Stone Avenue. In addition, "young people did not find it attractive to have their program run in an old and crowded building and it was felt that the program would be more appealing if it could be operated in a newer facility." HES staff argued that moving the program to a facility west of the headquarters, and closer to East Flatbush, would enable it to continue to flourish, gaining "additional members who wanted to be served but could not because there was no facility in that area for young adults," and they secured a building on East New York and Ralph Avenues, in the extreme western section of Brownsville, an area that was still white. This early relocation of an important HES program foreshadowed the increasing pressures on the organization during the 1950s as the neighborhood's racial balance changed. In the mid-1950s, HES staff also abandoned plans to build an addition to their main facility. While HES staff argued throughout the following ten years that the organization was still relevant to the community, they did not have enough confidence in the future of the neighborhood to make any new investments.[74]

Brownsville and Racial Change in Urban America

In the summer of 1955, the *New York Times* published a series of articles titled "Our Changing City" that described the transformation of the five boroughs. Much of the series focused on the construction of skyscrapers, cultural facilities, and new housing that signaled the city's growth. When the series described Brownsville, however, its focus shifted. "Desperation is the mood of most residents in the Brownsville–East New York section. The vast majority of inhabitants in this predominantly tenement area would, if they could, gladly follow tens of thousands of others who have gone," the article stated. Unlike other areas discussed in the series, no new development, other than public housing, was being undertaken in Brownsville. In this declining area "condemned buildings are not uncommon and many tenements seem ready to have boards hammered across the windows." Even though the area was still "eighty percent Jewish," the article noted that blacks and Puerto Ricans had been streaming into it. "In five years, ten at most, this will be another Harlem," stated Councilman Sam Curtis. Throughout the 1950s, Brownsville activists had worked to secure resources and create a positive atmosphere in the community. But, as the *Times* series revealed, their efforts had failed. Brownsville was viewed by New Yorkers as a future black and Latino ghetto.[75]

In American cities across the country, racial animosity among white working-class residents shaped urban development. Whites reacted violently to the arrival of blacks in their neighborhoods, and this response influenced the placement of public housing and other government programs in these cities. While many neighborhoods "fell" to black "invasion" despite the efforts of whites, public and private agencies restricted the opportunities of African-Americans to obtain housing, and black ghettos expanded around the central city.[76]

Housing options for black and Puerto Rican New Yorkers were extremely limited, and local realtors prevented minorities from buying or renting in several neighborhoods by informal but strict practices. These racially motivated restrictions placed increased burdens on neighborhoods like Brownsville, where whites responded peacefully to the arrival of new residents and attempted to create an atmosphere where the races could coexist. The efforts of Brownsville leaders were successful in the sense that there was almost no racial violence in the area. But public policies continued to reinforce segregation across the city and denied the resources necessary to make Brownsville attractive to whites. Brownsville activists hoped to create a viable, integrated community, but they had neither the organizational infrastructure nor the influence to achieve their goals.

Advocates of segregated neighborhoods could easily support their position by reference to then prevalent social science theory, which, particularly in the 1930s and 1940s, posited that cities were "naturally" divided by race. Most academics argued that diverse areas were inherently unstable, and well into the 1950s, the majority view was that integrated neighborhoods were an impossibility. Diverse neighborhoods were those "in transition" from white to black, and once the process commenced it was irreversible. Attempts at integration, according to this theory, were futile. At the same time, the federal government supported and deepened racial segregation through its lending policies. Federal Housing Administration guidelines established in the 1930s divided city neighborhoods by race and refused mortgage insurance to banks that lent to mixed areas. Federal guidelines reinforced the separation of the races and provided economic incentives to segregate. This "redlining" did not change until the early 1970s.[77]

Religion also played a role in Brownsville's transformation. Moses and other politically aware planners kept public housing out of Catholic areas in Brooklyn because they feared a backlash from those constituencies. In fact, recent studies have confirmed the planners' belief that Jews were more upwardly mobile and would leave their old neighborhoods more easily than Catholics. John T. McGreevy, for example, argues that much of Catholic identity was based in the parish community. The Catholic Church made major investments in Catholic neighborhoods, building schools, hospitals, and recreation centers. As a result, Catholics had more incentives to remain in their neighborhoods, and they often violently opposed the incursions of blacks and Latinos. Brownsville's Jews had fewer physical ties to the community than Brooklyn's Italian and Irish populations. There were few significant institutions, and most of the synagogues were small and decrepit. But the emotional ties to the community were strong for many Brownsville residents, as evidenced by the intensity of social activism during this period. Although Jews were more willing to leave aging neighborhoods, government hastened these decisions through its neighborhood improvement policies. In the 1950s public housing was considered a negative investment, while new schools and parks were viewed as positive resources. Brownsville received much of the former and almost none of the latter. Even assuming that policymakers were correct in their views that Jewish neighborhoods could turn over less violently, their decision making contributed to a self-fulfilling prophecy.[78]

New York's liberal communities also played a role in Brownsville's transformation. With the exception of the American Labor Party, few of New York's advocates for the poor questioned Moses's urban renewal plans. Organizations like the Upper West Side's American Jewish Committee attempted to mute criticisms of renewal programs by labeling opponents of slum clearance Communists. The city's labor unions were too embroiled in factional politics to give the plight of Brownsville residents much consideration. Even organizations like the NAACP and the Urban League, whose mandates were to support integration, were slow to appreciate the impact of urban renewal. The Brownsville Neighborhood Council enlisted the support of all these organizations in its efforts to revitalize the community, but it received little assistance.

Compounding the problem, as the case of Henry Fields shows, the Red Scare of the 1940s and 1950s had a powerful influence on activism for progressive causes in New York. Throughout these years, hundreds of the city's established community organizers were accused of Communist sympathies, party affiliation, or worse and were excluded from New York's social and political life. The repressive atmosphere fostered by this inquisition silenced alternative views and narrowed the political debates over the shape of postwar America. The anticommunist crusade in New York, even more than most other cities, paralyzed liberals and their institutions, rendering them unable to cope with community change. Brownsville's history as a leftist community contributed further to its marginalization in the context of McCarthyite hysteria. Brownsville was, since its founding, labeled a Red district, and as a result, Brownsville leaders were unable to gain the support of local government or private institutions for their efforts. "During the Korean War and McCarthyism," according to Rae Glauber, "fear was so great that many organizations disappeared. . . . Fear crippled everything. People were afraid to sign any statement."[79]

Powerful forces shaped urban communities in the 1950s. The half-century-long dispersion of the urban middle class, and the businesses they controlled, accelerated in this decade, causing fiscal crises in many cities. The massive migration of African-Americans from the South to the North, coupled with the migration of Puerto Ricans to cities like New York, taxed city services in a period of political turmoil. City governments were unprepared to deal with these unprecedented changes. Even without the disruption caused by public housing and urban renewal, Brownsville faced serious problems in the 1950s. Its infrastructure was crumbling, and successful residents had been leaving for more than two decades.

Unlike organizations in Chicago, Detroit, and other cities across the country, most Brownsville institutions endorsed integration as a positive goal rather than viewing it as a threat to community viability. Through the Brownsville Neighborhood Council, the Brownsville Boys Club, and other organizations, Brownsville residents worked to develop coalitions between black, white, and Latino residents. Many Brownsville activists were social workers, and many more were familiar with the then prevalent philosophies of the discipline. They believed that with cooperation the community could overcome its problems, and they worked hard to organize Brownsville residents. However, despite significant efforts, Brownsville in 1960 was worse off than in 1940. The schools were more deteriorated, the streets dirtier, and the recreational facilities more decrepit. Most Brownsville leaders realized that the difficulties facing the neighborhood were not primarily the fault of the new residents, but of a government that failed to respond to their needs. Decades later, many former Brownsville residents, their memories clouded by nostalgia, pointed to the migration of African-Americans and Latinos as the cause of their neighborhood's deterioration. The reality was more complicated.

The failure of New York's political and institutional leaders reveals the limitations of postwar liberalism. The Democratic Party platform of 1948 recognized civil rights as an important issue for the first time in the history of the party, heralding a significant change in the government's treatment of blacks and other minorities. Yet fears of Communism combined with racism to overwhelm movements toward integration. In contrast to Brownsville activists, most whites in the United States were opposed to integration in the 1950s. But because of the inaction of political elites, interracial cooperation failed even in the comparatively favorable racial climate of Brownsville.

Figure 16. St. Timothy Holy Church. Originally Chevra Torah Anshei Radishkowitz. Courtesy Jeffrey D. Hoeh.

5

Racial Change in a Progressive
Neighborhood, 1957–1965

Paul Chandler was born in Brooklyn and raised in Brownsville during the 1950s. As a black youth, he spent much of
his time with the Jewish children in the neighborhood.
"We used to play football in the area down near where the
Jimmerson Houses are now, because there was a lot of
open space. I made a lot of good friends there, and I
was welcome in their homes." Chandler remembered a
vibrant, interracial community where people got along.
"But when the public housing began to decline in the
1950s, the rest of the neighborhood began to change.
Whites left the area in the early 1960s, and the neighborhood wasn't the same." Bea Seigel was one of the residents
who left Brownsville during the 1950s. She was born and
raised in the community, and she met her husband at a
Brownsville Boys Club event. While Seigel continued to
love the neighborhood, after World War II she felt it
changing. "I used to take strolls with the carriage," she remembered, "and after I had my second child I started to
see things occurring where I wasn't comfortable. I started
to hear about incidents, and when I would walk with the
two of them I would get flirtatious comments that were

not too comfortable." Seigel was sad to leave Brownsville, but she felt she had no choice.[1]

Unlike other neighborhoods, there was no violent confrontation in Brownsville—the neighborhood transformation happened quietly but swiftly. "You didn't even see them go," recalled Chandler. "They just kind of snuck out and you'd look up and there was another black family." Change was particularly rapid in the large apartment buildings to the south and west of the oldest section. "We used to call them the 'Jewish Apartment Houses,' because only Jews lived in the large buildings." Blacks, by contrast, lived in the smaller, older frame houses. Chandler and his friends used to play handball on the walls of the large buildings. "On Sundays and evenings, they used to congregate in front of the building, and we couldn't play handball. But after a while we could play anytime we wanted to."[2]

Despite the efforts of local activists and the best intentions of community residents, in the early 1960s Brownsville became part of Brooklyn's black and Latino ghetto. Several Brownsville residents, like those involved in the Brownsville Neighborhood Council and other organizations, tried to adapt to the changes in the neighborhood. Many of these residents were raised as socialists and taught to identify with blacks and other exploited minorities. While significant numbers of whites remained, many of those who prided themselves on their liberal attitudes felt themselves forced out as they saw their neighborhood turning into what they considered to be a war zone. Emblematic was the story of one Jewish woman, a veteran of socialist politics, who remained in Brownsville public housing long after most of her contemporaries had moved out. Despite her active role in civil rights and community organizations, she felt compelled to leave after she was beaten by a black woman while doing her laundry in the basement of the project.[3]

In 1957, the Census Bureau conducted a special survey of the city. It found that Brownsville's total population had declined since 1950 by about 2,500 (to 85,328), but its black population grew by almost 50 percent (from 14,177 to 21,584). A year later, relying on the census report, the Community Council of Greater New York conducted an extensive survey of the city's neighborhoods. It noted the increase in black residents and discussed the more striking growth of the area's Puerto Rican residents. The 1957 census did not categorize Puerto Ricans (most of whom listed themselves as "white"), but using birth data and school records, the Community Council estimated Brownsville's Puerto Rican population to number 12,000. Whites, with about 60 percent of the population, were still a majority in the neighborhood, but their dominance declined dramatically during this period.[4]

Other statistics also revealed a changing community. In all but one local school, blacks and Latinos were in the majority. Many white families with young children had moved out by the late 1950s, the parents afraid to send their kids to local schools that were decrepit in addition to being majority black and Latino. Other white parents sent their kids to private schools (a few small Jewish schools had opened in the late 1950s) or had them transferred to other districts. As a result of the departure of young families, the age gap between whites and nonwhites widened. By the early 1960s the majority of whites remaining were elderly. The Community Council estimated that 46,000 whites had left the Brownsville/East New York area between 1950 and 1958. Many more were to leave in the next five years. By 1962, only 80,000 people lived in Brownsville, and more than 75 percent of these residents were black or Puerto Rican. By 1970 Brownsville was 77 percent black, 19 percent Puerto Rican, and only 4 percent white.[5]

Other Brooklyn communities experienced similar transformations. As the Bedford-Stuyvesant ghetto expanded east into Brownsville, it also moved west, into Fort Greene. The south Brooklyn neighborhoods of Flatbush, Bensonhurst, and Bay Ridge remained closed to blacks and Latinos because of racial steering by realtors and violent attacks on minorities who ventured into these areas. As a result, the ghetto grew along the east-west axis of Atlantic Avenue into areas such as Crown Heights and East Flatbush. Brownsville, already declining, was particularly affected by the increase of the mostly poor minority populations uprooted from other areas of New York City. Urban renewal, public housing, and the development of affordable housing in other areas all played a part. Locally rising crime rates (as well as the perception of rising crime), declining housing stock, and deteriorating conditions in public schools made Brownsville increasingly unattractive to whites, who had other housing options.

Every family that moved from Brownsville considered many factors in making its decision. Change began at the level of the family but quickly affected Brownsville's social and religious organizations. Synagogue closures accelerated during the late 1950s and early 1960s. Several old congregations were demolished in the expansion of the city's public housing program, while others sold their buildings to the burgeoning Baptist and other Christian congregations in the area. At the same time, the Hebrew Educational Society (HES), the neighborhood's predominant educational and religious institution since the 1910s, struggled with changes in Brownsville's racial makeup. HES leaders debated for more than a decade whether to leave Brownsville, and when the organization did close, the Jewish community was officially extinguished. For six decades the HES served as a community center, a linchpin for community organizing, and a resource upon which residents depended for bringing badly needed social services to the area. Its departure in 1965 formally marked the end of the old neighborhood.

Though social scientists have been interested in neighborhood racial transition for more than fifty years, theories explaining the process are extremely speculative. Few researchers have attempted detailed studies of neighborhood transformation, and most theories are untested. Social scientists in the 1950s posited an inevitable process of neighborhood change typified by four stages. (1) "penetration," the initial entry of blacks; (2) "invasion," the subsequent settlement of a large number of blacks; (3) "consolidation," the departure of whites from the neighborhood; and (4) "piling-up," the subdivision of units by landlords taking advantage of continuing demand by blacks to increase profits. This four-step process, and the pejorative terms describing the stages, was widely accepted by academics in the early postwar years. Racial prejudice certainly shaped early theories of racial succession, but even those who supported integration accepted the inevitability of the four-stage process. Sociologists argued that racism was frequently a secondary factor in neighborhood transformation, but even areas with liberal views toward blacks experienced racial change. Social scientists asserted that white residents typically left neighborhoods because of "natural mobility" resulting from increases in income and opportunities for better housing. Racial change occurred, according to theorists, when neighborhoods were no longer able to attract new white residents.[6]

Studies of racial change in the 1950s often focused on middle-class neighborhoods where middle-class blacks seeking to escape the ghetto attempted to buy homes. Brownsville, by contrast, was designated a "slum" long before blacks entered it in significant numbers. Citing inadequate facilities and better housing opportunities in newer neighborhoods, Brownsville's second-generation residents were moving to better parts of Brooklyn and to the suburbs for more than two decades. This migration simply accelerated in the 1950s as new areas opened in Brooklyn, Queens, and Long Island. Large numbers of Brownsville whites moved to Canarsie, whose population swelled from 47,000 in 1958 to 104,000 in 1963. Often purchasing houses for the first time, Brownsville residents moved to new, more luxurious dwellings.[7]

The most frequent cause for departure from the neighborhood was social mobility. "The minorities were used as a scapegoat by a younger generation ready to cut its ties to the past," argues sociologist Jonathon Reider. Brownsville housing and facilities did not compare to the newer areas of Brooklyn and Long Island. When people secured the resources to improve their material situation, they took advantage of the opportunity. However, as the 1950s ended, increasing numbers of residents left for racial reasons. As more and more neighbors moved out, the pressure on those who remained increased. In many communities the term "block-busting" became common in this period, as unscrupulous real estate agents used white fears and black demands for housing to reap profits in changing neighborhoods. The impact of direct racial appeals was not as significant in Brownsville as it was in other areas, because the majority of the dwellings in Brownsville were apartments. Most Brownsville residents were not concerned about declining property values because they did not own their own homes.[8]

Blacks and Latinos moved into buildings that were rapidly deteriorating. In the late 1950s and early 1960s, fire deaths occurred more frequently than ever. In August 1959, four people were killed and more than forty made homeless by a fire that destroyed two buildings on Watkins Street. Officials determined that vagrants had accidentally set the fire, but the deteriorated condition of the building exacerbated the damage. In February 1960, a fire on Powell Street that began in the middle of the block and quickly spread in both directions destroyed seven buildings. A *New York Amsterdam News* reporter found decrepit conditions in several Brownsville tenements. "There are rows of run-down, wooden buildings which would, if a fire broke out, make the Chicago fire look like a bonfire," the paper said. Many had no running water or heat.[9]

By 1960, whites were the minority in the oldest sections of Brownsville. Only the areas to the west and the extreme south contained a white majority. In the early 1960s, most whites in these places also departed. As vacancies arose in apartments and houses, landlords rented to blacks and Latinos desperate for affordable units. Crime and juvenile delinquency in the area combined with an expanding black and Latino presence to push more whites out of the neighborhood. Most crimes in Brownsville occurred to the north, along East New York and Saint Mark's Avenues as well as in the public housing complex. But white residents had to travel through these troubled areas, and they feared that violence would spread into their blocks.

Figure 17. Abandoned apartment on Powell Street. Courtesy BBC Alumni Association.

As a result, in a period of five years, Brownsville went from being two-thirds white to 80 percent black and Puerto Rican.

The Unholy Trinity: Race, Crime, and Public Housing

In 1960 Jack Feinberg, a white tenant of the Van Dyke public housing project in Brownsville, wrote to his congressman, Emmanuel Celler, requesting assistance in getting a transfer to the Pink or Breukelen Houses in East New York. Although the letter complained about the asthma and other diseases of his children that were exacerbated in the troubled project, Feinberg's main problem was that Van Dyke was "80 percent minority." Feinberg clearly struggled with this request. "I have collected money for CORE, NAACP, Jewish charities . . . and many others. I am a Democrat and I believe in the rights of all people," he said. However, because of the transformation the project was undergoing, he believed that the addition of the Tilden project to the area would make it "impossible to properly bring up a child." Feinberg's dilemma was created by two decades of government policy that reshaped New York into two separate societies—one white, the other black and Latino.[10]

Former Brownsville residents often cited increasing crime as the main reason for their departure. Scholars of neighborhood change argue that "once individuals decide that their neighborhood has begun to decline, they become more generally helpless and more generally fearful, and they select evidence around them that reinforces this view." Indicators of neighborhood health—crime, conflict in public housing, deteriorating schools—all told whites that Brownsville was not a good place to live. According to a 1962 report for the first six months of the year, the Seventy-third Precinct, which was contiguous with Brownsville's borders, witnessed 8 homicides, 8 rapes, 147 assaults, 73 robberies, and 166 burglaries during that period. Brownsville suffered 990 felonies (placing it fourteenth out of eighty-three precincts), and had 2,653 misdemeanors, the fifth highest number in the city. Brownsville's total of 4,015 crimes was also the fourteenth highest in the city.[11]

Both New York City and the borough of Brooklyn experienced a dramatic increase in crime during this period. In 1957, there were 314 murders in the New York City. That number rose to 390 in 1959, to 483 in 1961, and to 637 in 1964. The number of murders in Brooklyn more than doubled from 88 to 206 during the same period. The total number of felonies and misdemeanors in New York City was 173,830 in 1957. By 1964, the figure jumped to 375,155. Among the boroughs, Manhattan had the highest crime rate, but Brooklyn was a close second. Brooklyn reported 111,346 crimes in 1964, 30 percent of the city total. Brownsville was part of a much larger trend that grabbed the attention of New York residents.[12]

The New York Police Department destroyed almost all precinct-level data for the years prior to 1970, making a full examination of the impact of crime on Brownsville impossible. But other statistics revealed a rise in disorder during the late 1950s. Between 1957 and 1963, juvenile arrests increased significantly, rising by 20 percent in the northeast corner of the neighborhood where the Howard Houses were located. They climbed by more than 15 percent in and around the Brownsville, Van Dyke, and Tilden Houses. In 1963, Brownsville ranked first in the city in juvenile crimes, and the area's rating of 130 offenses per 1,000 juveniles was substantially higher than the statistics for Harlem and more than twice the citywide rate of 50.6. These data are not an entirely reliable guide to criminal activity—juvenile delinquency rates often fluctuated not according to increases or decreases in crime but in relation to the changing attitudes of the adult population—but the rise in youth arrests strongly affected many white residents.[13]

The largest percentage increases in juvenile delinquency were in the western and southern sections of Brownsville—areas where whites were still a majority. In these sectors, the offense rate more than doubled between 1957 and 1963. It remained lower than in the minority sections, but the increase in delinquency exacerbated the fears of Brownsville whites over the area's changing racial composition. The section south of the Brownsville Houses was shifting most rapidly from white to black during the late 1950s and early 1960s. Conflicts between white, black, and Latino youths resulted in desperate demands by residents for additional police protection.[14]

While they were responsible for only a small percentage of total crimes, gangs attracted increasing attention from residents, journalists, and politicians. In the late 1950s, city newspapers reported a constant stream of gang conflicts, particularly in the changing areas of Manhattan, Brooklyn, and the Bronx. Whites continued to join gangs in the 1950s, but the black and Puerto Rican youths who crowded into the city's declining ghettos formed the majority of the serious gangs. Gangs battled over turf, for scarce resources such as parks and swimming pools, and for the respect of their peers, but they rarely preyed upon adults. Gang violence was targeted against competing groups of youths. These struggles seldom resulted in death, but an increase in gang violence coincided with rising crime rates to heighten fears in racially changing neighborhoods.[15]

A 1960 investigation by reporters from the *New York World Telegram and Sun* found sixty-two "active" gangs in Brooklyn, eleven of which were in Brownsville. While many of them were involved in criminal activities, most of these groups, said reporters, were "organized primarily for street fighting" among themselves. In response to increasing concerns over gang violence, the New York City Youth Board announced a special project to spend $250,000 to send workers into Brownsville and a few other hot spots to calm gang tensions. The Youth Board called Brownsville a "high hazard" area. "The problem of drugs, excessive drinking, gambling, and sex parties is seen in the Brownsville area as a community problem which, at times, involves a great many youngsters," asserted Youth Board officials. The biggest gangs were the "Roman Lords," a predominantly Puerto Rican gang; and the "Frechmen" and "Johnquils," predominantly black gangs. Both were based in the northern section of Brownsville, along East New York Avenue, Saint Mark's Avenue, and Prospect Place. Another major gang in the area was the "Corsair Lords," based in the nearby Kingsborough Houses. These groups battled for turf and over the expanding drug trade, particularly heroin.[16]

Gang violence usually involved only gang members, but innocent bystanders also became victims. In July 1959, a father of ten was fatally stabbed trying to protect others from harassment by the Corsair Lords. Whites had long before vacated the areas contested by the gangs, but many white Brownsville residents worked in the area in factories along East New York and Atlantic Avenues, and in commercial businesses along Fulton and Rockaway Avenues. Many others had to cross the area from the Fulton Avenue subway line to their homes in the southern section of Brownsville. Robberies and muggings along the Rockaway Avenue corridor were a daily occurrence. In March 1960, police charged one local man (not identified as a gang member) with thirteen armed holdups in just a few months. In the remaining white sections, violent crime was less frequent, but neighbors complained about vandalism and other petty crime. One landlord on Powell Street complained that a "gang of Puerto Ricans ages 10–15 have broken windows, doors, tiles, bulbs, roof tops, poles, [and] set fires to fences, ash cans, [and mattresses]." Because of the gangs, the anonymous complainant continued, some landlords were giving up on their buildings, allowing the youths to take over. Since the police did nothing to stop the boys, "they have become so brazen that they have even thrown rocks and bags of water off the roof at everyone that passes by." Police officials responded that they were well aware of the problem and had taken steps to increase police presence in the area, but they did not consider the situation serious.[17]

Although crimes occurred throughout New York City, public housing projects became a lightning rod for attention. During the late 1950s and early 1960s, NYCHA officials deflected accusations that their buildings were crime-ridden. Newspaper articles frequently described gang battles and other criminal activities in public housing, which became increasingly identified with violence at they same time that they were becoming predominantly occupied by minorities. NYCHA officials argued that the stories were not true—that the projects were among the safest areas in the low-income neighborhoods that most frequently surrounded them. "There is not, and there never has been, any crime wave in public housing in New York City," argued NYCHA Chairman William Reid. "Captains of various precincts in the city have consistently reported that there are fewer crimes and incidents in public housing developments than in the surrounding areas making up the balance of the precincts." According to NYCHA staff, the 1961 crime rate for felonies and serious misdemeanors was 3.8 per thousand persons in the projects, almost half the 6.3 crime rate for the city as a whole. In 1961, there were 23 homicides at authority-managed projects (out of 483 citywide), 660 assaults (out of 11,021), 124 burglaries (out of 483), and 67 rapes (out of 1,211). While denying the existence of a major crime wave, the NYCHA expanded security measures across the city. The housing authority police force more than doubled from 313 officers in 1958 to 712 (plus 200 private "security officials") in 1962. The NYCHA also added over 500 paid staff and 750 volunteers during the summer of 1962 to operate recreational programs designed to combat juvenile delinquency.[18]

Crime might have been lower in projects across the city, but in Brownsville the NYCHA's units were among the city's most troubled. According to 1961 statistics, the arrest rate at the Van Dyke Houses was the highest in the city at 14.1 per thousand persons. The arrest rate at Brownsville Houses was 9.5, the third highest in public housing, almost triple the NYCHA average of 3.8. Both the recently opened Tilden Houses and the Howard Houses had arrest rates lower than the city average (2.7 and 3.1 respectively). For many Brownsville residents, the Van Dyke Houses became the emblem for all of the neighborhood's problems, and housing authority staff constantly reported to high-level officials about small and large conflicts at Van Dyke. Numerous confrontations between black and Puerto Rican youths and housing police officers occurred, especially during the summer months when teenagers and young adults congregated outdoors. On three separate occasions in July 1961, local youths assaulted police officers attempting to disperse crowds. In one incident, according to NYCHA security, "large groups of Negroes and Puerto Ricans became disorderly at Livonia and Powell Street." A "riot call" was sent to New York City police and twenty-three people were arrested. Security officials argued that most of the troublemakers were not public housing tenants—that they lived in the neighborhoods surrounding the projects. "Large groups of adults loiter about in the daytime, many of them drinking in the streets and engaging in drunken brawls. There also seems to be wide-spread drug addiction," the report concluded.[19]

By 1962, just eight years after the Van Dyke Houses opened, federal officials raised concerns about the project, and they frequently questioned the NYCHA about its plan to quell disturbances. Authority officials responded that the New York City Youth Board was working with the gangs, the Youth Employment Service with other area teens, and that they initiated a "special consultant team of social workers" to organize tenants associations and "related self-help programs." NYCHA staff assisted "multi-problem families" and worked with Brownsville organizations to coordinate the response of social service agencies. NYCHA officials acknowledged that their plan "may not bring immediate radical change to the conditions" in the area, but they had no better response. Racial tensions in the project increased along with crime during the early 1960s. Many minor and several more significant incidents between black and Latino youths and elderly white persons drew the attention of housing officials. Often, according to housing officials, the seniors would reprimand the youths for being loud and inconsiderate, and the incident would escalate from there. "There are no sitting areas exclusively for the use of the aged and teenagers playing don't look where they throw the ball," reported one staff member. "When the oldsters scold them, they retaliate with insults." After one such confrontation, three elderly white women residents were "bombarded by a group of fifteen teenagers with rocks, old shoes," and other projectiles. One woman asserted that when she tried to flee to the elevator, one teenage girl held the door while others pelted the woman.[20]

Managers of the projects downplayed the incidents with such comments in their reports as "things aren't quite this bad." But white residents at Van Dyke actively sought transfers to other projects, and the number of requests skyrocketed in the early 1960s. One family requested a transfer after their son was beaten up in the stairwell of their building by "Negro boys who called him 'poor white trash' and 'dirty Jew.'" A mother in another white family wrote repeatedly to authority staff and other government officials, asking for a transfer out of Van Dyke. The tenant argued that the conditions were "deplorable" and stated that "bottles came flying out windows, balloons filled with water from the roof and my children get bombarded with them from undesirables here." Black youths, according to the tenant, also threw rocks at her husband. "When we moved in six-and-a-half years ago," she said, "I made up my mind to get along with all. Now the Negro children feel they outnumber us completely and they pick on us Jew whites and call us filthy names. . . . The project itself is causing racial wars here."[21]

Authority staff argued that these differences could be overcome by a tenants organization "to teach understanding for others." But most white residents had little faith in the ability of housing officials to increase understanding and respect within the projects. One elderly tenant requested a transfer even though "the services were excellent." The tenant argued that "she was fearful of leaving the apartment for fear of being hurt by youngsters while playing." The woman said she had been very active in the community, but that she saw no point in remaining in the area. Another tenant felt that she was a "prisoner in a golden cage. The apartment is lovely, but she is afraid to go out," reported NYCHA staff. The tenant argued that only an increase in white tenants would make it possible for her to stay. "If there were enough families no one group would feel the project belonged to them. However, when there were so few whites the Negroes seemed to resent their presence."[22]

Many families, black, white, and Latino, left public housing for private accommodations in this period; people on public assistance or social security, however, had fewer options and so they hoped to move to other projects. White residents at Van Dyke in the early 1960s tried several avenues to achieve their goal of a transfer. According to housing officials, the white tenants' first request often noted the changing racial character of the projects. A subsequent request would state a medical condition with a "vague diagnosis" and later statements would involve "unkind remarks hurled at them by Negro adults and children, or about the lack of playmates for their children, or of incidents that have taken place which make them feel unwanted." Project officials realized that eventually the families would find an acceptable argument for transfer and that when a unit became available they would leave. By 1963, only twenty-five white families (there were additional elderly single persons) remained at Van Dyke Houses, and all of them were trying to get out.[23]

White families were not the only ones desirous of leaving Van Dyke. Many black and Puerto Rican families also requested transfers in the early 1960s. One black family of five that was crowded into a four-room unit complained that they and other minority tenants were denied transfers to the same projects where whites were approved. Another tenant argued that the NYCHA offered black tenants "only segregated projects in areas with bad schools." Project managers responded that large families had longer waiting periods because of the lack of large apartments. They noted that "because of the greater availability of small apartments, small (usually white elderly) families are more likely to be successful in getting apartments in projects of their choice (Pink, Breukelen, Marlboro)." While a small number of large apartments were available in new buildings, these were most frequently in segregated areas, and many blacks rejected them. "Most tenants," staffers acknowledged, "white and non-white, who transfer . . . also wish to live in a better neighborhood." But because the NYCHA continued to develop in slum areas, this was frequently impossible, especially for blacks and Puerto Ricans.[24]

Forging a New Ghetto

The same year that Jack Feinberg wrote to request a transfer out of the Van Dyke Houses, the tenants of the Brownsville Houses organized a protest at the New York City Housing Authority. The tenants looked at the new Tilden project through the jaundiced eyes of those who had already witnessed racial transformation, and they demanded that the Tilden Houses be integrated. "Segregated housing," they argued, "naturally brings about segregated schools, and the children who attend these segregated Negro and Puerto Rican schools are receiving an education of very low quality. Their chances for a bright successful future are being sabotaged. This disgraceful situation cannot continue." Brownsville tenants believed that the NYCHA planned a segregated community. At the time, Tilden was the most integrated of the housing projects. Over 30 percent of its tenants in 1962 were white. By 1970, however, Tilden was as segregated as the Brownsville Houses.[25]

While it was widely praised in its early years, by 1960 public housing was a failure in the minds of the American public, where the unholy trinity of racial minorities, crime, and public projects became intertwined. In fact, the majority of housing project tenants (in New York City and across the country) were white, the crime rate in projects was lower than outside, and these units provided desperately needed housing to the "worthy poor" (working, two-parent families)—but these data were lost in the increasing animosity against these programs. Statistics for Brownsville projects during the early1960s revealed that public housing continued to serve the working poor, even though they were of a different color. At Brownsville and Howard Houses, only 18 percent of tenant families received public assistance. At Van Dyke Houses, 16 percent were on welfare, and at the higher-income Tilden project only 8 percent received aid. The overwhelming majority of tenants in Brownsville public housing were from working families.[26]

Despite the fact that new tenants were also the "worthy poor," the increasing number of blacks and Puerto Ricans was the constant concern of New York politicians and bureaucrats. Brownsville was not the only community to experience neighborhood transformation in the late 1950s. Many areas were witnessing similar changes, and, like Brownsville, they often blamed the New York City Housing Authority for their problems. In the spring of 1957, in consideration of neighborhood complaints but primarily in response to allegations of corruption and mismanagement at the housing authority, Mayor Robert F. Wagner directed the city comptroller, Charles F. Preusse, to prepare an in-depth study of the operations of the NYCHA and to make recommendations for reform. Although Preusse cited no statistics to back his claim, his opinion was that the increase in minority tenants was directly related to the increase in "problem families": "We find the entrance of undesirable families into the projects, creating a hard-core of problem tenants which, while small in number, are the root of deep troubles both to their neighbors and to the Authority." In order to alleviate the concentration of troubled tenants, his report recommended "A far more careful screening of applicants" and an effort to create a "more balanced population, economically, which would tend to remove any existing stigma from low-income public housing and would also tend to raise the standards of social conduct within the projects."[27]

The changes in income rules proposed by Preusse served as a proxy for concerns over the racial makeup of public projects. For more than two decades, the NYCHA denied that race should play any role in housing decisions, but in February 1959 the housing authority initiated a new program that established goals for the racial composition of the projects and a plan to achieve greater racial balance in public housing. Under the plan, whites received preference for admission into predominantly minority projects, and blacks and Latinos had priority in projects with a white majority. In adopting the NYCHA's plan, Race Relations Consultant Madison S. Jones argued that "We're trying to kill the idea that public housing is minority housing. If we can get into this thing sensibly with the community groups, we can reverse the tendency towards segregation."[28]

In 1960, Bernard Roshco, a former NYCHA staff member, wrote an article criticizing the little-known integration plan. The policy, he argued, resulted in the housing authority holding apartments vacant, sometimes for months, in search of white applicants when eligible black and Puerto Rican applicants were in need of shelter. In several instances, four-room apartments, usually reserved for families with one or two children, were rented to childless white couples willing to accept them. "Whatever the long-range benefits that may accrue from the integration program," argued Roshco, "the immediate result for non-white applicants is a sharp reduction in the number of apartments available."[29]

The NYCHA, arguing that it had not made the plan public because "it might be misunderstood," quickly responded to Roshco's article by defending its integration efforts. Chairman Reid, within the same month as the release of Roshco's article, discussed the program with civil rights leaders, journalists, and the State Commission Against Discrimination. In his public statements, Reid asserted that the program had not drastically changed the composition of any project. Housing managers were authorized to hold apartments vacant only when applicants whose occupancy would further integration were in the process of approval. The number of apartments kept vacant for this purpose was very small. Only sixty-five apartments were reserved as of June 30, 1960, according to NYCHA statistics. "Race does not take priority over the criterion of housing need. There has been no reduction in the number of apartments available to non-whites. No apartments are restricted to whites only. There are no quotas on the number of families in any racial group which may be admitted to any project," Reid asserted. The chairman's statements only confirmed that the NYCHA program was having little effect. The majority of the housing authority's projects were, and would remain, segregated.[30]

The revelation of the integration program resulted in a flurry of interest within the city's liberal community. Because they were directly involved in crafting the plan, most of the city's civil rights organizations came to the support of the NYCHA. On August 27, 1960, twenty-six organizations, including the NAACP, New York State Conference, the New York Chapter of the American Jewish Committee, the New York Office of Labor Migration of Puerto Rico, the National Conference on Christians and Jews, and the Department of Social Relations of the Protestant Council of the City of New York, held a news conference to endorse the program. Said the organizations, "We fully support the objectives of the New York City Housing Authority, under the chairmanship of William Reid, in its efforts to achieve actual racial integration in the housing facilities it operates. We have worked with the housing authority to advance that objective in the past and will continue to do so in the future." Happy that the NYCHA finally accepted its social responsibilities, civil rights organizations chose to ignore thirty years of intransigence on the issue of integration.[31]

The actual effect of this program was negligible. Except for a few projects, the segregation of New York's public housing projects continued unabated. During 1960, twenty white families moved out of the Brownsville Houses—only two moved in. Forty-two white families left the troubled Van Dyke Houses, and fourteen moved in. Only in the Howard Houses, which already had the highest percentage of whites in Brownsville projects (35 percent), did the program have some success. There, twenty-three white families moved out during 1960, and sixty-four were admitted. These new families clearly took the place of black and Latino applicants—only six black and one Puerto Rican family were admitted. Several of the minority families rejected from the Howard Houses undoubtedly ended up in Brownsville or Van Dyke. Fifty-eight black families left Van Dyke in 1960, while seventy-three moved in. At Brownsville, sixty black families left, while seventy-four were admitted. The number of Puerto Rican families increased by a similar amount. Public housing in New York remained segregated, and by 1964 the NYCHA de-emphasized the program.[32]

The housing authority's integration program was handcuffed by two decades of indifference and active segregation on the part of project planners. By placing public housing in segregated neighborhoods or, as in the case of Brownsville, in areas on their fringe, the NYCHA ensured that its population would be racially divided. The relocation of thousands of poor blacks and Latinos by the urban renewal program also made the development of integrated, middle-income housing difficult. Despite the efforts of the BNC, when housing officials argued that middle-income projects were not viable, they were probably right. Given the NYCHA's policies, it was a risky investment to build such housing. White, middle-income New Yorkers had many housing options. Even the black middle class had options better than Brownsville. Why would they choose Brownsville, an area that the city had so clearly directed toward decay?

Moses and his staff had called Brownsville Houses a "Negro project" even when it was integrated. By 1962, their forecast had come true. At its initial 1949 occupancy, Brownsville Houses' population was 52 percent white and 46 percent black. In 1962 the project's tenantry was 81 percent black, 12 percent Puerto Rican, and only 7 percent white (almost half of the white population were older than sixty). The Van Dyke Houses' population experienced a similar change. In 1954, the first year of its operation, the project's population was 43 percent white and 57 percent black. In 1962, this project's population was 72 percent black, 15 percent Puerto Rican, and 16 percent white (60 percent of them older than sixty). Statistics were not available for the initial occupancy of Howard Houses, but in 1962 the population was 50 percent black, 19 percent Puerto Rican, and 30 percent white (this percentage would be cut in half by 1964). By 1965, all of Brownsville's projects, like the rest of the community, were segregated.[33]

Despite the promises of a new philosophy for project siting embodied in the 1957 Preusse Report, the NYCHA's plans for Brownsville were little different in the 1960s than they were in the previous decade. In 1963, after the Kennedy administration increased funding for the public housing program, the NYCHA announced plans for three additional public housing projects in Brownsville: the Seth Low Houses, with four high-rise buildings containing 536 low-income units; the Langston Hughes Apartments, with three high-rise buildings including 509 apartments; and Glenmore Plaza, a project of four high-rise buildings with 438 units of housing. These projects, thus comprising 1,483 units, were located in the industrial and tenement wasteland between the Howard Houses and the Brownsville Houses complex, creating a wall of public housing that stretched almost a mile from the northern end of Brownsville straight through the community. As before, city planning officials acknowledged the extreme concentration of units but argued that no other redevelopment was possible. "It does not appear to be feasible to utilize this area for middle-income housing and the only alternative to a continuation of the present deplorable conditions would appear to be redevelopment with public housing," they argued.[34]

Unlike the reaction to earlier projects, there was little opposition to the NYCHA's plans from the community or the Citizens' Housing and Planning Commission (CHPC). While CHPC staff continued their philosophical objections to such concentrations of low-income units, a staff memo argued that "occupancy in public housing is considered to be a step upward in this neighborhood; and the leadership of the Negro and Puerto Rican groups in the area were tenants in public housing projects." Many Brownsville leaders did support the development of additional housing. Some saw it as an answer to the significant housing needs of the community; others agreed with city officials that public housing would be much better than the squalid slums that existed in the area to be redeveloped. While some activists continued to lobby for the development of middle-income housing, groups like the BNC and the Brownsville Committee on Youth had dissolved, and new organizations that would emerge during the War on Poverty were yet to coalesce. As a result, the economic and racial segregation of Brownsville's housing continued. Swift change in Brownsville housing combined with increasing segregation within local schools to accelerate neighborhood transition.[35]

New Yorkers viewed Brownsville's public projects as minority housing by the late 1950s, and local schools were not far behind. Debates over integration in New York's public schools were fierce in the 1950s and 1960s, and they affected Brownsville's transformation. In the aftermath of the U.S. Supreme Court's 1954 decision invalidating segregated schools, the New York NAACP and other civil rights organizations in the city increased their efforts to integrate the public school system, which at the time was almost as segregated as those in the South. The Brooklyn NAACP chapter, working with an association of liberal organizations called the Intergroup Committee on New York's Public Schools, lobbied the board of education to use its new school construction program to build schools that would draw from diverse populations. They fought for the placement of schools in fringe areas that bordered Bedford-Stuyvesant, particularly Flatbush and Brownsville. In 1956 a heated battle ensued when the board of education chose to locate the planned Junior High School 258 within the Bedford-Stuyvesant school district and refused to adjust the boundaries of the district to support integration by drawing on the surrounding communities. The board did promise advocates that in the future integration would be made a priority. However, despite the work of these groups, school officials remained opposed to planned integration, and Brooklyn's public schools by the late 1950s were more segregated than they had been at the beginning of the decade.[36]

Brownsville residents were a significant part of the school integration movement. These activists did not use the Brownsville Neighborhood Council as their medium, however, because it was almost defunct, and its remaining energy was devoted to preventing any further damage to Brownsville's remaining white population. While a few BNC members continued to live in Brownsville, most had moved out or to the extreme western end of the neighborhood. Even Irving Tabb, the last BNC president, had moved to East Flatbush, and under his continued leadership, from 1958 until it disbanded in the early 1960s, the BNC served primarily to protect the interests of whites on the borders of Brownsville. The group made no attempts to reach out to or organize the blacks and Puerto Ricans who had recently moved to the area, and in fact the minority membership of the group declined during this period. One Youth Board worker argued that most white activists "think only in terms of the problems of their area," and not about the concerns of the larger community. In 1958, only two of thirty-four BNC directors were black, and neither was active in the group.[37]

Despite Brownsville's negative atmosphere and the feeling among most whites that racial change was inevitable, in the late 1950s a small number of progressives, including BNC members Rae Glauber, Sarah Goldstein, and Irene Eisenberg, joined with African-American and Puerto Rican activists, including Winnie Coalbrooke and Fanette Urgo, to form the Brownsville Council on Youth (BCY). This organization, affiliated with the New York City Youth Board, was founded to combat juvenile delinquency, but it took on an expanded portfolio of activity with the primary goal of maintaining integration in the neighborhood. To this end, the BCY devised a project to coordinate the activities of public and private agencies and prominent individuals to actively promote the idea of an integrated community in Brownsville. The group proposed that the NYCHA make special efforts to integrate the Tilden project by focusing on attracting "normal families (both parents in home, mother not working)" and assigning an intake person to the Hebrew Educational Society "since maximum 'push' needs to be to encourage white families to apply." Activists planned a large campaign with mass mailings, posters, films, and newspaper articles to generate interest in the community and to convince white people to move into the projects and to remain in the area. And in an effort to decrease racial tensions, the program also included the distribution of instructional materials to local schools. However, despite the efforts of Brownsville activists in planning their program, they were unable to convince local or citywide institutions to support the project, and it was never initiated. While NYCHA officials in 1958 had pledged to increase their efforts to integrate projects across the city, housing administrators made no specific promises to BCY members.[38]

The integration struggle continued in the early 1960s when Brooklyn civil rights groups joined with Brownsville residents to lobby the board of education to build a planned junior high school, JHS 275, in an area where it would draw students from Brownsville, East New York, and Canarsie. Reverend Helen Archibald of Saint Luke's Congregational Church, Alex Efthim of the Jimmerson Houses Committee for Cooperative Living, and Thelma Hamilton, president of the Brownsville Houses Tenants Council, joined others to create the "Emergency Committee for the Integration of Junior High School 275." They argued that an integrated school could support their efforts to maintain diversity in Brownsville housing, but many white residents in the area opposed the plan. In an ironic twist, these parents organized through the near-defunct Brownsville Neighborhood Council to oppose the development of JHS 275 in a fringe area between the communities and argued that it should be built in the heart of Brownsville. BNC President Irving Tabb asserted that the immediate need for new facilities in Brownsville outweighed the longer-term goals of integrated schools, but the real motive behind the BNC's lobbying was to keep Brownsville's black and Latino students separate from the white youths of Canarsie and East Flatbush. These former Brownsville residents wanted a separate junior high school built in Canarsie.[39]

The local school board also opposed the integrated site. Thelma Hamilton argued that the board was unrepresentative (it was made up entirely of residents from Canarsie and East Flatbush) and that twenty-five hundred residents had joined her committee in favor of the fringe site. Rae Glauber, who had been a leader of the BNC, was in 1962 a member of the Brownsville Council on Youth. She remembered that the conflict over the location of the new junior high school lasted two years and sharply split the community. "The integrated site won, for those who favored it were the new, emerging forces, the Negroes and Puerto Ricans; and the new white people planning to remain in Brownsville, who were the Jimmerson Cooperative residents." The Jewish War Veterans and the local American Jewish Congress also supported integration. Succumbing to this pressure, the board of education finally agreed to build at the site proposed by integration advocates. During its construction, however, education officials decided to change the district that the school would serve. Integrationists once again organized to protest that the school as planned would be 90 percent black and Latino instead of the intended fifty-fifty ratio between whites and the other ethnic groups. After a long debate with education officials and white parents, a zoning plan was drafted to create a school that was more integrated than most Brooklyn schools—but the majority of its student body continued to be blacks and Latinos. The failure of local activists to achieve integrated schooling ended the possibility of a diverse Brownsville. For more than a decade, many Brownsville residents worked to secure resources that would promote the neighborhood as a place of racial and economic integration. But the combination of bureaucratic inertia and opposition from white former residents denied this possibility.[40]

Religious Institutions and White Flight

Neighborhood change affected all Brownsville institutions, including its religious organizations. As they had for the previous two decades, Brownsville synagogues continued closing during the 1950s. The staff of the Brownsville branch of the Brooklyn Public Library listed eighteen Brownsville congregations in their 1959 community survey. While most congregations lost significant membership and were on their last breath by the late 1950s, urban redevelopment contributed to their demise. Congregation Chevra Thilim Kesher Israel, one of the oldest synagogues in the neighborhood, was uprooted by the Brownsville Houses in 1946. When the city condemned their building, they merged with Ohev Sholom, another neighborhood institution located down the street. The city condemned that synagogue in 1963 for the construction of the Langston Hughes Houses. "We were very sad to lose our building," remembered Ronald Kantrowitz. "My father was President, and he continued to worship every morning, even after we moved to East Fifty-seventh Street in East Flatbush in the early 1950s." Unlike others, Thilim Kesher Israel was still active, with more than seventy-five members in the late 1950s. While many of them had moved out of Brownsville years before, they continued to return for Sabbath and holidays. "My father walked from East Flatbush, and towards the end we yelled at him to stop," Kantrowitz said. "We said he was taking his life into his hands, but he didn't listen." While members returned for special services, few were as committed as Kantrowitz's father. "Not many people went to morning services," his son remembered, "and often my dad had to go around the corner to the Belmont Avenue Market to pull together a minyan [ten people necessary to worship]. He had to offer the pushcart vendors breakfast to get them in the synagogue." When the synagogue was taken by the city, the remaining congregants disbanded.[41]

Other religious groups followed in the late 1950s and early 1960s. The synagogues of Congregation Austrian Gemilath Chasidim and Congregation Tifereth Aaron V'Israel were demolished for the construction of the Tilden Houses. Founded in 1902, Austrian Gemilath had a three-story building with a large sanctuary. While the congregation once had more than one hundred members, few remained by the late 1950s. When the city bought the building, the congregation put the funds in its account to use for the burial society and other purposes. There were not enough people left to purchase another building, recalled Jack Baum, president of the congregation's burial society, "so we had meetings at the Young Israel of Eastern Parkway Synagogue." The few remaining members of Tifereth Aaron were "happy at the time that the city bought their property because they couldn't get anything for it," said Abraham Reiss, its burial society president. The synagogue was a branch of a larger congregation that also had facilities on the Lower East Side and in Williamsburg. During the 1950s, all these groups merged into the synagogue in Borough Park, Brooklyn, which is still active today. "There were only three or four members left in Brownsville when the building closed," Reiss recollected. "They had left long before the synagogue was sold." Agudath Achim Anshei Libowitz, founded in 1906, had 250 members in 1939, but it too was condemned by the city in 1958 and was demolished for the Tilden project. Like the other congregations, its few surviving members chose not to purchase another building.[42]

Most Brownsville congregations operated in small, rented facilities. When they closed, they sold their torahs and other religious materials, and their history died with their last members. Only a few of Brownsville's congregations owned their buildings, and several of those that were not bought by the city were purchased by the newly established Baptist and Pentecostal churches serving the area's new residents. Between 1959 and 1965, at least nine synagogues were sold to Christian churches. Ohel Abraham of Zitomer had ninety-five members in 1939, but by 1959 fewer than a dozen remained. In that year the congregation sold its two-story frame building to the Pentecostal Church of the Assembly of God for $14,000. "They were happy to get something for the building," remembered Ruth Lurie, daughter of a former member. "For years we continued to meet at my parents' house in Oceanside, but we never reestablished a synagogue. The members had moved to different places."[43]

Two of Brownsville's most distinguished synagogues, and two of the few with architectural importance, Chevra Torah Anshei Radishkowitz and Beth Israel of Brownsville, sold their buildings in 1965 and 1966 respectively. Beth Israel's four-story synagogue went to Noah's Ark Baptist Church for $65,000. The trustees said that they did not have the financial ability to maintain the structure, which was constantly subject to vandalism because it was vacant at "increasingly frequent intervals." The members of Anshei Radishkowitz sold their facility to the Archdiocese of New York for $45,000. The building was one of the most beautiful synagogues in the area, according to former residents. Its sanctuary, large enough to hold several hundred congregants, had the most stained glass windows of any Brownsville synagogue. Like Beth Israel, the membership dwindled to only a few by the early 1960s. By that time, none of Anshei Radishkowitz's seven trustees lived in the area (they had all moved to other parts of Brooklyn), and their synagogue became St. Timothy Holy Church (see fig. 16).[44]

Other Brownsville congregations struggled with the same concerns over maintenance of buildings that could no longer be supported by their memberships. Ahavath Achim Anshe sold its building on Riverdale Avenue to the Seventh Day Adventist Church. By that time, the congregation's membership had declined to seventy. Of that number, only about twenty attended Sabbath services and only twelve attended the synagogue during the week. The congregation's trustees argued that the surrounding neighborhood had "deteriorated and changed in the past five years, and a further change is anticipated in the future." Only two of the eight trustees lived in Brownsville and all believed that it would be impossible to maintain the building with the declining membership. Like the others, Chevra Poale Zedek Anshe Lomze, founded in 1911, gave up on the area and sold its building to a Pentecostal congregation for $14,000 in 1963.[45]

The sale of synagogues to Christian churches violated Jewish doctrines and was criticized by many religious Jews. Brownsville was not the only area witnessing racial transition in the early 1960s, and the Union of Orthodox Rabbis made a formal statement condemning the transfer of Jewish religious institutions. But these critics offered no alternatives. Unlike Catholic parishes, where the citywide Archdiocese owned and supported the parish facilities, each congregation had complete authority to dispose of its own synagogue. Some synagogues that found selling their buildings to churches distasteful instead transferred them to real estate agents—who then sold them to churches. Shomrei Emanuei and Anshe Dokshitz each sold their buildings to local agents for $10,000 in the early 1960s. Anshe Dokshitz had held services only sporadically during the past four years, and the member-

Figure 18. Bethany Gospel Chapel. Originally Hebrew Ladies Day Nursery. Courtesy Jeffrey D. Hoeh.

ship of the congregation had declined to seventeen, only six of whom lived in Brooklyn. In light of the frequent vandalism committed on the building, the congregation felt it had no choice but to sell the building for the best offer. But Brownsville Jews realized that what one rabbi called the "transparent subterfuge" of selling to an agent did not resolve the moral issue.[46]

Most Brownsville Jews attended synagogue infrequently at best. The majority of Brownsville's congregants were senior citizens whose children had little desire to preserve their congregations. According to one Brooklyn rabbi, only two Brownsville congregations established new synagogues after they sold their buildings. The others "lacked a minimal quorum of active members to warrant relocation." After dissolution, the congregation frequently distributed the remaining burial plots held by the mutual benefit society to the remaining congregants and disbursed other funds in accordance with the congregation's bylaws. Several continued to exist as mutual benefit associations for the remaining members and their children.[47]

Like individual congregations, the Hebrew Educational Society (HES) struggled with neighborhood change. By the late 1950s, the HES facility, now approaching fifty years old, was in desperate need of repair. In 1958, the HES told representatives of the United Jewish Appeal that the men's bathroom needed to be completely renovated, the handball courts were crumbling, and "the kitchen had deteriorated almost to the zero point." Despite the problem it faced, the HES continued to insist upon its relevance to the community. If anything, argued HES leaders, the transformation of the neighborhood heightened the importance of the HES to those who remained. Finding that at least twenty-one thousand Jews continued to live close to the HES headquarters in 1959, Director Landesman argued: "As we consider our present role in our community we find that we are very much needed. In a changing metropolitan neighborhood like ours, with many of our people in better economic condition moving to the suburbia or to adjacent areas, our institution assumes an important role. We must 'stay put and serve' the on-going needs of the large Jewish population in Brownsville. The larger numbers of remaining residents most of whom are in the low economic income group require intensive service by such agencies as the H.E.S." The HES dedicated itself to programs to deal with juvenile delinquency, intergroup relations, improvement and integration of public schools, the difficulties faced by the elderly, the rising crime rate, increases in the numbers of people suffering from emotional problems, and the teaching of the Jewish faith. The society also pledged to work with other community organizations to address these problems. Indeed, it was hoped that the opening of the Jimmerson Houses, with their large Jewish population, would revitalize the HES.[48]

HES staff continued to hold onto a slim optimism about the Jewish community in Brownsville, noting that many Jews from Europe, Israel, and Latin America moved into the neighborhood along with the new black and Puerto Rican residents. They found that several yeshivas in the neighborhood were overcrowded, serving more than fifteen hundred children. In addition, the student body of the HES Hebrew School was larger than it had ever been in the past. "Since the H.E.S. remains the only Jewish agency with a full leisure and educational program in this area in which still resides a vast Jewish population," its staff argued, "we find ourselves serving a need as great as ever." As other Brownsville Jewish organizations followed their members to new communities, the HES expanded its program to meet new needs. Despite changes in the neighborhood, or perhaps because of them, HES membership grew during the late 1950s and early 1960s. As neighborhood institutions closed, the remaining Jewish residents depended increasingly on the organization. But external pressures from financial supporters along with internal pressures from staff and members eventually pushed the HES out of Brownsville.[49]

In 1961, as the community's transformation continued, the concerns of Brownsville's white residents about crime and violence were increasingly important to HES operations. "Due to the population changes in the community and the early sunset during the winter months," staff reported, "parents have become very fearful of having their children walk the streets at night and, therefore, it has become necessary to provide transportation." In order to keep their program going, HES began busing children and chaperoning students to and from the headquarters. In addition, the staff shifted programs that had operated during the evenings to the weekends or afternoons because members were afraid to walk Brownsville's streets at night. Activities for specific groups, teen programs in particular, ceased to function. Even the Fellowship program, which had been relocated to a "more stable area," was at risk. Several confrontations, muggings, and fights between Fellowship members and neighborhood youths concerned HES officials: "The problem now faced by the agency is that the streets immediately surrounding it are changing ethnically to such a degree that the agency now appears to be an island." Though the staff believed that between twenty and thirty thousand Jews still lived in Brownsville, most of them resided in the western half of the neighborhood. The only way to persuade people to come to its headquarters, located in the center of Brownsville, was by offering them transportation there on HES buses.[50]

As the Jews remaining in the neighborhood became the minority, many Jewish youths became increasingly angry about changes in the neighborhood, and delinquency rates among that group rose. Their parents, whom HES staff felt were paralyzed by Brownsville's transformation, did not know how to deal with their children. As a result of their inability to motivate themselves to change their family situation, an unusually large number of children attending the Center displayed problems that seemed directly related to their family situations. According to HES staff, the Jews remaining in Brownsville were "almost entirely from the lowest socio-economic strata of the Jewish community," and "their needs are great." To help these residents, HES began a cooperative effort with the Jewish Family Service (JFS) in 1961. The project sought to aid families "who realistically feel left behind in a community that has already changed. These are people who are not as yet acting out their anxieties to the point where the Youth Board may be involved but at the same time are fraught by a great deal of insecurity." The goal of the program was to provide Jewish residents with the support they needed to enable them to leave Brownsville.[51]

By this time, it had become clear to most involved with the HES that it too should depart. Having witnessed for over a decade the dissipation of the Jewish population, and having struggled to create programs that would bring former members back to their building, the board decided "to continue a rich and creative program at the Main Building, explore the possibility of extension programming in rented facilities in the Brownsville area, [but plan] for possible relocation within a five year period." No specific event brought about the decision to move. The board's decision was based on "criminal activities and the present population, vandalism and assaults committed upon those using H.E.S. facilities in our main building and our Fellowship building," as well as the departure of most of Brownsville's Jews and the fact that the "Jewish families who had girls in the family would especially not live in the area for fear of assault upon them." While HES was successful in keeping membership numbers constant through transportation programs and shifting schedules, the organization was tiring from this effort.[52]

To most board members, Canarsie seemed the most appropriate place for the relocation of the HES. An analysis of membership, undertaken by the staff in 1961, found that while fewer than 30 members lived in the twelve-block area surrounding the facility, and fewer than 80 people in the 4,754 units of Brownsville public housing were members, more than 150 residents of Canarsie participated in HES programs. By 1963, Canarsie had a population of 104,000, and at least 75,000 of them were Jews. Because the neighborhood had grown so quickly, like Brownsville had several decades before, it suffered from a deficit of recreational, social, and educational opportunities. Canarsie residents aggressively lobbied HES officials to expand their programs in the area, emphasizing that 80 percent of the neighborhood's Jewish families had at one time or another come from Brownsville.[53]

The HES's proposal to move to Canarsie was overwhelmingly approved by the UJA trustees, who also agreed to fund a large percentage of the construction costs of a new facility. In 1965, the HES opened up a storefront office in Canarsie, in anticipation of the opening of its new building then under construction. Writing in the magazine of the Jewish Welfare Board, HES Executive Director David Kleinstein explained that the organization's decision was best for both the Jewish community and for Canarsie: "What does a Jewish Community Center do when the neighborhood in which it has been located for 66 years has changed so radically that the entire Jewish population of the area has moved elsewhere? The answer is that it moves as soon as it can to the area where its services and programs are needed by its former members." Kleinstein explained that the HES board had chosen Canarsie because it was a Jewish neighborhood with similar economic, cultural, social, and recreation needs to Brownsville, and that Canarsie was "the area of greatest need . . . a lower, middle-class and middle-middle class Jewish community which had become the lowest rung on the ladder of the upsurging economic and social life and whose needs were as fundamental as their earlier Brownsville predecessors."[54]

The HES sold its buildings to the Catholic Diocese of Brooklyn. Despite some misgivings among board members about transferring the HES facilities to a Christian organization, former director Alter Landesman argued that the move was appropriate, and that the former HES building would continue to serve the community. "The new non-Jewish groups that have moved into the section need social services as much as the older Jewish elements who are now leaving it. The Catholic Diocese of Brooklyn has taken over by purchase both Hebrew Educational Society buildings . . . and are using them as religious, recreational, and educational centers for the population presently residing in the neighborhood," stated Landesman. These buildings continued to serve the community, but the departure of the HES was an important event in the history of Brownsville, signifying the end of the Jewish era. By 1965, when the organization moved to Canarsie, almost no whites remained in Brownsville. From then on Brownsville would be populated only by blacks and Puerto Ricans, who would have to create their own institutions.[55]

The Hebrew Educational Society was the last vestige of a neighborhood founded in the late 1800s. When it departed in 1965, there were no other significant institutions left from the community created by Charles and Elias Kaplan. By the mid-1960s, Brownsville was known citywide as an African-American and Puerto Rican ghetto, a place to be avoided. Many poor blacks and Latinos, however, had no place else to live, and they did not give up hope for Brownsville's revitalization. During the 1960s, many new residents joined with veteran activists and attempted to forge a new Brownsville. Like their predecessors, they battled government inertia, and they faced the entrenched racism of New York's political system. In the context of the expanding civil rights movement and the recognition of urban poverty by the federal government, this new class of Brownsville activists achieved some significant victories. One success was the 1962 battle of Beth-El Hospital workers.

Figure 19. Local 1199's Beth-El Hospital Strike Office. Photograph by Sam Reiss. Courtesy 1199 Archives, Kheel Center, Cornell University.

6

A Northern Civil Rights Movement:
The Beth-El Hospital Strike of 1962

In 1962, the workers at Beth-El Hospital, the largest employer in Brownsville, commenced a strike led by the newly invigorated Local 1199 of the Hospital Workers of America. After almost two months on the picket line, the workers achieved union recognition and higher wages at the hospital. In the midst of the southern civil rights revolution, the Beth-El strike revealed the promise of a northern movement that crossed racial and ethnic lines, as members of New York's liberal community vigorously backed the Jewish-led union and their predominantly black and Puerto Rican rank and file. The Beth-El strike is significant on many levels—as a chapter in New York labor relations, for its role in the history of Local 1199, but especially because the conflict awakened the whole Brownsville community to the possibility of organization and helped bring about the political maturation of this rapidly changing neighborhood. In addition, the strikers brought to the forefront the racial conflicts that would occupy the attention of Brownsville, New York City, and America throughout the 1960s.[1]

By 1962, the Brownsville neighborhood had become

a black and Latino ghetto. The Beth-El Strike, then, occurred at an important moment not only in Brownsville history but in the racial history of New York City. Six years later, Brownsville again gained the attention of the city as the focal point of the battle over community control of local schools that led to the New York teachers' strike of 1968. This conflict, in which charges of racism and anti-Semitism abounded, and which strained relations between blacks and whites throughout the city, stands in stark contrast to the cooperation evident in the Beth-El Strike of 1962.

Hospitals were a major growth field in the United States after World War II. Supported by the Hill-Burton Act and other federal programs, hospital construction boomed in the 1950s. In New York, this funding was matched by state and local funding, and New York City's medical sector expanded dramatically. Across the city new hospitals were built while existing hospitals expanded their facilities. This growth brought increasing demand for both highly skilled health care professionals (doctors, nurses, and technicians) and less-skilled assistants (aides, orderlies, and the like). By 1960, health care was one of the fastest growing sectors of New York's economy. This expansion created new opportunities for many New Yorkers. Through the Veterans Administration and other federal programs, young whites (many of them second- and third-generation immigrants) received advanced degrees in medicine and other sciences and used their credentials to join the professional class. Blacks and Latinos also benefited from the less-skilled employment opportunities, and health care was a field that many entered. Across the country, hospitals employed more than one million people, and New York led the nation in health care employment.[2]

While its racial makeup changed in the late 1950s, Brownsville's occupational distribution remained remarkably stable. In 1960, more than one-third of Brownsville workers toiled in manufacturing jobs, and about half of these workers were in the textile or apparel trades. Blacks and Puerto Ricans replaced whites in textile shops along Brownsville's industrial fringe. Many Latinos were drawn to Brownsville in the 1950s by these shops. Originally they commuted from Manhattan to their jobs, but over the decade many moved to the area. The retail trades were another significant occupation of Brownsville workers in the 1960s, both within the area and throughout Brooklyn. But one of the fastest growing fields according to the 1960s census was health care. More than eight hundred Brownsville residents worked in that sector, most of them at Beth-El Hospital.[3]

The opening of Beth-El Hospital in 1921 was the culmination of a communitywide effort to bring health facilities to the neighborhood. According to its promoters, the facility was one of the few causes that brought all segments of the community together. "The project received the support of every civic and social organization in the community, as well as of every element of the population, of the radical Socialists as well as the strict Orthodox," remembered Alter Landesman, and more than ten thousand residents participated in the hospital's funding campaign. Throughout the 1910s, volunteers collected donations, mostly nickels and dimes, for the hospital fund. Many street corners in the neighborhood also held coin collection boxes to encourage participation by community residents. After a decade of fund-raising, the five-story facility, the Brownsville and East New York Hospital, as it was originally called, opened. The hospital changed its name to Beth-El Hospital in 1933, and it grew dramatically over the years. In 1928, the hospital added a maternity pavilion, and it completed a nurses' residence in 1942. In 1952, Beth-El finished a six-story addition housing a 130-bed surgical pavilion (increasing total bed capacity to 334) and a residence hall. While the Brownsville residents continued to support the hospital as it grew, Beth-El became increasingly dependent upon the financial support of wealthy philanthropists, businessmen, and, most importantly, government funding. The Hill-Burton program and other resources enabled Beth-El to become a regional facility that served much of southern and eastern Brooklyn. But the expansion of Beth-El's facilities increased the size of its bureaucracy and weakened ties between management and workers, as well as with the Brownsville neighborhood in general.[4]

Large and small voluntary hospitals like Beth-El depended upon low-skilled workers for the majority of their functions. While the professionals who ran "voluntary" (not-for-profit) hospitals were among the most respected and well-paid in the country, "nonprofessional" workers—orderlies, cooks, aides, janitors, craftsmen, laborers, and others—were consistently the worst paid and the most overworked. Voluntary hospitals were exempted from minimum wage laws by statute. In 1959, New York hospital workers received average starting salaries of $0.90 per hour for females and $1.03 per hour for males—both well below the national minimum hourly wage of $1.30. Many voluntary hospitals, outgrowths of the paternalistic religious orders that created them, treated their workers as charges, requiring them to live in dorms with little privacy, forcing them to work long hours, and paying them subsistence wages. Citing lack of privacy, supervision away from work, and long hours without overtime, one study of hospital workers noted the "paradox that a charitable institution should tend to treat its employees in such a manner as to make them potential objects of charity."[5]

Most voluntary hospitals in the 1950s disdained attempts to rationalize the workplace, forgoing innovations like personnel departments and labor force management studies. There were few guidelines or written personnel policies, and unskilled workers often faced arbitrary supervision and swift punishment. A worker's situation was almost completely dependent on his or her direct superior, who had the responsibility of assigning tasks and hours, and who could hire and fire service workers on a whim. A nonprofessional often had no higher authority to which he or she could appeal. These indignities, added to the low wages paid by hospitals, resulted in a high turnover rate at most institutions. This turnover, combined with skill divisions among hospital workers, made labor organizing difficult at voluntary hospitals. In addition, the conservative, antiunion attitudes of administrators and trustees, coupled with the patriarchal attitudes of the doctors and nurses who supervised the nonprofessionals, stymied the efforts of union organizers. Adding to these organizational difficulties were New York state laws that exempted voluntary institutions from obligations to bargain collectively with duly-elected workers' representatives.[6]

Despite the long list of obstacles facing the organization of hospital workers, in 1957 the officers of Local 1199 of the Retail Drug Employees, a small union of pharmacists and drug clerks led by Leon Davis, undertook a campaign to bring collective bargaining rights to these nonprofessionals. The first hospital targeted by Local 1199 was Montefiore Hospital, a large institution located in the north Bronx. In December 1958, after a year of organization and negotiation, the union secured recognition by hospital management as the representative of Montefiore's nonprofessionals. Compared to the struggles that would follow, the fight at Montefiore was bloodless. The unexpected ease of victory may have pushed union leaders and members to move too quickly to organize other hospitals. Less than a year later, thirty-five hundred Local 1199 members struck six separate hospitals in New York: Mount Sinai, Beth-Israel, Beth-David, Bronx, Brooklyn Jewish, and Lennox Hill.[7]

After several months of negotiation that involved city politicians, AFL-CIO leaders, and several members of New York's civil rights community, union officers and hospital managers settled the strikes, but not on terms that fully satisfied the union. The settlement did not provide for collective bargaining and did not recognize Local 1199 as the representative of the workers. Instead, the compromise brokered by Mayor Wagner created a Permanent Advisory Committee (PAC) that included six hospital representatives and six representatives from the public. This body, to which three union representatives were added in 1960, was responsible for establishing wages and work conditions for the nonprofessionals at the six hospitals. In return for the hospitals' agreement to abide by the decisions of the PAC, the union agreed not to strike any of the hospitals. By the standards of most labor struggles, the strike was a failure. Workers had not won the most important goal, union recognition. However, the strike had energized hospital employees throughout the city and convinced them that better wages and working conditions were possible. The strikes at these six hospitals also served as a model for future efforts at Beth-El Hospital.[8]

Local 1199 leaders did not view the settlement as an end but rather as a beginning. They realized that the PAC was not equivalent to bargaining rights for hospital workers, but they also recognized that they did not have the power to achieve any more at the time. This setback was only temporary, however, and over the next year Local 1199 organized hundreds of workers at additional hospitals. A pattern developed: when the union had organized a substantial portion of the workers at a particular hospital, the managers of that institution typically would agree to join the PAC, which would give them protection from a strike. Because this prevented the union from achieving its goal of collective bargaining, in August 1961, Leon Davis, now union president, notified the mayor that the union was rescinding its no-strike pledge from any hospital that was not a PAC member. Davis declared that the thirty-nine New York hospitals in this category could not use its protection to avoid unionization in the future. Beth-El was not a member of the PAC, and union officials targeted that hospital as the location of the battle to restructure labor relations within New York's voluntary hospitals.[9]

The union had been active at Beth-El since the fall of 1960, when organizers first began handing out flyers and getting signatures on union cards. In less than two weeks, the union asserted, they had recruited one hundred nonprofessionals. By November 1960, meeting often in neighborhood locations like the Brownsville Community Center, the organizers felt that they were close to getting a majority of the workers to join. In March 1961, 248 workers voted for union representation. Soon after the vote, the union established a local office in Brownsville for the Beth-El workers. This office was the center for strike activity, as well as a community resource where workers and their supporters in the community met to strategize and socialize. Many Brownsville residents who were later active in other neighborhood organizations acquired their first experiences in community action at this facility. A large majority of the nonprofessional staff at the hospital were black or Latino, and most of these people were residents of Brownsville or other areas in Eastern Brooklyn who had moved to the area in the 1950s.[10]

In the early 1960s, much of the nation's attention focused on the growing movement for equal rights in the South. From the beginning of their organizing efforts, union leaders used the civil rights movement as their model, basing their appeal on the argument that black and Puerto Rican workers deserved "fair pay" and "equal rights." In December 1961, forty hospital workers and union officials picketed Beth-El's black-tie fund-raiser at the Waldorf Astoria. The flyer the protesters distributed to the dinner attendees appealed to their sense of morality, emphasizing that workers subsisted on below-poverty wages:

> Tonight, you will hear lofty-sounding phrases about the humanitarian work performed by Beth-El Hospital. But the ugly truth about our starvation wages and the Trustees' arrogant refusal to even meet with us will be conveniently swept under the rug. You won't be told that the workers who clean, cook and help serve the patients receive as little as $42 a week; that many of us are forced to apply for supplementary relief assistance to feed, clothe and house our families. . . . Most of us are Negroes and Puerto Ricans and we cannot help [but] feel that this is one of the reasons the Trustees have refused to even meet with us.

While attempting to get hospital officials to negotiate with them, union leaders developed more creative ways to apply pressure to Beth-El management. In January 1962, hospital workers protested at the home of Morrell Goldberg, executive director of Beth-El, and informed his neighbors that while Goldberg portrayed himself as a liberal, he had consistently refused to negotiate with the union and had not even acknowledged its existence. "Morrell Goldberg treats his workers as if this were Mississippi not New York. Apparently, Morrell Goldberg believes that he can take advantage of us because we are members of a minority group; that he can intimidate and threaten us into giving up what we know is right and just—our demand for higher wages and union representation." The union also picketed the Famous Restaurant on Pitkin Avenue, owned by trustee Paul Bluth, asking customers not to patronize his business.[11]

As union officials expected, in January 1962, after a year and a half of organization, Beth-El decided to join the PAC and gain the protection of the no-strike clause. Local 1199 officials responded that this action was taken only to confuse workers and avoid collective bargaining. The union declared that it would not acknowledge the hospital's decision, and the workers began to prepare for a strike. In the months following Beth-El's affiliation with the PAC, union officials attempted to create as much goodwill for the workers as possible, undertaking a media blitz to communicate the employees' story to the public. Local 1199 press releases emphasized the fact that hospital workers, as one of the only groups of American workers that did not have the right of collective bargaining, were denied equal rights. "All workers have a constitutional right to leave their jobs to protest for a redress of grievances. Anything else is involuntary servitude," asserted a union release. "It is incredible that in the year 1962, low-wage minority group workers should be compelled to strike to win the elementary right to be represented by a union of their own choice—a right accorded all other workers in our city, state and nation." Davis described the hospital's decision to join the PAC as "too little and too late," and set a February 12 strike date.[12]

The hospital responded to the threat by securing an injunction from the New York Supreme Court prohibiting the walkout. Davis announced that the workers would not respect the injunction, because the hospital had ignored all their requests to meet. At the eleventh hour, the president of the Board of Trustees, Benne Katz, met with Local 1199 officials and, according to them, "said he would recommend that the hospital's trustees accord the union the right to bargain collectively for nonprofessional workers." As a result of this promise, one ultimately not kept, the strike was delayed. After two more months of protest by the union and delay by the hospital trustees and management, on May 21 the hospital's Board of Trustees voted to refuse to recognize the union and to stay with the PAC. On May 23, the union declared a strike. Union officials reported that the situation was "chaotic" and that between 275 and 300 of the nonprofessional workers were on strike while hospital officials stated that operations were normal and that fewer than 50 workers had walked out.[13]

Once it started, the strike quickly gained the attention of the whole city. Picket-line violence erupted frequently, and on the first day of the strike, five picketers were arrested during a clash between strikers, nonstriking hospital workers, and the police. Union officials charged the police with racism and brutality in connection with this arrest. The two black and one Puerto Rican arrestees among the five were charged with more serious offenses than the whites, and the blacks were also taken into the vestibule of the hospital and beaten severely before being taken to the police station. On May 29, Leon Davis was sentenced to thirty days in jail for ignoring the Supreme Court's injunction against striking. Davis refused to influence the strikers to end the walkout, and he remained in jail for the whole sentence. Throughout this period, confrontation continued on the picket line. Brownsville residents were a major presence at these protests. "We were very supportive of the strikers," said Maurice Reid, a Brownsville activist who participated in the picketing. Community members walked the picket line, called and wrote local officials, and brought food and drinks to the strikers. Five additional picketers were arrested in a fight on June 3, and on June 5, police detained twenty-four college students during a sit-down protest they held in the hospital lobby. A second sit-down of twenty additional college students occurred on June 12.[14]

These students were typical of the cross-section of support received by the strikers. Like the union, the students connected the goals of the black and Puerto Rican strikers to the battle for civil rights in the South. In the press release issued by the protesters, they stated that

> Many of us have been on freedom rides and sit-ins in the North and South. Some of us spent time in jail in Jackson, Mississippi for taking part in the fight which the Negro people of the South are waging for human dignity, human equality and human freedom. The struggle of the Beth-El workers and of all voluntary hospital workers to win the same rights that other American workers enjoy—union representation and collective bargaining—is part and parcel of the struggle for civil rights for Negroes, Puerto Ricans and other minority peoples throughout the country. The battle against economic exploitation is inseparable from the campaign for the right to vote for Southern Negroes and from the struggle to integrate bus terminals.

More than sixty students from City College, Brooklyn College, Queens College, New York University, Hunter College, Columbia University, and the New School were arrested during the strike.[15]

Civil rights leaders and organizations also actively supported the Beth-El workers. The local and national chapters of the NAACP gave monetary assistance and vocal support, as did the Congress of Racial Equality (CORE), which contributed funds and sent letters to all its local members asking them to join the picket line. Other groups, such as the "Committee for the Employment of Negro Performers," also supported the walkout. A month into the strike, more than fifty of the leading civil rights activists in the city joined together to form the "Committee for Justice to Hospital Workers" and pledged to aid the workers "with money, mass demonstrations and political action." The committee asserted that the "hospital strikes symbolize in most dramatic form the second-class citizenship status and sweatshop wages of all minority group workers in our city" and concluded that "the public can no longer tolerate a condition in which community supported institutions are controlled by a group of self-perpetuating trustees whose archaic and outmoded labor policies result in hardships to the patients the employees and the public at large." Among the members of the committee were James Baldwin; A. Philip Randolph; Joseph Monserrat, director of the Migration Division of the Puerto Rican Labor Department; Percy Sutton, president of the New York NAACP; James Farmer, director of CORE; the leaders of Ministers Associations in the Harlem Community; Juan Mas, president of the Federation of Spanish Societies; and Gilberto Gerena Valentin, president of the Congress of Puerto Rican Municipalities.[16]

The strikers also received the strong support of New York's minority-owned media. Both the *New York Amsterdam News* and *El Diario* devoted substantial attention to the strike. A *New York Amsterdam News* editorial reserved particular criticism for Brooklyn Borough President Abe Stark and Congressman Emmanuel Celler, both of whom were Beth-El trustees. The editorial argued that both these men called themselves "Liberals," and that both would "mount a platform at the drop of a hat and declare to the world that they are the greatest friend of the working man the world has ever known. Yet they sit on the board of this hospital while the hospital pays these people starvation wages and refuses to bargain." In light of the battles in Birmingham and other parts of the South, the mainstream media was well attuned to the racial factors of the conflict, and several radio stations also issued editorials in support of the strikers. WCBS urged the hospital to "open its eyes to the facts of life of the American labor movement" and allow the workers the right of collective bargaining. Another radio station argued that it was wrong to deny workers a right that is "standard for every kind of worker from stevedores to Hollywood directors" and criticized the hospital management for using the patients as "moral hostages in an economic war."[17]

The strikers also received the assistance of many sectors of the Jewish community, which clearly caused problems for hospital trustees and management. Representatives of the Jewish Labor Committee stated that the hospital was preventing workers "from exercising their democratic rights" and petitioned Governor Rockefeller to intercede in the conflict. An editorial in the *Jewish Daily Forward* raised the issue the trustees wanted to avoid: that Jews had a special obligation to be fair to workers. Acknowledging that all thirty-six trustees of the hospital were Jewish, and that a number of them were known as philanthropists, the editorial stated that the trustees "do not know or seem to forget that 'Charity begins at home.'" The editorial concluded that the strike "brings no honor to the Jewish community of Brooklyn" and asked the trustees to "realize that their stand is wrong and not humanitarian in relation to the striking workers."[18]

As they had in previous strikes, the city's major labor unions supported Local 1199. Among the most active and vocal was the United Federation of Teachers—which only six years later, during the conflict with the Ocean Hill–Brownsville Community School Board, would battle many of the same people it now supported. The UFT held a special picket of more than fifty of its members at the hospital in support of the strike, and several UFT locals, including many teachers in Brownsville schools, pledged additional economic aid. Labor support for the Beth-El strikers came from a wide spectrum of New York unions. In a report to New York City AFL-CIO President Harry Van Arsdale, Leon Davis listed fifty-six different unions that had donated a total of $10,698 to Local 1199's strike fund.

The assistance of the AFL-CIO's New York City Council was critical to the success of the strike. In recognition of the increasing importance of service workers to the AFL-CIO, Harry Van Arsdale himself did much of the negotiating between political leaders and trustees for the union. Because Davis spent much of the strike in jail (he was not released until June 28), Van Arsdale's support was crucial. Organized labor also assisted the workers by backing the union's decision to pull out of the PAC. The AFL-CIO, through its representatives on the PAC, had provided a veneer of respectability to that body, but after spending a month attempting to settle the strike within the structure of the PAC, the AFL-CIO officially pulled out of the committee in late June, and this action greatly weakened the PAC's influence. On June 23, to increase the pressure on Beth-El's management, Van Arsdale organized a protest at the hospital of more than one thousand AFL-CIO members, including many of the top officials of the city's largest unions.[19]

Labor leaders also attacked the hospital's misrepresentation of its financial situation. The union published an internal study that disclosed that thirty-four of fifty-four families of strikers at Beth-El would have been better off on government relief than on the wages paid by the hospital. The union argued that at the same time the hospital management said it could afford no more than subsistence wages, it had spent $40,000 on strikebreakers, more than $10,000 a week. Davis emphasized that much of the money for replacement workers came from local government though city subsidies to New York's voluntary hospitals. New York's labor community also increased the pressure on the trustees who were politicians, asking Emmanuel Celler to "use your good offices to make a peaceful settlement possible that will safeguard the rights of the workers and secure for them a measure of economic justice," and telling Stark that he had "the right and duty to speak up on this outrageous denial of rights to low-paid Negro and Puerto Rican workers." Both men were especially susceptible to such pressure as they depended on the labor vote to win their strongly democratic districts.[20]

And still Beth-El's Board of Trustees refused to budge. From the beginning, the hospital took the position that while wages were low, they were the best the hospital could offer. Beth-El management appealed to the moral standards of the workers, reciting their obligation to the sick. When the hospital decided to join the PAC and increased wages to the levels determined by the committee, they put this forth as evidence of management's good faith, stating, "Give yourself a fair chance with PAC. You will find that it will help provide you with improved wages, better working conditions, important fringe benefits, and a sense of dignity and purpose in knowing that you are carrying out part of the job of caring for the sick." Throughout the strike the hospital continued to operate with temporary employees and volunteers. In memos to staff and trustees, the management asserted that few workers had walked out, but in fact management was uncertain just how many strikers there were. A day after the strike began, management stated that "only a handful" of workers had failed to come to work, but three days later the hospital reported that fifty workers had failed to show up. Managers asserted that many of them had "remained at home because of union intimidation rather than out of sympathy with the strike." According to the administrators, only about thirty "hardcore" members were picketing.[21]

During the first month of the strike, the hospital denied that the walkout had any impact on operations. On June 1, Executive Director Goldberg reported that all the hospital's patient services continued at a normal level. "Since the so-called 'strike' was called on Wednesday, May 23rd, 201 new patients have been admitted to the hospital, 140 babies have been born in the Maternity Wing, 98 operations have been performed, 557 sick and injured people have been treated in our Emergency Room and 1400 indigent patients have been given medical care in the hospital's outpatient clinic," Goldberg asserted. By the second week of June, the number of strikers reported by hospital management had reached ninety, but according to management this had not affected operations. Hospital administrators may have believed that Beth-El was handling the walkout without problems, but several trustees were under intense pressure. Congressman Celler, who had actively supported Local 1199 in many of its earlier actions, was especially concerned about the hospital's position. Hospital management and several trustees argued that collective bargaining was inappropriate "because of the purpose and financial structure of a voluntary hospital." Behind this stand, however, was another reason for their intransigence: many of the trustees were businessmen who dealt with unions daily, and in retrospect hospital administrators later acknowledged that at least some of them were taking out their antiunion feelings on the hospital workers. Celler, in response to the intransigence of the businessmen on the board, argued that "the matters of a living wage and working conditions have no relation to the classification of the organization." Voluntary hospital or not, workers had a right to fair compensation.[22]

Under pressure from many liberal colleagues and constituents, Celler released his concerns to the press. In an open letter to Board President Katz, he stated that hospital workers should not be treated differently than industrial workers. "They, too, are entitled to organize for their common good. They, too, are humans, interested in better wages and hours with the wish to live decently and bring up their children properly. Paltry wages and sweatshop conditions prevent this." Making his opposition public, Celler concluded, "I regret to state that my fellow Trustees of the Beth-El Hospital are being myopic and are as wrong as a two-foot yardstick." Theodore Shapiro, a Brooklyn businessman and philanthropist, was so strongly opposed to its actions and management that he resigned from the board, stating that if the hospital continued to deny the rights of the workers to collective bargaining, "the noble ends toward which the hospital has been dedicated [would] now become perverted and violated." Shapiro was particularly unnerved by the number of police at the hospital, which made "it appear more like a prison in revolt than an institution for the sick."[23]

On July 16, almost two months into the strike, and after he had personally tried to mediate between the parties, State Supreme Court Justice A. David Benjamin sentenced Davis to six months in jail for failing to end the walkout at Beth-El Hospital. Davis's sentence heightened fears of picket line violence and accelerated the ongoing behind-the-scenes political negotiations to end the conflict In late June, New York's labor and civil rights communities increased pressure on Governor Nelson Rockefeller to intervene, and several civil rights leaders hinted to the governor that a settlement was necessary to avoid a riot among New York blacks and Latinos. Local 1199 had from the beginning desired to use the strike as a means to achieve changes in state law to allow collective bargaining in hospitals, and they used this goal to force a compromise.[24]

On July 17, the governor announced that he had settled the strike. Under the agreement, Local 1199 workers returned to work, and Rockefeller vowed to introduce and support legislation that would provide collective bargaining rights for all New York hospital workers. The governor said he had intervened because he felt "the situation was getting explosive and had very serious implications in the city" as a result of "racial considerations and the tensions that might develop from them." Both sides also agreed to binding arbitration of their disputes. Material gains followed quickly. Less than six months after the settlement of the strike, the Beth-El workers had achieved a minimum wage of $1.35 an hour and recognition of Local 1199 as their bargaining agent. In addition, Local 1199 had attained its larger goal of legislative approval for the right to collective bargaining. While the workers were not able to secure all their demands, they were able to increase wages and benefits to more acceptable levels. As a result of this victory, by the end of the decade Local 1199 comprised some thirty thousand members.[25]

The strike at Beth-El hospital was a significant event not only for the members of Local 1199 but also for the Brownsville community. The non-professionals at Beth-El, overwhelmingly black and Puerto Rican, were heretofore unorganized and invisible. Like their neighbors in Brownsville, many of them were newcomers to the area who had yet to form strong connections within the neighborhood. The Beth-El strike was the first time

Figure 20. Beth-El Hospital picket line. The Beth-El workers were supported by a wide variety of New York unions. Courtesy 1199 Archives, Kheel Center, Cornell University.

that these community members joined in a single cause. Local activists, including Alex Efthim, Thelma Hamilton, and Rae Glauber, were strong supporters of the strikers, and the battle sparked new efforts at community organization. The conflict at the hospital was fought by the whole Brownsville community, not only the Beth-El workers. Of the 20 union stewards at Beth-El in 1962, 14 lived in Brownsville. More than a third of the 240 registered union members lived in the heart of Brownsville, and over three-quarters of the workers lived either in Brownsville or in areas of East New York and Bedford-Stuyvesant close to Brownsville. These workers involved their families, their friends, and their neighbors in the battle, walking the picket line and donating food.[26]

In contrast to the strikers, who lived in the declining areas north and east of the hospital, most of the doctors and other professionals on the Beth-El staff lived in Eastern Parkway, in Canarsie or Flatbush, areas to which many of Brownsville's successful white residents had moved. These were people who had "made it" but, according to Local 1199 members and their supporters, were trying to prevent those below them from obtaining economic security. The strike exploited the guilt of those who had benefited from the economic boom of the 1950s. Granting economic concessions to hospital workers was a small price to pay to ameliorate the racial tensions that were increasing in changing neighborhoods such as Brownsville, and fit well within the liberal agenda of support for collective bargaining. In framing the issue as a battle of poor minorities against wealthy professionals, the Beth-El strikers presented a relatively easy decision for New York liberals. Beth-El's minority workers were only seeking the rights that had been accorded all other Americans. They were being denied the benefits of American law by hospital management, just as the "Freedom Riders" in the South were denied their constitutionally protected right to vote. Presented in such stark terms, New York's liberals threw their support overwhelmingly to the side of the strikers. The backing of this coalition was vital to the workers' success. Brownsville's remaining white residents were especially active in supporting the strikers; residents of the Jimmerson Houses not only frequented the picket line but also donated cans of food and money to the strike fund. Like the black and Puerto Rican residents who supported the strike, these people realized that in order for Brownsville to prosper, its residents needed to earn a decent wage. As one resident wrote: "Properly represented employees working under modern Union conditions are better employees making a better hospital and better community."[27]

The philosophy of Local 1199 was the civil rights model of interracial cooperation. The union sponsored dances, lectures, and theatrical performances and attempted, as historians Leon Fink and Brian Greenberg argue, to heighten members' "sense of belonging to and participating in [the] social environment so necessary for creating a fuller and happier life." Local 1199 members were active in their support of the civil rights movement in the South, sending funds to the Southern Christian Leadership Conference, and the North, where they participated in the picketing at Woolworth's stores. Many members of the union remembered that when Local 1199 became involved, workers of different races socialized for the first time. That the union counted among its supporters groups as disparate as the American Jewish Congress, the NAACP, and the Nation of Islam is testimony to its efforts. Many New York liberals viewed the example set by Local 1199 and the workers at Beth-El Hospital as "the answer" to the race problems facing changing neighborhoods like Brownsville. By 1962, however, few whites remained in Brownsville to participate in interracial programs.[28]

CONFERENCIA CONTRA ARRABLES ATRAE CONCURRENCIA RECORD
Pagina Espanol (2)

THE BROWNSVILLE COUNSELLOR

FREE GRATIS

VOL. 2 NO. 5   PUBLISHED BY · THE BROWNSVILLE COMMUNITY COUNCIL, INC.   MAY, 1967

WAR ON SLUMS DRAWS OVERFLOW CROWD

Part-of huge crowd that attended P.S. 41 Housing Conference take time out to tour the blighted areas. This scene is on Powell St. Tour was led by BCC Board Members Andrew Batts & Horace Clark.

A record crowd of slum-weary Brownsville residents turned out to find out what was in store for them in the building of the New Brownsville. On Saturday, April 22, at P.S. 41, Riverdale Avenue and Osborn Street, the first Southeast Brownsville Housing Conference was held.

Four (4) panels, a guided tour of South East Brownsville, a movie on Urban Renewal, and a Summary meeting made up the six hour conference. Each panel included prominent City, State, or Housing Redevelopment Board officials, and dealt with separate phases of the redevelopment process. The first panel, "Legal Financial and Technical problems of the Redevelopment Corporation, "11:30 a.m. until 1:00 p.m. was moderated by Kenneth Weatherspoon of B.C.C. Housing Committee and featured a question and answer period, following an address by each panel member. Room #108 where panel #1 was

(Continued on page 4)

Mr. Norman Badillo, Bronx Boro President headed a group of Puerto Rican leaders who attended the rally organized by Accion Civica de Hispanos Inc., one of the delegate organizations of B.C.C. Luis Hernandez, former City Collector, Rev. Ruben Dario Colon, Chairman of the Puerto Rican Development Corporation, Joe Arenas Brooklyn Coordinator for the same agency, joined Community leaders in a well attended conference held at Bristol Family Club, 1753 Pitkin Avenue. Alfredo Jorge is the Chairman and Ralph Lopez is secretary.

FINAL PLANS FOR OSBORN NEWPORT AREA

On Monday, May 6th, at 8:00 P.M., a Housing and Redevelopment meeting was held at P.S. 41, 411 Thatford Avenue. The final plan for the Brownsville Urban renewal, project (Area 15).

The meeting was convened in order to provide an opportunity for questions and answers about the plan.

The public hearing on the Brownsville project before the City Planning Commission is scheduled for Wednesday, May 24. The Planning Commission Meeting starts at 10:00 A.M. and is held in the Board of Estimate Chambers, City Hall.

PROGRAM NOTES

Submitted by: John D. Morrison

The day camp registration at Brownsville Boys Club has been most gratifying. Over two hundred youngsters were referred to the Boys Club for scholarships. At this writing we do not know how many youngsters will be actually given scholarships. Registrations and applications are still being accepted. Junior Counsellors are needed. No pay is involved but Junior Counsellors get a share of the tips. Counsellors 18 or older and entering or in college are also needed. The pay is $320.

The other services available at the Boys Club are of great interest and should be taken advantage of by community residents. Among these are remedial reading for grades 4-8 younster Tuesday - Friday from four until five.

Rooms are available both afternoon and evenings for youth and adult groups that have their own leadership. Woodworking in the evening for adults 7 - 10 P.M.

Special programs for youth: arts and crafts, woodworking cooking. For information contact the Brownsville Recreation Center.

Podiatry (foot care) for everyone and specialized dental services for children are also available.

Brooklyn Womens Hospital

(Continued on page 3)

BROWNSVILLE STUDENT WINS ART AWARD

Once again, a Negro girl proved that Negro students are as intelligent, if not more, than any other children. Miss Dorothy Lee, age 13 has been awarded a scholarship to the High School of Music and Arts. She will go directly from eight grade to High School, and then to College.

Miss Lee is now attending classes at Junior High School 275. While she was at P.S. 144 her art teacher, Mrs. Ruth Green became so interested in the girl's ability to paint, that she gave the girl personal instructions after school hours Thanks to Mrs. Green, Dorothy got her scholarship and that is not all, she plans to pay all expenses to see Dorothys way through College. Mrs. Green

has a class of predominantly Afro-American children.

Dorothy lives with her parents at 123 Riverdale Avenue. She has four brothers and one sister. Her older brother is now serving in the U.S. Marines. Mr. and Mrs. Lee are very proud of their daughter. They almost cried with joy when they received the letter informing them that Dorothy had won the scholarship.

During her spare time, Dorothy goes to the Brooklyn Museum of arts. The Museum had 15 of her 18 paintings.

Since she does not have a place to paint, she paints in their finished basement, but she hopes that someday she will have her own studio.

13 year old Dorothy Lee, 123 Riverdale Ave. displays one of her prize winning paintings.

PUBLIC SCHOOL 284

On Wednesday April 19, 1967 a meeting was held in the office of District Superintendent, Dr. Max B. Meyers in P.S. 268 - 155 E. 53rd St. to attempt to settle some recurrent problem in P.S. 284.

P.T.A. 284 President Lillian Carter, B.C.C. Education Committee Chairman, Zedia Harrington; B.C.C. President Thelma J. Hamilton; Brownsville Counsellor Editor, William O. Marley, Lavinia Brown P.T.A. members, seven (7) teachers from P.S. 284 and Principal William Emmer met with Dr. Meyers in a four hour meeting.

A list of demands to settle

(Continued on page 4)

CRISIS OF P.S. 189

Public School 189, Rockaway and East New York Avenues, has an enrollment of 1,390 students, 90% of them Afro-American or Puerto Rican Yet, there is not one Afro-American or Puerto Rican in this school's executive board.

This is only one of many grievances aired by many parents at a Sunday meeting held recently at Catholic Center of Brownsville, 1212 East New York Avenue, and at other meetings at Tilden Community Center, 630 Stone Ave.

Among the other grievances are: threatened transfer of students to inferior schools

(Continued on page 4)

Figure 21. *The Brownsville Counsellor.* Courtesy Major Owens.

7

The Brownsville Community Council:
The War on Poverty in Brownsville, 1964–1968

Maurice Reid was a newcomer to Brownsville in the early
1960s, but his interest in the community led him to devote
his life to it. "A basketball game brought me to Brownsville," Reid remembered. "I played in the CYO (Catholic
Youth Organization) League, and we had a game there. I
met a girl, and when I would come to visit her, I met all of
these interesting people—people like Willa Webster and
Thelma Hamilton. There was so much history here that I
kept coming back." While the neighborhood was changing in the early 1960s, Brownsville remained an area full
of activism. The people Reid met were at that time co-
alescing into a new organization they named the Brownsville Community Council (BCC), which later became a
powerful force for improvement in the neighborhood
during the 1960s. By 1963, most of the whites had left the
neighborhood, but activism did not end: the remaining
whites, blacks, and Latinos in the area would pass on their
knowledge to newly emerging reformists. At the time they
had no idea that their neighborhood would become a focal
point for citywide political and racial conflict only a few
years later.[1]

New York City can claim many firsts, and in 1964 the city led the nation with the commencement of the decade's many "hot" summers of urban rioting. The incident began on July 16, 1964, when Thomas Gilligan, a white police lieutenant, witnessed an altercation in Harlem between a white building superintendent and some black teenagers. According to his own account, when Gilligan intervened in the conflict, James Powell, a fifteen-year-old black youth, darted at him with a knife. Gilligan then fatally shot the teenager. He argued that the shooting was in self-defense, but other witnesses stated that there was no reason for lethal force. A crowd gathered at the scene and began throwing rocks, bottles, and garbage can lids at the arriving police officers, beginning the first major riot of the decade. Mobs roamed the streets of Harlem and Brooklyn's Bedford-Stuyvesant area for six nights, attacking police and looting stores. By week's end, 1 rioter was dead, 118 were injured, and 465 had been arrested. The New York riots, however, were small compared to those that would afflict other American cities. From 1965 to 1968, Los Angeles, San Francisco, Cleveland, Detroit, and Newark all experienced severe violence, with hundreds of people killed or injured and hundreds of millions of dollars in property damaged. Race rioting even occurred in smaller cities like Waterloo, Iowa, and Dayton, Ohio. No American urban area emerged from this period unscarred.[2]

In August 1964, immediately after the riots, the *New York Times* published an editorial in support of the Economic Opportunity Act of 1964, the centerpiece of President Lyndon Johnson's "War on Poverty." "The antipoverty bill," argued the editors, "is also an anti-riot bill. The members of the House of Representatives would do well to bear that in mind when the time comes for a vote." The *Times* editorial board shared the concerns of many New York elites. Desperation in New York's poor areas was increasing, and protests for better services and equal treatment were growing louder. Racial conflict certainly affected the antipoverty effort, but the origins and goals of Johnson's War on Poverty remain controversial. While the initiative was identified with the black urban poor, Adam Yarmolinsky, one of the creators of the program, asserted that race was an insignificant factor in the deliberations of the Kennedy and Johnson administrations. The focus of federal officials, he contended, was to end poverty in rural areas. Richard Cloward and Frances Fox Piven have contested this view, arguing that the strategy of Johnson and other Democrats was to use federal funding to increase black political participation and to co-opt community protest by including blacks within the system. Others contend that Johnson's program was shaped by his desire to do "something big" to distinguish himself from President Kennedy. When he took office, Johnson pushed his administrators to quickly formulate a bill. With Sargent Shriver at the head of the Task

Force of the War Against Poverty, policymakers cobbled together a proposal of many disparate ideas that Congress passed without much consideration. Some of the programs in the Economic Opportunity Act, like Head Start and Upward Bound, received wide support from both parties. Others, such as the Job Corps, got mixed reviews, but none received as much attention as the Community Action Program (CAP).[3]

While policymakers debated antipoverty proposals, activists in Brownsville were already organizing a group that became one of the nation's first federally funded community programs. Brownsville residents were invigorated by an atmosphere of optimism in the aftermath of the victory at Beth-El Hospital, the 1963 March on Washington, and the passage of the Civil Rights Act of 1964. Building on such triumphs, they founded the Brownsville Community Council, the organization that soon thereafter became the focal point for Brownsville's antipoverty program. In 1968, Major Owens, the BCC executive director who would later become the area's congressman, recalled that "A few years ago Brownsville was powerless and voiceless. Today Brownsville is a leader among poor communities. United effort of various people and organizations combined to produce a slogan of 'Power in Unity,' and an organization—the Brownsville Community Council—to breathe life into the words."[4]

The Creation of the Brownsville Community Council

In the late 1950s, while local businesses and many members of the Brownsville Neighborhood Council were fighting the construction of the Tilden Houses, other activists were trying to create an atmosphere in which the project would make a positive contribution to the neighborhood. These men and women, including Thelma Hamilton, Willa Webster, Rae Glauber, Ida Posner, Bill Marley, Ken Cave, and Helen Efthim, most of whom lived in the area's public housing projects, organized the Tilden Tenants Council in 1960. They drew on a long history of neighborhood involvement. "Thelma Hamilton and Willa Webster were my mentors," remembered Maurice Reid. "All of the activists were just wonderful people, committed to improving the neighborhood." Willa Webster was a homemaker active in many Brownsville causes throughout the 1950s. Thelma Hamilton and Ida Posner were garment workers who had strong ties to left-wing activism in New York City. "Thelma Hamilton and Ida Posner were inspirations to me," recalled Paul Chandler, another young activist who played an important role in Brownsville during the 1960s. "They were the Rosa Parkses of Brownsville. Both had a lot of contact with the left, and they transferred a lot of their knowledge to the people in the community." In the early 1960s, the group was primarily concerned with the issues that plagued Brownsville for decades: poor schools, inadequate sanitation, and negligible government services in general. "One of the things that was so evident in the change from being a predominantly white neighborhood to an African-American one was that the city services went down," argued Maurice Reid. "So a lot of the focus was to maintaining or recouping city services." Over the decade they expanded their involvement to many other neighborhood concerns.[5]

Political agitation also played an important role in the activities of these residents. Bill Marley, a postal worker and journalist, was one of the leaders in the effort to increase black voting power in Brooklyn and to attack the entrenched and unresponsive Democratic machine. Marley was a leader in the United Negro Voters League, created by members of the Student Nonviolent Coordinating Committee (SNCC) and the Congress of Racial Equality (CORE) to increase voter registration and turnout among black Americans. The most famous offshoot of this effort was the Mississippi Freedom Democratic Movement, whose unsuccessful attempt to seat delegates at the 1964 Democratic Convention attracted worldwide attention. Members of Brooklyn CORE had at the same time organized the Brooklyn Freedom Democratic Party to elect blacks to local offices. Based in Bedford-Stuyvesant but active in Brownsville, the most significant candidate supported by the group was Major Owens, chairman of Brooklyn CORE, but who lost his 1964 bid to become a New York City councilman.[6]

During these political campaigns, many local activists also discussed ways to improve their neighborhood. Residents began to consider other issues of common concern, like inferior schools, inadequate trash collection, and limited government services. After the elections, several groups—the Tilden Tenants Council, the United Negro Voters League, local Parent-Teacher Associations, block associations, and churches—coalesced into a new group that they named the Brownsville Community Council. "Just about every local group became a part of the BCC, regardless of where they were politically or what their primary focus was," argued Reid. "It was all these individuals, and everyone was so focused on improving the community, and they weren't going anywhere, so it had to get better here. It was just a unique combination of individuals." The ideas of the group mirrored some of the philosophies then shaping President Johnson's War on Poverty.[7]

Several different strands of thought merged into the Community Action Program. In the late 1950s, social scientists Lloyd Ohlin and Richard Cloward developed a theory of juvenile delinquency arguing that poor youths participated in gangs because they were excluded from participating in "normal" institutions. Their "opportunity theory" posited that programs that provided stability and a protective atmosphere for troubled youths prevented children from becoming delinquent. With the support of the Ford Foundation, Ohlin and Cloward helped to form Mobilization for Youth (MFY), a program based in the Lower East Side to furnish services and recreational programs to poor youths. MFY provided job training, educational programs, and neighborhood organization to remove the obstructions to opportunity in the neighborhood. Through the agitation of social scientists and the Ford Foundation, seventeen programs across the nation in 1962 received grants to test Ohlin and Cloward's theory.[8]

At the same time, social scientists from the University of Chicago promoted other reforms. These academics argued that poor areas lacked the institutional infrastructure to function effectively and that their neighborhoods needed assistance to create these necessary organizations. Planners and urban sociologists also participated in discussions on urban problems. They asserted that city systems were so complex that they inhibited efforts to help the urban poor. Planners advocated wholesale change to urban institutions and asserted that grassroots participation was vital to the new conceptualization of the city. Still others argued that community-based institutions would help the poor by coordinating social service provisions so that government funds would be spent more efficiently. These strands shared a belief in resident organization and empowerment to bring about changes in poor areas, but to varying degrees. Some policymakers just wanted neighborhood input in planning social services. Community action advocates argued that "maximum feasible participation" empowered the poor to demand better services and more resources, giving them the opportunity to participate more successfully in society.[9]

All these theories played some role in the development of the War on Poverty. Despite the fact that none of the ideas were tested, federal policymakers pushed for the inclusion of a Community Action Program in President Johnson's legislative package. Johnson's advisers argued that with federal funding, locally based Community Action Agencies could plan poverty programs, coordinate the activities of social service agencies, and mobilize the poor to demand better services. To the chagrin of many established social service providers and local government officials, this program gave power directly to neighborhood groups. While mayors welcomed more resources for schools, job training, and other services, they were very concerned about the potentially subversive aspects of the CAP. During 1964 and 1965, mayors across the country pushed the Johnson administration to rein in the activities of federal administrators from the Office of Economic Opportunity (OEO) who were trying to include residents in the planning of the poverty initiative. Mayor Richard J. Daley of Chicago called it a "folly" to think that the poor could design a program, and New York Mayor Robert Wagner demanded that "local autonomy be respected" by federal officials.[10]

While politicians complained about federal interference in local programs, the political infrastructure in New York controlled much of the poverty program. Mayor Wagner filled the board of the newly created Council on Poverty with his cronies, and only the OEO's threat to withhold funding forced him to allow the participation of neighborhood representatives. In the spring of 1965, Wagner announced that designated poverty areas would hold elections to create local boards that would craft and implement the poverty program, subject to approval by his administration. To prevent true grassroots control and to protect the interests of institutional elites, Wagner required that local board members be chosen by delegates from neighborhood-based institutions such as social service agencies, YMCA's, churches, and block associations. As a result, most antipoverty boards were stacked with middle-class professionals and politically connected persons. Few poor people were elected.[11]

The BCC was launched concurrently with the creation of the CAP and before it was clear what form the latter program would take. Originally a volunteer coalition, the BCC was among the first organizations to apply when CAP funds became available. In the summer of 1965, the BCC received a four-month planning grant of $20,000 to hire a consultant and organize a "social action program." One analyst of the program argued that successful antipoverty efforts depended on a preexisting, indigenous leadership, and two years of effort from Brownsville activists gave the BCC a head start in program development. Even though many of them were professionally trained, BCC leaders made much of the fact that their organization was run by community members, not outsiders. "The poor will take a hand in their own affairs," stated Board Chair Major Owens in the announcement of local elections. But Brownsville's professional leadership cadre maintained control in neighborhood elections overseen by the OEO. In August 1965, delegates from Brownsville organizations selected board members for the Brownsville–East New York Community Action Committee, which would oversee the area's poverty program. Later that year, delegates chose the directors of the BCC, the organization chosen to implement the program. Among the BCC directors were Reverend Luis Carreras of Our Lady of Mercy Church; Ken Cave, president of the Van Dyke Houses Residents Council; Alex Staber, president of the Jimmerson Houses Tenants Council;

Bill Marley of the Tilden Tenants Council; and Angel Rivera, director of the Puerto Rican Organizations of Brownsville and East New York. The delegates also elected Willa Webster, Thelma Hamilton, and Rae Glauber to the BCC board.[12]

The BCC board included three businessmen, two social workers, two insurance investigators, two postal clerks, and two homemakers. Other members were working class, but they were not the disenfranchised poor. In describing the group, William Marley candidly admitted, "there are no poor people as such on the committee at present. . . . But there is another side of the coin: this committee has to work, and in order for it to work there must be people on it who have proven that they know how to get things done. These are such people . . . and the fact that many of them are either in professional or semi-professional occupations should be no cause for criticism. On the contrary, Brownsville–East New York is fortunate to have such people." While the majority of the BCC board members were black or Latino, five directors were white, which made this organization a very diverse group. "When I moved to this community in the early 1960s, blacks, whites and Latinos were working together in many organizations," remembered Maurice Reid. "It was always assumed that any community activities would be interracial."[13]

The election of the BCC board spurred a power struggle, as local political leaders fought to gain control of the organization through the placement of their associates. Assemblyman Samuel Wright, one of the first black elected officials in the area, for example, tried to use the elections to consolidate his power in Brownsville. But when Wright and several members of his political club offered themselves for election to the BCC board of directors, all were defeated. Brownsville residents long felt neglected by the Democratic leadership, and they were skeptical about the newfound interest of party officials. "The BCC is involved in the antipoverty program, and the community is determined not to allow the program to become infiltrated either by politicians or by political appointments to jobs," Bill Marley argued. "The community is equally determined that, by and large, only community residents shall sit on the Board or hold Executive Office." Although rebuffed in the short term, Wright, who lived in the area, continued to play a major role in Brownsville politics and was a force with which the BCC would frequently contend. OEO staffers praised the Brownsville elections for their efficiency and fairness. "This was the showpiece, and it came off well: good attendance, orderly procedure, no demonstrations, the majority pleased with the whole thing," the regional office reported.[14]

Throughout late 1965 and early 1966, the BCC organized neighborhood residents and planned its program, scheduled to begin in the summer. The group received an additional grant of $25,000 in October 1965 and another in March 1966 to continue the planning process. In accordance with the CAP directives, the BCC envisioned the creation of four Community Action Centers to focus on revitalization. These centers, located throughout the neighborhood, were responsible for coordinating services and developing new initiatives to meet area needs. Early in their deliberations, BCC board members realized that they needed someone with political acumen and a strong understanding of local government. Such a person could protect the program from politicians like Wright and government bureaucrats who did not support the idea of community action. In January 1966, the board hired Major Owens as "Project Consultant." Owens, a librarian educated at Morehouse College, was active in many organizations in the area. In addition to his leading role in the highly active and sometimes radical Brooklyn CORE, Owens was an organizer of the Brooklyn Tenant Organization and the Rent-Strike Coordinating Committee, two groups that fought for better maintenance of Brooklyn tenements. He was also a leader in the fight against police brutality in Bedford-Stuyvesant and an advocate for increased employment opportunities for blacks—particularly in the 1963 battle over the construction of the Downstate Medical Center. Blacks picketed this project, one of the largest construction projects ever undertaken in the borough, because it had no black workers. While the protesters failed to secure construction jobs, this fight, like that at Beth-El Hospital, galvanized the black community to demand greater job opportunities. Owens brought many skills to the BCC, but more importantly, as a self-styled "responsible militant," he was able to talk to both activists and career bureaucrats. This ability served the BCC well and quickly made it one of the most organized Community Action Agencies in the city.[15]

Upon taking the leadership of the organization, Owens outlined his program as one that sought nothing less than the rebirth of Brownsville. The BCC's efforts focused on creating "socially useful jobs for people who need them," aiding in "the development of the attitudes and habits needed to acquire the education which enable individuals to enter the larger competitive society on an equal footing," conveying to residents "the know-how needed in solving day to day problems of city life," relieving "immediate physical and mental suffering in every way possible," and assisting in "the development of small businesses in order to provide financial resources to support independent community institutions." During the next three years, Owens and other Brownsville activists made the BCC one of the strongest antipoverty programs in the city.[16]

The Program of the Brownsville Community Council

The CAP placed much hope in the ability of poverty-area residents to plan a better neighborhood administered by a complex hierarchy of organizations. Although the majority of funds went to nationwide programs such as Head Start, Job Corps, and Legal Aid, the New York City Council on Poverty worked with city agencies to fund and oversee neighborhood-based programs, while the local Community Action Committee assessed neighborhood needs and available resources, and developed a strategic plan. These committees were also expected to coordinate existing services and develop new projects to serve unmet needs. All these new services were to be provided by Community Action Agencies like the BCC that operated Neighborhood Action Centers located in each poverty area. "The neighborhood service center is the focal point of the CAP program," argued Sar Levitan, a CAP creator. With federal funds, the BCC employed professionals to manage programs and poor residents to provide outreach, clerical, and other services.[17]

While in principle these initiatives were vital to the CAP, most local groups struggled to design efficient Neighborhood Action Centers: hiring staff and coordinating the program presented serious organizational and political problems for fledgling groups. During the first year of the program, most focused their efforts on the administration of already existing programs, particularly Head Start and Job Training. The first BCC program was Head Start, and two centers, with a combined budget of $250,000 and serving a total of 390 Brownsville children, were established in 1966. Because of the power of New York's entrenched political institutions, even the operation of a Head Start program presented difficulties. Before 1966, Head Start was administered by the board of education, "the people most responsible for much of the problem," according Maurice Reid, who was hired by the BCC to run its children's education programs. Activists had to fight the board of education for several months before they won control of the program.[18]

The BCC leadership had an advantage over many neighborhood agencies because they had been working together for some time in analyzing neighborhood needs. As a result, the BCC planning process proceeded faster than most local poverty groups. By the spring of 1966, and after dozens of neighborhood meetings and input from local leaders and BCC board members, Major Owens and consultant Alex Efthim presented the "Total Action Plan of the Brownsville Community Council." The Total Action Plan was a smorgasbord of community action programs that made the

BCC the focal point for all social services, economic development, and urban renewal that was to take place in Brownsville. In addition to its administrative programs, the Total Action Plan sought to bring hope to community residents and foster in them the belief that the poor could take care of themselves. "The Total Action Plan will create an atmosphere in Brownsville where apathy is dispelled and community pride is encouraged because there is faith in the orderly processes of our society and there is know-how to make use of these processes," stated the plan's introduction.[19]

In most proposals, the Total Action Plan took existing ideas and adapted them to the particular circumstances of Brownsville. The Head Start program was established by 1966, as were juvenile delinquency programs like those proposed by the BCC. In addition, the Federal Manpower Demonstration and Training Act funded locally based job training for several years, and the BCC program was similar to these efforts. What was significant about the Total Action Plan was the power that it gave the group. If accepted by OEO officials without revision, the BCC would quickly be transformed from an organization with fewer than five staff members and a budget of less than $50,000, to a major institution with a staff of well over one hundred and a budget in excess of $2.5 million.[20]

The BCC's initial program focused on youth and adult education. In addition to Head Start, summer camp, and college preparation, the group created a Neighborhood Adventure Corps, recreational activities for preteen boys and girls, a Brownsville Sports League for athletic competition, and a Young Adults Council to enable youths to learn about and participate in civic affairs. To reach troubled youths, the BCC formed the Brownsville Cadet Corps, which mixed military training with recreational programs and remedial education. The plan argued that the Cadet Corps would connect with teens by rejecting the "middle-class values" of the educational system, teaching young adults about their culture and heritage. In 1967, more than two thousand children and young adults were served through these after-school and summer projects. The organization also created an adult education program with child care and tutorial support to residents studying for their GEDs. Offerings to persons with high school diplomas included training in medical occupations (nursing and geriatric aides) and food preparation and catering; as well as "enrichment" programs in black history, literature, music, and drama. A similar project in Puerto Rican culture offered classes in Puerto Rican history along with training in English and Spanish. To spur interest in these programs, BCC leaders emphasized that all trainees were eligible for both administrative and outreach positions within the organization. Two other programs, the Small Business Development Project and the Housing Rehabilitation and Maintenance Project—

which merged job training in the construction trades with rehabilitation of local tenements—were also included in the Total Action Plan, but they were never implemented.[21]

Evaluations of the CAP later argued that few Community Action Agencies actively promoted the political organization of poor residents. Most simply provided social services to their constituents. From its inception, however, BCC activists claimed that the mobilization of the poor was vital. "Casework by professionals will not be emphasized," argued the Total Action Plan. "Instead, block workers, other area workers, and workers attached to specific organizations will tackle the problems of the poor." Block workers, who staffed the Neighborhood Action Centers, performed outreach to the community that helped them craft the BCC program. In addition, the group supported existing neighborhood groups and organized communitywide activities that created "community spirit, solidarity and joint action in social emergencies."[22]

Federal and local officials disagreed about the purposes of the Community Action Program, and from the beginning the program was plagued by competing definitions of the term "community action." Many neighborhood activists saw the CAP as a means to liberate poor communities. Most local politicians viewed the program as a way to keep things quiet during the hot New York summers, particularly after the riots of 1964. As a result, a large share of New York's community action dollars were allocated for youth programs. For instance, almost half of the BCC's total grant for fiscal year 1967 was spent on summer initiatives, including the Brownsville Baseball League, the Young Adults Council, the Youth Remedial Day Camp, the Delinquency Prevention Project, the Brownsville Cadet Corps, and the Career and College Club. Government officials also funded two of the five Neighborhood Action Centers requested by the BCC, and many of the group's summer programs were given funds to continue limited operations during the year. The BCC did not immediately become the all-encompassing institution envisioned by the Total Action Plan, but BCC administration and community action programs were funded at levels sufficient to keep the dream alive in the minds of the group's leadership. These hopes were realized in January 1967 when the New York City Council on Poverty designated the BCC as Brownsville's Community Poverty Corporation, making the organization the official umbrella agency responsible for coordinating all antipoverty programs in the area. According to its staff, the BCC was the first program in the country to complete the process of incorporation.[23]

By the spring of 1967, the group had opened two additional Neighborhood Action Centers, which, according to activists, would "stimulate the poor to use the resources made available to them, . . . supervise the services built into the Total Action Plan, and . . . mobilize the entire community behind total community solutions to its social problems." These centers were on the frontlines of the organization of the neighborhood and were the places where new community activities gestated. "All of the centers were vibrant," remembered Annie Nicholson, who worked at Action Center Three. "These were the places that we organized protests, gave out consumer information, and provided training to area residents." While the organization continued to receive a large portion of its funding for summer youth programs, many other activities were undertaken through these community action centers. For example, the BCC organized senior citizens and made them aware of new resources available to them through the recently enacted Medicare program. Seniors also mentored and tutored children at the center's after-school program. Job training and employment referrals were another mission of the centers. The group received more than $250,000 from the Federal Manpower and Career Development Agency to operate a job training program. One of the many curricula was an office skills program to train secretaries, clerks, and paralegals. Three hundred people participated in this program during the summer of 1967.[24]

The BCC also involved itself in the more traditional projects of a community organization. Like Brownsville groups before it, the BCC fought for more middle-income housing in Brownsville, opposing the redesignation of a site on Rockaway Avenue for low-income housing. "Low-income housing is needed, yes, but there is only so much that one community can reasonably absorb. Brownsville already has all that it can handle if it is to push its fight for quality schools, higher employment, and a reduction of the crime rate with any success," BCC leaders argued. Like the Brownsville Neighborhood Council a decade before, the organization fought to improve sanitation in the area by organizing tenants to pressure landlords and the local government. The group also battled to increase recreational facilities, urging the NYCHA to use the neglected community centers in the Brownsville and Tilden Projects. In September 1966, one hundred Brownsville residents closed down a block of Herzl Street, demanding that it be turned into a play area. Adults and children, with the support of Thelma Hamilton, director of their Neighborhood Action Center, barricaded the block with lawn chairs and ordered the police department to close it to traffic. In 1967, the BCC boasted, Neighborhood Action Center One alone resolved more than three thousand welfare problems, four thousand tenant problems, and registered hundreds of new voters. In addition, the group supported the creation of new block clubs, provided job training for hundreds of residents, and included thousands of residents in neighborhood parades and cultural festivals.[25]

In early 1967, the BCC began publishing a biweekly paper, *The Brownsville Counselor,* to inform neighborhood residents of the progress of its activities. Each edition of the paper included reports on BCC events, local news, columns by local residents, and information on government programs. Through *The Brownsville Counselor,* the group reached out to Brownsville residents in additional ways, prodding them to become more active and to use their talents to help themselves and the organization. One article stated, "We would like to take this opportunity to seek out some of those fine artists, writers, carpenters, and other specialists in the community. Maybe you have tried in vain to find a job in your profession and have been turned down for reasons other than qualification. If this has happened to you, please come in and let the Brownsville Community Council help you." Articles also gave information to Brownsville residents to protect them from financial scams such as installment credit plans.[26]

A year into its existence, in April 1967, the BCC completed its second Total Action Plan, which proposed an expanded community organization effort. The 1967–68 Total Action Plan included the existing program and several additional projects geared to uplifting Brownsville residents: the Afro-American Intensified Cultural Education Program, the Afro-American Intercultural Education Project, the Puerto Rican Culture Action Project, the Puerto Rican Consumer Workshop Project, the Howard Houses Self-Help Workshop, Operation Open City Brownsville (a Fair Housing project), the creation of the Brownsville United Block Association (a group to organize and support block clubs in the area), and a mental health action project. In addition, as required by the newly established New York City Community Development Agency, the BCC in 1967 decentralized its operations and contracted out many services to smaller local groups. Among these organizations were the Leatherneck Cadet Corps, which managed the juvenile delinquency project; PROBE (Puerto Rican Organizations of Brownsville), which operated the Puerto Rican cultural and educational project; the United Block Associations, which organized block clubs in the neighborhood; the East Brooklyn Mental Health Project, which lobbied for and operated clinics in the area; and Christians and Jews United for Social Action, which organized tenants in the area.[27]

In setting forth the second Total Action Plan, the BCC made a tactical decision that Brownsville needed more than youth programs. Although many government officials viewed the Community Action Program as a youth-centered venture, adults became the main focus of BCC activities. In his presentation of the plan, Owens stated, "Since millions of dollars for youth programs are available through such sources as the board of education, the Department of Parks and other public and private institutions, the BCC will spend only a small percentage of its community action funds for youth programs. . . . The greatest percentage of funds will be spent for activities which encourage the organization of adults, the P.T.A.'s, block associations, churches, cultural organizations. Organized adults will be able to get the needed services for youth." The 1967 program reveals a changing focus within the organization toward more sophisticated community action, as well as a greater focus on the cultural aspects of poverty. But these proposals also reveal the maturity of the existing BCC program. Having succeeded in establishing viable summer camp and youth programs, activists looked to the larger needs of Brownsville.[28]

During its second full year, BCC leaders increased their focus on consumer education, resident organization, and educational reform, and shifted their priorities from social services to activism and institutional change. According to the Total Action Plan, the only youth programs that would be supported were those that "demonstrate to the board of education and other institutions what can be done in the sphere of youth motivation." The organization also committed itself to the still-developing concept of "community control," stating "to achieve after-school and weekend activities, Community Schools will be demanded for every school in Brownsville." Each group funded by the BCC was required to work with local schools and organize parents. In addition, each had to have a program for voter registration, even though Congress banned this activity for antipoverty groups in 1966. To create a mobile force of neighborhood activists, all delegate agencies were required to publicize meetings of the board of education, the Council on Poverty, the Board of Estimate, and other government agencies, and each group had to have a plan to mobilize residents to attend the meetings when necessary. Consumer education, including "buying clubs" and "comparative shopping projects," was another requirement for all BCC-funded groups. In 1967, the BCC opened the Brownsville Credit Union and actively solicited membership through its delegate organizations.[29]

Brownsville activists were energized by the resources and attention coming to their area, but the neighborhood continued to suffer serious crime and housing problems. Outside observers labeled it a disaster area. In the mid-1960s, Brownsville and East New York were often grouped together as the worst of New York City's trouble spots, placed high on a list of areas designated "flammable" by Mayor John Lindsay's administration. Random crime and violence in both neighborhoods increased during the decade. In 1967, the New York City Police Department reported that the number of homicides in Brownsville skyrocketed from ten in 1960 to more than thirty in 1966. Total arrests, according to the precinct, rose from 1,883 in 1956 to 3,901 in 1966. The report noted that the climb in crime was mostly attributable to those over twenty-one years old, and the most frequent crime was grand larceny. "Don't come out this way by subway," one detective told reporters. "Brownsville is one of the toughest areas in Brooklyn, if not the whole city. You could be mugged getting off the train in broad daylight." Police administrators stated that the precinct was averaging five arrests per day. In addition, local activists made the startling assertion that more than 85 percent of crimes in the area went unreported. While Brownsville reformers worked to revitalize the neighborhood with government assistance, reporters saw an area devastated by crime. Beleaguered businessmen reported daily robberies and even the ubiquitous metal gates on Pitkin Avenue stores could not prevent the crime. According to reporters, many of the gates were "either bent open from the bottom, probably with crowbars," or "twisted wide enough for a man to get his hand through a broken plateglass window." Large numbers of stores on Pitkin Avenue and other commercial streets gave up on the area and closed. Reporters noted that New York cabdrivers, afraid of being mugged, refused to take people into the area.[30]

Increasing violent crime was not the only measure of the neighborhood's decline. As in the 1950s, Brownsville continued to suffer serious problems in the areas of sanitation and housing. A 1964 exposé by the *New York World Telegraph and Sun* found more than sixty housing code violations in a single building on Belmont Avenue. Tenants consistently complained that negligent or corrupt inspectors ignored these violations. In response, Thelma Hamilton, Paul Chandler, and other activists organized a program to investigate housing violations. Their report sharply criticized both city agencies and housing court judges who gave "automatic adjournments to slumlords . . . thus giving landlords a license to operate." Local activists demanded that the city place severely neglected buildings in receivership. City officials who cared enough to visit the area were shocked at the circumstances in which Brownsville residents lived. Said Parks Commissioner Thomas P. F. Hoving, "Conditions here are absolutely wretched. It makes you sick. If I had to live in some of these places, I think I'd be a drug addict myself." Long in decline, Brownsville dwellings deteriorated to the point that local officials gave the area the dubious distinction of having the worst housing in the city. City officials bore much responsibility for these problems, the worst of which were in the designated urban renewal area. Landlords had few incentives to maintain properties soon to be demolished. The city's housing and welfare departments, responsible for ensuring the habit-ability of these units, failed miserably. During one period of bitter cold, dozens of families had to be evacuated to area armories. Fires were also fre-quent in these buildings, and New York Fire Department officials called Brownsville's Forty-fourth Battalion, which responded to an average seven thousand calls per year, "the busiest in the world."[31]

Gangs continued to flourish in the area, and during the 1960s black and Puerto Rican gangs competed violently for "turf" in Brownsville, particu-larly along its eastern border. In the summer of 1966, these incidents esca-lated, and several blacks caught in the crossfire in one tenement were forced to seek shelter and protection at a local church. Few whites remained in Brownsville by the mid-1960s, so racial tensions there did not involve whites. Next door in East New York, however, whites were the aggressors in the area's severe racial conflict. During the summer of 1965 an eleven year old black youth was gunned down in a dispute between blacks and a self-styled group of white youths who called themselves SPONGE (Society for the Prevention of Negroes Getting Everything). These mostly Irish and Italian youths protested the recent arrival of blacks and Latinos in East New York, organizing vigilante groups to threaten and intimidate "outsiders" who moved into their area. Unlike Jews in Brownsville who lived in rental property, large numbers of East New Yorkers owned their homes—and they did not respond peacefully to their new neighbors. These whites were attached both economically and socially to their neighborhood and were not going to relinquish it without a fight. More than one thousand police officers were dispatched to enforce order in the neighborhood. Over the summer, several incidents erupted between black and white youths, and dozens were arrested.[32]

The problems that troubled Brownsville were the result of decades of unplanned development and government neglect in the area. Public hous-ing, urban renewal, deteriorating private housing, as well as failing schools and inconsistent social services, all played a role in the neighborhood diffi-culties. As a newly founded group, the Brownsville Community Council was not equipped to address all the problems immediately, but Brownsville activists were optimistic that over time, with continued government sup-port, they could revitalize the neighborhood. Through the empowerment of Brownsville residents, BCC leaders argued that they could secure the private and public resources necessary to make Brownsville a showpiece of the War on Poverty. By 1970, much of this optimism would dissipate in the face of government bureaucracy and the intractability of neighborhood distress.

The BCC and the Contradictions of Black Power

In early 1968, Major Owens wrote a short article for the *Brownsville Counselor*, explaining the purpose of the organization's many parades and festivals. "What do parades have to do with all of this? Parades are key tools in the building of community unity and power," argued Owens. "Parades reach the unreachables. They inspire the apathetic. They bring a lot of cynics back to the fold. Without an Afro-American Day Parade and a Puerto Rican Day Parade to inspire and carry a message of uplift, there are thousands who would never lift-up their heads long enough to see that there are job training programs, and there are factories and stores where they can obtain employment if the community insists that the doors be opened." Owens and other activists viewed the group as a means to empower poor residents to take control of their lives, of their neighborhood institutions, and of the political system. Through the BCC, Brownsville residents gained access to social service jobs and government resources. These victories caused Brownsville residents to reshape their attitudes toward New York City government.[33]

Before the 1960s, the term "Black Power" had little meaning to most Americans. However, by 1968, after several years of protest and riots by African-Americans, the country was familiar with the term. "Black Power" represented many different things to different people. Some viewed the philosophy as no more than the logical extension of the civil rights movement's goal of equality. Others saw Black Power as the creation of a separate black nation. Almost all advocates agreed that at a minimum the idea meant the transfer of control of governmental and private organizations in black neighborhoods from whites to blacks. Across the country, black leaders called for the transformation of the nation's institutions—political, economic, and social—in order to make them representative of the people that they served. Black activists sought to make government more accountable by putting local people in charge of public services. One had only to look at the negative effects that programs like public housing and urban renewal had on Brownsville to understand the motivations behind the community control movement. City, state, and federal agencies failed dramatically in providing services to urban residents, advocates argued, and locally run organizations could only bring improvement. The goal of Black Power activists, according to William Van Deburg, was "to completely reorient the institutions that were most central to their daily living. They sought to bring schools, hospitals, and government agencies closer to the people by atomizing existing centers of power." As a neighborhood-based group, the

BCC was in the forefront of this movement to empower black and Latino Americans and to create new opportunities for their political participation.[34]

One of the greatest successes of the CAP was its inclusion of blacks and Latinos within the political system through government jobs. From its inception, the BCC was primarily concerned with creating job opportunities for Brownsville residents. Blacks and Latinos, those with educational credentials and those without, had long been barred from employment in New York City government institutions; and even in Brownsville's first Head Start program, city officials, who at the time controlled the newly created program, gave most of the administrative jobs to whites who lived outside of the area. The BCC therefore focused on this problem almost immediately after the group's founding. Board member Bill Marley criticized Head Start bureaucrats in his weekly *New York Recorder* column. "Brownsville is getting the run-around because several well-paying jobs are at stake, most of which were supposed to have gone to community residents," Marley wrote. "The significant thing here is that, with the possible exception of some of the teachers, all of these other jobs could very well have been filled by reasonably intelligent community residents. . . . Brownsville can, and must, reclaim these scores and scores of jobs that rightfully belong to its residents; and any organization that pretends to represent Brownsville, be it political or civic, is a farce unless it gives proper attention to this most basic of problems." Throughout the 1960s, BCC leaders worked to ensure that local residents benefited from federal funding with increased employment opportunities. While not all local agencies were responsive, the organization often succeeded in this effort, and dozens of Brownsville residents entered the public sector.[35]

The group faced a similar battle with the New York City Housing Authority and its programs. Blacks and Latinos had long sought opportunities with the NYCHA, one of the largest public employers in the city. As with the Head Start program, BCC members complained that the NYCHA used irrelevant criteria for prospective applicants to deny opportunities to low-income residents. Since most of them did not have high school diplomas or college degrees, they were eliminated from consideration early in the hiring process. But like the NAACP Legal Defense Fund, which made similar arguments in lawsuits around the country, activists asserted that residents were more than qualified for these positions. BCC leaders argued that many of the additional federal resources that were provided to organizations like the NYCHA were secured with their assistance and that local residents therefore should receive the benefits of employment. By attacking "credentialism" within local social service programs, the BCC sought to create practical economic benefits for Brownsville residents. Years before affirmative action gained national attention, the BCC fought established hiring systems and sought to place local residents in government-funded jobs. This debate also played an important role in the conflict over community control of public schools. Brownsville blacks and Latinos, long held back by what they viewed as arbitrary requirements, responded harshly to criticisms that they were not "qualified" to administer their children's schooling. By attacking barriers to jobs, the BCC revealed to Brownsville residents the possibility of neighborhood transformation through economic empowerment.[36]

The CAP's framers hoped it provided a mechanism for the poor to participate in democratic society, and in rhetoric and often in practice, the BCC captured these intentions. But a closer analysis of the group reveals a more complicated story. Many Brownsville residents could finally participate in civic affairs through the BCC, and several hundred local residents secured jobs in the previously closed social service and government sectors. But frequently those who benefited most from these opportunities were middle-class residents or working-class persons with particular skills. Many have argued that the CAP helped only those at the top of the hierarchy in these neighborhoods—"creaming" the best and brightest while leaving the poor behind—and this was often the case in Brownsville.[37]

BCC criticism of public agency hiring practices, which often focused on jobs that were taken by "middle-class people" who did not live in Brownsville, presented a conundrum for the leaders of the group. While they often portrayed the neighborhood as completely lower class, many neighborhood activists had advanced schooling and held professional occupations. Evaluations of the CAP have argued that it co-opted indigenous protest movements by hiring activists to run social service programs. Many of the BCC's senior staff were local activists, and many of the board members and their families worked for the organization or in its delegate agencies. Twenty-one board members worked for the BCC, including Thelma Hamilton, who was paid $8,000 a year to direct Neighborhood Action Center Number One; Ken Cave, director of personnel (at a salary of $10,500); Rae Glauber, assistant coordinator of training ($6,500 annually); and Bill Marley, coordinator of information (at a salary of $10,000). In addition, seventeen family members of directors were employed by the BCC. Board member Angel Rivera had three family members on the staff. In 1968, the regional OEO declared the group in violation of its regulations and demanded that these employees resign from their board positions, which they did.[38]

The hiring of local activists was a nationwide phenomenon. Welfare activists around the country faced such criticism, which would be turned against them in the 1970s when conservatives labeled them "poverty pimps." Throughout the early years of the Community Action Program, activists and administrators debated what role poor people should play in neighborhood-based organizations. Although the BCC's leadership remained predominantly middle class, employment for all local residents continued to receive significant attention from activists. In 1967, the BCC established a personnel committee "to see that as many of the needy residents of Brownsville as possible, who possess the minimum qualifications, receive employment in the BCC." This group focused on low-skilled jobs and assisted residents who lacked educational credentials. Brownsville residents secured many positions with BCC departments and with the organizations the group funded. With BCC support, they also made small inroads into low-skilled jobs in government. While the BCC's efforts were not completely successful, compared to other programs around the country the group helped many poor residents move into the economic mainstream.[39]

BCC leaders also championed the ideology of resident empowerment, which, according to several analysts of community action, was rare for the program. Later analysts found that grassroots organization at most CAPs across the nation was not seriously pursued. Only 5 percent of the groups in one study demonstrated concern for institutional change through resident organization. An internal OEO report discovered that only twenty-eight out of one hundred neighborhood service centers emphasized neighborhood organizing, and another found only three out of twenty cities where CAPs sought to mobilize the poor. Most programs were concerned with individual change, not broader societal transformation. But Brownsville's middle-class leaders struggled throughout the 1960s to incorporate poor residents into their activities. Their philosophy was that block organization offered the best opportunity to empower poor residents, and BCC leaders made these activities a priority. The "Operating Principles" adopted in 1967 stated that "An attempt will be made to spread the Community Action funds to as many Brownsville Organizations as possible" and to "spread funds geographically to cover the entire area of Brownsville." "As far as is possible," the document asserted, "all new programs should be contracted to independent community organizations or subcontracted to semi-independent organizations."[40]

Owens and his staff devoted a great deal of effort to locating and training block groups and other small organizations throughout Brownsville.

They believed that the resolution of neighborhood problems would take place through the empowerment of residents at the grassroots level, from which ideas and proposals to address neighborhood concerns should come. According to the Total Action Plan, these groups would focus on neighborhood problems and "would include those activities to help enrich neighborhood life, such as motivation in self worth thru the availability of books on the study of Negro life and history or other minority group history." Owens stated that it was "mandatory that the poor themselves play a more active role in the fight for Economic, Educational and Social equality." As the BCC's program expanded, staff devoted increasing effort to the cultivation of grassroots organizations, pushing them to undertake a greater role in social service programs and to have greater responsibility for their operations.[41]

But even the organization of block groups presented difficulties. The BCC did not establish block groups itself; rather it provided certification and financial support to those interested in participating in the program. As a result, a majority of the most active block groups were in the western section of Brownsville, which was more middle class and had a higher percentage of homeowners. Few of the most troubled blocks in the neighborhood were members of the United Block Associations, an umbrella group funded to support grassroots organization. In addition, while the Tilden Tenants' Council was a leader in the BCC, the tenant groups at the Howard, Van Dyke, and Brownsville Houses were less active.[42]

One grassroots organization that focused on the poorest Brownsville residents was Christians and Jews United for Social Action (CUSA), formed in 1965 by local clergy and student volunteers. The group was a local chapter of the national ecumenical organization Christians United for Social Action, which was created by liberal clergy to assist the civil rights movement; it was supported by Catholic Charities, the Episcopalian Church, and other denominations. CUSA was a force in neighborhood organizing in several cities around the country, and, owing to the special circumstances of the Brownsville area, the local chapter called itself "Christians and Jews United for Social Action." In the early 1960s, this group assisted hundreds of Brownsville tenants, helping them to use both legal action and public protest to improve the services provided by their landlords. Using student volunteers, the organization canvassed the neighborhood, taking complaints and providing advice to tenants in Brownsville tenements. When at least one-third of the tenants in a troubled building agreed to join together, CUSA organized rent strikes against their landlord. CUSA members and local residents also put pressure on landlords by picketing them at their homes and lobbying city officials for additional inspections based on carefully compiled statistics on neighborhood trouble spots.[43]

Thelma Hamilton, Father John Powis, and Delores Torres were among the leaders of CUSA. From CUSA's storefront on Strauss Avenue, they and other organizers worked to decentralize and integrate local schools, to increase services to the area, and to empower residents to secure better treatment. "They feel that we have this office and we can get some action," Hamilton said. "You can't give people leadership and don't follow through." At CUSA events, sound trucks rolled through the neighborhood asking tenants to bring their complaints to the organization. Said one observer, "The rallies, addressed by priests, laymen and young Negro and Puerto Rican leaders CUSA has been developing, are moving toward the solid base of support necessary for taking on the slumlords on even terms. They are beginning to attract real attention." The group also used other nonviolent protest tactics, including sit-ins at local government offices, to pressure officials to respond to its complaints.[44]

Paul Chandler was one of the young activists in CUSA. "One tactic we used was that we would hold our own landlord court," Chandler remembered. "We would get testimony from tenants and convict the landlords of failing to meet their obligations." Such protests resulted in greater attention to the area by city building inspectors, but the increased government oversight was short-lived. Frequently landlords would just abandon their buildings, leaving the tenants to fend for themselves. Housing conditions continued to deteriorate, and tenants suffered in cold, dangerous apartments. While grassroots organizations like CUSA often worked with the BCC, they frequently criticized the group for not taking a strong enough position against city agencies or private parties. The BCC was much more concerned about its relationship with New York's political system than were Chandler and other activists. "I had no problem putting a rat in Mayor Lindsay's face," recalled Chandler. He believed it was the only way to get attention to serious problems. But "responsible militant" Major Owens and other BCC leaders opposed such tactics. Chandler argued that more conservative organizations privately supported their efforts, because they benefited from such incidents. "We were used a lot by other groups to get more funding for them," Chandler remembered. "They would tell the city 'you better support us, or we'll sick those guys on you.'"[45]

Grassroots organization served many purposes. First and foremost, it met the BCC's primary responsibility of organizing the poor. Second, it helped facilitate the group's efforts in recruiting participants to its programs and volunteers for its activities. Third, block clubs and other local organizations lobbied for further funding for BCC programs. Finally, these small groups enabled residents to see immediate results from their activities and helped the BCC to fight the apathy and resentment believed to be holding down the neighborhood. Major Owens testified, "This can be the turning point in the Brownsville community. The base has now been set for the persons living here to reach out for the many aspirations which before had seemed too much beyond their grasp. No one can overlook the many causes which [have] contributed to the apathy which exist in the community. However the time is ripe for these causes to be alleviated as much as possible." Through resident empowerment, the BCC strove to transform the nature of social service provision and economic development. With this accomplished, activists hoped, the neighborhood would grow from within and would not repeat the mistakes of government bureaucracies.[46]

The BCC also used public events to create interest in the organization and its activities. Several times a year the group held fairs and parades and sponsored black and Latino cultural festivals. These programs were widely attended. Such activities, argued Owens, were vital to combating the skepticism and apathy of the neighborhood. Parades, festivals, and these meetings paved the way for other organization activities, including ethnic art exhibitions, voter registration drives, sports programs, and other types of entertainment. The purpose of these affairs, according to organizers, was "to display the harmony and unity achieved in this summer's Total Action Programs." The celebration of the contributions of blacks to world culture was a major aspect of the Black Power movement. Through greater understanding of African-American cultural heritage, blacks would develop self-pride, argued advocates like Kwame Ture and Charles V. Hamilton. In the past, blacks were told they "had no cultural heritage worthy of respect," but the Black Power movement sought to change that attitude. "Black people must redefine themselves, and only they can do that. . . . Throughout the country, vast segments of the black communities are beginning to recognize the need to assert their own definitions, to reclaim their history, their culture, to create their own sense of togetherness." In accord with this philosophy, the BCC created numerous cultural programs, including the screening of movies and the presentation of plays and literature of African-American and Latino interest. For example, the Career and College Club toured the area showing the film "Slavery" starring Ossie Davis and Ruby Dee. The BCC also sponsored a communitywide tribute to Langston Hughes, which culminated in the naming of a recently completed NYCHA project the Langston Hughes Houses.[47]

Through their African-American and Puerto Rican cultural programs, the BCC sought to educate Brownsville residents on their heritage and history. These efforts included both indigenous programs and performers from around New York City. The group's description of the Puerto Rican Cultural Action Project aptly describes the goals of all the programs: "This program aims to enrich through entertainment and education the lives of 40,000 Puerto Rican residents of Brownsville who have no other means of contact at hand with their cultural heritage. It also aims to bring about a better understanding on the part of other ethnic groups as to the human values and beauty of Puerto Rican culture."[48]

In addition to providing educational and recreational opportunities for local youths, the BCC sought to empower them to play a part in the revitalization of Brownsville. For example, in the Neighborhood Youth Corps, young adults were hired to care for younger children in after-school programs. By giving these young people significant responsibilities, the BCC hoped to make them recognize their own abilities. Similarly, the Remedial Education and Youth Aspiration Project sought to help "those students who have been or are in the process of being alienated by the traditional methods of a middle-class oriented school system," and to "create an atmosphere of dedication to excellence among those students who have average and unusual abilities but who are not provided with the proper stimulation and motivation." Leaders believed that through community organization they could change the psychology of Brownsville residents. They did not blame local youths for their lack of drive. Rather, like many advocates of Black Power, they faulted "middle-class white institutions" for failing to provide young people with the tools to succeed. Most of the BCC leaders, as well as those active in the community control movement, were professionals with mainstream credentials. However, in shaping their programs for local youths, these activists rejected the importance of such training, arguing that it was based on "white middle-class values." One of the goals of area leaders was to embrace black culture as a rejection of the "culture of poverty" theory developed by Oscar Lewis and others. BCC activities played an important role in this effort.[49]

No aspect of the BCC program better exemplified the cultural orientation of the organization than the Brownsville Cadet Corps. BCC leaders envisioned the Cadet Corps as a means to provide educational and recreational opportunities to Brownsville youths within a group that would foster discipline and self-esteem. The plan for the corps described it as "a program for deprived young people which exploits the positive appeals of the quasi-military, and reduces to a minimum the social class and exclusion

factors, [and] will be a valuable program for the deprived youth of Brownsville." A participant in the program would emerge "with less frustration, less
confusion about the complex society which baffled him before," and with "a
new pride in groups and self, with new ambitions and some idea of how their
ambitions may be achieved through study and work." They would also gain
"new attitudes and work habits which facilitate the orderly pursuit of their
goals." This mixture of liberal psychology and conservative discipline, rem-
iniscent of the Black Panther Party, may have seemed a contradiction to
outsiders, but to BCC leaders it represented the empowerment of poor
youngsters. In some ways the Brownsville Cadet Corps was a continuation
of the ideas promoted twenty years before by the Brownsville Boys Club
(BBC). Like the BBC, the group sought to empower young residents and to
reveal to them opportunities for advancement. But unlike BBC leaders
twenty years before, staff believed that before youths could take advantage
of educational and cultural opportunities, they had to be "deprogrammed"
and to reject the atmosphere of failure in which they lived.[50]

By creating a milieu in which poor residents were empowered to organize themselves and create programs for neighborhood improvement, the
BCC played a major role in the cultural reorientation of Brownsville. BCC
leaders were conscious of this fact and geared their activities toward such a
transformation. "With the proper motivation and inspiration adults as well
as children are able to solve most of their own problems, teach themselves,
protect themselves from the vicious forces of oppression in society and generally seize opportunities as they occur. Cultural activities, self-image improving activities are not luxuries but vital necessities for the poor," argued
the Total Action Plan. All of these efforts provide a context in which to understand the conflict over the community's control of public schools. To
BCC leaders and the residents of Brownsville, no other area was of greater
importance than the education and development of their children. For this
reason, they demanded control over local schools. But although Brownsville residents had already assumed responsibility for many other aspects of
government services and succeeded in revitalizing them, the board of education and the United Federation of Teachers presented more formidable
obstacles.[51]

The BCC and Modern Brownsville

In January 1969, U.S. Senator Walter Mondale (Democrat, Minnesota) visited the BCC' offices. "I have heard so much about the Browns-

ville Community Council's program that I had to come see it in operation," the senator said. Mondale's visit was an attempt to cultivate support for the continuation of the Community Action Program, imperiled by the election of President Richard Nixon, but by that time the War on Poverty had run out of steam. In 1968 the organization was a major, year-round operation; its budget was $1.94 million, almost twice the budget for 1967. The group grew quickly, but unlike many other organizations, the BCC did not face allegations of mismanagement or misuse of funds. In fact, city officials pointed to the group as a model for other antipoverty agencies. However, 1968 was the high point for the BCC, as it was for Community Action Programs across the country. Significant budget cuts from Washington resulted in a decrease in New York City CAP funds. And Congress also drastically reduced the amount of discretionary funds—those not directed at Head Start, Legal Aid, or other specific programs. These funds paid for the administration of groups like the BCC, as well as for the staffing of the Neighborhood Action Centers. As these dollars dried up, staff levels declined and new programs could not be developed. George Nicolau, the head of New York's Community Development Agency (CDA), noted in 1968 that "declining commitment at a time of sharply rising expectations creates nothing less . . . than a devastating whipsaw for both the responsible leader and the poor alike. It is, I am convinced, the most important contributing cause of the racial tensions which now exist in New York and other major cities of the United States." Throughout Brownsville, resentment increased as a result of the federal government's abdication of responsibility.[52]

The curtailing of the Community Action Program seriously hurt the BCC, but it also changed New York's antipoverty program in a way that ensured the group's continuation. In January 1968, in protest of the federal cuts, Nicolau resigned. Lindsay replaced him with the BCC's executive director, Major Owens. Lindsay had supported greater neighborhood participation and the hiring of activists into the city bureaucracy. As a result, the CDA was an organizing base for black and Latino activists. Lindsay chose Owens because he believed Owens was less "militant" than alternative candidates for the position. Owens served as CDA commissioner until 1972, when he was elected to the state assembly. Throughout his tenure as commissioner, Owens remained active in Brownsville and supportive of the BCC's program. So despite CDA budget cuts, the BCC continued to receive funding.[53]

In three short years the Brownsville Community Council was transformed from a volunteer organization of a dozen Brownsville residents to a $2 million organization with several facilities and more than one hundred

Figure 22. Major Owens in the 1970s. Courtesy Major Owens.

full-time staff. Throughout the 1960s, the BCC had a major impact on the Brownsville community, bringing in new resources, creating new jobs, serving the neighborhood's youths and adults, and organizing residents. The group also played a major role in the political maturation of the Brownsville population, and this would significantly affect the neighborhood, and all of New York City, during the battle over community control of schools.[54]

Critics of the Community Action Program later argued that it muted neighborhood protest by incorporating black and Latino activists into established political institutions and giving them a stake in the system. Over time, Community Action Agencies became entrenched bureaucracies themselves, more focused on administration of programs than neighborhood outreach. During the early 1970s, many BCC staffers moved into government positions, and the organization itself narrowed its focus, devoting increasing attention to the development of badly needed affordable housing in the neighborhood. The hiring of local activists by government agencies certainly benefited those individuals and provided many Brownsville residents with stable employment. The emergence of a black and Latino class of bureaucrats also helped residents by making government agencies more responsive to the needs of poor, minority neighborhoods. So an assessment of the success of the Community Action Program in Brownsville depends upon the criteria used. Community action did not bring about a radical alteration of the power structure. But it did result in concrete advancements for many residents through jobs and improved social services.[55]

Some assert that the CAP failed because it did nothing to counteract the structural forces responsible for urban poverty. Black poverty was the result of declining economic opportunities in cities; it would not be solved by increased funding for social services. Activists in the Brownsville Community Council believed that the empowerment of the poor at the local level would increase their political strength and lead to greater economic opportunities for Brownsville residents. But the connection between local protest and macroeconomic change was tenuous at best. In his assessment of the Community Action Program, Daniel Patrick Moynihan criticized Community Action Agencies for unrealistically raising the expectations of ghetto residents that they would control local government—when that was never the intention of the program. Such expectations, argued Moynihan, led to greater resentment when community action failed to achieve significant improvements in the lives of the poor. Despite the BCC's efforts, Brownsville continued to suffer from disturbingly high rates of unemployment and crime in addition to the myriad other social problems that afflict most urban ghettos. Brownsville's plight was the result of decades of decisions by public and private actors, who excluded blacks and Latinos from economic and housing opportunities in the suburbs and other parts of the city and created a segregated ghetto in central Brooklyn. The small amounts of funding provided did little to change these macrolevel disabilities.[56]

But on a more immediate level, the impact of the Community Action Program in Brownsville was significant. Put simply, the CAP supported indigenous protest movements and helped them grow more quickly than they would have in its absence. By activating the apathetic and creating a large and organized neighborhood-based institution, BCC leaders persuaded residents that they could increase their influence over local agencies. In some areas, such as health care, recreation, and housing, the BCC delivered on its promise to bring new resources to the area. The BCC represented the high point of optimism surrounding the civil rights movement and the War on Poverty. The organization was crucial to the psychological reorientation of black and Latino Brownsville residents, who increasingly demanded greater control of education and social service resources in their neighborhood, as well as greater political accountability from local government. The

BCC gave meaning to the term "Black Power," which became a rallying cry in many poor neighborhoods. The political and cultural maturation of Brownsville residents led to the creation of the Ocean Hill–Brownsville School Demonstration Project, which became the focal point of the 1968 New York teachers' strike.

Figure 23. Supporters of community control block entrance to Junior High School 271. JHS 271 was the center of conflict in the Ocean Hill–Brownsville school district. Photograph by Sam Reiss. Courtesy Sam Reiss Collection, Robert F. Wagner Labor Archives, New York University.

8

The Ocean Hill–Brownsville Community and the 1968 Teachers' Strike

After graduating from the Immaculate Conception Roman Catholic Seminary on Long Island in 1959, Father John Powis became pastor in the Fort Greene section of Brooklyn. Four years later, he transferred to Our Lady of Presentation Church on Eastern Parkway, the border between Ocean Hill and Brownsville. Upon his arrival in 1963, Powis immediately saw that the local schools were in trouble. "There was this tremendous burst of population," Powis said. "I remember walking the streets and seeing a tremendous number of people, especially children. I realized that the schools would be in crisis at that moment because there were not enough school buildings." Delores Torres's four children were in these crowded classrooms, and she was upset at the way they were neglected by the New York City Board of Education. "People were getting anxious because their children were going to school at split times, no children were going full time." Torres said. More than six thousand area children were on what the board of education called "short time" during the 1960s. Two of Torres's children attended school in the morning, while the others went to class in the afternoon. The problems of local schools, created by decades of neglect and bureaucracy, brought Powis, Torres, and other activists together, and the battle they waged affected schools across the city.[1]

In the fall of 1968, Brownsville and its neighbor, Ocean Hill, became the focal point for a citywide conflict over public education. The battle, which drew national attention, centered on the issue of "community control" of local schools; a proposal to allow parents to shape the curriculum and staffing of schools in their neighborhoods. Frustrated after years of attempts to integrate New York's public schools, many activists shifted their focus from racial equality to local parental control over their children's education. This idea emerged out of the "Black Power" movement and was supported by much of New York's elite, but it conflicted with the goals of the recently formed United Federation of Teachers (UFT). The UFT represented the largest teaching force in the nation, and the union feared that community control would threaten recently won job protections. In response to the attempts of Ocean Hill–Brownsville parents to consolidate control over local schools, UFT members struck the city system three times in the fall of 1968, and ultimately succeeded in ending the experiment in community empowerment.

The battle over community control received a great deal of attention from journalists and social scientists at the time. Indeed, the controversy remains a focus of writings on modern race relations and urban problems. None, however, discuss the vital role of the Brownsville Community Council (BCC) in the struggle. While the community control board was a separate entity, the BCC provided organizational support for community control advocates, and many BCC leaders, particularly Thelma Hamilton, Bill Marley, and Delores Torres, were also leaders of the community control movement. BCC-supported groups, including Christians and Jews United for Social Action (CUSA), also played an important role in the struggle as advocates for the community board. BCC staffers were also energetic participants in local schools during the strikes, and they provided organizational support to the activities of the governing board.[2]

However, the BCC programs were small in comparison to the gigantic operation that was the New York City Board of Education. In providing social services, local groups competed with private volunteer organizations like the Health and Welfare Council of New York and the Jewish Board of Guardians. While these organizations protested the usurpation of their power, they were already in decline by the 1960s. Many private social service agencies had retrenched during the 1950s, unable to cope with the needs of New York's new minority poor. Within Brownsville, groups like the Jewish Welfare Services and the Jewish Board of Guardians had pulled out along with the Jewish population, and other organizations failed to evolve. The BCC filled a vacuum in the area of social services; it did not displace existing groups.

Local schools, by contrast, had very strong institutional structures in the board of education and the UFT. Organized in the early 1960s, the UFT replaced the much smaller, left-leaning Teachers' Union (TU) as the main protector of public school teachers. During the 1940s and 1950s, the TU supported the integration of New York's school system and other efforts to improve educational opportunities for blacks and Latinos. The UFT was also liberal in orientation, but it was more focused on the bread-and-butter needs of its members. Led by Albert Shanker, New York teachers gained significant increases in pay and won other protections regarding promotion and management of the system during the early 1960s. The objectives of the union were consonant with the goals of its upwardly mobile, mostly second- and third-generation immigrant teaching force. Community control was in direct conflict with the union's aspirations. The UFT was still a fledgling organization in the 1960s, and it would have been disastrous for the union as an organization if it failed to respond to attempts to weaken the recently created administrative structure. In this context, the UFT and Ocean Hill–Brownsville residents soon found themselves in conflict.[3]

The demand for community control emerged from a two-decade effort to achieve racial equality in New York schools. Across the city, schools with black and Latino majorities received fewer resources, were overcrowded, and were often saddled with teachers who had failed to perform adequately in other schools. The school situation for blacks and Latinos deteriorated throughout the 1960s, as more whites left the school system. Activists believed that integrated schools would ensure more money, improved facilities, and better teachers for minority children, and they demanded that bureaucrats work toward this goal. Despite years of effort by civil rights leaders to improve educational opportunities for blacks through integration, by the mid-1960s almost all New York City schools were segregated. Brownsville's were no exception. The battle over school integration become so heated in the early 1960s that it strained relations among New York's civil rights organizations. Frustrated after a decade of attempts to secure support from the board of education for integrated schools, in 1964 the New York NAACP, CORE, and the Parents Workshop organized the City-Wide Committee for Integrated Schools, with former Brooklyn NAACP head Milton Galamison as the leader.[4]

The committee proposed a boycott of New York City schools to protest the continuing segregation and the intransigence of school officials. On

February 3, 1964, 464,000 students, 45 percent of the student body, were absent. The majority of the participants were black and Latino, and 90 percent of Brownsville's students joined in the boycott. Many attended "Freedom Schools" organized by the demonstration leaders. Taught by a racially diverse collection of college professors, clergy, and social workers, these schools focused on African-American and Latino history and culture, and they served as models for similar efforts during the 1968 strike. When board of education officials failed to respond to the demands of the demonstrators, Galamison called a second boycott. As the rhetoric of protest leaders escalated, liberal groups such as the Catholic Interracial Council and the American Jewish Committee condemned Galamison's activities, and the New York NAACP and CORE withdrew, calling the boycott counterproductive. The action had little impact on the plans of the school board.[5]

Civil rights groups and integration activists also failed to attain a much more ambitious goal that they believed would solve the problem of segregation. Throughout the early 1960s, these groups called for the creation of an "Educational Park" in the Flatlands section of Brooklyn near Brownsville, East Flatbush, and Canarsie. The proposed park for junior high and high school students replicated a college campus and included several educational facilities from which Brooklyn youths could choose. Advocates argued that construction of a complex serving ten thousand or more students was more efficient than building several small schools, because the campus could provide state-of-the-art facilities (science labs, libraries, theaters) that were not feasible at individual schools. The proposed campus also eliminated neighborhood districts, thereby removing the biggest obstacle to school segregation—residential segregation. From 1964 to 1966, Educational Park advocates pushed their program at city hall and at the board of education. They secured three thousand signatures from area parents and the support of many liberal organizations, including the American Jewish Committee, the American Jewish Congress, the NAACP, the Urban League, and the Catholic Interracial Council.[6]

After much agitation, activists convinced the board of education to study the idea, but a plan was never implemented. Many white parents' groups opposed the Educational Park. Among the most vocal critics was the local school board in eastern Brooklyn, which was controlled by white parents from Canarsie and East Flatbush (including former Brownsville Neighborhood Council Chair Irving Tabb). Parent leaders on the local school board called the plan ill-conceived and opposed the busing of their children out of the neighborhood. They argued that the Educational Park would "cause a further mass exodus of white children from our schools." Several local school board members were active in the Democratic Party, and they used their power to scuttle the project. Councilman Sam Curtis, who represented Canarsie and part of Brownsville, opposed the idea and accompanied Canarsie homeowners groups to school board meetings. State Assemblyman Alfred Lama, who represented Canarsie and Brownsville, also pressured board of education officials to reject the idea.[7]

Brownsville activists were the strongest supporters of the Educational Park idea, and Willa Webster, BCC member Helen Efthim, and others spoke at school board meetings in favor of the proposal. They also complained about their neighborhood's lack of representation on the local board. The board of education, with the advice of local groups, appointed local school board members, and BCC leaders tried, without success, to secure Bill Marley's selection. While giving tepid support to the idea of school desegregation, the white parents on the local board opposed every practical measure put forth by integration activists. Schools, in their view, were not the place to achieve integration. "Integration is a housing program, not a school program," one board member stated. In rejecting the Educational Park they argued that white parents "did not want to send their children into dangerous areas," which they equated with any school with minority kids. While publicly praising the idea, board of education officials never seriously considered the Educational Park. The board hired a consultant to develop a plan, but he soon resigned when he realized that the administration would never implement it. According to the consultant, most board of education staff viewed the idea as a "mild form of insanity." Political scientist Harold Savitch, who studied the battle for the Educational Park, concluded that public hearings by the school board "were nothing but pro forma ratification ceremonies to justify the rejection." Later in 1965, through the intervention of East Brooklyn politicians, the New York City Commerce Department chose the proposed site to develop an industrial park.[8]

In February 1966, Brownsville activists filed suit against the board of education, seeking to stop its plan to build several new elementary and junior high schools in eastern Brooklyn. The suit alleged that the board's plan discriminated against Brownsville youths by constructing schools that increased segregation within the area. The lawsuit further claimed that the board refused to follow its own integration plan and demanded that the plans for an Educational Park be followed. Despite neighborhood protests, the board of education defended its school construction program on the grounds that the Educational Park proposal was unfeasible, Brownsville schools were overcrowded and decrepit, and the immediate needs of local children had to take priority over the long-term goals of integration advocates. Brownsville activists continued to press for the Educational Park, and in July 1966, BCC President Thelma Hamilton, Vice President Alex Staber, and Angel Rivera, head of Puerto Rican Organizations of Brownsville and East New York, led more than a thousand residents in a protest of the groundbreaking for the Flatlands Industrial Park. Staber and several others were arrested when they interrupted the ceremonies by shouting "Jim Crow Must Go" and "Industrial Park No, Educational Park Yes." While public officials and businessmen stood by waiting for photographers who were to memorialize the groundbreaking, Mayor John Lindsay calmed the crowd, but the industrial development continued.[9]

One of the few efforts at integration to which the board of education agreed in the early 1960s was a voluntary program to bus children from overcrowded schools to schools in other parts of the borough with unfilled seats. Many Brownsville residents, led by Father John Powis and other local activists, helped facilitate the busing program. In the fall of 1965, several hundred Brownsville youths traveled to Canarsie, Bay Ridge, and Bensonhurst to begin the school year. But whites in these areas responded violently to the program. Powis described the events at several of the schools as a "scene out of hell." In Bay Ridge, parents and children pelted the children and Powis (in his vestments) with eggs and called them niggers. When the children entered the schools, they were put into separate classes, persecuted by the white students, and ignored by the staff. After several weeks of abuse, most of the students transferred back to Brownsville schools.[10]

Brownsville activists increasingly viewed integration efforts as frustrating and fruitless. Instead, they decided that if the board of education could not provide a decent education to their children, they would do it themselves. Though the concept of community control seems at odds with the goal of integration, Brownsville activists moved easily from one to the other. Several Brownsville activists cite frustration as the major reason for their changing orientation. "It was a natural evolution," reflected Maurice Reid. "The outside folks were not going to protect us, so you turn inward." Many Brownsville activists had volunteered their own children for the busing program. Their kids were traumatized, and the parents were disheartened by the response. "When you have that experience, it leads you to conclude, hey, we could do better ourselves," Reid argued. The parents also demanded control because they had been consistently thwarted by local school boards controlled by whites. In their view, white parents enjoyed influence over the operations of schools, but minorities did not. Even after redistricting in 1965, Ocean Hill and Brownsville parents lacked representation on local boards. As one community control advocate asserted, "if the decision makers are not responsive to the needs of the children they are charged with educating, why not change the decision makers? Why not put decisions in the hands of those with the greatest stake in the achievement of the children, their parent and local community leadership?" Proponents of community control hoped that parental involvement would make teachers and administrators more accountable. They argued that parents would force New York's educational bureaucracy to devote more money to struggling schools and that the funds would be used more efficiently by locally controlled boards. Advocates also believed that parents could help solve problems like overcrowding and lack of resources by volunteering in their children's classrooms.[11]

The move toward community control also benefited from the changing ideological climate of the late 1960s and its impact on civil rights organizations. Brooklyn CORE, for example, was a staunch advocate of integration and fought for the Educational Park. However, by the late 1960s, as the organization became increasingly separatist in orientation, Brooklyn CORE leaders, liberated by their expulsion from the national organization, dropped their advocacy of integration and aggressively supported the creation of local school districts. Kwame Ture and Charles Hamilton argued in their 1968 book *Black Power* that black communities "must devise new structures, new institutions to replace those forms or to make them responsive. There is nothing sacred or inevitable about old institutions; the focus must be on people, not forms." Many activists believed that neighborhood control of all institutions was vital to African-American development. For almost two years, the BCC had put this philosophy into action, replacing private and public agencies and assuming the role of a comprehensive neighborhood social service institution. Responsibility for youth programs, recreation, job training, housing and economic development, and other government functions had already devolved to local institutions by this time. It was only logical to Brownsville activists that the educational system do the same.[12]

Some civil rights leaders, however, questioned community control. Bayard Rustin, an organizer of the 1964 school boycott, vocally criticized the idea, calling it an example of the "politics of frustration." Rustin argued that community control offered "the illusion of 'political self-determination in education,' to those 'so alienated that they substitute self-expression for politics.'" He believed that the path to black liberation was through alliances with labor organizations and other groups, not through separatism. However, in the heated atmosphere of the late 1960s, few activists heeded Rustin's advice.[13]

The coordinated effort for community control coalesced after a 1966 meeting of the board of education. Activists from around the city, including Thelma Hamilton, Father John Powis, Delores Torres, Maurice Reid, and Paul Chandler, attended the meeting to protest the board's continued neglect of their schools. When one of the activists attempted to take the floor, she was told that her comments were out of order. A protest ensued, and the board members canceled the meeting and left the room. In response, activists took the board member's' seats, beginning what would become a three-day sit-in at the board of education. Naming themselves the "Ad Hoc People's Board of Education," activists argued that the only way for real educational improvement was for neighborhood leaders to personally take control of the schools.[14]

During the 1960s, many education reformers called for the decentralization of control over public schools, which they defined as moving authority from the central bureaucracy to smaller, hopefully more efficient management at the district level. The education system stifled experimentation and handcuffed teachers in dealing with the changing needs of students, Devolution of authority to smaller units, advocates asserted, revitalized schools by giving teachers and administrators greater flexibility in developing educational programs. Neighborhood activists in Brownsville reformulated this idea and demanded local, parental control over individual schools. The BCC argued that community-based educational programs created an experience relevant to previously disregarded students, guaranteeing that all children were treated as "educable beings, endowed with creative capabilities and potential." "Decentralization provides the framework for change," the BCC's 1967–68 Total Action Plan argued. Community control freed teachers and principals "from bureaucratic red tape" and would "enable school districts to innovate." In addition, Brownsville activists reasoned, the transfer of authority gave "parents a viable role in the educational process." By decentralizing the operations of New York's schools and giving responsibility to parents, children whom the system failed would now be rescued.[15]

While opponents asserted that community control would exacerbate the problem of school segregation by pushing whites out of the public school system, advocates concluded that the battle for integration needed to be refocused. BCC leaders argued that residents "must look at integration in a different light than we have in the past five years. Movement of children by central direction has not worked. Decentralization attempts to build strong communities in New York City with an aim toward promoting solid community support for integration when it is tried." In demanding local control, Brownsville activists reversed their priorities: in 1960, they had argued that integration would bring about better schools; by 1965, they advocated better schools as a means to integration.[16]

Community control coalesced with the plans of many education policymakers in New York City who were working to secure a decentralization program to transfer responsibility of schools to smaller units. As a result of pressure from parent activists and lobbying by officials of the Ford Foundation, the New York state legislature in the spring of 1967 directed Mayor Lindsay to develop a plan for school decentralization. To ensure that a more radical proposal was not adopted, the board of education announced a trial community control plan of its own, selecting three districts—the IS 201 educational complex in Harlem, the Twin Bridges District on the Lower East Side, and the Ocean Hill–Brownsville District in Brooklyn—to participate in this program. The original plan of the People's Board of Education was to demand a citywide program for community control, but several local chapters of the organization made more progress in this area than others, and they were chosen to implement the experimental effort. The Ocean Hill–Brownsville group was the furthest advanced in developing a community-oriented school program. Before the board of education's announcement of the experiment, Father Powis was in contact with Mario Fantini, a program director at the Ford Foundation involved in antipoverty programs supportive of community control. With Fantini's assistance, the Ocean Hill–Brownsville People's Board of Education secured a grant of $44,000 from the Ford Foundation in July 1967.[17]

Throughout the spring and summer of 1967, Powis's group worked with parents, teachers, local leaders, and education reformers to craft their program. They received little support from the board of education; after all, the administration did not really want the program to succeed. To operate the experiment, the group proposed a "governing board" to include one parent from each school selected by school Parent-Teacher Associations; one teacher from each school, chosen by the teachers; two administrators, one university representative, and five "community representatives" chosen by the parent representatives. The governing board, according to the plan, was responsible for hiring a unit administrator; selecting principals for local schools; setting curriculum, goals, and standards for classrooms; recruiting and selecting staff; and determining budgetary needs and allocating funds among local schools. While the New York City Board of Education envisioned a slow planning process, community control activists wanted to implement their ideas immediately. Without the board of education's agreement or support, the Ocean Hill–Brownsville People's Board of Education held elections for their governing board. Parents' representatives were chosen on August 4, and parents elected five "community representatives"— Herbert Oliver, minister of the Bedford Central Presbyterian Church, Assemblyman Sam Wright, Father John Powis, Delores Torres, and Walter Lynch—on August 10. The governing board selected Brownsville minister C. Herbert Oliver as chair. (He defeated State Assemblyman Samuel Wright for this position.) Next, the board chose Rhody A. McCoy, a teacher and administrator in New York City schools for eighteen years, as unit administrator. Despite the fact that they had not authorized the elections, board of education officials agreed to work with the governing board.[18]

The 1967–68 school year was a period of positive change in Ocean Hill–Brownsville schools, according to the Ford Foundation and other evaluators. Ford reviewers felt that Rhody McCoy was "strong and capable," and the board was "consistent in its approach." Given its limited financial support, the governing board appeared to be functioning "as well as can be expected." The New York City Commission on Human Rights (CCHR) also reported positive changes at Ocean Hill–Brownsville schools. The governing board appointed, over the objections of the UFT, five new principals: one white, two black, one Chinese, and the first Puerto Rican in the city. The Latino principal, Luis Fuentes, struggled to gain the support of the teachers, but, according to the CCHR, he "quickly gained the respect of the students, parents and the community." By establishing a rapport with Spanish-speaking parents, the principal served students for whom English was a second language. Parent participation increased dramatically as a result of his efforts. The governing board also implemented several programs to support literacy in the schools, including a bilingual reading campaign; trained more than three hundred parent aides; initiated several after-school programs; and created a community newspaper staffed by students. As a result of these efforts, many more parents and children were involved in their schools.[19]

Despite these successes, throughout the 1967–68 school year, the governing board and McCoy battled not only board of education officials but also with many teachers and administrators at local schools. Conflict between the governing board and local teachers began early in the experiment. Teachers envisioned the governing board as an advisory group that recommended—not implemented—changes in local schools. Teachers were involved in the planning of the Ocean Hill–Brownsville experiment, but most were inactive in the summer months leading up to the August elections. When the teachers returned to work, they found that the governing board had made significant progress in implementing its plan for community involvement. Several teachers joined the governing board in the fall of 1967, but most quickly resigned and accused the governing board of ignoring their views. The remaining governing board members responded that the teachers were critical of every aspect of community involvement. The teachers, Powis argued, were also upset about the selection of Rhody McCoy as unit administrator, because McCoy was not on the board of education's approved list for the position.[20]

While some teachers supported the idea of community "involvement," they opposed many aspects of the experimental district. UFT President Albert Shanker feared that community control would "Balkanize" the school system and allow a small but vocal neighborhood minority to dominate schools to the detriment of both students and teachers. Many teachers, fearful of losing their recently hard-won pay increases and job protections, opposed any change in the system. Teachers also objected to many of the decisions made by McCoy and the governing board with regard to curriculum and personnel, particularly hiring teachers and principals outside of the approved lists. Administrator McCoy made what some teachers felt were arbitrary decisions regarding assignments, and some simply refused to follow his directives. In September 1967, the UFT staged a twelve-day citywide strike concerning operations at city schools. Though the strike did not directly raise the issue of community control, those involved in the experiment believed that the strike was directed at them. Ocean Hill–Brownsville schools remained open during the strike, staffed by volunteers.[21]

Conflict between the governing board and certain teachers increased throughout the 1967–68 school year, and on May 9, 1968, the governing board sent notices to thirteen teachers and six supervisory personnel, accusing them of subverting the community control program. The letters informed these staff that their services were no longer required, and they were directed to the board of education to find other positions. The UFT argued that the governing board's actions were in contravention of the collective bargaining agreement, and School Superintendent Bernard Donovan agreed, immediately reinstating them. But the governing board refused to grant the teachers permission to return to work, and parents in Ocean Hill and Brownsville supported the governing board's actions. On May 15, as a result of several demonstrations against the reinstatements at Ocean Hill–Brownsville schools, the board of education closed three of the eight schools in the district. A week later, 350 of the teachers in the district went on strike in support of the ousted employees. On June 20, Unit Administrator McCoy sent dismissal notices to all 350 striking teachers.[22]

Negotiations throughout the summer failed to resolve the dispute, and 93 percent of the city's teachers walked out on September 9, 1968. The board of education promised to immediately reinstate the teachers who wanted to return to their Ocean Hill–Brownsville schools, and the teachers agreed to return to work on September 11. But again the governing board refused to accept the directives of the board of education and rejected the reinstatement of the teachers who, in its opinion, had "voluntarily left our children for seven weeks last year." Over the summer, with the support of the BCC, the governing board recruited dozens of teachers to replace those who were released for striking the prior spring. They were predominantly young and inexperienced, but they believed in the idea of community control. According to the governing board, there was a waiting list of teachers who wanted to teach in Ocean Hill–Brownsville schools, and in early fall it reported that "Our 8 schools are all open and operating beautifully for the first time. We hope to now be able to work in a peaceful relationship with our teachers for a new day in educational excellence."[23]

As a result of the governing board's refusal to reinstate the teachers, the UFT called a second strike, which began on September 13 and lasted through September 30. Brownsville schools continued operating during the strike with replacement teachers. When Mayor John Lindsay agreed to station New York police at Ocean Hill–Brownsville schools to protect the returning teachers, the UFT agreed to end the second strike. But the governing board refused to allow the striking teachers to return to the classroom. McCoy told the returning teachers that they had to take a "sensitivity" course before reinstatement. Several Ocean Hill–Brownsville schools allowed the teachers into their buildings, but administrators did not give them classroom assignments. When teachers entered the schools, tensions increased. The teachers who supported the governing board ostracized the returning teachers, and protesters outside the schools attempted to intimidate them.[24]

Figure 24. Confrontation between teachers and community control advocates. Paul Chandler is in center of picture. Courtesy United Federation of Teachers Archives, UFT Photo Collection. Robert F. Wagner Labor Archives, New York University.

During October, conflicts at Ocean Hill–Brownsville schools became an everyday occurrence. Several schools had large police forces and rows of barricades to separate the factions from each other and from the students. One former student remembered that "we'd look out on the rooftops, across the street from the school the cops were there with their riot helmets and their nightsticks and helicopters, and the playground was converted into a precinct, and walking up to the school you just have mass confusion." On October 1, police arrested six people after an altercation outside of JHS 271, the center of the conflict in Ocean Hill. Prior to the arrests, several hundred residents massed outside the school to protest the returning teachers and to prevent their entrance into the building. The confrontation continued even after several teachers supporting community control asked the protesters to disband. Because of tensions outside the school, the board of education closed JHS 271 for several days during the fall.[25]

As a result of the strikes, racial tensions escalated in Brownsville and across the city to the point that Mayor Lindsay publicly voiced his fears that a riot would occur. Even though 70 percent of the Ocean Hill–Brownsville replacement teachers were white and 50 percent were Jewish, many viewed the conflict between the UFT and the governing board as a battle between white and black (and Puerto Rican). Black and Latino parents accused the teachers of racism, both for walking out and for failing to effectively teach their children while in the schools. Racial strain increased dramatically when the UFT called attention to several anti-Semitic flyers that were distributed throughout Brownsville and in several schools. The origin of these flyers was hotly disputed, but the UFT used them to rally support behind its cause. The most widely read document demanded that all the Jewish teachers resign and threatened the teachers with violence. "Get Out, Stay Out, Staff Off, Shut Up, Get Off Our Backs, Or Your Relatives in the Middle East Will Find Themselves Giving Benefits to Raise Money To Help You Get Out From Under The Terrible Weight Of An Enraged Black Community." The union distributed 500,000 copies of the flyer, and, as a result of its inflammatory statements, the New York Association of Rabbis and the Jewish Anti-Defamation League became actively involved in the strike. Other Jewish groups, such as the American Jewish Committee and the American Jewish Congress, also followed the strike closely.[26]

The governing board publicly stated that it never condoned anti-Semitism in any form and that the UFT was using these documents to kill the experimental district. The board cited a New York Civil Liberties Union report, which found no connection between the anti-Semitic statements and the governing board. "They looked through all their files for anything that was anti-Semitic or antiwhite from any district in the city . . . and most never came from Ocean Hill–Brownsville," said John Powis. "They created in this city a fear . . . that here was a bunch of crazy people that were determined to take over the schools." The charges of anti-Semitism badly hurt the community control effort. "We were the bad guys now, and they were the good guys," remembered Paul Chandler. According to Maurice Reid, race was not an important issue in the deliberations of the governing board but the UFT used the issue to weaken the experimental district. Union leaders were looking for a way to gain the support of New Yorkers, "so they reached out to things that were said or done by folks that really were not involved directly in the day-to-day operation of the district or the decision-making of the district to make it seem that this was a black-white issue." The experimental district attracted activists of many differing ideologies. Jitu Weusi, a JHS 271 teacher, was prominent in the battle, and he created a major controversy when he read one of his student's poems on WBAI radio. Most New Yorkers viewed the poem, titled "Anti-Semitism, Dedicated to Albert Shanker," as a direct attack on Jews. Weusi argued that the poem expressed feelings that deserved recognition, but the incident galvanized support for the teachers.[27]

Throughout the months of September and October, board of education officials waffled, sometimes stating that the governing board was never officially recognized and sometimes working with the governing board to achieve a resolution to the dispute. While classes continued in Ocean Hill–Brownsville, most of the city's schools were paralyzed. The board of education officials pleaded with government officials to intervene, asking Mayor Lindsay as well as the New York State School Commissioner, James Allen, to resolve the conflict. The board of education suspended and reinstated the governing board several times, but the community control effort continued in Ocean Hill—Brownsville schools.[28]

BCC staff and board members were active participants and leaders in this struggle, and several were arrested in protests at local schools. During the conflict, BCC staff members helped organize parent volunteers in the classrooms, pulled together groups of protesters to support the governing board at local schools, and published several "fact sheets" on the conflict. One such missive stated that "Albert Shanker is a power hungry dictator whose agents (19 teachers) deliberately undermined the programs in the Ocean Hill–Brownsville school district in an attempt to sabotage and destroy the demonstration district and thereby declare community control a failure." According to striking teachers, BCC leaders were instigators in many violent altercations. They accused BCC President Thelma Hamilton of spreading a false rumor that police had shot a child during a school protest, and they also claimed that Hamilton, accompanied by Sonny Carson of the Brooklyn CORE, went into a school and threatened teachers with physical harm. BCC board member BCC Marley, according to striking teachers, grabbed the camera of a teacher and went after another teacher with a beer can. The strikers charged Major Owens with condoning violence against teachers by supporting the workers who attacked striking teachers. "How is it possible," they asked, "that federal funds are given to such men," who "incite riots, intimidate people," and "assault teachers." Owens, the teachers complained, backed these people. "[Y]et," said one critic, "he is now a City Commissioner in overall charge of anti-poverty groups around the city. Is it any wonder, then, that attacks by anti-poverty workers on teachers have become even more intense this school year?"[29]

The BCC and the governing board were so closely connected that several people protested to federal officials about the affiliation. Congressman Emmanuel Celler received several letters objecting to the federal government's support of the BCC and, indirectly, the governing board. Celler, who actively supported the UFT, also protested the activities of the BCC to the Office of Economic Opportunity. OEO officials, however, cognizant that the BCC's involvement was in accordance with the principle of "Maximum Feasible Participation," responded that BCC staff and leaders had every right to join in this struggle. "We are not unmindful of the complaints of those who infer that local anti-poverty workers should be restrained from endeavoring to provision certain communities with substitute educational outlets during the ongoing teachers' strike," reasoned the OEO staff. "But, at the same time, as citizens and members of the community, anti-poverty workers cannot ignore the legitimate and explicit concerns and objectives of the community they serve. Such concerns have been manifested in attempts to provide children of some communities with the education they are now being denied because of the school dispute."[30]

On October 14, citing concern over the safety of its teachers, the UFT struck New York City schools for the third time in two months. The strike lasted until November 19, when the board of education secured the intervention of New York State Education Commissioner Allen, who suspended the governing board and put the Ocean Hill–Brownsville school district under state trusteeship. The trustee reinstated the teachers, transferred three principals, and ran the schools for four months, at the conclusion of which he reinstated the governing board. Soon after that, however, the New York state legislature adopted a school decentralization plan that created thirty districts across the city, each with approximately twenty thousand students. The bill was strongly supported by the UFT; but most community control advocates opposed the plan, because it resulted in districts too large for significant experimentation with parental control and protected the established system of advancement for teachers and administrators. And the decentralization legislation eliminated the Ocean Hill–Brownsville experimental district.[31]

The crisis at Ocean Hill–Brownsville was a major event in New York City, capturing the fervent attention of the local media, civic leaders, and local politicians. The conflict caused a serious rift among the city's liberals. Many of the organizations that supported the Brownsville residents during the Beth-El strike were now divided between the teachers and the neighborhood. In 1962 the Jewish Labor Committee, the American Jewish Congress, the AFL-CIO, the NAACP, the Urban League, the Anti-Defamation League, and several other groups had formed a mighty coalition to support Brownsville workers in their battle with Beth-El hospital management. By 1968, many of these groups were on opposite sides—the AFL-CIO understandably supported the UFT, one of its strongest members, while leaders of the newly independent Brooklyn CORE were active in support of the governing board. Many other organizations, in particular the NAACP and the American Jewish Congress, found themselves paralyzed—sympathizing with competing causes. Journalists and other commentators still refer to the conflict as the breaking point of the "liberal coalition" of civil rights groups and Jewish organizations. Many argue that the wounds exposed during the battle for community control have yet to heal.[32]

Like the Beth-El strike, the Ocean Hill–Brownsville crisis galvanized the community. Once apathetic residents followed the negotiations closely and participated in the demonstrations at local schools. Parents who were not active in their schools became teachers' aides and nonprofessional assistants. In the end, despite their efforts, the expectations of these residents to create a system to support the educational needs of local children were frustrated because local activists overestimated their ability to outmaneuver politically powerful organizations such as the UFT and the board of education. Once outsiders, by 1968 New York's teachers were an organized force capable of commanding support from New York's labor organizations and local politicians. No government institution in the city was more entrenched than the board of education. The community control program envisioned by Brownsville activists directly threatened the power of these institutions, and made the conflict inevitable.

Historian Jerald Podair argues that the conflict affected not only New York schools but all city residents by destroying the illusion that New York was a pluralist society whose residents shared core values. The struggle over community control became a focal point for advocates of varying ideologies. Black Power advocates saw the community control movement as the vanguard of efforts to create an "Afrocentric" curriculum that, they believed, was better attuned to the needs of blacks. Leftist intellectuals saw it as a means to empower poor Americans through political engagement. Others saw the idea as the end of the liberal experiment, because it contradicted the ideals of opportunity and merit. They worried that community control would result in a system that awarded political connections to the detriment of quality. Critics also warned that community-based power increased the parochialism of education in the city and suppressed minority rights. While many New Yorkers had prided themselves on the "humanism" of the city's residents, by the late 1960s whites and blacks had widely divergent views on the meaning of terms like "equality," "pluralism," and "middle-class." The 1968 teachers' strike, Podair concluded, exposed these conflicts, and they have yet to be resolved.[33]

While the debates around community control continue to draw attention from many perspectives, to Brownsville activists the battle for public schools posed much more mundane concerns. Unlike intellectuals who joined the effort, most Brownsville parents were not focused on the larger philosophical meanings of community control. They were seeking to move a gigantic bureaucracy forward in the hopes of improving education for their children. Most Brownsville residents rejected efforts to subsume the battle for local schools under a broader agenda of race-based ideology. In March 1969, the leaders of the Detroit-based "Republic of Africa" announced that the group would hold elections in Ocean Hill and Brownsville. The goal was to consolidate black ghettos and rural areas into a self-governing federation. As a focal point of racial conflict, Brownsville was an attractive place to begin the movement, the leaders believed. But when they attempted to organize the area, they were rebuffed by the overwhelming majority of residents. "People told them 'I'm an American, and that's where I'm staying,'" Paul Chandler recalled. The goal of residents was to secure greater accountability from local government, not to establish a competing infrastructure.[34]

The majority of Brownsville blacks and Latinos continued to hold to the ideals of an integrated, pluralist society. Thousands left the neighborhood in the 1960s and 1970s in search of integrated neighborhoods. But the reality of segregated schools in the late 1960s made activists modify their goals to those they believed were more achievable. The failure of Brownsville residents to secure what they thought were reasonable requests to influence their children's education was a bitter pill to swallow. Yet it did not end the efforts to improve the community.

Figure 25. Loew's Pitkin Theater. The theater closed in the 1970s. Courtesy Jeffrey D. Hoeh.

9

A Modern Ghetto? Brownsville since 1970

On June 11, 1970, Richard Green and Charles Wheel, two Brownsville residents fed up with the failure of the Sanitation Department to pick up the neighborhood's trash, set fire to a large pile of garbage in front of their building. Green and Wheel were then arrested, setting in motion what would be called the "Brownsville Trash Riots." Over the next two days, dozens of people set fires, smashed windows, and looted stores in the neighborhood. Garbage pickup in the area, always irregular, had become increasingly sporadic—from pickups six days a week to no more than twice a week by 1970. Because of the density of population and the amount of trash produced daily, the inconsistent schedule made it impossible to keep the streets clean. Sanitation Department representatives faulted broken equipment for the decline in services, stating that 30 percent of the city's garbage trucks were out of service at any given time.[1]

But Brownsville residents blamed local government and argued that the Sanitation Department neglected the area because the residents had no political clout. In addition, residents asserted, sanitation workers and their union discriminated against the neighborhood, refusing to work there because they felt it was unsafe. Brownsville residents had complained about the trash situation for years, and the Brownsville Community Council organized several demonstrations that spring, to no avail. In the summer of 1970, peaceful protests turned violent. Several stores were destroyed on Sutter Avenue, and many owners said they would not return to the neighborhood. "We were fire-bombed two weeks ago and we've been held up 30 times in the last two years," said Arthur Janholovits, owner of Key Food Store. His grocery store would not reopen. Along Sutter Avenue, Pitkin Avenue, and other commercial strips, vacant stores proliferated. By 1970, only five of the sixteen shops on the 100 block of Sutter Avenue were operating.[2]

While most Brownsville residents did not support the violence, they were quick to note that the riots had resulted in greater attention from Mayor John Lindsay and the Sanitation Department. "You see every sanitation truck in the city here this morning," one youth told a reporter. Despite the increased effort, the trash situation in Brownsville remained severe. Years of garbage had piled up in the streets and in the hundreds of lots left vacant by yet-to-be-completed urban renewal projects. Brownsville residents were justifiably skeptical about statements of concern by city officials. They had heard them before. "It's a damned disgrace," said BCC president Henry Fuller. "Everybody gives you lots of words and reports upon reports that wind up on somebody's desk. We're the most deprived community in the whole city—deprived in every shape and form imaginable."[3]

In contrast to other urban conflagrations that were criticized by New York's press, most of the city's newspapers were sympathetic to the Brownsville protesters. Pete Hamill wrote in his *New York Post* column that the garbage burning was a "civilized measure" that was "the act of people who felt the city had abandoned them." Since the city had failed to serve the neighborhood, Brownsville residents, in Hamill's view, "reacted the same way the middle-class would have reacted: they did the job themselves." A follow-up article in the *New York Times* verified the predictions of Brownsville residents, reporting that "two weeks, three days and several extra garbage pickups since . . . the Brooklyn neighborhood remains filthy." The main thoroughfares like Pitkin Avenue witnessed some short-term improvements, but the smaller streets remained deep in refuse. While city officials did increase collections in the area, BCC leaders reported that the number of sanitation trucks fell far short of the need. A BCC report on sanitation in the area calculated that 175 sanitation trucks were required to adequately serve the neighborhood, but only 140 were made available. Exacerbating the problem, more than half of these trucks were often out of service.[4]

In the fall of 1970, following the Trash Riots, the BCC held a news conference to announce that the group would ask the government to designate Brownsville a federal disaster area. Local leaders joined with officials of the Brooklyn Model Cities program to request additional financial assistance from the government. "This is a disaster area, no question about it," said BCC spokesman Bill Marley. "Many of the buildings here are occupied although they have no water. And with cold weather coming on, they have no heat." The group protested the recent federal cuts in the Community Action Program, which would, they argued, result in the layoff of nineteen BCC staffers. The organization never did officially apply for disaster designation, but it did prevent the proposed budget cuts in the short term, as city funds replaced some of the decrease in federal support.[5]

The following May, Brownsville erupted once again. This time the violence grew out of a planned, nonviolent protest against state budget cuts that drastically scaled back public assistance, Medicaid, and other payments to New York's poor. In response to the cuts, BCC leader Maurice Reid organized a demonstration blocking traffic at the corner of Stone and Sutter Avenues. Several thousand people turned out to hear speakers and participate in the citywide "Strike Day" called by the Black Coalition. Most local stores, informed in advance of the rally, were closed. The protest began peacefully, but when the police attempted to clear the intersection, several young men scuffled with the officers. The conflict quickly escalated: a number of young men set fires in abandoned cars and buildings in the area; others looted Brownsville stores. By the end of the day, firemen had fought more than one hundred fires, at least twenty of them major. Forty-two people were arrested, at least twenty residents were injured, and eighteen policemen were hurt. Thirteen firemen also received medical treatment. Most of them were injured by bottles, rocks, and other objects thrown at them by rioters.[6]

For the rest of the summer, reporters for city papers ventured into the neighborhood to describe its demoralized state. Many journalists treated Brownsville as though it were an exotic foreign land and they anthropologists studying the natives. Their articles portrayed Brownsville's problems in dramatic terms, arguing that "private enterprise has almost completely withdrawn" and reporting, incorrectly, that "four of five families are on welfare." Columnists compared the neighborhood to an ancient archeological site and portrayed Brownsville residents as "hardy ghosts among the ruins." The reporters were educated by local residents, who told them that they had been "pushed to the point of desperation." Area leaders talked of "genocide" in describing the treatment of local residents by New York government. Mayor Lindsay took several big-city mayors on a tour of the neighborhood, and they proclaimed it the worst place they had ever seen. Mayor Kevin White of Boston called Brownsville "the first tangible sign of the collapse of our civilization." Anarchy ruled the area, according to reporters. Looting became a "condition of life," accepted by residents as a viable means of existence.[7]

Throughout the 1970s, local reporters returned often to Brownsville to file similar reports. The articles became increasingly repetitive as each recited the litany of problems—decrepit housing, spiraling crime and drug abuse, failing schools—afflicting Brownsville. Reporters often compared the neighborhood's condition to the old Jewish neighborhood and found present-day Brownsville wanting in every respect, and it was not difficult for them to find a former resident who would wax nostalgic about old Brownsville. "It is hard for a visitor not to notice the rubble and the remnants of the elegance that once was," one reporter stated. "The Loew's Pitkin Theater, at the corner of Legion Street, still looms over the scene, but its Baroque glory has faded." The more insightful stories noted that the working-class Jewish community had also struggled with crime and other social problems, but most drew the same conclusions: "once a temperate Jewish ghetto, Brownsville today is little more than char, rubble, filth and the residue of violence."[8]

In the early 1900s, Brooklyn's upstanding citizens looked upon the rough, dirty Brownsville neighborhood with disdain, and since 1970, many New Yorkers continued to view the area as a place to be avoided. In addition to the dirty streets that plagued the neighborhood for decades, Brownsville schools remained overcrowded and underfunded, and Brownsville residents continued to struggle with intermittent employment, juvenile delinquency, and violent crime. However, while much remained the same, several aspects of Brownsville society changed. Brownsville's indices of crime, delinquency, and health, always among the city's worst, became firmly entrenched at the bottom of New York City's registers. Brownsville residents were far behind their peers in every quality-of-life measurement. In 1970, the area's poverty rate was the highest in the city, and its crime rate ranked second. Modern Brownsville became a symbol of urban blight, drawing journalists from around the world to study the neighborhood.

But the story was more complicated than the stereotypical tale of an urban "underclass." While Brownsville dwellings and businesses declined in the 1970s, much of the neighborhood's housing and commercial sector was rebuilt in the 1980s and 1990s. New construction, supported by public funds, created new opportunities for working-class residents. Brownsville continued to serve the same function it had for a century: it was a transitory neighborhood for working-class New Yorkers. With half the population it had in 1920, Brownsville continued to face many serious problems. Crime, poverty, drug addiction, and other types of social distress plagued the area, and only recently improved. But while the neighborhood struggles against political and social apathy, many community institutions continue to work for area improvements. Brownsville has remained a poor neighborhood with all the promise and problems common to such areas.

Urban Renewal and the Destruction of Brownsville

Little remains of the Brownsville built in the early 1900s. A few synagogues, schools, and some large apartment buildings are scattered throughout the area, and several blocks of single- and two-family homes along the southern and western fringes still exist. These, in addition to the stores of Pitkin Avenue, are the only reminders of the old neighborhood. During the 1950s, 1960s, and 1970s, property neglect and abandonment ravaged the area. As the number of very poor families in the neighborhood increased, Brownsville's housing stock declined precipitously, forcing the city to take over dozens of buildings to prevent their further deterioration. Many of the buildings were not salvageable, and the city demolished them. As a result, Brownsville's population declined by a staggering 35 percent in the 1970s, as twenty-five thousand people settled elsewhere. Visitors to Brownsville in the 1970s compared it to Dresden, Germany, after World War II.

No aspect of Brownsville's decline was more deplorable than the failure of the city-sponsored urban renewal program. In 1961, the City Planning Commission picked a half-mile area in southern Brownsville to participate in a program of new construction and rehabilitation. Brownsville residents lobbied hard for the designation, believing that it would bring new resources to the area. Local activists had no idea how much damage the urban renewal program would cause to the neighborhood over the next three decades. With Brownsville housing already dilapidated, the much-delayed program resulted in decreased apartment maintenance and increased housing abandonment in the renewal area, because landlords would not invest in units soon to be demolished. During the late 1960s and early 1970s, dozens of blocks of housing disappeared, along with thousands of people that occupied them. A 1973 report concluded that the result of the program's failure was that "Brownsville has never really been renewed. . . . Urban renewal has fostered rapid and irreversible decay in those areas which the City had intended to save."[9]

Brownsville's urban renewal program was beset with problems from the beginning, and government officials stymied Brownsville residents' attempts to participate in the process. City planners delayed presenting specific renewal proposals for years, and Brownsville's housing continued to decline during the interim. Throughout the 1960s, planning officials constantly defended themselves against charges of delinquency in the management of Brownsville's renewal. In 1966, residents forced Brooklyn Borough President Abe Stark to intervene and push the planning staff along to prevent the federal government from withdrawing its share of funding. Some five years after the formal designation, planning officials were just finishing the "Preliminary Final Plan" for submission to the City Planning Commission.[10]

In 1967, six years after the area was designated an urban renewal area, planners announced an initiative to spend $72 million on 2,000 new units and 458 rehabilitated apartments in the area. The most significant project in the urban renewal area was the Noble Drew Ali Plaza, a development sponsored by the Brownsville Community Council and the Moorish Science Temple, a local Muslim institution, that would provide 385 units of housing. A second development was the Riverdale and Osborne Towers, a middle-income complex with two nine-story buildings to be built by the Brownsville Housing Association, a coalition of local religious groups. Both projects were funded by the Federal Housing Administration under its new Section 236 program for urban development, with attempts to house low-income and middle-income families together by basing rents on income levels. These projects, however, opened more than ten years after the urban renewal designation.[11]

In addition to bureaucratic inefficiency, the urban renewal area competed from the beginning with the plans of the newly formed Central Brooklyn Model Cities program (CMBC). Created in 1967 by the city to secure funds under the federal Model Cities Demonstration Act, the Central Brooklyn Model Cities district included all of Brownsville, Bedford-Stuyvesant, and a large part of East New York. The leaders of the CMBC chose a different area of priority for Brownsville, and in 1968 they announced their own "Marcus Garvey Urban Renewal Area," which covered the whole northwestern quarter of the neighborhood. The group planned to build 3,000 new apartments and to acquire 1,000 dilapidated apartments for rehabilitation. Thus Brownsville's two urban renewal areas together represented more than half the acreage of the neighborhood.[12]

The Model Cities plan was part of a larger effort to revitalize the city's slum areas. In 1969, the City Planning Commission completed a comprehensive study of every neighborhood in the five boroughs. Titled the *Plan for New York City*, it proposed spending several billion dollars on the renewal of neighborhoods throughout the city. Calling itself a new approach to city planning, the report criticized the prior efforts of government officials, arguing that "projects were not coordinated with each other or with new schools, adequate recreation space, health facilities or job training. The buildings replaced slums, but they helped institutionalize poverty and the ghetto." The report also blamed city welfare agencies for making Brownsville a "dumping area for many of the city's poor." The decline of Brownsville's housing was clearly evident by the time the plan was completed. According to city officials, the city demolished five hundred Brownsville tenement buildings during the 1960s, causing the dislocation of thousands of tenants. To replace these units, the plan trumpeted the Marcus Garvey Urban Renewal Area, but it ignored the original urban renewal district. Planners envisioned a total of 3,600 new apartments and the rehabilitation of 600 apartment units of low- and middle-income housing. To complement improved housing, the plan proposed additional recreation centers, early childhood facilities, a "multi-service center" for welfare families, as well as elementary and intermediate schools for the area. Despite all these proposals, no new housing opened in this period. Brownsville was the subject of much planning but little actual development.[13]

After numerous complaints about delays in the urban renewal process, in 1973 the State Study Commission for New York City commenced an examination of the program in Brownsville. In a scathing fifty-page report, the commission criticized every aspect of urban renewal management, accusing the city of demolishing thousands of units of housing and dislocating hundreds of families while failing to complete a single unit of new housing in the twelve years since the designation. "Block after block has been left vacant for years, forming a wasteland of gutted carcasses of buildings and rat-filled rubble," the study asserted. The original proposal recommended that most of the units in the urban renewal area be "conserved"—rehabilitated instead of demolished. However, because the city failed to submit renewal plans to the federal government until 1968, and because of difficulties in administering and managing rehabilitation, large numbers of previously sound buildings deteriorated beyond redemption. As of January 1973, only 13 buildings out of 236 originally designated for renewal had been rehabilitated. Almost all the units originally designated for renewal had been demolished.[14]

The city's code enforcement program, meant to force landlords to maintain these buildings, exacerbated the area's decline. Urban renewal officials announced in the early 1960s that the city would acquire properties that had been allowed to deteriorate. This notice served as an incentive for property owners to allow their units to decline further and then to sell them to the city—frequently, according to the report, at a price "in excess of the market price which they could realize, given the rapid deterioration of the neighborhood." By the time the city acquired the buildings on the renewal site, most were in serious disrepair. City officials hoped to secure additional funding in the future to build new housing, so they decided to demolish the buildings rather than hold them for rehabilitation. In the early 1970s, however, federal support for housing construction declined and these parcels lay vacant, many for more than two decades. Other property owners abandoned their buildings to the Federal Housing Administration (FHA), which held their mortgages. The FHA demolished several of these properties because they were imminently dangerous, and this added to the decline of the area. They became trash-strewn lots where people abandoned cars and other junk, as well as havens for drug addicts and prostitutes.[15]

While accurate in depicting the city's mismanagement of the urban renewal program, the 1973 report ignored several other issues contributing to the decline of Brownsville's housing stock. Landlords allowed area buildings to decline for several reasons, and racism played an important role in their decisions. Many building owners had lived in the neighborhood when it was white, and they felt a greater obligation to maintain buildings occupied by people they knew. As the owners became "absentee landlords," and their long-standing tenants left to be replaced by blacks and Latinos, their feelings of responsibility to the area declined. Other, nonracial, factors were also relevant to Brownsville's abandonment. Many landlords sold their buildings in the 1960s, and the new owners soon realized that the income they were receiving was declining while the maintenance needs were increasing. Rental payments became even less consistent in the 1960s, because tenants faced periodic financial crises and because welfare agencies were slow to forward public benefits. Declining revenues made it difficult for even the most conscientious owners to maintain their buildings. The urban renewal designation added to the area's stigmatization, and as a result many landlords stopped spending money on repairs and waited for the city to bail them out.[16]

In 1973, the *New York Post* published a six-part series describing life in Brownsville, focusing on the trials and tribulations of the Harris family, a married couple and their five children who lived in the urban renewal zone.

Long neglected by its landlord, the Harrises' apartment on Howard Street was among the worst of the units remaining in the renewal area. There were "gaping holes in the floor and ceiling," and paint was "so old and faded that the original color [was] hardly recognizable." The building next door, though it had no rear wall, still housed several people. "Some blocks are so scarred with half burned, half demolished structures they have the eerie appearance of an ancient ruin," the reporters stated. Like many other Brownsville residents, the Harrises placed their hopes on reaching the top of the long public housing waiting list. "The projects are better for the kids. . . . They paint every three years and the rent is okay and the gas and electricity isn't so high." Unfortunately, the *Post* reported, given that 155,000 New Yorkers were on the waiting list, the Harrises' chances were slim.[17]

Throughout the 1970s, the increasing number of vacant and declining properties became the site for a troubling increase in fires, at least some of them deliberately set. While Brownsville did not experience the coordinated "arson-for-profit" destruction of blocks that occurred in the Bronx, fires were frequent in area apartments. Brownsville's housing stock, especially the most decrepit units, had long been fire hazards, and fire officials noted that most blazes occurred because of faulty electrical wiring. Local youths also set many fires, sometimes as retaliation against a member of a rival gang or to punish people who had informed on them. Fires occurred mostly in what fire officials described as vacant buildings, but vacancy was difficult to determine, because many extremely poor persons lived in buildings with no windows or roofs. In August 1972, the city papers reported a sensational story of one woman who claimed to have set more than two thousand fires in the Brownsville area. The woman, a heroin addict who lived on Belmont Avenue, said that she had been lighting two to four fires a week for more than twelve years because she "liked to see flames and got a thrill from watching the fire equipment rolling up to a burning building" (she claimed that she would torch buildings only after she inspected them to make sure they were vacant). While all the city's newspapers picked up the story, neither the reporters nor the police were able to substantiate her tale.[18]

Fires destroyed dozens of local buildings, but others declined more slowly, with their tenantry intact. During the 1970s, property neglect forced the city to take over thousands of vacant and occupied buildings in Harlem, the South Bronx, Bedford-Stuyvesant, and Brownsville to prevent further destruction of these areas. Under city law, buildings could be taken by the city if they had tax delinquency in excess of three years. In 1976, the city council changed the law to allow seizure after one year. While officials hoped that this action would spur owners to pay up badly needed tax revenues in the midst of the city's financial crisis, the opposite occurred: hundreds of landlords abandoned their buildings. By the early 1980s, New York City, through its Department of Housing Preservation Development (HPD), managed four thousand buildings across the city comprising more than twenty-six thousand units. The city also held an additional twenty thousand units in vacant buildings. Forced to become the landlord of last resort, the city attempted to bring occupied buildings up to code standards, to rehabilitate structurally sound buildings, and to demolish those that were unsalvageable. From the late 1970s through the 1980s, more than $200 million annually in city funds subsidized the operations of the department.[19]

Within Brownsville, housing abandonment accelerated during the decade. In 1970 there were 31,793 occupied housing units within Community Planning District 16 (which includes Brownsville and Ocean Hill). In 1980, only 23,815 remained, a decrease of 25 percent. At the same time, the number of vacant housing units increased from 1,634 to 3,380. In 1979 the HPD estimated that more than 60 percent of the units in Community District 16 were either held by the city or at risk of becoming city property.[20]

In order to reduce the demands on its overextended administration, the HPD created several programs to promote private management and ownership of the properties in receivership. The authority turned over several buildings to the tenants to manage, with the expectation that they would become cooperatives. Another program, the Community Management Program, released city properties to local nonprofit corporations. These groups also received funding through the federal Community Development Block Grant Program to rehabilitate the units. One Brownsville agency to participate in this program was the Ocean Hill–Brownsville Tenants Association. Founded in the late 1960s by Father John Powis and other activists, the group originally sought to compel private landlords to improve building services. When many local buildings became city property, the association pressured the city to allow the tenants to manage the units. By 1979, the association controlled twelve buildings with 250 units. Local residents rehabilitated the buildings with support from federal job training programs, and many Brownsville residents served as maintenance workers. The group owned and operated more than 2,000 units by the 1990s. The association also helped create more than 200 low-income cooperative units in the area.[21]

During the late 1970s, nonprofit companies completed several other housing developments in Brownsville, all with government subsidies. But fewer than 500 units were produced by local groups in the late 1970s, and they did not compensate for the more than 8,000 units lost to abandonment. While urban renewal and Model Cities officials celebrated these successes, they continued to fend off criticism about inefficiency and corruption in their programs. In 1975, city officials announced the funding of the Noble Drew Ali Plaza II, a $27.4 million, 584-unit project adjacent to the original buildings completed in 1973. However, that same year the development was tabled when the FHA foreclosed on the mortgage of Noble Drew Ali Plaza I. For the next eight years, state and federal officials alleged corruption in the management of the project, but they filed no charges. The second project did not open until 1987 (completed by another developer), twelve years after it was approved.[22]

New York City's public housing also underwent significant changes, many of which affected Brownsville units. In the early 1970s, congressional amendments to the program set rents in public housing at 25 percent of tenant income (later raised to 30 percent), and this change brought about an increase in rent to those with good incomes and a decrease in rent to those on assistance. As a result, many working families, who could find better housing at the same high prices, moved out. The percentage of public housing tenants on public assistance increased and caused a decline in NYCHA revenues. While federal subsidies made up some of the gap, with rents no longer covering operating expenses maintenance suffered accordingly. Within Brownsville, as in other projects, elevators broke down, upkeep of public space ceased, and other facilities deteriorated. Broken windows and lights went for months without replacement. These policy changes also exacerbated the racial and economic segregation of public housing by pushing working families out of the projects.[23]

Brownsville's vacant lots and crumbling tenements continued to provide development opportunities for the NYCHA. In 1975, the authority opened the Marcus Garvey Houses, one of the few efforts to change the dismal architecture of Brownsville public housing. Working with the Institute for Architecture and Urban Studies, the project attempted to provide, according to architectural historian Robert A. M. Stern, "high density settlement in low-rise structures that would revive the successful urbanism of the traditional city." The Marcus Garvey Houses, completed in 1975, consisted of 909 units in a six-square-block area. The buildings were four-story, townhouse-like structures, and parts of the development were turned inward to create a "mews." The idea was to create public spaces that could be defended and used by project residents, unlike the sterile, dangerous open spaces typical of high-rise public housing. In the construction process, housing officials eliminated some amenities like front stoops and balconies that would have helped to create positive use of the public spaces, and the NYCHA increased the density of the project to allow more units. In later years, architectural critics noted that the buildings were better maintained than most public projects, but that the complex was only a moderate success in meeting the goal of integrating the housing into the neighborhood. The prospective tenants of the Marcus Garvey Houses were pleased with the apartments, and thousands applied for admission. This development, along with the Noble Drew Ali Plaza and the Riverdale and Osborne Towers, completed in 1973, all provided desperately needed new housing in the area, but Brownsville's housing needs were still increasing at a time when federal housing support declined.[24]

In 1977, Roger Starr, New York's housing development administrator, created a short-lived furor when he recommended that the city cut back services in certain areas—he pointed to Brownsville in particular—so that the government could focus resources on neighborhoods that were still salvageable. In the midst of the fiscal crisis that almost put New York in bankruptcy, Starr argued that the administration did not have the money to maintain services in all the city's troubled sections, and that it would be better to allow certain areas to lose their population so that the government could focus its efforts. Residents in areas like Brownsville would receive "inducements" to move to other neighborhoods, and the areas they left would remain vacant "until new land uses present themselves," Starr reasoned.[25]

Many people were offended by Starr's suggestions of "planned shrinkage," and charitable organizations, the press, and other government officials all criticized his proposal. While Starr's bosses distanced themselves from his remarks, the city was actually doing to Brownsville just what he proposed. In the 1970s, Brownsville's population declined by one-third, a net loss of twenty-five thousand persons. Some residents left because their economic prospects improved, and because the knot of housing segregation loosened a little during the decade. But many residents were forced out by government policies that exacerbated housing decline and denied other public services to the community. Brownsville was never an attractive neighborhood, but housing deterioration and abandonment marked the area as an urban wasteland.

Hitting Rock Bottom: Brownsville Society in the 1970s

The deterioration of Brownsville's infrastructure was just one aspect of the serious problems facing the neighborhood. In 1970, more than 30 percent of Brownsville residents earned incomes below the poverty level, and in several census tracts the percentage exceeded 40. In 1973, 30 percent of

Brownsville's males were unemployed. Twenty-five percent of area families were on public assistance in 1977. To provide for their dependents, many Brownsville residents operated in the underground economy, performing odd jobs and hustling to pay the bills. According to a 1973 *New York Post* report, one man made his money by street-peddling goods he bought through the mail. By frequently changing his address, the man was able to avoid paying for the goods. The opportunities of area residents were also limited by continuing discrimination. One *New York Post* informant worked as a print shop assistant for several years but lost his job because he was unable to join the printers union. "I never thought I would be on welfare," he said. "They say there's no jobs 'cause you need skills. And when you have the skills they say you need something else."[26]

Economic turmoil in Brownsville mirrored the problems facing many urban areas during the 1970s and 1980s. In his 1987 book *The Truly Disadvantaged*, William Julius Wilson describes the impact of the changing American economy of the 1970s on inner-city blacks. "Urban minorities have been particularly vulnerable to structural economic changes, such as the shift from goods-producing to service-producing industries, the increasing polarization of the labor market into low-wage and high-wage sectors, technological innovations, and the relocation of manufacturing industries out of the central cities," he asserts. Only a relatively small number of educated blacks, Wilson argues, participated in the expansion of the service and professional sectors, and they moved out of ghetto neighborhoods as soon as they could. The departure of middle-class blacks left the remaining residents with even fewer connections to the mainstream economy and society. Across the nation, the participation of black men in the labor force declined dramatically in the 1970s. Accelerating unemployment led to escalating poverty rates as well as to increasing crime and drug abuse.[27]

The restructuring of the American economy dramatically affected New York's industrial workers. New York City lost 525,000 manufacturing jobs between 1953 and 1980. As jobs moved to the N.Y. suburbs, the South, the West, and farther, the entry-level jobs needed by unskilled New York residents dried up. In 1975, 15 percent of New Yorkers lived below the federal poverty level. By 1987, the number increased to 23 percent of the population (twice the national average). Brownsville families were especially hard hit by the economic decline. Forty-two percent of Brownsville families lived in poverty in 1980. New York firms created 650,000 new jobs in the "service sectors" during these years, but many Brownsville residents did not have the required education or training to take advantage of these opportunities.[28]

Economic troubles were not new to Brownsville, but the extreme violence of the decade was. Disorder across the city increased dramatically during the 1970s. Except for 1978, the crime rate went up by more than 10 percent every year between 1974 and 1981. A record 1,841 people were killed in New York in 1981, and Brownsville was at the forefront of this crime wave. Throughout the 1970s, the Seventy-third Precinct was consistently among the fifteen worst divisions in the city, and near the top of the list in Brooklyn. Crimes against the person (murder, rape, robbery, and aggravated assault) were especially high in the area. Fifty-three people were murdered in the precinct in 1970, thirty-seven people in 1975 (tenth highest in the city), forty-six in 1976 (eighth), and thirty-one in 1977 (tenth). Brownsville's rates of robbery and aggravated assault were also among the worst in the city.[29]

The crime wave hit public housing projects severely. Between 1974 and 1975, crime within NYCHA housing rose at a rate three times faster than the city as a whole. NYCHA projects reported a crime rate of 18.4 per 1,000 persons in 1974, a rate that was probably much higher because crimes reported to the NYPD may not have been included in the housing authority's statistical records. As they did in the 1950s and 1960s, Brownsville projects continued to suffer crime more than the average in public units. The Van Dyke Houses rate of 28.9 crimes per 1,000 persons made it the seventeenth most dangerous project, and the Brownsville Houses and Langston Hughes Houses had rates of 23.5 and 24.3 respectively. Although the most dangerous projects during the 1970s were on the Lower East Side, in Harlem, and in the Bronx, Brownsville's projects were not far behind. Because of their notoriety, Brownsville projects were the focus on an important study by architect Oscar Newman. In his book *Defensible Space*, Newman used the Brownsville and Van Dyke projects, where violent crime was an everyday occurrence, to support his argument that high-rise buildings were more dangerous than low-rise structures.[30]

Despite the efforts of journalists to depict the neighborhood as bereft of hope, Brownsville retained the community activism that had marked the neighborhood for a century. The Brownsville Community Council continued to organize the neighborhood and fight for new services and economic opportunities throughout the early 1970s, and in 1971 the organization employed more than 350 residents. The battles of the late 1960s and early 1970s, however, took their toll on the group, and several activists, including founders Thelma Hamilton and Willa Webster, pulled away. "I guess if there was a weakness it was that there wasn't another generation behind them to keep the organization going," said Maurice Reid. "I think it was part of having the money." Government funding, in Reid's mind, took away some of the vibrancy of the organization. The BCC was no longer a grass-roots-based community group—it was part of New York's web of social service agencies. "The money spoiled us," said Reid. "It took away some of the enthusiasm to struggle until 2:00 in the morning." The 1973 State Study Commission Report on Urban Renewal in Brownsville criticized the organization for failing to protect the interests of local residents in the implementation of the urban renewal program. The BCC, the report argued, was more concerned with the fees it would receive as project sponsor than with the impact of the relocation process on Brownsville tenants.[31]

Throughout the 1960s the BCC avoided the debilitating internal disputes and charges of corruption that handcuffed other community action programs. But in 1973 the group received much unwanted attention because of a struggle for control that pitted local assemblyman Sam Wright against city administrator Major Owens. Wright, who had created his own local Democratic machine, had attempted for several years to garner control of the BCC. He succeeded in 1972 when his slate, led by Fred Wilson, won a majority of the seats on the board. However, the Community Development Agency (CDA), which oversaw the CAP program and was run by Owens, declared the elections null and void. The CDA ordered new elections, but Wilson canceled them, arguing that they had not been properly planned. At a subsequent vote, Wilson's slate once again carried the vote, and in the fall of 1973, the CDA voided the BCC's $2.5 million contract, declaring the elections "riddled with gross violations and corruption." In its place the CDA funded the newly created Brownsville Community Action Agency, led by Joseph Francois, former BCC chair. While BCC staff continued to operate programs under the new agency, the conflict raged in court and sapped the energy of the group. The battle was rendered moot in 1974 when the Nixon administration eliminated the Office of Economic Opportunity and drastically slashed the CAP program. The organization declined just as Brownsville's needs intensified.[32]

Despite the attention directed to them in the late 1960s and early 1970s, area public schools continued to struggle in educating Brownsville children. Nor did the New York state legislature's creation of a decentralized school system end the conflict. Assemblyman Sam Wright, who took control of Local School Board 23 in 1970, used his influence to provide jobs and contracts to his political backers. But local activists, including Thelma Hamilton and Father John Powis, contested Wright's power, and in 1971 they filed formal complaints with the school board. In a scathing indictment, the deposed "People's Board of Education" charged Wright with "using his position and community school board funds to further his interests as a State Assemblyman, co-leader of the United Political Club, politician and attorney." Activists alleged that seven of the nine local school board members and more than fifty school officials were members of Wright's political club, in violation of federal law that barred political influence in the distribution of educational funds. Funds controlled by the local board, Hamilton asserted, were spent without the required consultation of parents in the district. In short, Wright had created his own fiefdom.[33]

In the fall of 1972, schools again became a battlefield in Brownsville. This time the struggle pit blacks in Brownsville and East Flatbush against whites in Canarsie. Since 1961, to promote integration and relieve overcrowding in Brownsville schools, the children from the Tilden Houses had been assigned to schools in East Flatbush and Canarsie. However, in the summer of 1972, under pressure from white parents, the local school board refused to admit new students from Tilden to Canarsie schools. The board argued that their schools, already more than one-third black, would "tip" if any more minorities were admitted. In an ironic response to those in Brownsville who had supported community control, Canarsie parents asserted that the decentralization program gave them the right to set the standards for admission to local schools. While the number of students involved was extremely small (90 out of a district of 20,000), Canarsie parents closed all their schools to prevent the black students' admission. As they had in 1968, board of education officials waffled, fearing the wrath of white parents while cognizant that failing to take a stand was reneging on promises to promote integration. Throughout the fall, the school board shifted the black students among schools in the district. When they arrived in Canarsie, protesters pelted the children's buses with objects and racial slurs. After a monthlong boycott by white parents, the board capitulated to their demands, ruling that all future applicants from the Tilden Houses would be denied admission but would have the option to go to other "integrated" schools in Brooklyn.[34]

The board's decision testified to Brownsville's continued marginalization in the city's political system. As in many other American cities, blacks in New York began to gain political influence just as financial crises engulfed the city and limited the options of local government. Brooklyn's black population won increasing representation in city, state, and federal legislatures in the 1970s, but real power remained elusive. Brownsville, like most working-class neighborhoods, and like the Jewish ghetto that preceded it, was not an area that received much attention from New York's power structure. In 1972, the city council voted to expand the number of council districts to increase black and Latino representation. One of the new districts covered Brownsville and part of Bedford-Stuyvesant. Its first councilman was Sam Wright. By far the most important politician to emerge from the area in the 1960s, Wright allied himself early with Meade Esposito, head of the Brooklyn Democratic Party. Wright created a local political club modeled on the traditional machine system. Members of Wright's club received jobs or government contracts; those who opposed him were frozen out. Wright did not ignore the problems facing Brownsville. In 1971, he and his staff put together a proposal for a $200 million program to revitalize area schools and housing. But the proposal went nowhere. "Sam Wright was a blessing and a curse," said Maurice Reid, who often tangled with Wright's machine. "He was a very smart man, and he could have done so much." Wright frequently criticized city government for failing to provide adequate services in Brownsville, but he remained loyal to the Democratic Party. His political power ended in 1978 when he was convicted of soliciting a bribe from a company seeking a contract with the local school board.[35]

Many Brownsville activists continued to fight Wright and his cronies throughout the 1970s. Major Owens was the most successful of local progressives in winning political power. Elected to the state senate in 1974, Owens ran an insurgent campaign against the candidate chosen by the party. With the support of many former Brownsville Community Council (BCC) members, Owens ran a grassroots campaign critiquing the party's attempts to co-opt black political power by offering a few jobs to black residents. During the 1970s and 1980s, Owens and Assemblyman Albert Vann organized a movement that ran several candidates against the machine. In 1982, Owens was elected to the House of Representatives, a position he still continued to hold in 2001. His district included Brownsville, Crown Heights, East Flatbush, Eastern Parkway, and parts of several other neighborhoods. While Major Owens received much support in the area, most Brownsville residents remained suspicious of local politicians, and turnout in elections was among the lowest in the city. In view of the overwhelming problems facing the neighborhood in the 1970s, few residents believed that black representation could revitalize Brownsville.[36]

A Partial Rebirth: Brownsville since 1980

In the late 1970s, after a decade of reporting from troubled neighborhoods like Brownsville, the "urban underclass" became a familiar term in the country. Much debated among academics and policymakers, the popular perception of many American cities was that they were filled with poor, black, and Latino persons mired in a "culture of poverty" that prevented them from joining the mainstream of American life. According to social scientists, journalists, and pundits, inner-city neighborhoods lacked even a semblance of structure. Middle-class residents pulled out, social institutions failed, and government proved unable to pull blacks and Latinos out of their situation. "They are the unreachables," a 1977 *Time* magazine article called this group. "Their bleak environment nurtures values that are often at odds with those of the majority—even the majority of the poor." Liberals lamented the lack of funding for social programs to help this marginalized segment, while conservatives like Charles Murray argued that government funding actually intensified the problems of the people it was supposed to assist. According to many analysts, the underclass was a self-selected group of the poor responsible for a disproportionate amount of crime, delinquency, drug addiction, teen pregnancy, and other social problems. Michael Katz and other critics of the "underclass debate" noted that definitions of the underclass often ignored the one issue that all the group's supposed members have in common—poverty.[37]

Brownsville's social indicators of poverty, crime, and drug use all offered dramatic evidence to those who viewed the area as emblematic of the underclass community. But many other aspects of Brownsville society contradicted the assumptions and prejudices of these theories. In the 1980s and 1990s, Brownsville continued to support a variety of social institutions, both religious and nonsectarian. These organizations, along with government-supported programs, provided an infrastructure that helped many Brownsville residents deal with social and economic dislocation. While most Brownsville residents struggled against poverty, the neighborhood was not devoid of hope, and many groups worked aggressively to improve the area's resources and infrastructure.

The 1970s were particularly bad years for Brownsville. Housing declined, crime increased, and public services waned. In the 1980s and 1990s, however, public and private investment rebuilt much of the area that was destroyed. The NYCHA completed several public housing projects, designed with more consideration of their neighborhood impact than those built in the 1950s and 1960s. Nonprofit tenants' associations and for-profit owners rehabilitated apartment buildings and erected new houses for homeownership in the area. The amount of public investment in the neighborhood since 1980 dwarfed the private funds that created the original community. And this investment brought significant returns. That some of these houses sold in 1999 for more than $160,000 was testament to the improvements in Brownsville's physical landscape.

While many groups participated in the reconstruction of Brownsville, the organization most credited with the neighborhood's rebirth was the Eastern Brooklyn Congregations (EBC), a coalition of local Catholic, Lutheran, and Baptist churches and synagogues led by Catholic priests Leo Penta and John Powis, and Reverend John Youngblood, pastor of Saint Paul's Community Church. The group was affiliated with the Industrial Areas Foundation (IAF), an advocacy group founded by Saul Alinsky, and with the IAF's assistance it brought many new resources to the area.[38]

The major focus of the organization was the construction of affordable housing. In 1981, the group met with veteran developer I. D. Robbins, who had built thousands of houses on Long Island and spent his retirement telling anyone who would listen that he could build affordable housing in the city if provided with vacant land. After talking with Robbins and getting financial support from their church hierarchies, the EBC members announced the "Nehemiah Plan," named after the biblical prophet who rebuilt Jerusalem. The principle of the Nehemiah Plan was that homeownership was necessary to stabilize Brownsville and East New York, and the group proposed to build five thousand single-family homes. Robbins said that he needed large parcels of land so that he could build efficiently, Levittown-style, and the group argued to city officials that the still-vacant urban renewal area was perfectly suited to such a development. With the support of Brooklyn Catholic leader Bishop Francis Mugavero, the EBC raised $12 million in loan funds to support the development, and after much pressure on local politicians, it secured title to the vacant land from the city. In addition, the group won a $10 million subsidy from the city to lower the sale prices of the homes by $10,000 each.[39]

Nehemiah's two- and three-bedroom row houses had small front yards and forty-five-foot backyards. At 1,130 square feet, the houses were small by modern standards but luxurious for Brownsville. Several thousand people were on the waiting list when ground was broken for the first house in 1982, and the EBC completed its 1,000th house in 1987. Difficulties in assembling land and securing title from the city delayed the project, which the EBC hoped would produce 1,000 houses annually. However, the EBC continued to build these small rowhomes, completing more than 2,200 homes in eastern Brooklyn by 1999. Forty percent of the buyers of the original thousand houses came from local public housing projects; many of the home buyers were members of churches in the EBC.[40]

Figure 26. The Nehemiah Houses. Courtesy Jeffrey D. Hoeh.

While most agreed that the Nehemiah Plan was a success, critics argued that it was not a long-term solution to New York's affordable housing problem because the densities were too low and the prices too high to make them available to poor residents. The average income of the original buyers was $25,000. However, the developments made a major difference in the physical landscape of Brownsville, where, fifteen years after the first buyers moved in, the *New York Times* reported that the homes "remain attractive and well-kept." Homeowners raved about their houses. "I feel grateful, blessed free," one told reporters. Others moving from the projects to their new homes said it was "like moving to paradise." One resident told reporters that the homes were "like getting a stake in your neighborhood, your country, a stake in everything you believe in, and it gives you hope."[41]

Most newspaper articles on the neighborhood examined the dark side of Brownsville, but journalists returned from the Nehemiah houses with stories of hope. The streets of Brownsville "throb with life, life restored by tiny rowhouses built under the Nehemiah program," reported Samuel Freedman, one of the first to chronicle the story of the EBC in his book *Upon This Rock: The Miracles of a Black Church.* The development was the subject of features in newspapers across the country, and the program was replicated by the federal government when Congress passed the HOME Act, which funds the creation of homeownership opportunities for working-class people. The Nehemiah houses added to the stability of the neighborhood and combined with New York's booming real estate market to make Brownsville a location for settlement for new residents. Between 1980 and 1990, for the first time in sixty years, Brownsville's population increased by almost ten thousand people. Housing prices rose by 30 percent in the late 1990s as first-time homebuyers desperate for affordable accommodations became willing to move into what realtors call "fringe areas" like Brownsville. "If houses are priced right, they are moving as soon as they come on the market," reported one local realtor. Vacant lots continued to dot the Brownsville neighborhood, but throughout the 1990s they were slowly filled with housing and commercial ventures. Brownsville at the end of the century was not a luxurious community, but it provided affordable, decent housing to thousands of working-class New Yorkers.[42]

Public housing remained an important part of Brownsville's infrastructure. Four additional public projects opened in the late 1980s and early 1990s. The newer projects brought the total number of NYCHA residents in Brownsville to a staggering 21,302, almost 30 percent of the residents in the neighborhood. The NYCHA also managed many small and medium-sized apartment buildings that were taken from landlords by the city, so the total number of tenants in publicly owned units in Brownsville exceeded twenty-five thousand in 2000. Many thousands more lived in NYCHA projects in nearby Ocean Hill and East New York. Others lived in federally subsidized, privately owned units. In all, more than half of the area's sixty thousand residents lived in publicly supported housing.[43]

In the 1980s and 1990s, scandals, corruption, maintenance deficiencies, and rising crime rates marked the nation's public projects, particularly in places like Chicago, Detroit, Newark, and New Orleans. But unlike housing authorities in other cities that became targets for the backlash against public housing, the NYCHA maintained a good reputation and was regarded by many as the best-run large authority in the country. While far from luxurious, experts viewed New York's public housing as markedly superior to that in other cities. Because demand for housing remained high in New York during the 1980s (while it declined in other cities), public housing continued to draw working families. In addition, while concentrated in certain areas like Brownsville, Harlem, and the South Bronx, public projects in New York were less isolated than in other big cities, and as a result they were more attractive to prospective tenants. New York compared favorably with other cities like Chicago, renowned as the worst example of public housing segregation. There, the overwhelming majority of projects filled a corridor of South Chicago bounded by a ten-lane interstate expressway and railroad tracks. NYCHA units, on the other hand, were dispersed throughout New York (even though large sections of the city, particularly

Figure 27. Map of Brownsville Public Housing. Brooklyn Community District 16 map used with permission of the New York City Department of City Planning. © New York City Department of Planning. All rights reserved.

Queens and South Brooklyn, had few projects). These factors made New York's public housing exceptional.[44]

However, the NYCHA continued to face several challenges. Much of the housing stock was approaching fifty years old and required billions of dollars for modernization. The tens of millions of dollars in federal support to rehabilitate aging projects met only a fraction of the need. In addition, as the city's homeless population exploded in the 1980s, the NYCHA accepted a larger percentage of people from shelters. This led to increasing economic and racial segregation and to declining revenues. Public housing was originally designed to be self-sustaining, but by the 1990s the federal government provided 50 percent of NYCHA's annual operating costs. Within Brownsville, the housing authority modernized several projects, but maintenance problems persisted. Racial segregation also continued to intensify. In 1985, the racial distribution of NYCHA projects was 13 percent white, 56 percent black, and 27 percent Puerto Rican. By 1995 the white population declined to 8 percent. Brownsville's projects were exclusively occupied by minorities.[45]

The area's crime problem was much more difficult to solve than its housing woes, but Brownsville also made progress in this area. After a lull in violence during the early 1980s, crime in the neighborhood once again shot up. The crack cocaine epidemic was responsible for a new wave of violence. Across the city, precincts reported record numbers of serious crimes in the late 1980s. The number of murders increased from 1,385 in 1985 to a record 1,849 in 1987, and, according to police, almost half of the slayings were drug related. Brownsville was hit especially hard by the crisis, and city papers frequently reported tragedies emanating from gang drug battles. In one year alone, 1992, four tenants of the Noble Drew Ali homes were murdered in drug-related incidents. The area's public projects became havens for local addicts and drug dealers, who attacked and intimidated elderly residents to prevent them from interfering with the trade. A 1994 *New York Newsday* article reported that "the staccato of gunfire is part of the daily rhythms of life in Brownsville." Local residents became immune to the violence. "If you don't hear a gunshot, you're amazed at the quiet. It started five years ago, and in the last two years it's become outrageous," one tenant reported in 1993. Sixty-three people were killed in the Seventy-third Precinct in 1992, down from seventy-eight the year before. In 1992 the Seventy-third Precinct and the adjacent Seventy-fifth Precinct covering East New York were together responsible for a quarter of the homicides in all of Brooklyn. Children and adults were frequently caught in the crossfire between warring gangs, particularly in and around the projects, which tenants labeled "war zones."[46]

In the early 1990s, journalist Greg Donaldson spent more than a year visiting Brownsville, getting to know its residents, particularly teenagers and the police who patrolled the crime-ridden neighborhood. In his book, *The Ville: Cops and Kids in Urban America*, Donaldson showed the random violence with which local residents and police struggled, and he sympathetically portrayed the struggles of neighborhood youths like Sharron Corley, who Donaldson described as a typical "son of Brownsville." "In the Ville," Donaldson argued, "it is almost impossible for a young man to behave in a way that will keep him untouched by trouble. It is not healthy to stay in the background and appear passive. But it is not such a good thing to stand out on merit, to excel." Because of the constant fear of violence, neighborhood youths attempted to blend in with their peers. Achievement, in Donaldson's view, is not often rewarded, and it is often cause for punishment by area thugs. In the 1920s and 1930s, Brownsville had more than its share of gangsters, but the neighborhood was also famous for producing Aaron Copeland and Danny Kaye. In the 1990s, residents still achieved economic success despite the difficulties facing the neighborhood, but Brownsville was known to most as the rough-and-tumble community that produced heavyweight champions Mike Tyson and Riddick Bowe. Both men have said that they learned to fight on the streets of Brownsville and that the toughness of the neighborhood brought out the killer instinct in them. "Bummy Mike," as Tyson was known as a youth in Brownsville, was constantly in and out of juvenile detention. Tyson's image solidified the perception of Brownsville as a place of danger. Resident concern over crime in Brownsville was further exacerbated by a 1994 scandal that revealed a ring of corrupt NYPD officers at the Seventy-third Precinct. The officers stole cash, drugs, and guns from drug dealers and extorted money from others. Investigations of the ring revealed that the Seventy-third Precinct was viewed by many as a "dumping ground" for cops who had failed in other precincts.[47]

After 1994, however, crime decreased dramatically in the area, as it did across the city. In the early 1990s, the Seventy-third Precinct consistently recorded in excess of sixty murders a year, but in 1994 there were forty-six killings in the area. This number dropped to twenty-seven in 1995, then to six in 1997 (before rising again to twenty-one in 1999). These declines corresponded with citywide statistics. The reasons for the easing of crime are much disputed by experts, but they include more police and better strategies to prevent crime, the decline in the crack trade, the rise in the number of people incarcerated, and improvements in the local economy, which began to benefit the poor. The merger of the NYCHA police force with the NYPD supported an increased focus on local projects, which had a beneficial impact on the neighborhood as a whole. The easing of violent crime significantly improved Brownsville residents' quality of life, and the police presence on the streets made people feel comfortable using public spaces again.[48]

Community organizations grew significantly in the 1980s and 1990s. Many BCC activists continued to contribute to the neighborhood in the years after the dismantling of the Community Action Program. In the mid-1970s, several BCC leaders, including Maurice Reid, formed the Brownsville Community Development Corporation (BCDC) to secure funds from the newly created federal Community Development Block Grant Program. The BCDC focused on improving health care in the area, and it operated the Brownsville Multi-Service Family Health Center, which provided on-site care to thousands of local residents. The group, run by Maurice Reid, also performed outreach at local schools and facilities, and worked with tenant councils in housing projects. In 1993, the BCDC opened a renovated 26,000-square-foot facility on Rockaway Avenue, the original site of the BCC, that provided adult and pediatric care, testing services, counseling and mental health services, and treatment for substance abuse. In 1998, the organization had an annual budget in excess of $7 million.[49]

The Ocean Hill–Brownsville Tenants Association (OHBTA) and the Eastern Brooklyn Churches (EBC) also played major roles in improving neighborhood resources. The OHBTA focused on the organization of tenants associations within the area's private apartment buildings to enable residents to fight for better services from landlords. To protect local tenants from landlord discrimination, the association prepared information on the eviction process and offered tenants referrals to legal services agencies. The group also provided housing counseling to area residents and helped them wade through the bureaucracy and paperwork of the dozens of housing programs available in New York City. In later years, the OHBTA added housing management to its portfolio, and its buildings coupled affordable shelter with social services to tenants. While its primary purpose was the rehabilitation and maintenance of affordable housing, the group was also an advocate for the neighborhood, demanding more resources from city officials. The group's job training, social service, and educational programs served thousands of Brownsville residents.[50]

In the 1990s, the organization turned over management of several of its properties to other companies and shifted its focus back to advocacy and economic development. The group's "Youth Collective" worked with area teenagers at risk of dropping out of school and provided counseling, job training, and internships. As a grassroots organization, the OHBTA was involved in many battles with city agencies. In 1992, the Youth Collective assisted local teens in taking over and clearing out an abandoned firehouse in Brownsville to use as a recreation center. This effort led to conflict with local politicians and city agencies, who closed the building but promised to devote new resources to the area. Other educational programs run by the OHBTA included a Montessori school. The group initiated economic development programs to support entrepreneurship among local residents, and it also created a for-profit construction company that employed one hundred workers.[51]

The East Brooklyn Churches (EBC) also promoted grassroots protest and activism. In the 1980s, the group organized a program to oversee local merchants accused of price gouging and spoiled food. Like the OPA inspectors during World War II, members of EBC churches prowled the aisles of local stores looking for high prices and defective products and threatened boycotts of local stores that failed to meet acceptable standards. The EBC expanded its portfolio in other ways, creating programs in community policing, education, and economic development. To improve the quality of life in East Brooklyn, the group worked to develop relationships with local police and pressured city agencies to close drug-dealing operations in the area. In the field of education, the EBC created two charter schools and gave thousands of dollars in college scholarships to local youths. EBC leaders, however, consistently battled with the New York Police Department and the board of education over these programs. Because of bureaucratic intransigence, and differences over policy, neither agency supported the EBC's proposals, and relationships between the group and city agencies remained strained.[52]

Like the Jewish community that preceded the modern neighborhood, Brownsville teemed with religious institutions, and Christian churches took the place of synagogues. A 1998 inventory by the City Planning Commission listed 167 religious institutions in Brownsville and Ocean Hill. Sixty-one churches were in Brownsville proper, and a staggering 106 dotted the triangle of Ocean Hill, an area not much larger than one square mile. In Brownsville some churches occupied former synagogues, others storefronts on Pitkin and Rockaway Avenues and other thoroughfares. Many of the churches in Ocean Hill inhabited the small storefronts that line Rockaway and Fulton Avenues. The majority of local congregations were Baptist, but there were also a large number of Pentecostal and other evangelical churches. Brownsville churches had many similarities to the synagogues that preceded them. Most were very small, and their sanctuaries could not comfortably accommodate more than a hundred members. Like their Jewish counterparts, many congregations relied on the entrepreneurial talents of their ministers to stay afloat. A large number of the ministers worked in other occupations during the day and devoted evenings and weekends to religious activities. A small number of newer churches joined long-standing congregations (Mount Ollie, First Baptist, Brownsville Community Baptist, Tabernacle Baptist) in building substantial institutions, but most remained small and undercapitalized. Only a small number of ministers, one of whom was Reverend Spurgeon Crayton of Mount Ollie Baptist Church, were active in community organizations. Crayton was instrumental in the development of several area facilities, including the R. D. Brown houses, a seniors home on Saint Mark's Avenue.[53]

While religious groups generally avoided large-scale social programs, government agencies were much more active in modern Brownsville than they were in the old community, and government facilities, both wanted and unwanted, proliferated in the area, particularly along East New York Avenue. The Brownsville Multi-Service Facility, for example, a $2.4 million building that occupied the whole block of Thomas Boyland (formerly Hopkinson Avenue) between Pitkin and East New York Avenues, housed many community groups and provided job training, educational programs, employment assistance, and technical and financial assistance to small businesses. In 2000, there were seven primary care health facilities, five drug and alcohol addiction facilities, sixteen job training and education programs, twelve after-school programs, nine day-care centers, and nine senior centers in the area, almost all supported by local, state, and federal funding. While these facilities still failed to meet the overwhelming needs of the neighborhood, they represented a marked improvement in local resources.[54]

Brownsville also had several facilities that housed and provided social services to the homeless, mentally disabled persons, and substance abusers. Residents vehemently opposed the continued development of such facilities and argued that Brownsville had more than its fair share of programs for very poor persons. In the early 1990s, neighborhood activists also protested the construction of a juvenile detention facility in the area. The $40 million project, with 124 beds in addition to educational and recreational facilities, covered a whole block of northern Brownsville. It was next to the new offices of the Seventy-third Precinct and formed a compound that residents referred to as "the fort." Brownsville residents were particularly upset about the development of the detention facility, because it was built on land they thought would be used for a new public high school. Chanting "schools, not jails," local residents held several demonstrations against the center, which opened in 1997. To Brownsville activists, the millions spent on criminal justice facilities while educational needs went unmet was evidence of racism toward Brownsville's predominantly black population.[55]

As it did for a century, Brownsville continued to suffer from a lack of sanitation and recreational resources. The "Community Needs Assessments" produced annually by Brownsville's Community Planning Board consistently complained about inadequate trash pickup and the need for parks and other recreational facilities. In 1984, the city announced the closure of the Brownsville Recreation Center (formerly the BBC clubhouse), the only significant indoor center in the area. Only after complaints by local residents and politicians did the city rescind the decision and agree to spend $9 million to renovate the building. In the past few years the city has also spent several million dollars renovating the pool and other facilities in Betsy Head Park.[56]

The school battles of the late 1960s and 1970s continued to haunt the neighborhood. Few of Brownsville's community control activists supported the city decentralization program when it was approved, and the intervening decades supported their skepticism. Stories of corruption, patronage, and inefficiency at local school boards were common in the 1970s and after. A 1990 study of local school boards found a system built to support the economic and political aspirations of board members without consideration of the needs of students. In many districts, board members distributed principalships and other positions in return for political favors and sometimes cash. Parents in many neighborhoods responded with apathy, and participation in local school board elections averaged less than 10 percent of eligible voters. In Brownsville, parental involvement was among the lowest in the city, hovering around 2 percent. After three decades of failing schools, the New York state legislature voted in 1996 to curb the authority of local school boards and return control to the chancellor of schools. When interviewed about the change, most Brownsville activists and parents expressed support for the new system.[57]

Brownsville schools had continued to hover at the bottom of the list by most standards of achievement. In 1996, only 26 percent of local children read at grade level, the third worst rating in the city. While many parents and their children continued to be isolated from the system, several Brownsville activists remained involved in the struggle to improve education. Paul Chandler, a leader of the community control movement, now served as a director of the Jackie Robinson Center for Physical Culture. This group, based in Bedford-Stuyvesant, provided after-school and weekend programs at several Brownsville schools. Children aged eight to eighteen received tutoring and counseling and took part in recreational programs that included athletics, music, dance, and drama. More than five thousand youths participated annually.[58]

In the 1990s, the educational system also made small strides. While violence continued to plague the area's high school, many intermediate schools became havens for local children. In the 1970s, Brownsville schools had to rely on temporary staff because they had difficulty attracting full-time teachers. That changed in the last decade of the century, and school performance began to improve. One district official noted, "You can see the narrowing of the gap, but it's going to take changing the outside environment." The construction of the Nehemiah homes gave stability to the area, but many of Brownsville's schools, several of which were built one hundred years ago, continued to require significant maintenance. Seven of the schools still used coal-burning furnaces. The increase in population resulting from the new public and private housing exacerbated overcrowding. At the same time, inefficiency and budget crises within the board of education left one local school, PS 156, vacant. Closed in 1993 because of asbestos, the school remained shuttered into the next decade despite the efforts of local parents who took over the building to protest the constant shifting of their children from school to school.[59]

Increasing economic opportunities gave Brownsville residents a reason to demand better schools. During the 1980s, despite economic growth in New York, unemployment in Brownsville was consistently more than double the city average. In 1980, the unemployment rate was 18.6 percent for men and 15.3 percent for women. By 1990, the rates had climbed to 21.5 and 19.4 respectively. At the same time, the number of Brownsville residents moving up the economic ladder increased, and many relied on the public sector to assist them. In the 1970s and afterward, black employment in New York's public sector (particularly the post office, mass transit, and public hospitals) rose significantly, and offered the only distinctive "ethnic niche" that blacks could use to help others gain stable employment. In 1980, 30 percent of Brownsville workers had government occupations, a percentage which has since increased. Many Brownsville residents worked in the health care and education fields, and their participation in the retail and finance, insurance, and real estate sectors also increased in the last two decades of the century. Brownsville's improving occupational profile was the result of increasing educational attainment. Between 1980 and 1990, the number of high school graduates in the area increased by 56 percent, while the number of persons with at least some college experience increased by 159 percent. As a result, the percentage of Brownsville residents living in poverty decreased from 42.0 to 37.6 during the decade. While many middle-class residents did leave the area in the 1970s, not all Brownsville residents lived in abject poverty, and the construction of the Nehemiah Houses increased the number of middle-class persons in the area.[60]

Better jobs helped improve the business climate within Brownsville. In the 1970s, crime, riots, and economic decline had a major impact on Brownsville's commercial sector, but while many old merchants sold out, most of their stores remained open. The people who bought them, Brownsville's emerging merchant class, were not Jewish but Asian, Arab, Caribbean, and African-American. A 1979 article from the magazine *New Brooklyn* countered stories of the street's demise and stated that Pitkin Avenue had "throngs of shoppers," who were "pleasant and orderly." Several major retail chains opened stores on the block, including Thom McCann, Florsheim, and Stride Rite. Many clothing stores continued to serve Brooklyn shoppers on Pitkin Avenue, some long-standing and some new, along with the numerous furniture stores that persisted on the block. Belmont Avenue also continued to provide a location for inexpensive clothing and food stores. The area's commercial growth was the result of the investment of a new merchant class, most of them recent immigrants. As they did in other areas of New York City, these business people obtained credit through informal networks, family, ethnic societies, and small banks, and they purchased or rented stores in an area that continued to draw a large number of customers. Brownsville was no longer the Fifth Avenue of Brooklyn, but its commercial sector provided a variety of goods and a significant number of jobs to local residents.[61]

Local businesses also received assistance from city and state agencies to promote Brownsville's commercial sector. In 1980, Belmont Avenue underwent a $700,000 facade renovation program, and local merchants received public funds to expand their operations. More recently, Belmont Avenue merchants celebrated the opening of "The Ville Fleamarket," an open-air vendor's lot. The market, created to remove street vendors from major thoroughfares, rented space to individuals for $10 a day. Fifty years after Brownsville activists proposed a facility for area peddlers, the lot provided space to twenty-three vendors, many of them immigrants from the Caribbean or Africa. In the 1990s, businesses also benefited from the creation of the Pitkin Avenue Business Improvement District (BID). In the 1990s, BIDs—self-taxing districts that supplemented city services by pay-

Figure 28. Pitkin Avenue. Courtesy Jeffrey D. Hoeh.

ing for sanitation, security, and other business services—became a popular means for businesses to work together to fund street improvements, promotions, and other common interests. In New York City, BIDs were a multimillion-dollar business, operating in Times Square, on Wall Street, and in other commercial districts. Some critics charged BIDs with violations of wage and civil rights laws, as well as corruption and inefficiency, but they remained a growing sector of New York's economy. The Pitkin Avenue BID, created in 1993, covered Pitkin, Rockaway, Belmont, and Sutter Avenues. It was among the smallest in the city, with an annual budget of approximately $120,000. The organization used these funds for security, lighting, graffiti removal, and promotion of the area, and it recently began a program for facade improvements and other modernizations of Brownsville stores.[62]

The industrial district that divided Brownsville from East New York was also reborn. In 1980, the East Brooklyn Industrial Park opened, covering the industrial corridors along the Long Island Railroad Tracks as well as Atlantic and Linden Avenues. With government funds, the park acquired and demolished several buildings, widened and repaired streets, and updated utilities. By clearing large parcels of land, the industrial park made the area attractive to businesses in the area with expansion needs and to businesses from other areas looking for industrial sites. The group developed business incubators, provided funding and technical assistance to growing companies, and helped entrepreneurs secure economic incentives from the city and state government. Several dozen businesses relocated to the area or expanded their operations, including the Brooklyn Bottling Company, Don's Truck Sales, and Legion Lighting Company. There were sixteen garment factories, thirteen companies producing metal wood and plastic displays of different varieties, and several other manufacturing firms. Together they employed several thousand people.[63]

Brownsville today is a study of contrasts. Along Rockaway Avenue, small bodegas struggle to exist alongside large swaths of vacant land. On Belmont Avenue, the grimy business of fishmongers and butchers continues unchanged from the beginning of the century. Along Pitkin Avenue, almost every store is occupied, the newly refurbished sidewalk shines, and colorful banners line the street. Most of the stores are discount operations with names like Bargains on Pitkin, 99 Cent Town, and C&N Bargain Express. But there are also newly renovated chain stores such as Lane Bryant and Ashley Stuart, in addition to the ubiquitous Rite Aid, McDonald's, and Kentucky Fried Chicken. The street is clean and orderly and it serves many of the neighborhood's needs.

As Brownsville begins the twenty-first century, there is an atmosphere of hope on the streets. Services have slowly improved, parks are being renovated, new residents are moving in, and new stores are following. Brownsville has benefited from the "trickle-down effect" of New York's booming economy. Residents don't know what the impact of the next, inevitable, economic downturn will be. If the past is any predictor, Brownsville will once again struggle, and indices of social problems will rise. Such is the state of working-class communities. They are frequently the last to profit from economic growth, and the first to suffer from economic dislocation. Right now, however, Brownsville is once again a vibrant, working-class community.

Epilogue

Each year the Brownsville Boys Club (BBC) holds a reunion. But none of the attendees live in Brownsville, so the event is held in Queens, the home of many former members. These retired men and their wives (many of whom also grew up in Brownsville) enjoy getting together to relive old times and share reminiscences of a neighborhood long gone. Unlike the organization that these men created, the BBC reunion is not an interracial event: only whites attend. "We've drifted apart," said one member. "We've made no attempt to bring in black people, neither has there been an attempt to keep them out. It just seems to be the natural way." Though the memories of a racially integrated childhood are strong, few group members maintained these relationships after they left the neighborhood.[1]

In July of each year, the Brownsville Recreation Center—originally the BBC clubhouse—is the focal point of another reunion. Many of the fete's organizers—they call it "Old-Timers Week"—are also former BBC members. For these black men, the event is a chance to get reacquainted with former and current Brownsville residents. The weeklong program includes a parade, a charity basketball game, and a night of singing and dancing; it is the highlight of the summer for many natives. "Most of us don't live in Brownsville," said one organizer, "but we come back every year to try to give back to the neighborhood." Like the whites who preceded them, the men and women who sponsor Old-Timer's Week moved to other parts of Brooklyn or the suburbs. Many still attend church in the area and support other local institutions, but their ties to Brownsville have weakened over the years.[2]

The separation of these men, black and white, from their former home—the one they say generates so many positive memories—demonstrates the difficulties of developing sustaining urban institutions in modern America. The United States is a transitory society—the average family moves once every five years, a rate that has remained relatively consistent for more than a century. Americans are constantly aspiring to better surroundings and leaving behind less desirable neighborhoods. This mobility weakens all types of organizations, but it is particularly damaging to working-class associations, because poor neighborhoods face greater social and economic problems.[3]

These stories of estrangement also illuminate the complex nature of the word "community." Americans employ this concept frequently to describe groups of people sharing common interests, but Brownsville's history shows that the term often obscures more than it reveals. In the years before World War II, New Yorkers ridiculed and ostracized Brownsville residents because of their working-class status. Brownsville immigrants remained isolated from the broader "New York community" for decades. Jewish Americans who worked to assimilate into society also tried to distinguish themselves from their Brownsville brethren; to describe the area's residents as part of a larger "Jewish community" distorts the reality of their relationship to the outside world. The important role of leftist activists in the neighborhood served to further marginalize the neighborhood from mainstream society. In the postwar years, perceptions of the area and its residents inhibited cooperation between Brownsville leaders and citywide public and private institutions.[4]

Brownsville citizens also struggled with the idea of community. The activists in Brownsville Neighborhood Council, the BBC, and other postwar neighborhood organizations were steeped in the ideology of modern liberalism. They believed in the sanctity of individual rights, and they held to the ideals of equal opportunity for all people. Brownsville's heritage of leftist organization infused this liberalism, and gave it an aggressive cast. Local organizations argued that society, through its government and private organizations, had an obligation to make sure that all Americans received the support necessary to maintain a decent standard of living. However, despite their vocal opinions on societal responsibility, Brownsville's liberalism did not frequently extend to interpersonal relations, and Brownsville remained racially segregated even during the optimistic 1940s. BNC leaders frequently spoke of soliciting support from Brownsville's "black community," an entity separated psychologically, but seldom physically, from the broader "Brownsville community." Local groups struggled to achieve more than token black participation, but white and black adults remained socially divided. Institutions led by blacks were primarily based in racially segregated churches, and this placed additional barriers between neighborhood whites and blacks. In the United States of the 1940s, for blacks and whites to live in close proximity without conflict was an exceptional event. Brownsville differentiated itself as a neighborhood where people of different races "got along," but most residents were unable to conceive of a society without racial distinctions.

The civil rights movement in the 1960s forced many whites to expand their definitions of community and acknowledge the rights of minorities to fully participate in society. Brownsville activists drew upon this ideology and continued working to create a truly integrated neighborhood. Like the union leaders who organized the workers at Beth-El Hospital, these residents argued that segregation would continue unless aggressive efforts were made to bridge the gaps between the races. A small number of labor organizations such as Local 1199 succeeded in creating integrated institutions, but within Brownsville such a program was impossible because few whites remained to participate in the project.

The decades-long struggle for integration reached a crisis in the late 1960s, when, despite the heroic efforts of civil rights activists and notwithstanding millions of dollars in War on Poverty funds, American society remained socially and economically divided. In this context, some blacks rejected the integrationist philosophy. The rise of Black Power ideology changed the rhetoric of American race relations, but its impact on the actual program of neighborhood organizations in Brownsville was less dramatic. To the uninitiated, the demand for community control seemed like a significant step away from the program of equal opportunity, but most Brownsville residents saw it as a chance to share with whites the ability to shape public institutions.

Brownsville blacks also had complicated relationships with Brooklyn's self-defined "black community." In the 1940s and 1950s, most black leaders lived in Bedford-Stuyvesant, and they frequently distanced themselves from their poorer brethren in Brownsville. In the 1960s, black and Latino activists, with the support of community action funds, worked to organize the disenfranchised, but even these organizations were segregated by class. Government programs helped all Brownsville minorities, but they provided the greatest benefits to black and Latino professionals. The opportunities that arose during that period of easing discrimination also damaged neighborhood institutions, because most blacks left the neighborhood when financial success and increasing housing opportunities made this possible.

Social barriers certainly inhibited Brownsville's integration, but public policies created the entrenched racial ghettos of postwar New York. Throughout the twentieth century, urban elites expressed concern over the state of poor neighborhoods. Their solutions to these problems most frequently involved destroying the districts and starting over. Elites were unable to see any value in these neighborhoods, nor were many able to comprehend that the differences between these areas and their well-tended sections were primarily economic. During the twentieth century, urban immigrants provided unskilled labor for factories, construction, and service occupations, and most enterprises depended on these poorly paid workers. But while urban elites recognized the importance of the poor to the urban economy, they complained about the negative impact of these groups on the city. Poor residents, argued city leaders, were responsible for decrepit housing, dirty streets, and the social problems of the slum areas where they lived. Millions of first- and second-generation immigrants achieved middle-class status during the century, but working-class neighborhoods persisted because the demand for cheap housing among poorly paid residents endured. Throughout the twentieth century, urban elites attempted to erase physically decayed neighborhoods. They failed because the slum was an integral part of urban society.

In the early 1900s, efforts at city revitalization were locally funded. The private sector undertook rehabilitation of city neighborhoods when and where it was profitable, and publicly supported projects were infrequent. In the postwar years, federal funding dramatically reshaped the process of urban development. Initiatives like public housing and urban renewal brought millions of dollars in additional resources to cities, enabling the demolition and reconstruction of many urban areas. These programs created vital resources (Lincoln Center, for example) and they kept (or brought back) thousands of middle-class residents. They also provided desperately needed modern housing to millions of poor Americans, and were successful in modernizing many neighborhoods. But because local elites implemented these programs, they continued to reflect the philosophy that the slums could be eliminated with bricks and mortar.[5]

The entry of African-Americans and Latinos into American cities during the 1940s added yet another complication to urban revitalization. Slums like Brownsville that already bore a stigma because they housed poor people now suffered from the additional marginalization caused by the racial background of their new inhabitants. Like their predecessors, blacks and Latinos journeyed to cities to find economic opportunities, and they took their place at the bottom of the social ladder. Shortly after their arrival, however, changes in New York's economy eliminated many of the low-skilled occupations that provided subsistence wages to the working class. The supply of low-wage workers exceeded the demand, and this left many workers unable to support their families. Economic restructuring exacerbated the already serious problems of working-class neighborhoods.

The postwar era was a period of significant movement in New York City as people left declining urban areas for new neighborhoods in the suburbs. At the same time, renewal programs reshaped the city's geography by uprooting hundreds of thousands of residents. This process, the result of decisions by private developers, government officials, and the individual choices of families, caused fiscal and social turmoil. The migration of blacks and Latinos coincided with the departure of white residents. New York's new residents did not create the slum or the racial ghetto, but their arrival increased awareness of these areas and heightened the fears among whites that their cities were in crisis. Concerns about the impact of racial minorities on New York society persisted into the twenty-first century.

As urban areas continue to deal with the impact of national economic and social changes, critics argue that public housing and urban renewal are responsible for the decline of the city. But these programs did not create ghettos; they only gave these areas new form. Public housing and urban renewal "failed" because they were not designed to address the root causes of the slum—economic inequality and racial discrimination. Until American society tackles these serious problems, the ghetto will persist.

Notes

Introduction

1. On the city as immigrant magnet, see John Bodnar, *The Transplanted: A History of Immigration in Urban America* (Bloomington: Indiana University Press, 1985); Donna R. Gabaccia, *From Sicily to Elizabeth Street: Housing and Social Change Among Italian Immigrants, 1880–1930* (Albany: State University of New York Press, 1984); George Sanchez, *Becoming Mexican American: Ethnicity, Culture and Identity in Chicano Los Angeles, 1900–1945* (New York: Oxford University Press, 1993).

2. Though one of the nation's largest cities in its own right, Brooklyn has received scant attention from historians. For overviews of Brooklyn history, see Myrna Frommer, *It Happened in Brooklyn: An Oral History of Growing Up in the Borough in the 1940s, 1950s, and 1960s* (New York: Harcourt Brace, 1983); Ralph Foster Weld, *Brooklyn Is America* (New York: Columbia University Press, 1950). While the borough remains neglected, the lives of African-Americans in Brooklyn have received greater attention, particularly in the past decade. Clarence Taylor, *The Black Churches of Brooklyn* (New York: Columbia University Press, 1994); Clarence Taylor, *Knocking at Our Own Door: Milton A. Galamison and the Struggle to Integrate New York City Schools* (New York: Columbia University Press, 1997); Craig Steven Wilder, *A Covenant With Color: Race and Social Power in Brooklyn* (New York: Columbia University Press, 2000); Harold Connolly, *A Ghetto Grows in Brooklyn* (New York: New York University Press, 1977); Barbara Habenstreit, *Fort Greene, USA* (Indianapolis: Bobbs-Merrill, 1974).

3. On the 1968 strike, see Jerald Podair, "Like Strangers: Blacks, Whites and the Ocean Hill–Brownsville Crisis, 1945–1980" (Ph.D. diss., Princeton University, 1997); Clarence Taylor, *Knocking at Our Own Door*; Daniel Perlstein, "The 1968 New York City School Crisis, Teacher Politics, Racial Politics and the Decline of Liberalism" (Ph.D. diss.: Stanford University, 1994); Melvin Urofsky, *Why Teachers Strike: Teachers' Rights and Community Control*

(Garden City, N.Y.: Doubleday, 1970); Maurice Berube and Marilyn Gittell, *Confrontation at Ocean Hill–Brownsville: The New York School Strikes of 1968* (New York: Praeger, 1969); Mario Fantini, Richard Magat, and Marilyn Gittell, *Community Control and the Urban School* (New York: Praeger, 1970). On the impact of the strike on Black-Jewish relations, see Albert Vorspan, "Blacks and Jews," in James Baldwin, ed., *Black Anti-Semitism and Jewish Racism* (New York: Richard Baron, 1969); Andrew Hacker, "Jewish Racism, Black Anti-Semitism," in Paul Berman, ed., *Blacks and Jews: Alliances and Arguments* (New York: Doubleday, 1994), 154–163; Johnathon Kaufman, *Broken Alliance: The Turbulent Times between Blacks and Jews in America* (New York: Simon and Schuster, 1995); Murray Friedman, *What Went Wrong? The Creation and Collapse of the Black Jewish Alliance* (New York: Free Press, 1993).

4. On the rise of the suburbs, see Kenneth Jackson, *Crabgrass Frontier: The Suburbanization of the United States* (New York: Oxford University Press, 1985); Robert Fishman, *Bourgeois Utopias: The Rise and Fall of Suburbia* (New York: Basic Books, 1987). On the emergence of the service economy, see Roger Waldinger, *Still the Promised City? African-Americans and New Immigrants in Postindustrial New York* (Cambridge: Harvard University Press, 1996); John Mollenkopf and Manuel Castells, eds., *Dual City: Restructuring New York* (New York: Russell Sage Foundation, 1991).

5. On deindustrialization, see Thomas J. Sugrue, *The Origins of the Urban Crisis: Race and Inequality in Postwar Detroit* (Princeton: Princeton University Press, 1996); William Julius Wilson, *The Truly Disadvantaged: The Inner City, the Underclass, and Public Policy* (Chicago: University of Chicago Press, 1987); John Cumbler, *A Social History of Economic Decline: Business, Politics, and Work in Trenton* (New Brunswick: Rutgers University Press, 1989). On the migration of African-Americans to the North, see Nicholas Lemann, *The Promised Land: The Great Migration and How It Changed America* (New York: Knopf, 1991). On housing discrimination, see Arnold Hirsch, *Making the Second Ghetto: Race and Housing in Chicago, 1940–1960* (New York: Cambridge University Press, 1985); John Bauman, *Public Housing Race and Renewal: Urban Planning in Philadelphia, 1920–1974* (Philadelphia: Temple University Press, 1987); Dominic Capeci, *Race Relations in Wartime Detroit: The Sojourner Truth Housing Controversy of 1942* (Philadelphia: Temple University Press, 1984); Douglas Massey and Nancy Denton, *American Apartheid: Segregation and the Making of the Underclass* (Cambridge: Harvard University Press, 1993).

6. On the development of public housing, see Hirsch, *Making the Second Ghetto;* Bauman, *Public Housing, Race and Reform;* Sugrue, *Origins of the Urban Crisis;* Capeci, *Race Relations in Wartime Detroit.* Also see Joel Schwartz, *The New York Approach: Robert Moses, Urban Liberals and the Redevelopment of the Inner City* (Columbus: Ohio State University Press, 1993); Peter Marcuse, "The Beginnings of Public Housing in New York," *Journal of Urban History* 12 (August 1986): 349–373; Gail Radford, *Modern Housing for America: Policy Struggles in the New Deal Era* (Chicago: University of Chicago Press, 1996); Gwendolyn Wright, *Building the Dream: A Social History of Housing in America* (New York: Pantheon, 1981). On criticism of public housing, see A. Scott Henderson, "Tarred with the Exceptional Image: Public Housing and Popular Discourse, 1950–1990," *American Studies* 36 (1995): 31–52.

7. On the creation of the new ghetto, see Hirsch, *Making the Second Ghetto;* Sugrue, *Origins of the Urban Crisis;* Schwartz, *New York Approach.* Also see Raymond Mohl,

"Making the Second Ghetto in Metropolitan Miami, 1940–1960," *Journal of Urban History* 21 (1995): 395–427; Charles F. Casey-Leninger, "Making the Second Ghetto in Cincinnati: Avondale, 1925–1970," in Henry Louis Taylor, ed., *Race and the City: Work, Community and Protest in Cincinnati, 1820–1970* (Urbana: University of Illinois Press, 1993).

8. Robert Caro, *The Power Broker: Robert Moses and the Fall of New York* (New York: Knopf, 1974). For an opposing view on Moses, see Leonard Wallock, "The Myth of the Master Builder: Robert Moses, New York and the Dynamics of Metropolitan Development Since World War II," *Journal of Urban History* 17 (1991): 339–362; Jon Teaford, *Rough Road to Renaissance: Urban Revitalization in America, 1940–1985* (Baltimore: Johns Hopkins University Press, 1990).

9. Allen Matusow, *The Unraveling of America: A History of Liberalism in the 1960s* (New York: Harper and Row, 1984); Charles Murray, *Losing Ground: American Social Policy, 1950–1980* (New York: Basic Books, 1984); Fred Seigel, *The Future Once Happened Here: New York, D.C., L.A., and the Fate of America's Big Cities* (New York: Free Press, 1997). For opposing views, see the articles in Michael Katz, ed., *The Underclass Debate: Views from History* (Princeton: Princeton University Press, 1993).

Chapter 1

1. Samuel Tenenbaum, "Brownsville's Age of Learning," *Commentary* 8 (1949): 174; William Poster, "Twas a Dark Night in Brownsville," *Commentary* 9 (1950): 461.

2. Alfred Kazin, *A Walker in the City* (New York: Harcourt Brace, 1951), 12; Deborah Dash Moore, "On the Fringes of the City: Jewish Neighborhoods in Three Boroughs," in Olivier Zunz, ed., *The Landscape of Modernity: New York City, 1900–1940* (Baltimore: Johns Hopkins University Press, 1992), 252; Poster, "Twas a Dark Night in Brownsville," 458.

3. Henry Stiles, *History of Kings County* (New York, 1884), 307; Rae Glauber, *All Neighborhoods Change: A History of Brownsville, Brooklyn* (Brooklyn: Author, 1963); Alter Landesman, *Brownsville: The Birth, Development, and Passing of a Jewish Community in New York* (New York: Bloch Publishing, 1969).

4. Stiles, *History of Kings County*, 307; Landesman, *Brownsville*, 40; Eleanora Schoenebaum, "Emerging Neighborhoods: The Developments of Brooklyn's Fringe Areas, 1850–1930" (Ph.D. diss., Columbia University, 1977), 99; Irving Ripps, "Jews of New York," 28 May 1941, Papers of the Writers Project, Works Progress Administration Papers, New York City Municipal Archives, roll 164, 1–2.

5. Landesman, *Brownsville*, 40; Moore, "On the Fringes of the City," 252.

6. Margaret Freeman, *The Children's Branch of the Brownsville Library: Its Origins and Development* (Brooklyn: Brooklyn Public Library, 1940), 13; Moore, "On the Fringes of the City," 254.

7. Moore, "On the Fringes of the City," 257; "Some Phases of Life in Brooklyn's Ghetto," *Brooklyn Eagle*, 2 July 1899; Schoenebaum, "Emerging Neighborhoods," 125–127.

8. Moore, "On the Fringes of the City," 257.

9. Schoenebaum, "Emerging Neighborhoods," 117–120.

10. Walter Laidlaw, *The Population of the City of New York* (New York: Cities Census Commission, 1932), 549–555.

11. Ibid., 549–555; Henry Roth, *Call It Sleep* (New York: Avon, 1934).

12. Tenenbaum, "Brownsville's Age of Learning," 173; Poster, "Twas a Dark Night in Brownsville," 460.

13. Schoenebaum, "Emerging Neighborhoods," 101–110, 257; Landesman, *Brownsville*, 83; "Real Estate Boom: 82 Acres Sold in a Day," *Brooklyn Eagle*, 3 January 1904.

14. "Modern Tenement City Is Brownsville City," *Brooklyn Eagle*, 29 November 1908; "Builders Angry with President Coler Regarding Flimsy Building Charges," *Brooklyn Eagle*, 11 November 1906.

15. "Insurance in Brownsville," *Brooklyn Eagle*, 24 September 1908; "Increase in Violations of the Tenement House Law," *Brooklyn Eagle*, 5 May 1907.

16. Kazin, *Walker in the City*, 15; "Brownsville Aims to Get Playground," *Brooklyn Eagle*, 16 February 1913; Florence Adamson, *A Study of the Recreational Needs of Brownsville, Brooklyn* (Brooklyn: Brownsville Neighborhood Council, 1940), 7.

17. Sharon Zukin and Gilda Zwerman, "Housing for the Working Poor: A Historical View of Jews and Blacks in Brownsville," *New York Affairs* 9 (1985): 8; Landesman, *Brownsville*, 55.

18. Poster, "Twas a Dark Night in Brownsville," 459.

19. Landesman, *Brownsville*, 5–6.

20. Samuel Abelow, *A History of Brooklyn Jewry* (New York: Scheba Publishing, 1936), 52–53; Daniel Soyer, *Jewish Immigrant Associations and American Identity: 1880–1925* (Cambridge, Mass: Harvard University Press, 1997), 79; Max Halpert, "Jews of Brownsville" (Ph.D. diss., Yeshiva University, 1959), 171–179; Irving Howe, *World of Our Fathers* (New York: Harcourt Brace Jovanovich, 1976), 183–184; see also Moses Rischin, *The Promised City: New York Jews, 1870–1914* (Cambridge: Harvard University Press, 1962); Nathan Kazanoff, "The Jewish Landsmanschaftn in New York City Before World War I," *American Jewish History* 76, no. 1 (September 1986).

21. Howe, *World of Our Fathers*, 188; Soyer, *Jewish Immigrant Associations and American Identity*, 51–61.

22. Halpert, "Jews of Brownsville," 172–174.

23. "Local Organizations," *American Jewish Yearbook*, 1919–1920 (Philadelphia: Jewish Publication Society); Works Progress Administration, "Historic Records Survey, Church Records," 1939; New York City Municipal Archives, Rolls 319–320; see also Hannah Kliger, *Jewish Hometown Associations and Family Circles in New York* (Bloomington, Ind.: Indiana University Press.

24. Adamson, *Study of the Recreational Needs of Brownsville*, 60; John McGreevy, *Parish Boundaries: The Catholic Encounter with Race in the 20th Century Urban North* (Chicago: University of Chicago Press, 1996); Gerald Gamm, *Urban Exodus: Why the Jews Left and the Catholics Stayed* (Cambridge: Harvard University Press, 1999).

25. Adamson, *Study of the Recreational Needs of Brownsville*, 60; Deborah Dash Moore, *At Home in America: Second Generation New York Jews* (New York: Columbia University Press, 1981), 128–134.

26. Halpert, "Jews of Brownsville," 176; David Kaufman, *Schul with a Pool: The Synagogue Center in American Jewish Life* (Waltham, Mass.: Brandeis University Press, 1999), 250.

27. Gerald Sorin, *The Nurturing Neighborhood: The Brownsville Boys Club and Jewish Community in Urban America* (New York: New York University Press, 1990), 42; Lizabeth Cohen, *Making a New Deal: Chicago Workers, 1919–1939* (New York: Cambridge University Press, 1993); John Bodnar, *The Transplanted: A History of Immigrants in Urban America* (Bloomington, Ind.: Indiana University Press, 1985).

28. "Modern Tenement City Is Brownsville," *Brooklyn Eagle*, 29 November 1908; "Women Planning to Aid Nursery," *Brooklyn Eagle* 21 January 1913; "Brownsville Wants a New B. R. T. Station," *Brooklyn Eagle*, 29 August 1917; "Brownsville Boasts New Civic League," *Brooklyn Eagle*, 9 September 1917; "Brownsville Plans a New Group," *Brooklyn Eagle*, 22 August 1923.

29. David Kaufman, *Schul with a Pool*, 89–91; Landesman, *Brownsville*, 179.

30. Daniel Soyer, "Elite Philanthropists and Immigrant Constituents at the Hebrew Educational Society of Brooklyn, 1899–1929," unpublished paper, in possession of author; HES, *Annual Report*, 1909.

31. Soyer, "Elite Philanthropists," 24; Landesman, *Brownsville*, 171, 190; David Kaufman, *Schul with a Pool*, 116.

32. Sorin, *Nurturing Neighborhood*, 29–30.

33. Tenenbaum, "Brownsville's Age of Learning," 176; Margaret Freeman, *Children's Branch of the Brownsville Library*, 22–34.

34. Arthur Granit, *I Am From Brownsville* (New York: Philosophical Library, 1985), 222; Sorin, *Nurturing Neighborhood*, 40.

35. Adamson, *Study of the Recreational Needs of Brownsville*, 40; Moore, *At Home in America*, 29, 96.

36. Poster, "Twas a Dark Night in Brownsville," 465; Landesman, *Brownsville*, passim.

37. Landesman, *Brownsville*, 162; "Pitkin Avenue Being Transformed into a Miniature Bowery," *Brooklyn Eagle*, 26 January 1907; "Plenty of Counterfeit Coin in Brownsville," *Brooklyn Eagle*, 23 July 1907; "Riot Outside Charles Kaplan's Saloon, Police Rescuers Called Out," *Brooklyn Eagle*, 9 July 1907.

38. Susan Glenn, *Daughters of the Shtetl: Life and Labor in the Immigrant Generation* (Ithaca: Cornell University Press, 1990), 92, 111.

39. Ibid., 121; see also Steven Fraser, "Combined and Uneven Development in the Men's Clothing Industry," *Business History Review* 57 (winter 1983) 528–537.

40. Schoenebaum, "Emerging Neighborhoods," 160, 185; Committee on the Regional Plan of New York and Its Environs, *Regional Plan of New York and Its Environs, Vol. 1B: Clothing and Textile Industries, Wholesale Markets and Retail Shopping and Financial Districts* (New York: Regional Plan of New York and Its Environs, 1928), 41, 73; *Trow's Business Directory: Borough of Brooklyn* (New York: Trow's, 1912).

41. Adamson, *Study of the Recreational Needs of Brownsville*, 37; Landesman, *Brownsville*, 101; Zukin and Zwerman, "Housing for the Working Poor," 8.

42. Kazin, *Walker in the City*, 38; Irving Ripps, "Jews of New York."

43. Landesman, *Brownsville*, 125, 130; Moore, *At Home in America*, 46; "Riot in Brownsville," *Brooklyn Eagle*, 2 December 1908.

44. Kazin, *Walker in the City*, 38–39; Tenenbaum, "Brownsville's Age of Learning," 174.

45. Kazin, *Walker in the City*, 35; Poster, "Twas a Dark Night in Brownsville," 460.

46. Marquee Picture Profile: "The Pitkin Theater Brooklyn," *Marquee* 16, no. 3 (1984): 11–14.

47. Brooklyn Edison Company, *Brooklyn Market Survey* (Brooklyn Edison Company, 1936); Landesman, *Brownsville*, 86.

48. Brooklyn Chamber of Commerce, *Manufacturing Firms With More than 100 Employees* (Brooklyn: Brooklyn Chamber of Commerce, 1942); Poster, "Twas a Dark Night in Brownsville," 459.

49. New York Herald Tribune, *New York City Market Analysis* (New York: New York Herald Tribune, 1933); Carol Bell Ford, *The Girls: Jewish Women of Brownsville Brooklyn 1940–1995* (Albany: SUNY Press, 2000), 41.

50. Ford, *The Girls*, 3; U.S. Census Bureau, *Census of Population and Housing by Health District, 1940* (Washington, D.C.: Government Printing Office, 1942), 77–78.

51. U.S. Census Bureau, Census *of Population and Housing by Health District, 1940*, 77–78. These categories were (1) Craftsmen, foremen and kindred workers; (2) Operatives and kindred workers; (3) Domestic service workers; (4) Service workers, except domestic; and (5) Laborers.

52. Margaret Sanger, *Autobiography* (New York: Doubleday, 1971), 211–220; Ellen Chesler, *Woman of Valor: Margaret Sanger and the Birth Control Movement in America* (New York: Simon and Schuster, 1992), 150–151.

53. Moore, *At Home in America*, 206; Jeffrey Nathan Gerson, "Building the Brooklyn Machine: Irish, Jewish and Black Political Succession in Central Brooklyn, 1910–1964" (Ph.D. diss., City University of New York, 1990), 89.

54. "Brownsville Has Riot Over Its Red Flag Day," *Brooklyn Eagle*, 2 May 1907; "Borough Hall Clerks Escape a Ghetto Mob," *Brooklyn Eagle*, 3 July 1908.

55. Tenenbaum, "Brownsville's Age of Learning," 177; Sol Hurok with Ruth Goode, *Impresario* (New York: Random House, 1946), 24; Harlan Robinson, *The Last Impresario: The Life, Times and Legacy of Sol Hurok* (New York: Viking Press, 1994); "Brownsville Labor Lyceum Reopened," *Brooklyn Eagle*, 20 October 1917.

56. Brownsville Labor Lyceum, "The Lyceum Bulletin," January 1923, Vertical Files, Tamiment Collection, New York University; interview with Dudley Gaffin, 1 December 1999.

57. Kenneth Teitlebaum, *Schooling for Good Rebels: Socialist Education for Children in the United States, 1900–1920* (Philadelphia: Temple University Press, 1993), 64–70; Paul Buhle, Mari Jo Buhle, and Dan Georgakas, *The Encyclopedia of the American Left* (New York: Garland, 1990), 724.

58. "Abraham I. Shiplacoff, The Spirit of Brownsville," Vertical Files, Tamiment Collection, New York University; "A. I. Shiplacoff, 56, Labor Leader, Dies," *New York*

Times, 7 February 1934; "Shiplacoff, 56, Enemy of War, Socialist, Dies," *New York World Telegram*, 7 February 1934.

59. Charles Leinenweber, "Socialist in the Streets: The New York City Socialist Party in Working-Class Neighborhoods," *Science and Society* 17 (summer 1977): 152–171.

60. Gerson, "Building the Brooklyn Machine," 105; "Co-operative Bank for Brownsville," *Brooklyn Eagle*, 24 September 1919; "Five Brownsville Families Evicted," *Brooklyn Eagle*, 17 May 1919; "Brownsville Faces Extremely Trying Housing Situation," *Brooklyn Eagle*, 1 August 1920; Joseph A. Spencer, "New York City Tenant Organizations and the Post—World War I Housing Crisis," in Ronald Lawson, ed, *The Tenant Movement in New York City, 1904–1984* (New Brunswick, N.J.: Rutgers University Press, 1986), 62–68.

61. Gerson, "Building the Brooklyn Machine," 104–113.

62. "Detectives Raid Socialist Rooms" *Brooklyn Eagle*, 28 November 1919; "Governor Orders Police to Probe Radical Meeting," *Brooklyn Eagle*, 24 April 1919; "Ousted Leaders All Win at Polls, But to Be Barred," *New York Times*, 17 September 1920; Gerson, "Building the Brooklyn Machine," 105.

63. "Hyman Schorenstein, Obituary," *Brooklyn Eagle*, 3 February 1953; Gerson, "Building the Brooklyn Machine," 107.

64. Mark Naison, "From Eviction to Resistance to Rent Control: Tenant Associations in the Great Depression," in Ronald Lawson, ed., *The Tenant Movement in New York City, 1904–1984* (New Brunswick, N.J.: Rutgers University Press, 1986), 123; Beth Wenger, *New York Jews During the Great Depression* (New Haven, Conn.: Yale University Press, 1996), 128–134; Moore, *At Home in America*, 220–228.

65. Kazin, *Walker in the City*, 58; Wenger, *New York Jews*, 110.

66. Interview with George Aronov, by Deborah Bernhardt, 12 December 1995, Workers in New York City Oral History Collection, Tamiment Collection, New York University; Peter N. Carroll, *The Odyssey of the Abraham Lincoln Brigade: Americans in the Spanish Civil War* (Stanford: Stanford University Press, 1994), 17.

67. U.S. Census Bureau, *Negro Population in the United States, 1790–1915* (Washington, D.C.: Government Printing Office, 1917); U.S. Census Bureau, *Negroes in the U.S. 1920–1932* (Washington, D.C.: Government Printing Office, 1934); Connolly, *A Ghetto Grows in Brooklyn*.

68. Glauber, *All Neighborhoods Change*, 12.

69. Connolly, *A Ghetto Grows in Brooklyn*, 24, 118; Brooklyn Urban League, *Annual Report*, 1919, 2–3.

70. Connolly, *A Ghetto Grows in Brooklyn*, 112; U.S. Census, Manuscript Census, 1920, New York Public Library.

71. Connolly, *A Ghetto Grows in Brooklyn*, 114; Thirteenth Census, Occupations, pp. 579–581; Fourteenth Census, Occupations, pp. 1165–1169. See also Craig Steven Wilder, *A Covenant with Color: Race and Social Power in Brooklyn* (New York: Columbia University Press, 2000), 159–174.

72. U.S. Census, Manuscript Census, 1920.

73. Ibid.

74. Connolly, *A Ghetto Grows in Brooklyn*, 22; Wilder, *Covenant with Color*, 178–183.

75. Clarence Taylor, *Black Churches of Brooklyn*, 75.

76. U.S. Census Bureau, *Census of Population, 1930* (Washington, D.C.: Government Printing Office, 1940); interview with Jacob Baroff, 13 December 1999.

77. Clarence Taylor, *Black Churches of Brooklyn*, 86; Samuel Freedman, *Upon This Rock: The Miracles of a Black Church* (New York: Harper, 1993), 159; interview with Reverend Spurgeon Crayton, 22 November 1999; "History of Universal Baptist Church," Universal Baptist Church, no date.

78. Kazin, *Walker in the City*, 141.

79. "The History of a Gang: A Tough Kid," *New York Post*, 8 April 1940; "Reles Made Crime Debut as Boy of 13," *Brooklyn Eagle*, 6 March 1940.

80. Albert Fried, *The Rise and Fall of the Jewish Gangster in America* (New York: Holt, Rinehart and Winston, 1980), 202–204.

81. Ibid., 204–206; "The Story of a Gang," *New York Post*, 9–10 April 1940.

82. Fried, *Rise and Fall of the Jewish Gangster*, 216–218; "Reles, Two of Gang Indicted in Killing as O'Dwyer Acts," *New York Times*, 3 February 1940; "Reles Confesses to Six Murders," *New York Times*, 16 May 1940.

83. "Lays Murder Ring's Birth to Brownsville Slum," *Brooklyn Eagle*, 19 March 1941; "O'Dwyer Is Ready to Purge Brownsville," *Brooklyn Eagle*, 14 May 1940; Goell, *Brownsville Must Have Public Housing*.

84. Irving Halpern, *A Statistical Study of the Distribution of Adult and Juvenile Delinquents in the Boroughs of Manhattan and Brooklyn* (New York: New York City Housing Authority, 1939); Sorin, *Nurturing Neighborhood*, 22; "Reader Complains of Hold Up Youths in Brownsville Section," *Brooklyn Eagle*, 30 August 1939.

85. Milton Goell, *For Better Health in Brownsville* (Brooklyn: Brownsville Neighborhood Council 1942); Poster, "Twas a Dark Night in Brownsville," 466.

86. Roth, *Call It Sleep*; Granit, *I Am from Brownsville*; Shulman, *The Amboy Dukes*.

87. Schoenebaum, "Emerging Neighborhoods," 228, 242; Moore, *At Home in America*, 24; New York Herald Tribune, *New York City Market Analysis* (New York: Herald Tribune, 1934), 24; *Census of Population, 1930*; *Census of Population and Housing, 1940*; Laidlaw, *Population of the City of New York*, 549–555.

88. "Brownsville, Stepchild of a Dozen City Administrations, Demands Civic Improvements for Its 300,000 Citizens," *Brooklyn Eagle*, 28 February 1935; "Residents Plan Model Housing in Brownsville," *Brooklyn Eagle*, 9 May 1929; "Better Stores Movement Starts in Brownsville Shopping Area," *Brooklyn Eagle*, 14 April 1935; "Public Spirited Citizens on Brownsville Committee," *Brooklyn Eagle*, 14 February 1935.

89. New York City Slum Clearance Committee, *Real Property Inventory* (New York: New York City Slum Clearance Committee, 1934), 51A—51B; Homeowners Loan Corporation, "City Survey," 1940, box 1958, National Archives, Record Group 195; Adamson, *Study of the Recreational Needs of Brownsville*, 23.

90. Adamson, *Study of the Recreational Needs of Brownsville*, 2.

Chapter 2

1. Glauber, *All Neighborhoods Change*, 52–54; "Study Issues, Vote, First Lady Tells 3,500," Brooklyn Eagle, 24 September 1944.

2. On the war at home, see Studs Terkel, *The Good War: An Oral History of World War II* (New York: Ballantine,1984); John Morton Blum, *V Was For Victory* (New York: Harcourt Brace Jovanovich, 1976).

3. See Sugrue, *Origins of the Urban Crisis;* Kenneth Jackson, *Crabgrass Frontier.*

4. Glauber, *All Neighborhoods Change*, 37.

5. Glauber, *All Neighborhoods Change*, 53, 57; "Consumer Group in Brownsville," *Brooklyn Eagle*, 13 March 1945; Joel Schwartz, "Tenant Power in the Liberal City, 1945–1980," in Ronald Lawson, ed., *The Tenant Movement in New York City, 1904–1984* (New Brunswick, N.J.: Rutgers University Press, 1986), 142; Meg Jacobs, "How About Some Meat?: The Office of Price Administration, Consumption Politics, and State Building from the Bottom Up, 1941–1946," *Journal of American History* (December 1997): 910–941, 923–925.

6. Robert Zeiger, *The CIO, 1935–1955* (Chapel Hill: University of North Carolina Press, 1995), 149.

7. Ibid.; Glauber, *All Neighborhoods Change*, 31.

8. "Tenant Group Is Aid Here," *New York Amsterdam News*, 13 September 1947; Glauber, *All Neighborhoods Change*, 57–58.

9. Robert Zeiger argues that IUC meetings were not well attended and that those who did participate were considerably to the left of union membership. Zeiger, *The CIO*, 150; Brooklyn Jewish Community Council, "Report of Community Relations Committee, 15 September 1943 to 31 December 1943," Papers of the Brooklyn Jewish Community Council, American Jewish Archives (hereinafter "BJCC Papers"), box 6, folder 4. Josh Freeman argues that Communists were so powerful in the Brownsville that labor leaders were afraid to confront them. Joshua B. Freeman, *Working-Class New York: Life and Labor Since World War II* (New York: The New Press, 2000), 58.

10. See also Mark Naison, "From Eviction Resistance to Rent Control: Tenant Action in the Great Depression," in Ronald Lawson, ed., *The Tenant Movement in New York City, 1904–1984* (New Brunswick, N.J.: Rutgers University Press, 1986), 129; also Schwartz, "Tenant Power," 143; Glauber, *All Neighborhoods Change*, 32–35.

11. Glauber, *All Neighborhoods Change*, 38; "Brownsville Women Work for Unity," *Brooklyn Eagle*, 15 February 1945; "Brownsville Youngsters Have Interracial Conference Here," *New York Amsterdam News*, 1 February 1947; "Good Will Oath Given by 2000 Youths at Rally," *Brooklyn Eagle*, 6 March 1944.

12. "Letter from Robert Moses to Lee Smith, Director of Real Estate," 24 July 1943, Records of the New York City Parks Department, New York City Municipal Archives, New York, New York (hereinafter "Parks Papers"); "Survey in Brownsville to Show Negro Youths' Recreation Needs," *Brooklyn Eagle*, 11 April 1950, 10; Adamson, *Study of the Recreational Needs of Brownsville.*

13. The story of the BBC is chronicled in Sorin, *Nurturing Neighborhood;* interview with Jack Baroff, 13 December 1999.

14. Interview with Jack Baroff, 13 December 1999.

15. Sorin, *Nurturing Neighborhood*, 40–45; interview with Doc Baroff, 13 December 1999; interview with Dudley Gaffin, 1 December 1999.

16. Sorin, *Nurturing Neighborhood*, passim; interview with Jack Baroff, 13 December 1999; interview with Irving Levine, 21 March 1998.

17. Interview with Jack Baroff by Richard Broadman, in possession of author.

18. Landesman, *Brownsville*, 92–93; "Notes on the Brownsville Neighborhood Health and Welfare Council," no date, Papers of the Brooklyn Council for Social Planning, Brooklyn Collection, Brooklyn Public Library, Brooklyn New York (hereinafter "BCSP Papers"); "Annual Report of the Brooklyn Council for Social Planning," April 1955, BCSP Papers.

19. David Suher, "The Brownsville Neighborhood Council" (master's thesis, New York University, 1949); "Notes on the Brownsville Neighborhood Health and Welfare Council," undated, BCSP Papers; "Field Worker's Report," 12 June 1948, BCSP Papers.

20. Glauber, *All Neighborhoods Change*, 40; "Obituary, Milton Goell," *New York Times*, 23 August 1971.

21. "Council Choices Named," *New York Times*, 1 June 1945.

22. "Field Worker's Report," BCSP Papers; Brownsville Neighborhood Council, "By-Laws," BCSP Papers.

23. Schwartz, *New York Approach*, 119; Peter Marcuse, "The Beginnings of Public Housing in New York," *Journal of Urban History* 12 (August 1986): 353.

24. "Letter from State Senator Jacob J. Shwartzweld to Nathan Strauss, United States Housing Authority," 10 July 1938, Papers of the New York City Housing Authority, La Guardia and Wagner Archives, La Guardia Community College, Queens, New York (hereinafter, "NYCHA Papers"), box 53E4, folder 5; "Letter from Joseph A. Solovei, Attorney, to Alfred Rheinstein, Chairman, NYCHA," 27 July 1938, NYCHA Papers, box 53E4, folder 5.

25. Milton Goell, *Brownsville Must Have Public Housing* (Brooklyn: Brownsville Neighborhood Council, 1940), 2; "Letter from George Brown, Assistant Technical Director, NYCHA, to Joseph Solovei," 19 November 1938, NYCHA Papers, box 53E4, folder 5; Schwartz, *New York Approach*, 119; "Housing Project Drive Hits Climax in Brownsville," *Brooklyn Eagle*, 6 May 1941; Brownsville Slum Clearance Plan Gets Wide Support," *Brooklyn Eagle*, 13 November 1940.

26. Sugrue, *The Origins of the Urban Crisis*; Hirsch, *Making the Second Ghetto*.

27. Milton Goell, *Brownsville Must Have Public Housing*, 19.

28. Ibid., 10.

29. Ibid., 17.

30. Ibid., 26–29.

31. Ibid.

32. Ibid.; "Construction of Housing Project Faces Long Delay," *Brooklyn Eagle*, 11 December 1941; "Brownsville Soon to Undergo Face Lifting" *Brooklyn Eagle*, 16 September 1945.

33. Goell, *For Better Health in Brownsville*, 11, 18; Goell, *A Postwar Plan for Brownsville*.

34. William O'Neill, *American High: The Years of Confidence, 1945–1960* (New York: Free Press, 1989).

35. Robert Fishman, "The Regional Plan and the Transformation of the Industrial Metropolis," in David Ward and Olivier Zunz, eds., *Landscape of Modernity: New York City 1900–1940* (Baltimore: Johns Hopkins University Press, 1992), 106–128; New York City Planning Commission, *Proposed Postwar Works Program* (New York: City Planning Commission, 1942). On postwar planning in general, see Peter Hall, *Cities of Tomorrow: An Intellectual History of Urban Planning and Design in the Twentieth Century* (Oxford: Basil Blackwell, 1988).

36. Goell, *A Postwar Plan for Brownsville*, 7.

37. Ibid., 29–31.

38. Ibid., 11, 16–17; "Brownsville Residents Irked by Laxity of R. R. After Two Deaths," *New York Amsterdam News*, 21 November 1946; "Death Waits Inside a Bare Wire for the Children of Brownsville," *Brooklyn Eagle*, 13 November 1946.

39. Goell, *A Postwar Plan for Brownsville*, 21–23.

40. Ibid., 13–14.

41. Ibid., 33.

42. "Plans for New Brownsville Deserve Thoughtful Study," *Brooklyn Eagle*, 9 February 1945.

43. Interview with Jack Baroff, 13 December 1999; Sorin, *Nurturing Neighborhood*, 164.

44. Lillian Lampkin, "Tentative Project to Help Meet the Needs of Young People in an Unserviced Neighborhood of Brooklyn," March 1947, BCSP Papers.

45. Zeiger, *The CIO*, 148, 272; Joshua B. Freeman, *Working-Class New York*, 78.

46. Schwartz, "Tenant Power in the Liberal City," 142; Glauber, *All Neighborhoods Change*, 56–57.

47. Eric Schneider, *Vampires, Dragons, and Egyptian Kings: Youth Gangs in Postwar New York* (Princeton: Princeton University Press, 1999), 54–55; James Gilbert, *Cycle of Outrage: America's Reaction to the Juvenile Delinquent in the 1950s* (New York: Oxford University Press, 1986); 25–34; "Plan Youth Center to Aid Campaign on Delinquency," *Brooklyn Eagle*, 21 December 1942; "McGarry Assures Brownsville on Child Delinquency Project," *Brooklyn Eagle*, 28 December 1944; "Test Irks Brownsville," *New York Times*, 28 December 1944; Sorin, *Nurturing Neighborhood*, 88–90.

48. Sorin, *Nurturing Neighborhood*, 109; "Youth Board Program in Brownsville," *Brooklyn Eagle*, 5 April 1949; "Rifles, Air Guns, Knives Offered to Youngsters," *Brooklyn Eagle*, 4 March 1949; "Stark Asks City-Wide Drive on Delinquency," *Brooklyn Eagle*, 3 March 1949.

49. "Stark Asks City-Wide Drive on Delinquency," *Brooklyn Eagle*, 3 March 1949; "Brownsville Parents Demanding Reforms to Curb Child Gangs," *Brooklyn Eagle*, 20 March 1949; "Boro Theft Insurance Rate Tops City—Firms Blackball Brownsville," *Brooklyn Eagle*, 7 April 1948.

50. "Crime Groups Open War on Youth Crime," *Brooklyn Eagle*, 12 May 1949;

"Want Schools as Youth Centers After Hours," *Brooklyn Eagle*, 10 March 1949; "Youth Board Program in Brownsville," *Brooklyn Eagle*, 5 April 1949.

51. Sorin, *Nurturing Neighborhood*, 100–102.

52. Ibid., 92.

53. Ibid., 111–118; interview with Irving Levine, 21 March 1998.

54. Interview with Irving Kantrowitz, 12 December 1999.

55. "Young People's Fellowship, Report to the Federation of Jewish Philanthropies," February 14, 1949, Papers of the United Jewish Appeal, New York, New York (hereinafter "UJA Papers"); Irving Shulman, *The Amboy Dukes* (New York: Avon Press, 1949); "Brownsville's Older Folks Enjoy 'Golden Age' Program," *Brooklyn Eagle*, 29 April 1951.

56. Brooklyn Jewish Community Council, *Report and Recommendations* (Brooklyn: Brooklyn Jewish Community Council, 1947), 14, 18.

57. *Report and Recommendations*, 51–55; "Adult Institute of Jewish Studies Starts 4 Courses," *Brooklyn Eagle*, 13 November 1948.

Chapter 3

1. "Mayor of Brooklyn: A Man Who Believes in God, Youth and Greens," *New York Amsterdam News*, 6 January 1951; "Mapping Brownsville Drive," *New York Amsterdam News*, 10 March 1948; "Church Notes," *New York Amsterdam News*, 18 May 1946; "Miller Voted 'Mayor' of Brooklyn," *New York Amsterdam News*, 27 December 1947; "John King Voted to Brooklyn Mayor," *New York Amsterdam News*, 12 January 1946; "Brownsville Businessman Lauded for Contributions," *New York Amsterdam News*, 21 November 1948.

2. Interview with Reverend Harold Burton, 2 December 1999; "Negro Groups Aid Clean-Up Drive in Brownsville Area," *Brooklyn Eagle*, 21 December 1948; "Mayor of Brooklyn: A Man Who Believes in God, Youth and Greens," *New York Amsterdam News*, 6 January 1951; "Mapping Brownsville Drive," *New York Amsterdam News*, 10 March 1948; "Church Notes," *New York Amsterdam News*, 18 May 1946; "Miller Voted 'Mayor' of Brooklyn," *New York Amsterdam News*, 27 December 1947; "John King Voted to Brooklyn Mayor," *New York Amsterdam News*, 12 January 1946; "Brownsville Businessman Lauded for Contributions," *New York Amsterdam News*, 21 November 1948; Lampkin, "Tentative Project."

3. Connolly, *A Ghetto Grows in Brooklyn*, 130; Wilder, *A Covenant With Color*, 169–174; Joshua B. Freeman, *Working-Class New York*, 26.

4. Lillian Lampkin, "Tentative Project to Help Meet the Needs of Young People in an Unserviced Neighborhood of Brooklyn," March, 1947, Papers of the Brooklyn Council for Social Planning, Brooklyn Collection, Brooklyn Public Library (hereinafter "BCSP Papers"); U.S. Census Bureau, Census of Population and Housing, 1940 (Washington, D.C.: Government Printing Office, 1942), 171.

5. "192-194-198 Osborne Street Found in Shocking Condition," *New York Amsterdam News*, 7 October 1950; "Editorial—Brownsville 'Loses Face' Again," *New York Amsterdam News*, 13 October 1945.

6. Samuel Freedman, *Upon This Rock*, 162–163.

7. Interview with Reverend Spurgeon Crayton, Mount Ollie Baptist Church, 24 November 1999; "Mt. Ollie Has Founders Day," *New York Amsterdam News*, 27 November 1940.

8. Interview with Reverend Harold Burton, Brownsville Community Baptist Church, 2 December 1999; interview with Reverend James Green, Universal Baptist Church, 13 January 2000.

9. Clarence Taylor, *Black Churches of Brooklyn*, 136.

10. Ibid.

11. "Brownsville Organizes Fight for Playgrounds," *Brooklyn Eagle*, 14 December 1940; "Drive Pushed to Erase Peril in L. I. R. R. Yards," *Brooklyn Eagle*, 16 November 1946; "Brownsville Residents Irked by Laxity of R. R. After Two Deaths," *New York Amsterdam News*, 23 November 1946; interview with Reverend Spurgeon Crayton.

12. "Memo From Mr. Wilkins to Mr. Pickens," 31 March 1941, Papers of the National Association for the Advancement of Colored Persons, Library of Congress, Washington, D.C. (hereinafter "NAACP Papers"); Lampkin, "Tentative Project."

13. Clarence Taylor, *Knocking at Our Own Door*, 48–49; "Memo from Herbert Hill to Gloster B. Current," 19 July 1951, NAACP Papers.

14. "Duo Held, in High Bail for Theft in Boro Synagogue," *New York Amsterdam News*, 19 July 1947; "Brownsville Man Awaits Grand Jury Cop Charge," *New York Amsterdam News*, 4 December 1948; "Cops Still Shield Name of Borough Gun Suspect," *New York Amsterdam News*, 25 May 1946; "Caretaker Is Slain in His Basement Apartment," *New York Amsterdam News*, 30 August 1947; "Brownsville Youth Bites Cop's Hands," *New York Amsterdam News*, 31 August 1946; " Homicides Top Brooklyn Police Crime Cleanup," *New York Amsterdam News*, 23 October 1948; "Hearing for Brownsville Slayer Set," *New York Amsterdam News*, 6 November 1946; "Two Wives Kill Mates," *New York Amsterdam News*, 20 November 1948; "Married Man Kills Brownsville Girl," *New York Amsterdam News*, 17 April 1948.

15. "3 Boys in Teen-Age Gang Battle," *Brooklyn Eagle*, 1 November 1949; "Brownsville Asks Police Aid in Gang Feuds," *Brooklyn Eagle*, 20 July 1947; "Brownsville Pastors War on Mobsters," *New York Amsterdam News*, 20 July 1947.

16. Connolly, *A Ghetto Grows in Brooklyn*, 137–138; Algernon Black, "The Role of the Police," 10 September 1974, Papers of Algernon Black, box 7, Manuscript Division Columbia University, New York, New York; Wilder, *Covenant with Color*, 197–199.

17. "Cop Attack Riles Brownsville," *New York Amsterdam News*, 16 June 1945; "Police Beat Up Case Sizzles," *New York Amsterdam News*, 23 June 1946; "Detectives Attack Youth," *New York Amsterdam News*, 24 January 1948; "Editorial—About Some 'Hoodlum' Cops," *New York Amsterdam News*, 24 January 1948; "Mass Rally Slated in East New York to Probe Police Brutality," *New York Amsterdam News*, 12 June 1948.

18. Interview with Reverend Spurgeon Crayton, 24 November 1999; interview with Leroy Crayton, 24 November 1999.

19. Interview with Reverend Harold Burton, 2 December 1999; interview with Daniel Culley by Richard Broadman, in possession of author; interview with Dudley Gaffin, 1 December 1999.

20. "Quell Brownsville Race Riot," *New York Amsterdam News*, 8 June 1946.

21. "White Mob Runs Wild in Borough," *New York Amsterdam News,* 10 August 1946; "Police Jail 65 Negroes Like Cattle," *New York Amsterdam News,* 17 August 1946; interview with Arthur Lawrence by Richard Broadman, in possession of author.

22. Goell, *For Better Health in Brownsville,* 10; "Poll Tax Is Life, Death Question Cacchione Warns," *Brooklyn Eagle,* 30 June 1943; "Brownsville Assails Jim Crow at Conference Here," *New York Amsterdam News,* 9 June 1945; "Brownsville Neighborhood Council Has Third Affair," *New York Amsterdam News,* 30 June 1945; "Brownsville Women Work for Unity," *Brooklyn Eagle,* 15 February 1945; "Good Will Oath Given by 2,000 Youths at Rally," *Brooklyn Eagle,* 6 March 1944.

23. Goell, *A Postwar Plan for Brownsville,* 10. For a discussion of similar efforts at integration in the Bronx, see Samuel Lubell, *The Future of American Politics* (Westport, Conn.: Greenwood Press, 1955), 93–96.

24. Goell, *A Postwar Plan for Brownsville,* 27.

25. "Youth Project Activities Report," May 1945, BCSP Papers.

26. Interview with Arthur Lawrence by Richard Broadman, in possession of author; interview with Raymond Lawrence by Richard Broadman, in possession of author; interview with Irving Levine by Richard Broadman, in possession of author; Sorin, *Nurturing Neighborhood,* 113–115.

27. Sorin, *Nurturing Neighborhood,* 92, 113–115.

28. Ibid., 113–115, 140–141; interview with Irving Levine by Richard Broadman, in possession of author.

29. "Memo from Flora Davidson to Judge McGarry," 6 November 1947, BCSP Papers.

30. "Letter from Edwin Salmon, Chairman, City Planning Commission, to Edmund Butler, Chairman, NYCHA," 14 May 1942, Parks Papers; "Construction of Housing Project Faces Long Delay," *Brooklyn Eagle,* 11 December 1941; "Release," NYCHA, 31 August 1947; "Brownsville Houses Opens," *New York Times,* 8 March 1948.

31. "NYCHA Racial Distribution at Initial Occupancy," 1955, NYCHA Papers, box 71B5, folder 2; "Letter from Walter White, Secretary, NAACP, to Alfred Rheinstein, Chairman, NYCHA," 7 August 1939, NYCHA Papers, box 54C4, folder 1; "Letter from Alfred Rheinstein, Chairman, NYCHA, to Walter White, Secretary, NAACP," 31 August 1939, NYCHA Papers, box 54C4, folder 1; Schwartz, *New York Approach,* 122.

32. "Letter from Alfred Rheinstein to Walter White"; "Memo from George Poehler to Frederick Ackerman Regarding Report on Survey for Brooklyn Negro Project," NYCHA Papers, box 54B4, folder 9; "Letter from George Poehler to Frederick Ackerman Regarding Meeting at This Office for Brooklyn Negro Project," 1 February 1939, NYCHA Papers, box 54B4, folder 9.

33. "NYCHA Racial Distribution at Initial Occupancy," 1955, NYCHA Papers, box 71B5, folder 2.

34. "Memo from George Spargo to Robert Moses," 24 January 1945, Parks Papers, box 102757; "Memorandum Regarding Future Federal and State Housing Projects," undated, Parks Papers, box 102757; Schwartz, *New York Approach,* 119.

35. Schwartz, *New York Approach*, 119–120.

36. "Rally Slated to Urge Erection of 4 New Brownsville Schools," *New York Amsterdam News*, 13 March 1948; "Brownsville Sets Rally to Demand 4 New Schools, *Brooklyn Eagle*, 14 March, 1948; Suher, 23, 31, 42, 99.

37. Martha Biondi, "The Struggle for Black Equality in New York City, 1945–1955," (Ph.D. diss., 1997), 33; see also Cheryl Greenberg, "Negotiating Coalition: Black and Jewish Civil Rights Agencies in the Twentieth Century," in Jack Salzman and Cornel West, eds., *Struggles in the Promised Land: Towards a History of Black-Jewish Relations in the United States* (New York: Oxford University Press, 1997), 159–161; on Truman's civil rights program, see Alonzo Hamby, *Beyond the New Deal: Harry S. Truman and American Liberalism* (New York: Columbia University Press, 1973); Stephen Lawson, *Running for Freedom: Civil Rights and Black Politics Since 1941* (Philadelphia: Temple University Press, 1991); Donald McCoy and Richard Ruetten, *Quest and Response: Minority Rights and the Truman Administration* (Lawrence: University of Kansas Press, 1973).

38. U.S. Census Bureau, *Census of Housing, 1950* (Washington, D.C.: Government Printing Office, 1952), 12.

39. Tom Sugrue, "Crabgrass-Roots Politics: Race, Rights and the Reaction Against Liberalism in the Urban North, 1940–1964," *Journal of American History* (September 1995): 551–578, 557–561; Hirsch, *Making the Second Ghetto*, 95.

Chapter 4

1. "Boro NAACP Blasts Reds: Works with D.A.'s Men on Brownsville Probe," *New York Amsterdam News*, 2 June 1951; "Press Release, Brownsville Citizens Committee of 2000," 20 July 1951, Papers of the New York American Labor Party, Special Collections, Rutgers University, box 55 (hereinafter "ALP Papers"); see also Biondi, "The Struggle for Black Equality in New York City, 1945–1955."

2. "Brownsville Leaders Fight Attempt to Smear Police in Negro's Slaying," *Brooklyn Eagle*, 28 May 1951; "Memo to Gloster B. Current from Herbert Hill Regarding Action on Fields Case," 19 July 1951, Brooklyn Branch Papers, NAACP Papers; Clarence Taylor, *Knocking at Our Own Door*, 51; "Boro NAACP Blasts Reds," *New York Amsterdam News*.

3. "Brownsville Citizens Committee of 2000 For Justice in the Case of Henry Fields, Jr.," "Lawyers Fight Case Ten Years," *New York Amsterdam News*, 24 June 1961; Biondi, 151; Clarence Taylor, *Knocking at Our Own Door*, 51. On the reticence of Jewish groups to participate in grassroots protest, see Cheryl Greenberg, "Negotiating Coalition: Black and Jewish Civil Rights Agencies in the Twentieth Century," in Jack Salzman and Cornel West, eds., *Struggles in the Promised Land*, 165–166.

4. Community Council of New York, *Brooklyn Communities: Population Characteristics and Neighborhood Social Resources* (New York: Bureau of Community Statistical Services, 1959), 163–165; U.S. Census Bureau, *Census of Housing and Population, 1950* (Washington, D.C.: Government Printing Office, 1952); U.S. Census Bureau, *Special Census of New York City, 1957* (Washington, D.C: Government Printing Office, 1958).

5. In 1953, the Brownsville Neighborhood Council merged with another local or-

ganization, the Brownsville Health Council, to form the Brownsville Neighborhood Health and Welfare Council. This organization will be referred to as the Brownsville Neighborhood Council, or BNC.

6. Interview with Dudley Gaffin, 1 December 1999; "Abe Stark, Obituary," *New York Times*, July 4, 1972; "Stark Wedged Himself into Politics and Stuck," *New York World Telegram and Sun*, 6 September 1956; "Abe Stark, Obituary," *Daily News*, 4 July 1972; Glauber, *All Neighborhoods Change*, 24–25; "Brownsville Man Lauded for Contributions," *New York Amsterdam News*, 21 November 1948.

7. Interview with Dudley Gaffin, 1 December 1999; "Stark Wedged Himself into Politics and Stuck," *New York World Telegram and Sun;* "Abe Stark, Obituary," *Daily News*, 4 July 1972.

8. The story of the BBC is chronicled in Sorin, *Nurturing Neighborhood.*

9. Sorin, *Nurturing Neighborhood*, 120–140; "Letter from Edgar Doubleday, Executive Vice President, Charles Hayden Foundation, to Abe Stark," 1 June 1950, BCSP Papers; interview with Irving Levine by Richard Broadman, in possession of author.

10. Sorin, *Nurturing Neighborhood*, 115–117, "Boys Club Funds Dip, Staff Cut," *Daily News*, 17 March 1954.

11. Sorin, *Nurturing Neighborhood*, 145–147; interview with Irving Levine, 21 March 1998.

12. Sorin, 148; *Nurturing Neighborhood*, "Letter from Fired BBC Workers," no date, BCSP Papers; "City Takes Over Brownsville Boys Club," *Brooklyn Eagle*, 20 September 1954; "Brownsville Club Reopens With Many Activities Listed," *Brooklyn Eagle*, 25 January 1955.

13. "Statement to Board of Estimate from Irving Tabb, President BNH&WC," no date, BCSP Papers; "Report on Brownsville Boys Club to BNH&WC from Irving Tabb, President," 22 February 1955, BCSP Papers; Sorin, *Nurturing Neighborhood*, 150.

14. "Letter from Arthur Hodgkiss, Executive Officer of the Department of Parks, to Francis McGarey, Chairman, Youth Activities Committee," 8 March 1946, Parks Papers; "Letter from Benjamin Lambert, Executive Director, BBC to Stewart Constable, Chief Park Designer," 8 December 1949, Parks Papers; "Letter from Stewart Constable, Chief Park Designer, to Benjamin Lambert, Executive Director, BBC," 13 December 1949, Parks Papers; "The Brownsville Boys Club," September, 1954, Parks Papers.

15. Interview with Jack Baroff, 13 December 1999; interview with Dudley Gaffin, 1 December 1999; interview with Irving Levine, 21 March 1998.

16. Sorin, *Nurturing Neighborhood*, 203.

17. "Letter from Irving Tabb, President, BNH&WC, to Philip Cruise, Chairman, NYCHA," 7 June 1955, Papers of the Citizen's Housing and Planning Commission, New York (hereinafter "CHPC Papers"); "Duo Admits Giving Teenagers Heroin," *New York Amsterdam News*, 18 February 1950; "Pretty Cop Helps Break Heroin Ring," *Brooklyn Eagle*, 5 January 1951; "Ex Model Traps Narcotics Suspects," *Brooklyn Eagle*, 12 January 1951; "Renew Holdup Wave: Failed in 1 of 2 Jobs," *Brooklyn Eagle*, 10 February 1951; "Thug Gets $1,400 in Auto Stick Up," *Brooklyn Eagle*, 7 April 1951; "4 Brownsville Stores Robbed in Vicinity of Police Station," *Brooklyn Eagle*, 25 May 1951; "Next Class of Rookies Coming Here," *Brooklyn Eagle*, 20 November 1951.

18. E-mail message from Bernard Lewin, 20 October 1999; "Trio Arrested in Brownsville Youth War," *New York Amsterdam News*, 2 September 1950.

Juvenile Delinquency Rates—Offenses/Rate per Thousand, by Health Area (HA)

	HA 56	HA 57	HA 58	HA 59	HA 60
1953	54/15.2	121/29.6	23/6.9	127/23.6	55/15.2
1954	53/14.9	144/34.2	34/10.4	195/34.1	130/35.9
1955	98/27.8	197/45.4	30/9.4	357/58.8	176/48.1
1956	113/32.1	304/68.2	50/16.1	477/74.4	223/60.4
1957	163/46.6	397/86.5	26/8.6	628/92.9	274/73.5
1959	180/48.9	424/87.2	35/11.6	601/88.4	226/57.3
1959	254/65.8	400/78	30/9.9	604/87.4	311/75.3
1960	272/67.3	439/81.3	44/14.6	696/97.9	432/99.8
1961	372/92	476/88.2	67/22.2	707/99.5	572/132.2
1962	375/92.8	549/101.7	87/28.8	796/112	649/150

Source: New York City Youth Board, *Youth Board Area Report*, 1964.

19. New York City Youth Board, *Youth Board Area Report*, 1964; "Letter from Irving Tabb to Philip Cruise"; "NYCHA Racial Distribution At Projects, June 1955," NYCHA Papers, box 71B5, folder 2.

20. "Initial Occupancy Statistics," NYCHA Papers, box 63E3, folder 8; Lawrence Friedman, *The Government and Slum Housing: A Century of Frustration* (Chicago: Rand McNally, 1968), 140–142.

21. Glauber, *All Neighborhoods Change*, 68; "Letter from Irving Tabb to Philip Cruise."

22. Peter Marcuse, 354–356; New York City Housing Authority, "1971 Guide to Housing Developments," NYCHA Papers, box 65D6, folder 16; Catharine Bauer, "The Dreary Deadlock of Public Housing," *Architectural Forum* 106 (May 1957): 140–142; Robert A. M. Stern, *New York, 1960: Architecture and Urbanism Between the Second World War and the Bicentennial* (New York: Manacelli Press, 1995); Leonard Freedman, *Public Housing and the Politics of Poverty* (New York: Free Press, 1969), 115–118; Lawrence Friedman, *Government and Slum Housing*, 121–122; Wright, *Building the Dream*, 234–235.

23. Initial Occupancy Statistics, NYCHA Papers, box 63E3, folder 8.

24. Leonard Freedman, *Public Housing and the Politics of Poverty*, 107–111; Lawrence Friedman, *Government and Slum Housing*, 121.

25. "Turnover at New York City Housing Projects," NYCHA Papers, box 66A1, folder 6.

Number of Families Moving Out of Federal Projects

	Total	Voluntary	Involuntary	Total Units	Turnover Rate
1950	1,138	475	603	14,161	7. 75
1951	1,214	688	526	14,161	8. 49
1952	1,157	714	443	16,633	7. 76

Number of Families Moving Out of Federal Projects (*continued*)

	Total	Voluntary	Involuntary	Total Units	Turnover Rate
1953	1,657	900	757	20,557	9. 16
1954	1,819	1,136	683	25,775	8. 00
1955	2,543	1,658	685	31,004	7. 87
1956	2,401	1,890	511	31,803	7. 54

26. Salisbury, *Shook-up Generation* (New York: Harper, 1958), 82; Schwartz, "Tenant Power"; Glauber, *All Neighborhoods Change*, 62–63; Lawrence Friedman, *Government and Slum Housing*, 125–130.

27. "Memo Re Eviction of Tenants for Excessive Income," NYCHA Papers, box 69B3, folder 1; Lawrence Friedman, *Government and Slum Housing*, 140; Wilder, *Covenant with Color,* 110. On housing discrimination and its impact on African-Americans, see Charles Abrams, *Forbidden Neighbors: A Study of Prejudice in Housing* (New York: Harper, 1955); Douglas S. Massey and Nancy A. Denton, *American Apartheid: Segregation and the Making of the Underclass* (Cambridge: Harvard University Press, 1993), 17–60.

28. "Tenants on Welfare Statistics, NYCHA," NYCHA Papers, box 66A1, folder 7; "Initial Occupancy Statistics," NYCHA Papers, box 64A2, folder 12; "Initial Occupancy Statistics," NYCHA Papers, box 63E3, folder 8; Lawrence Friedman, *Government and Slum Housing*, 121–122; Wright, *Building the Dream*, 234.

29. Interview with Arthur Lewin, 11 November 1999.

30. On Robert Moses and his "redevelopment machine," see Schwartz, *New York Approach*; Caro, *The Power Broker.*

31. Schwartz, *New York Approach*, 98, 124; Caro, *Power Broker,* 965–968.

32. Caro, *Power Broker,* 965–968; Schwartz, *New York Approach*, 124.

33. "Letter from Irving Tabb to Philip Cruise."

34. "Brownsville Health and Welfare Council, Housing Committee Statement," 6 April 1954, BCSP Papers; "Flyer—Wanted: A Middle Income Housing Project in Brownsville," 10 January 1955, BCSP Papers; "Open Letter from the Brownsville Neighborhood Health and Welfare Council," no date, BCSP Papers; "Announcement of BNH&WC Annual Conference on Housing," 14 November 1955, BCSP Papers; "Proposed Resolution of BNH&WC," 13 December 1954; "Housing Committee Statement, BNH&WC, 6 April 1954; "Conference on Housing Needs, BNH&WC," 8 March 1954.

35. Schwartz, *New York Approach*, 84–107, 126–128.

36. Ibid., 133–137; "Announcement of BNH&WC Annual Conference on Housing," 14 November 1955, BCSP Papers.

37. Schwartz, *New York Approach*, 144–169; see also Hirsch, *Making the Second Ghetto.*

38. Glauber, *All Neighborhoods Change*, 66.

39. "Press Notice," BNH&WC, 13 March 1956; "Flyer Announcing the Annual Dinner of the Brownsville Neighborhood Council," 24 May 1950, BCSP Papers; "Middle-Income Housing Demand Made for Brownsville Unit," *Brooklyn Eagle*, no date,

Subject files, Brooklyn Collection, Brooklyn Public Library; "Brownsville Neighborhood Health and Welfare Council Review," December 1955, BCSP Papers;

40. "City Asked to Extend Brownsville Houses," *Brooklyn Eagle*, 24 December 1953; "Memorandum—Brownsville South," 9 May 1955 and 13 May 1955, CHPC Papers.

41. "Letter from Ira Robbins, Executive Director, CHPC, to John Bennett, Chair, New York City Planning Commission," 16 May 1955, CHPC Papers.

42. "Letter from Irving Tabb to Philip Cruise," 7 June 1955, CHPC Papers.

43. "BNH&WC Review," January 1955; "Letter from Rae Glauber to NYCHA Executive Director Warren Moscow," 20 December 1955, BCSP Papers.

44. "BNH&WC Membership List," 1955, BCSP Papers; interview with Reverend James Green, Universal Baptist Church, 13 January 2000.

45. "Memo to Files from Madison S. Jones," 16 October 1958, NYCHA Papers, box 65E6, folder 1.

46. "Letter from Irving Tabb to NYCHA Commissioner Reid," 23 November 1958, Papers of Mayor Robert Wagner, New York City Municipal Archives (hereinafter "Wagner Papers"), box 130, folder 1909; "Vast Tilden Houses to Open January 16," *New York Amsterdam News*, 28 December 1960; "News Release from the NYCHA," 30 January 1961, Wagner Papers, box 130, 1909.

47. "Brownsville Health Council, Brief Summary of Projects Accomplished," 21 June 1951, BCSP Papers; "Minutes, Brownsville Health Council, New Junior High School Committee," 17 October 1950, BCSP Papers.

48. "Minutes, Brownsville Health Council," 13 June 1950, BCSP Papers; "Minutes, Brownsville Health Council New Junior High School Committee, 31 May 1950, BCSP Papers.

49. Clarence Taylor, *Knocking at Our Own Door*, 54; "Letter from Clara Tabb, Chairman Schools Committee, BNH&WC, to the New York City Board of Estimate," no date, BCSP Papers; "Statement to the Board of Estimate by BNHWC," 15 November 1954, BCSP Papers; "Letter from Mrs. Elizabeth Bauer, Chairman New Junior High School Committee, to George Pigott, Jr. Associate Superintendent of Education," 2 March 1951, Files of Mayor William O'Dwyer, New York City Municipal Archives, New York, New York (hereinafter "O'Dwyer Papers); "Letter from Blanche Gittlitz, Chairman New Junior High School Committee, to Mayor Vincent Impelleteri," 5 August 1952, Files of Mayor Vincent Impelleteri, New York City Municipal Archives, New York, New York (hereinafter "Impelleteri Papers").

50. "Letter from Clara Tabb to Board of Estimate"; "Minutes, Brownsville Health Council New Junior High School Committee," 13 June 1950, BCSP Papers.

51. "Brief Presented to the Board of Estimate by the BNH&WC," 18 November 1955, BCSP Papers.

52. "Flyer for Concert Rally for a New Junior High School in Brownsville," 29 March 1952, BCSP Papers; "Letter from Congressman Emmanuel Celler to Mayor Impelleteri," 9 June 1952, Impelleteri Papers.

53. "Letter from Clara Tabb to Board of Estimate"; "Statement to Board of Estimate by BNHWC."

54. "All Brownsville Turns Out to See New School Started," *Brooklyn Eagle*, 9

September 1955; "Statement to Board of Estimate by BNH&WC"; "Brief Presented to New York City Board of Estimate by BNH&WC," 18 November 1955, BCSP Papers; BNH&WC Press Release, no date, BCSP Papers.

55. Interview with Reverend Spurgeon, 24 November 1999; interview with Leroy Crayton, 24 November 1999; Connolly, *A Ghetto Grows in Brooklyn*, 130.

56. Interview with Alice Book, 13 January 2000; interview with Reverend James Green, 13 January 2000; Universal Baptist Church, "History of Universal Baptist Church," 1999.

57. "Souvenir Journal Dedicational Celebration of Universal Baptist Church," June 10–July 8, 1956; Universal Baptist Church, "History of Universal Baptist Church," 1999.

58. Clarence Taylor, *Black Churches of Brooklyn*, 134; Samuel Freedman, *Upon This Rock*, 163–165.

59. Protestant Council of New York, *Report on the Protestant Spanish Community in New York City* (New York: Protestant Council of New York, 1960).

60. Clarence Taylor, *Knocking at Our Own Door*, 50–51; Glauber, *All Neighborhoods Change*, 115–116; "Dear Neighbor Letter from John Newton, Chairman Community Relations Committee, BNH&WC," 19 April 1955, BCSP Papers. See also Biondi, "The Struggle for Black Equality," 425–432.

61. "Boise Dent Wins 1950 Brooklyn Poll," *New York Amsterdam News*, 20 December 1950; "1951 Mayor of Brooklyn Dead of Cardiac Arrest," *New York Amsterdam News*, 24 November 1951.

62. Glauber, *All Neighborhoods Change*, 62.

63. "Officers and Executive Board, BNH&WC," June 1956, BCSP Papers.

64. Interview with Irving Levine, March 1998; interview with James Green, 13 January 2000; Spurgeon E. Crayton, *God's Star in the East: The Story of the Eastern Baptist Association* (Brooklyn: Eastern Baptist Association, 1996); "Rev. Harten Committee Acts First," *New York Amsterdam News*, 13 June 1950.

65. "Flyer Announcing 13th Annual Dinner of Brownsville Neighborhood Council," 25 May 1950, BCSP Papers; "Brownsville Neighborhood Health and Welfare Council Bulletin: Brotherhood Meeting Highlights and Activities," 8 February 1954, BCSP Papers; "Dear Neighbor Letter from John Newton, Chairman BNH&WC Community Relations Committee," 19 April 1955; "Brownsville Council Honors NAACP for Schools Fight," *New York Amsterdam News*, 25 December 1954; "Brownsville Group Asks Employers Not to Discriminate," *Brooklyn Eagle*, 20 April 1955; "Brownsville Neighborhood Health and Welfare Council Review," January 1955, BCSP Papers; *BNH&WC Newsletter*, January 1955, BCSP Papers.

66. "Brownsville Neighborhood Health and Welfare Council Bulletin: Brotherhood Meeting Highlights and Activities," no date, BCSP Papers.

67. "Brownsville Neighborhood Health and Welfare Council Review," 3 November 1955, BCSP Papers; "Brownsville Neighborhood Health and Welfare Council, Notice of Public Meeting," 10 April 1956, BCSP Papers.

68. Interview with Irving Levine, 21 March 1998; E-mail message from Bernard Lewin, 30 October 1999.

69. "Brownsville Synagogues and Churches," no date, BCSP Papers.

70. "Jewish Council Asks for Job and Education Laws," *Brooklyn Eagle*, 31 January 1950; Gerald Benjamin, *Race Relations and the New York City Commission on Human Rights* (Ithaca, N.Y.: Cornell University Press, 1972), 71–72; "Flyer for the Brooklyn Jewish Community Council: What It Is, What It Does, How It Functions," October 1952, Papers of the Jewish Labor Committee, Wagner Archives, Bobst Library, New York University, New York, New York (hereinafter "JLC Papers"); Brooklyn Jewish Community Council, "Information Brooklyn Jewish Community Neighborhood Councils," no date, JLC Papers.

71. "Minutes of the Executive Committee of the Brooklyn Jewish Labor Committee," 5 May 1952, JLC Papers; Brooklyn Jewish Community Council, "Information on BJCC Neighborhood Councils," JLC Papers.

72. "Brownsville Changing But Not in Spirit," *Brooklyn Eagle*, 6 January 1952; "Hebrew Educational Society, Program of Activities, 1962–1963," no date, Papers of the Hebrew Educational Society, the Archives of the New York United Jewish Appeal, New York, New York (hereinafter "UJA Papers").

73. Hebrew Educational Society, *Annual Report*, 4 December 1956, Papers of the Hebrew Educational Society, Brooklyn, New York (hereinafter "HES Papers").

74. "Memo from HES to Distribution Committee," UJA, 1 April 1954, UJA Papers; "Minutes of the 1954–55 Budget Conference," 6 April 1954, UJA Papers.

75. "Our Changing City: Southeastern Brooklyn Area," *New York Times*, 29 July 1955.

76. Hirsch, *Making the Second Ghetto*; Sugrue, *Origins of the Urban Crisis*.

77. Even those urban academics, such as Morton Grodzins and the Taeubers, who wanted to build interracial communities accepted the racial turnover as a natural state of affairs. See Morton Grodzins, *The Metropolitan Area as a Racial Problem* (Pittsburgh: University of Pittsburgh Press, 1957), 6; Karl Taeuber and Alma Taeuber, *Negroes in Cities: Residential Segregation and Neighborhood Change* (Chicago: Aldine Publishing Company, 1969), 4. For a discussion of these views and a counterhypothesis, see John Ottensmann and Michael Gleeson, "The Movement of Whites and Blacks into Racially Mixed Neighborhoods, Chicago, 1960–1980," *Social Science Quarterly* 73 (1992): 645–662. This view was contested by academics in the 1950s, and many articles were published about neighborhoods seeking to maintain integration. Some argue that by the 1960s neighborhood change was the result more of economic than racial factors. See, for example, Eleanor P. Wolf, "The Baxter Area: A New Trend in Neighborhood Change?" *Phylon* 26 (1965): 344–353; William Frey, "Central City White Flight: Racial and Nonracial Causes," *American Sociological Review* 44 (1979): 425–448; Kenneth Jackson, *Crabgrass Frontier*, 166–186.

78. See John T. McGreevy, *Parish Boundaries: The Catholic Encounter with Race in the Twentieth-Century Urban North* (Chicago: University of Chicago Press, 1996), 20, 102; Gerald Gamm, "Neighborhood Roots: Exodus and Stability in Boston, 1870–1990" (Ph.D. diss., Harvard University, 1994); Yona Ginsberg, *Jews in a Changing Neighborhood: The Study of Mattapan* (New York: Free Press, 1975); Hillel Levine and Lawrence Harmon, *The Death of an American Jewish Community: A Tragedy of Good Intentions* (New York: The Free Press, 1992), 174–180. Gerald Gamm argues that racial

change in Boston's Jewish neighborhoods was led by homeowners, and that the fact that most Jews rented is not determinative of the pace of neighborhood change. In Brownsville 95 percent of families rented, so it is difficult to make comparisons between the actions of renters and homeowners. Gerald Gamm, *Urban Exodus: Why the Jews Left Boston and the Catholics Stayed* (Cambridge: Harvard University Press, 1999), 53.

79. Glauber, *All Neighborhoods Change*, 60. For a discussion of the impact of anti-communism on American leftists, see Paul Buhle, "Themes in American Jewish Radicalism," in Paul Buhle and Dan Georgakas, eds., *The Immigrant Left in the United States* (Albany: SUNY Press, 1996), 104.

Chapter 5

1. Interview with Paul Chandler, December 12, 1998; interview with Bea Seigel by Richard Broadman, in possession of author.

2. Interview with Paul Chandler, 2 February 2000.

3. Sorin, *Nurturing Neighborhood*, 163.

4. U.S. Census Bureau, *Special Census of New York City, 1957* (Washington, D.C.: Government Printing Office, 1958); Community Council of Greater New York City, *Brooklyn Communities: Population Characteristics and Neighborhood Social Resources* (New York: Bureau of Community Statistical Services, 1958).

5. *Special Census of New York City, 1957; Brooklyn Communities*, 167; U.S. Census Bureau, *Census of Housing and Population, 1970* (Washington, D.C.: Government Printing Office, 1972).

6. Otis Dudley Duncan and Beverly Duncan, *The Negro Population of Chicago* (Chicago: University of Chicago Press, 1957), 110–120; Wolf, 18; see also Karl Taeuber and Alma Taeuber, *Negroes in Cities* (Chicago: Aldine Press, 1965); Richard Morrill, "The Negro Ghetto: Problems and Alternatives," *Geographical Review* 55 (July 1965): 338–361; Chester Rapkin and William Grigsby, *The Demand for Housing in Racially Mixed Areas* (Berkeley: University of California Press, 1960); Richard Taub, D. Garth Taylor, and Jan D. Dunham, *Paths of Neighborhood Change: Race and Crime in Urban America* (Chicago: University of Chicago Press, 1984); Harvey Molotch, *Managed Integration: The Dilemmas of Doing Good in the City* (Berkeley: University of California Press, 1972); William Frey, "Central City White Flight: Racial and Nonracial Causes," *American Sociological Review* 44 (June 1979): 425–448.

7. David Kleinstein, "3 Miles and 66 Years: Why the HES Is Leaving Brownsville," *JWB Circle*, March 1965.

8. Sorin, *Nurturing Neighborhood*, 166; City Commission on Human Rights of New York, *Report by the City Commission of Human Rights of New York on Blockbusting* (New York: City Commission on Human Rights, 1963), 2–4; Jonathon Reider, *Canarsie: The Jews and Italians of Brooklyn Against Liberalism* (Cambridge: Harvard University Press, 1985), 15.

9. "No Violations Found By Investigators," *New York Amsterdam News*, 7 August 1959; "Neighbors Help Bury Four Fire Victims," *New York Amsterdam News*, 8 August 1959; "Four Brownsville Tenements Burn," *New York World Sun and Telegraph*, 9 February 1960; "Rev. Johnson Wars Against Slumlords," *New York Amsterdam News*, 17 March 1962.

10. "Letter to Representative Celler from Jack Feinberg," no date, Papers of Congressman Emmanuel Celler, Library of Congress, Washington, D.C. (hereinafter "Celler Papers").

11. Taub, Taylor, and Dunham, *Paths of Neighborhood Change*, 12; New York Police Department, "Crime Statistics, 1/1/62–6/30/62," Papers of the New York City Housing Authority, La Guardia and Wagner Archives, Queens, New York (hereinafter, "NYCHA Papers"), box 66C7, folder 5.

12. New York City Police Department, *Annual Reports*, 1957–1964; "Crime Rise in City Is Seen for 1958: Juvenile Rate Up," *New York Times*, 2 February 1959; "City Crime up 4. 5% in 1960, 7th Straight Year of Increase," *New York Times*, 17 February 1961.

13. New York City Youth Board, *Youth Board Area Report*, 1964; James Gilbert, *A Cycle of Outrage: America's Reaction to the Juvenile Delinquent in the 1950s* (New York: Oxford, 1986), 67–71.

14. See chapter 4, note 18.

15. Schneider, *Vampires, Dragons and Egyptian Kings*, 23–24, 67–74.

16. "City O.K.s Funds to Launch War on Brownsville Gangs," *New York World Telegram and Sun*, 23 June 1960; "Jury Is Picked in Teen Murder Trial," *New York Amsterdam News*, 21 February 1959.

17. "4 Admit Teen Gang Slaying," *New York Amsterdam News*, 18 July 1959; "2 Hold Up Duos Sent to Sing Sing," *New York World Telegram and Sun*, 30 August 1960; "13 Hold Up Suspect Picked Up on Tip," *New York World Telegram and Sun*, 1 March 1960; "Anonymous Letter to Mayor Wagner," 31 May 1962, Wagner Papers, roll 46; "Letter from George Murphy, Deputy Inspector, to Mayor Wagner," 22 October 1962, Wagner Papers, roll 46, Municipal Archives.

18. New York City Housing Authority, "Arrests," 1961, NYCHA Papers, box 70D3, folder 3; "Letter from NYCHA Chairman William Reid to Congressman Abraham Multer," 24 April 1963, NYCHA Papers, box 70D3, folder 3; "NYCHA News Release," 2 July 1962, NYCHA Papers, box 70D3, folder 3.

19. New York City Housing Authority, "Arrests," 1961, NYCHA Papers, box 70D3, folder 3; "Memo to William Reid from Security Division, NYCHA Re Situation at Queensbridge and Brownsville-Van Dyke," 1 August 1961, NYCHA Papers, box 90A4, folder 6.

20. "Memo from Blanca Cedeno, Senior Intergroup Relations Officer, to Henry J. Mulhearn, Assistant Director Re Tensions in Brownsville, Van Dyke, Tilden Area," 31 August 1962, NYCHA Papers, box 90A4, folder 6; "Memo from Bernard Moses, Manager of Van Dyke Houses, to Percy Frank, Chief Manager, Re Special Problems of the Elderly," 6 August 1962, NYCHA Papers, box 90A4, folder 6; "Letter from NYCHA Vice Chairman Francis Madigan to Public Housing Authority Regional Director Herman Millner," 6 August 1962, NYCHA Papers, box 90A4, folder 6.

21. "Memo from Alfred Waxman, Senior Intergroup Relations Officer, to Henry J. Mulhearn Assistant Director, Intergroup Relations Re Incident at Van Dyke Houses," 15 November 1962, NYCHA Papers box 90A4, folder 6.

22. "Memo from David W. Holland, Senior Intergroup Relations Officer, to Henry J. Mulhearn, Assistant Director Re Case Number 207," 2 September 1961,

NYCHA Papers, box 90A4, folder 6; "Memo from Blanca Cedeno, Senior Intergroup Relations Officer, Re Reassurance Visit to Two Elderly Families in Fear of Living Conditions at Van Dyke Houses," 5 September 1962, NYCHA Papers, box 90A4, folder 6.

23. "Memo from Marie Rogers, Senior Intergroup Relations Officer, to Henry Mulhearn, Assistant Director Re Transfer Requests at Van Dyke Houses," 28 March 1963, NYCHA Papers, box 90A4, folder 6.

24. "Memo from Bernard Moses, Manager, Van Dyke Houses, to Mr. Frank, Chief Manager, Division C, Re Tenant Transfer Requests," 3 September 1964, NYCHA Papers, box 90A4, folder 4; "Memo from Barbara Carter, Housing Assistant, Intergroup Relations, to William Valentine, Director, Intergroup Relations," NYCHA Papers, box 90A4, folder 4; "Memo from David Holland, Senior Intergroup Relations Officer, to William Valentine, Director Intergroup Relations," 5 December 1963, NYCHA Papers, box 90A4, folder 4.

25. "Minutes, Brownsville Houses Tenant's Council," July 1960, NYCHA Papers, box 89A6, folder 8.

26. "NYCHA Housing Statistics, 1962," NYCHA Papers.

27. Charles F. Preusse, "Report to Mayor Wagner," 16 September 1957, NYCHA Papers, 10–14.

28. Bernard Roshco, "The Integration Problem and Public Housing," *The New Leader*, 4–11 July 1960, 11–12.

29. Ibid., 13.

30. "Housing Integration Plan Given," *New York Daily Mirror*, 28 August 1960.

31. "Foes of Bias Hail Housing Agency," *New York World Telegram & Sun*, 29 August 1960.

32. "NYCHA Move-Ins and Move-Outs 1961," NYCHA Papers, box 71B5, folder 4.

33. "NYCHA Housing Statistics," 1962–1964, NYCHA Papers.

34. "Memorandum from Abraham Leshan, Director, Public Improvements Division, to Chairman James Felt, New York City Planning Commission," 7 January 1963, NYCHA Papers, box 90A1, folder 23.

35. "Minutes of the Board of Directors Meeting, Citizens' Housing and Planning Council," 23 January 1963, CHPC Papers; "Memorandum from Sylvia Stark, Chairman Site Review Committee, to the Board of Directors, Citizens' Housing and Planning Council," 19 January 1963, CHPC Papers.

36. The Intergroup Committee on New York's Public Schools was a veritable "Who's Who" of liberal organizations, including (in addition to the NAACP) the American Jewish Congress, the American Jewish Committee, Americans for Democratic Action, the Anti-Defamation League of B'nai B'rith, the Citizen's Committee on Children, the Council of Spanish-American Organizations, the New York Civil Liberties Union, and the Urban League. "Letter from Israel Laster, Vice Chair, Intergroup Committee on New York's Public Schools, to Mr. Charles Silver, President, Board of Education of the City of New York," 17 May 1956, Brooklyn Files, NAACP Papers; Connolly, *A Ghetto Grows in Brooklyn*, 214–215; Clarence Taylor, *Knocking at Our Own Door*, 64; Adina Back, "Up South in New York: The 1950s School Desegregation Struggles"

(Ph.D. diss., New York University, 1997), 88–153; "Rezoning of Schools for Integration in Bedford-Stuyvesant," July 1956, NAACP Papers; "Memorandum from June Shagaloff to Messrs. Wilkins and Current Re Public School Desegregation, Bedford-Stuyvesant, Brooklyn," 2 November 1956, NAACP Papers; "Statement to the Board of Education Hearing on Proposed School Construction," 21 June 1956, NAACP Papers; "Memorandum to the Board of Education of the City of New York and the Commission on Integration from the NAACP, Brooklyn Branch," 3 February 1956, NAACP Papers.

37. "BNC Membership List," 23 November 1958, Papers of the Brooklyn Council for Social Planning, Brooklyn Collection, Brooklyn Public Library (hereinafter "BCSP Papers"); Glauber, *All Neighborhoods Change*, 103–110: "Memo from Blanca Cedeno, Senior Intergroup Relations Officer, to Henry Mulhearn, Assistant Director, Re Neighborhood Contacts," 31 August, 1961, NYCHA Papers, box 90A4, folder 16.

38. "Letter from Aaron Solomon, Executive Director, Brownsville Committee on Youth, the William Reid, Chairman, NYCHA," 20 April 1999, NYCHA Papers, box 63C5, folder 4.

39. Glauber, *All Neighborhoods Change*, 107–119; "Executive Committee Asks That JHS 275 Be Integrated School," *Brownsville Reporter,* January 1959, NYCHA Papers, box 73C2, folder 10; "Letter from Aaron Solomon, Executive Director, Brownsville Committee on Youth, to William Reid, Chairman, New York City Housing Authority," 5 January 1959, NYCHA Papers, box 63C5, folder 4; "Letter from Irving Tabb, President BNH&WC, to Morris Blodnick, Assistant Superintendent Board of Education," Papers of the Board of Education, Teachers College, Columbia University, New York, New York (hereinafter "Board of Education Papers"), Local School Board Files; "Brownsville Schools Site Decision Nears," *New York World Telegram and Sun,* 24 March 1960; "Parents Fight to Integrate New JHS 275," *New York World Telegram and Sun,* 28 January 1960. Tabb lived at 9201 Kings Highway, in East Flatbush. The BNC letterhead was quickly put together, and many board members' names were crossed off, indicating that they opposed Tabb's position.

40. Glauber, *All Neighborhoods Change;* "Release from Rev. Milton Galamison," 1 March 1960, Milton A. Galamison Papers, Schomburg Collection, New York Public Library (hereinafter "Galamison Papers"); Brooklyn Student Congress of Racial Equality, "JHS 275—The Fight for 50/50," 11 April 1963, Papers of the Congress of Racial Equality, Library of Congress, Washington, D.C. (hereinafter "CORE Papers"); "Emergency Committee for the Integration of JHS 275, Why We Picket Today," undated, Board of Education Papers, Local School Board Files, box 21; "Letter from Helen Efthim, Emergency Committee for Integration of JHS 275, to Rose Shapiro, Member New York City Board of Education," 5 March 1963, Board of Education Papers, Local School Board Files, box 21; "Letter from Jack Zimmer, Chairman, Local School Board 41 and 42, to Bernard Donovan, Acting Superintendent of Schools," 24 March 1963, Board of Education Papers, Local School Board Files, box 21; "JHS Site Approved in Brownsville," *New York World Telegram and Sun,* 30 January 1960; "JHS 275 'Volcano' Still Smoldering: What Are the Issues?" *New York Amsterdam News,* 13 April 1963; "Ask Mayor to Make P.S. 275 Test Case," *New York Amsterdam News,* 1 June 1963; "Judge Holds Judgment on JHS 275 Case," *New York Amsterdam News,* 31 August 1963.

41. Interview with Ronald Kantrowitz, 1 February 2000; Brooklyn Public Library, Brownsville Branch Survey, 1959, Brooklyn Collection, Brooklyn Public Library.

42. Interview with Jack Baum, 12 January 2000; interview with Abraham Reiss, 11 January 2000.

43. Interview with Ruth Lurie, 11 January 2000.

44. "In the Matter of the Application of Chevra Torah Anshei Radishkowitz," Court Order, Supreme Court of New York, Kings County, 19 October 1965; "In the Matter of the Application of Beth Israel of Brownsville," Court Order, Supreme Court of New York, Kings County, 22 September 1966.

45. Brooklyn County Clerk's Office, Real Property Records; "In the Matter of the Application of Ahavath Achim Anshe Brownsville Unterstitzing Verein," Court Order, Supreme Court of New York, Kings County, 17 December 1964.

46. "In the Matter of the Application of Congregation Anshe Dokshitz," Court Order, New York Supreme Court, Kings County, 22 January 1962.

47. Abraham Block, "Synagogues for Sale," *Jewish Spectator,* April 1966, 20–22; see also Gamm, *Urban Exodus,* 134–143.

48. "Minutes of the 1958–1959 Budget Conference," 2 April 1958, Papers of the Federation of Jewish Philanthropies, United Jewish Appeal, New York, New York (hereinafter "UJA Papers"); "Memo from HES to UJA Distribution Committee," no date, UJA Papers; "Annual Report for 1959," undated, HES Papers.

49. "Memo from HES to Distribution Subcommittee re 1958–59 Budget," 20 March 1958, UJA Papers; *HES Annual Reports,* 1956–1965, UJA Papers.

50. "Minutes of the 1961–62 Budget Conference," 4 April 1961, UJA Papers; "Annual Report for 1961," no date, HES Papers; "Analysis of Geographic Distribution of Membership as a Result of Mapping Survey," no date, UJA Papers.

51. "Minutes of the 1962–63 Budget Conference," 28 March 1962, UJA Papers; "Joint Report of Hebrew Educational Society and Jewish Family Service to Moses L. Parshelsky Foundation," 23 August 1962, HES Papers; "Minutes of 1964–1965 Budget Conference," March 1964, UJA Papers; "Minutes of Meeting of Board of Directors," 9 May 1962, HES Papers; "Minutes of Parshelsky Fund Meeting," 1 March 1963, HES Papers.

52. "Minutes of Meeting of Board of Directors"; "Minutes of Parshelsky Fund Meeting."

53. "Analysis of Geographic Distribution of Membership as a Result of Mapping Survey," undated, UJA Papers; "Memo re Meeting With Mr. Isaac Schwartz and Mr. Theodore Ratner," 9 January 1963, HES Papers; David M. Kleinstein, "3 Miles and 66 Years: Why the H.E.S. Is Leaving Brownsville," *JWB Circle,* March 1965.

54. "Minutes from Board of Director's Meeting," 13 February 1963, HES Papers; "Minutes of the 1965–66 Budget Conference," 30 March 1965, UJA Papers; Kleinstein, "3 Miles and 66 Years."

55. Landesman, *Brownsville,* 199.

Chapter 6

1. The story of Local 1199 and their unique efforts to bridge racial and class differences to organize service workers during the 1950s and 1960s is ably told by Leon

Fink and Brian Greenberg in their book *Upheaval in the Quiet Zone: A History of the Hospital Workers Union, Local 1199* (Urbana: University of Illinois Press, 1989). Fink and Greenberg acknowledge the importance of the Beth-El strike in the union's quest for collective bargaining rights, but they devote only a few pages to the conflict in their book, preferring to give greater attention to the strikes leading up to the Beth-El struggle. *Upheaval in the Quiet Zone* describes the strategy and tactics of 1199 president Davis and his officers during the battles of 1959 at six major New York hospitals and analyzes the role of local politicians, civil rights leaders, and the media in shaping these conflicts. The Beth-El strikers followed the methods developed in these earlier battles, and for this reason the strike is less necessary for Fink and Greenberg's purposes. A close analysis of the Beth-El strike, however, is useful, because it highlights the role of urban change and race relations in shaping the conflict.

2. Rosemary Stevens, *In Sickness and in Wealth: American Hospitals in the 20th Century* (Baltimore: Johns Hopkins University Press, 1999), 228–229; Charles E. Rosenberg, *The Care of Strangers: The Rise of America's Hospital System* (New York: Basic, 1987).

3. U.S. Census Bureau, *Census of Population and Housing, 1960* (Washington, D.C.: Government Printing Office, 1963).

4. Landesman, *Brownsville*, 214–216; Tina Levitan, *Islands of Compassion: A History of the Jewish Hospitals of New York* (New York: Bloch Publishing, 1965).

5. Fink and Greenberg, *Upheaval in the Quiet Zone*, 6.

6. Ibid., 7.

7. Ibid., 56.

8. Ibid., 88.

9. Ibid.

10. "No More Waiting," 3 October 1960, Papers of the Hospital Workers Union, Local 1199, Cornell University Labor Documentation Center, Ithaca, New York (hereinafter "Local 1199 Papers"); "We're Near the Goal," 10 November 1960, 1199 Papers; "Make a Date With the Future," 18 April 1961, 1199 Papers; "Open House," 18 September 1961, 1199 Papers.

11. "A Message to Beth-El Contributors From Beth-El Hospital Workers, Members, Local 1199 Drug and Hospital Union," no date, 1199 Papers; "Love Thy Neighbor? What You Should Know About Morrell Goldberg!" 26 January 1962, 1199 Papers; "Please Read This Before You Go Into the Famous Restaurant To Eat!," no date, 1199 Papers.

12. "P.A.C.—Mr. Goldberg's Double Talk," 8 February 1962, 1199 Papers; "Press Release," 10 February 1962, 1199 Papers; "Press Release, Local 1199," 10 February 1962, 1199 Papers.

13. "Beth-El Hospital Facing Walkout," *New York Times*, 11 February 1962; "Strike at Beth-El Is Postponed Again," *New York Times*, 14 February 1962; "The Day of Decision at Beth-El," 1199 Papers, 6 March 1962; "Hospital Workers Strike at Beth-El," *New York Times*, 24 May 1962.

14. "5 Hospital Pickets Arrested in Melee," *New York Times*, 25 May 1962; "Press Release: Local 1199 Charges Police Brutality Against Negro and Puerto Rican Workers at Beth-El Strike," 24 May 1962, 1199 Papers; "Chief of Nonprofessional Local Held in Picket Ban at Beth-El in Brooklyn," *New York Times*, 31 May 1962; "5 Hospital Pickets

Jailed in Scuffle," *New York Times,* 4 June 1962; "24 Students Seized in Beth-El Show-down," *New York Times,* 6 June 1962; "20 Are Arrested in Beth-El Strike," *New York Times,* 13 June 1962; interview with Maurice Reid, 9 February 2000.

15. "Why We Are Sitting In at Beth El Hospital," 30 May 1962, 1199 Papers; "An Appeal to Students, Issued by Students Who Have Been Aiding Beth-El Strikers," no date, 1199 Papers.

16. "Memo to New York Area Contacts from James Farmer, National Director of CORE," 4 June 1962, CORE Papers; "Letter from Charles Gordone, Chairman, Com-mittee for the Employment of Negro Performers, to Leon Davis," 4 June 1962, 1199 Papers; "New Group to Aid Hospital Strike," *New York Times,* 30 June 1962; "Hospital Strike Backed," *New York Times,* 14 July 1962; "1199 Strike Bulletin," 13 July 1962, 1199 Papers.

17. "Editorial: The Liberals," *New York Amsterdam News,* 9 June 1962, 10; "570KC Radio Editorial—Hospital Labor Dispute," 26 June 1962, 1199 Papers; "WCBS Radio Editorial No. 157—Fight for Union Recognition by Non-professional Employees of Brooklyn's Beth-El Hospital Backed by Sam J. Slate, Vice President and General Manager of WCBS Radio," 4 June 1962, 1199 Papers.

18. "Press Release, Jewish Labor Committee," 13 July 1962, 1199 Papers; "Telegram from Adolph Held, National Chairman Jewish Labor Committee, to Gover-nor Nelson Rockefeller," 13 July 1962, 1199 Papers; "Editorial," *Jewish Daily Forward,* 16 June 1962.

19. "Press Release, UFT Supports Beth-El Hospital Strikers," 31 May 1962, 1199 Papers; "Letter from Emmanuel Fineberg, Chapter 68 Chairman, UFT, to Local 1199," 12 June 1962, 1199 Papers; "Letter from Leon Davis to Harry Van Arsdale," 24 July 1962, 1199 Papers; "Labor Abandons Hospital Panel," *New York Times,* 22 June 1962; "1,000 Pickets Aid Beth-El Strikers," *New York Times,* 24 June 1962; Joshua B. Freeman, *Working-Class New York,* 136.

20. "Unionist Scores Hospitals on Pay," 13 July 1962, 1199 Papers; "$40,000 for Scabs—Starvation for Workers," 18 June 1962, 1199 Papers; "Letter to Acting Mayor Paul Screvane from Leon J. Davis," 12 June 1962, 1199 Papers; "Letter to Congress-man Emmanuel Celler from Leon J. Davis," 24 May 1962, Celler Papers; "An Open Letter to Abe Stark from the Beth-El Strikers," 20 June 1962, 1199 Papers.

21. Memos from the Board of Trustees to Beth-El Employees: 12 March 1962, 22 May 1962, and 23 May 1962, 1199 Papers; "Memo from the Board of Trustees to Beth-El Patients and Visitors," 23 May 1962, 1199 Papers; "Memo to Board of Trus-tees from Morrell Goldberg," 26 May 1962, 1199 Papers.

22. "A Statement of the Position of Beth-El Hospital," 7 June 1962, 1199 Papers; "Memo from the Board of Trustees to the Medical and Nursing Staff," no date, 1199 Papers; "Letter from Benne Katz to Congressman Emmanuel Celler," 5 June 1962, Celler Papers; "Letter from Congressman Emmanuel Celler to Benne Katz," 29 May 1962, Celler Papers.

23. "News Release from the Office of Congressman Emmanuel Celler," 17 July 1962, Celler Papers; "Letter from Theodore Shapiro to Benne Katz," 28 May 1962, 1199 Papers; "Trustee Assails Struck Hospital," *New York Times,* 30 May 1962.

24. "Hospital Unionist Given Six Months," *New York Times,* 17 July 1962.

25. "Rockefeller Wins Hospital Accord," *New York Times*, 18 July 1962; Fink and Greenberg, *Upheaval in the Quiet Zone*, 28, 108.

26. Fink and Greenberg, *Upheaval in the Quiet Zone;* "Beth-El Hospital Medical Staff," 1960, 1199 Papers.

27. Fink and Greenberg, *Upheaval in the Quiet Zone;* "Letter from William Taylor (V. P. Local 1199) to the Jimerson Tenants," 15 June 1962, 1199 Papers; "Letter from Alex Efthim to Leon Davis," 13 June 1962, 1199 Papers; "Letter from Alex Efthim to Benne Katz," no date, 1199 Papers.

28. Fink and Greenberg, *Upheaval in the Quiet Zone*, 102.

Chapter 7

1. Interview with Maurice Reid, 9 February 2000.

2. Jon Teaford, *The Twentieth Century American City* (Indianapolis: Bobbs-Merrill, 1990), 127–131.

3. Frances Fox Piven and Peter Cloward, *Regulating the Poor: The Functions of Public* Welfare (New York: Random House, 1971), 249; Adam Yarmolinsky, "Beginnings of OEO," in James Sundquist, ed., *On Fighting Poverty: Perspectives from Experience* (New York, Basic, 1969), 134; Thomas F. Jackson, "The State, the Movement and the Urban Poor: The War on Poverty and Political Mobilization in the 1960s," in Michael Katz, ed., *The Underclass Debate: Lessons from History* (Princeton: Princeton University Press, 1993), 414. The literature of the War on Poverty is voluminous. See James Patterson, *America's Struggle Against Poverty, 1900–1994* (Cambridge: Harvard University Press, 1994); Matusow, *Unraveling of America;* Alice O'Connor, "Community Action, Urban Reform, and the Fight Against Poverty: The Ford Foundation's Gray Areas Program," *Journal of Urban History* 22 (July 1996); Paul E. Peterson and J. David Greenstone, "Racial Change and Citizen Participation: The Mobilization of Low-Income Communities Through Community Action," in Jewell Bellush and Stephen David, eds., *Race and Politics in New York City: Five Studies in Policymaking* (New York: Praeger, 1971); Daniel Patrick Moynihan, *Maximum Feasible Misunderstanding: Community Action in the War on Poverty* (New York: Free Press, 1970); Henry J. Aaron, *Politics and the Professors: The Great Society in Perspective* (Washington, D.C.: The Brookings Institution, 1978); Sar Levitan, *The Great Society's Poor Law: A New Approach to Poverty* (Baltimore: Johns Hopkins Press, 1969); Robert A. Levine, *The Poor Ye Need Not Have With You: Lessons from the War on Poverty* (Cambridge, Mass.: MIT Press, 1970); Jeannette Hopkins and Kenneth Clark, *A Relevant War on Poverty: A Study of Community Action and Observable Social Change* (New York: Harper, 1969); Kenneth Pollinger and Annette Pollinger, *Community Action and the Poor: Influence vs. Social Control in a New York City Community* (New York: Praeger, 1972); Ralph Kramer, *Participation of the Poor: Comparative Case Studies in the War on Poverty* (Englewood Cliffs, N.J.: Prentice-Hall, 1969); Peter Marris and Martin Reim, *Dilemmas of Social Reform: Poverty and Community Action in the United States* (Chicago: Aldine Publishers, 1973); Stephen David, "Welfare: The Community Action Controversy," in Jewell Bellush and Stephen David, eds., *Race and Politics in New York City: Five Studies in Policymaking* (New York: Praeger, 1971).

4. Major Owens, "Anti-Poverty Workbook," *The Brownsville Counselor,* 1 September 1967; Papers of Congressman Major Owens, Brooklyn, New York (hereinafter

"Owens Papers"); Peterson and Greenstone, "Racial Change and Citizen Participation," 241–257; Katz, *Underclass Debate*, 95–100.

5. Interview with Maurice Reid, 9 February 2000; interview with Paul Chandler, 8 February 2000.

6. Interview with Maurice Reid; "Greetings from the Brooklyn Freedom Democratic Movement," undated, 1964, CORE Papers; "Third Negro State Assemblyman Sure," *New York Amsterdam News*, 18 September 1960.

7. "Greetings from the Brooklyn Freedom Democratic Movement"; Bill Marley, "Brownsville News," *New York Recorder*, 31 July 1965; interview with Maurice Reid, 9 February 2000; "Brownsville Council Christening, January 1," *New York Amsterdam News*, 2 January 1965.

8. O'Connor, "Community Action, Urban Reform, and the Fight Against Poverty," 598–600, 619; Kramer, *Participation of the Poor*, 56–60; Patterson, *America's Struggle Against Poverty*, 138–140.

9. Ibid.; Marris and Rein, *Dilemmas of Social Reform*, 246–248; John Wofford, "The Politics of Local Responsibility: Administration of the Community Action Program, 1964–1966," in James Sundquist, ed., *On Fighting Poverty: Perspectives from Experience* (New York: Basic, 1969), 75–75.

10. Matusow, *Unraveling of America*, 246; Patterson, *America's Struggle Against Poverty*, 146–147.

11. David, "Welfare," 33–36.

12. "Brownsville Elects 20 to Poverty Board," *New York Amsterdam News*, 21 August 1965; "Press Release: Antipoverty News," 10 August 1965, Owens Papers; Bill Marley, "All About Brownsville," *New York Recorder*, 11 September 1965; interview with Maurice Reid; Thomas Jackson, "The State, the Movement and the Urban Poor," 417.

13. Bill Marley, "Brownsville News," *New York Recorder*, 31 July 1965.

14. Ibid.; "Third Negro State Assemblyman Sure," *New York Amsterdam News*, 18 September 1965; "Memo from Harry Miller to Bill Haddad, OEO, Re Brownsville East New York Convention," 16 August 1965, Papers of the Office of Economic Opportunity, Inspection Division, box 50, Record Group 381, National Archives, Washington, D.C. (hereinafter, "OEO Papers").

15. "Letter from Willa Webster, Corresponding Secretary, BCC, to William De-Marle, Community Development Coordinator, Economic Opportunity Committee," 14 January 1966, Owens Papers; "Greetings from the Brooklyn Freedom Democratic Movement." For an examination of the Downstate Medical Center campaign, see Clarence Taylor, *Black Churches of Brooklyn*, 139–163.

16. "Letter to Community Leaders from Major Owens," 17 January 1966, Owens Papers; "Executive Director's Report to the Board of Directors of the Brownsville Community Council," 12 January 1966, Owens Papers.

17. Levitan, *Great Society's Poor Law*, 128–129.

18. Interview with Maurice Reid, 9 February 2000.

19. Major Owens and Alex Efthim, "1966–1967 Total Action Plan of the Brownsville Community Council, Inc," Owens Papers.

20. Ibid.

21. Ibid.

22. Ibid.

23. "News Release, Office of Economic Opportunity," June 1966, Celler Papers; interview with Maurice Reid, 9 February 2000.

24. Interview with Annie Nicholson, 21 September 1996; "Senior Citizens Are Also Active Citizens in Program," *Brownsville Counselor,* 1 September 1967, Owens Papers; "Program Notes," *Brownsville Counselor,* 25 August 1967, Owens Papers; "1966–1967 Total Action Plan."

25. Bill Marley, "All About Brownsville," *New York Recorder,* 23 October 1965; "Action Center Number One," *The Brownsville Counselor,* 1 September 1967, Owens Papers; "Office Skills Program Active," *The Brownsville Counselor,* 1 September 1967, Owens Papers; "Tenants Demand Play Street," *New York Amsterdam News,* 3 September 1966

26. "Hidden Talents," *The Brownsville Counselor,* 7 May 1967, Owens Papers.

27. Brownsville Community Council, "1967–1968 Total Action Plan," Papers of the Brownsville Community Council, Brooklyn Collection, Brooklyn Public Library, Brooklyn, New York.

28. Ibid.

29. Ibid.

30. "Sharp Rise in Crime Alarms Brownsville Area," *New York Times,* 8 July 1967.

31. "Hoving Shocked by Brownsville," *New York World Telegram and Sun,* 8 February 1966; "Brownsville Slums Brace for a Long, Cold Winter," *World Journal Tribune,* 2 October 1966; "Only 18 Violations!" *New York World Telegram and Sun,* 10 February 1964; "Slum Report Urges Better Enforcement," *New York World Telegram and Sun,* 28 April 1964; "City Denies Brownsville Fire Threat," *New York Times,* 7 July 1966

32. "40 Negroes Leave Brooklyn Homes," *New York Times,* 20 July 1966; "1000 Police Move in to Stem Brooklyn Unrest," *New York Times,* 23 July 1966; "Anti-Negro Group Loosely Formed," *New York Times,* 23 July 1966.

33. Major Owens, "Antipoverty Notebook," *The Brownsville Counselor,* August 1967, Owens Papers.

34. Kwame Ture and Charles V. Hamilton, *Black Power: The Politics of Liberation* (New York: Vintage Books, 1967), 37; William VanDeburg, *New Day in Babylon: The Black Power Movement and American Culture, 1965–1975* (Chicago: University of Chicago Press, 1992), 115.

35. Peterson and Greenstone, "Racial Change and Citizen Participation," 262–264; Bill Marley, "Brownsville News," *New York Recorder,* 10 July 1965.

36. "Bill Marley, "Brownsville News," *New York Recorder,* 17 July 1965.

37. Kramer, *Participation of the Poor,* 261–267; Patterson, *America's Struggle Against Poverty,* 149.

38. "BCC Board of Officers and Board Members Who Are in Apparent Conflict With 23–A," 31 January 1968, OEO Papers.

39. Bill Marley, "All About Brownsville," *New York Recorder,* 11 September 1965; "The President Speaks," *The Brownsville Counselor,* 1 September 1967; Moynihan, *Maximum Feasible Misunderstanding,* 81–91.

40. "Brownsville Community Corporation Funding Principles," no date, Owens Papers; "Executive Director's Report to the Board of Directors of the Brownsville Community Council," 12 January 1966, Owens Papers; "Brownsville Community Council Newsreel, no date, Owens Papers; Matusow, *Unraveling of America*, 267–268; Kramer, *Participation of the Poor*, 262.

41. "1967–68 Total Action Plan."

42. Interview with Maurice Reid, 9 February 2000; Brownsville Community Council, *Brownsville Guide to Community Resources* (Brooklyn: Brownsville Community Council, 1969).

43. "Letter from James J. Graham, President, Christians and Jews United for Social Action, to Congressman Emanuel Celler," 17 February 1966, Celler Papers.

44. "Moerdler Drops Plan for Brownsville Check," *New York World Telegram and Sun*, 14 February 1966; "Uplift-cum-Realism in a Brooklyn Slum," *National Catholic Reporter*, 16 February 1966; "CUSA: A Fight Versus Housing Ills," *New York Amsterdam News*, 5 February 1966; "Angry Tenants Go on Rent Strike," *New York Amsterdam News*, 2 February 1966; "4 Buildings to Be Viewed," *New York Amsterdam News*, 19 February 1966.

45. Interview with Paul Chandler, 8 February 2000.

46. "Executive Director's Report to the Board of Directors of the Brownsville Community Council," 12 January 1966, Owens Papers; "Brownsville Community Council Newsreel," Owens Papers.

47. "Antipoverty Notebook," *The Brownsville Counselor*, 25 August 1967, Owens Papers; "War on Slums Draws Overflow Crowd," *The Brownsville Counselor*, 7 May 1967, Owens Papers; "Festival Sparks Brownsville," *The Brownsville Counselor*, 1 September 1967, Owens Papers; Ture and Hamilton, *Black Power*, 37; VanDeburg, *New Day in Babylon*, 27; "Brownsville Community Council Newsletter," 7 February 1967, Owens Papers; "A Tribute to Langston Hughes," *The Brownsville Counselor*, 25 August 1967, Owens Papers. On the role of black nationalism in 1960s mobilization, see Komozi Woodard, *A Nation within a Nation: Amiri Baraka (LeRoi Jones) and Black Power Politics* (Chapel Hill: University of North Carolina Press, 1999).

48. "1967–1968 Total Action Plan."

49. Ibid.; "Neighborhood Youth Corps," *The Brownsville Counselor*, 25 August 1967; see also Jerald Podair, "'White' Values, 'Black' Values: The Ocean Hill–Brownsville Controversy and New York City Culture, 1965–1975," *Radical History Review* 59 (1994): 36–59.

50. "1967–1968 Total Action Plan."

51. Ibid.

52. "U.S. Senator Mondale Visits Brownsville Council," *New York Amsterdam News*, 4 January 1969; Human Resources Administration, "Newsletter," Celler Papers; "Letter from George Nicolau Commissioner, Community Development Agency, to Mayor John Lindsay," 30 January 1968, Celler Papers.

53. "Brooklyn Negro Leader Named Head of City Poverty Agency," *New York Times*, 13 March 1968; Office of Economic Opportunity, "News Release," 25 November 1968, Celler Papers; David, "Welfare," 41–46.

54. "Council Helps Brownsville to Help Itself," *New York Times*, 5 December 1971; James Patterson, *America's Struggle Against Poverty*, 147; Thomas Jackson, "The State, the Movement and the Urban Poor," 420.

55. Peterson and Greenstone, "Racial Change and Citizen Participation," 264–265; Thomas Jackson, "The State, the Movement and the Urban Poor," 420. On the contradictions of the role of community action in political incorporation, see Adolph Reed, *Stirrings in the Jug: Black Politics in the Post-Segregation Era* (Minneapolis: University of Minnesota Press, 1999).

56. Thomas Jackson, "The State, the Movement and the Urban Poor," 429; Moynihan, *Maximum Feasible Misunderstanding*, 81–91.

Chapter 8

1. Interview with John Powis by Richard Broadman, in possession of author; interview with Dolores Torres by Richard Broadman, in possession of author; "Militant Priest of Ocean Hill Brownsville Decries Bureaucracy," *New York Times*, 1 December 1968.

2. The literature on the strike is voluminous. Podair, "Like Strangers"; Clarence Taylor, *Knocking at Our Own Door*; Daniel Perlstein, "The 1968 New York City School Crisis, Teacher Politics, Racial Politics and the Decline of Liberalism" (Ph.D. diss., Stanford University,1994); Urofsky, *Why Teachers Strike*; Berube and Gittell, *Confrontation at Ocean Hill–Brownsville*; Fantini, Magat, and Gittell, *Community Control and the Urban School*; on the UFT, see Marjorie Murphy, *Black Board Unions: The AFT, and the NEA, 1900–1980* (Ithaca, NY: Cornell University Press, 1990); Back, "Up South in New York."

3. Clarence Taylor, *Knocking at Our Own Door*, 188; on the Teachers Union, see Back, "Up South in New York," 170–197.

4. Clarence Taylor, *Knocking at Our Own Door*, 124–145.

5. "Memo from June Shagaloff to Roy Wilkins," 28 January 1964, NAACP Papers; "NAACP Refutes Charges of School Split in NYC," 18 February 1964, NAACP Papers; "Letter from Mrs. Nellie Baker to Roy Wilkins," 17 February 1964, NAACP Papers; "Manual for School Boycott," 3 February 1964, NAACP Papers; Clarence Taylor, *Knocking at Our Own Door*, 124–145.

6. "Memorandum from Naomi Levine to Members of the New York Conference on the Educational Park," 7 December 1966, Board of Education Papers; "Release, American Jewish Committee," 2 January 1968, American Jewish Committee Papers, New York, New York (hereinafter "AJCommittee Papers"); "Release, Brooklyn Congress of Racial Equality," 11 April 1963, CORE Papers; "Open Letter from Milton A. Galamison to Mayor Robert F. Wagner," 1 March 1960, Galamison Papers; "Parents for an Educational Park," no date CORE Papers; "Minutes of Conference for Educational Parks," 13 February 1967, CORE Papers; "Testimony Presented Before the Board of Estimate by James Farmer National Director, CORE," 23 September 1965, CORE Papers; Harold Savitch, "Powerlessness in the Ghetto," *Polity* (1973): 45.

7. Savitch, "Powerlessness in the Ghetto," 46–47.

8. "Local School Board 41–42 Minutes," 7 May 1964, Board of Education Papers;

"Local School Board Minutes," 6 February 1964, Board of Education; "Letter from Elizabeth Clark, Coordinator Local School Board, to Jack Zimmer, Chairman, Local School Board 41 & 42," 28 March 1965, Board of Education Papers; "News Release, American Jewish Congress," 2 January 1964, Board of Education Papers; Back, "Up South in New York," 435–436; Podair, "Like Strangers," 53–56; Savitch, "Powerlessness in the Ghetto," 48–49.

9. "News Release of the Parents Workshop," 17 February 1966, Galamison Papers; "Brownsville Opposes a New JHS," *New York World Telegram and Sun,* 22 February 1966; "General Minutes of Local School Board 41 and 42," 6 February 1964, Board of Education Papers; "Mayor Walks Into Angry Crowd and Draws Cheers," *New York Times,* 20 July 1966.

10. Clarence Taylor, *Knocking at Our Own Door,* 181; interview with John Powis by Richard Broadman; interview with Maurice Reid, 9 February 2000.

11. Interview with Maurice Reid; "Teachers for Community Control—Vote No on Strike!" AJCommittee Papers, 4 September 1968.

12. Ture and Hamilton, *Black Power,* 42.

13. Daniel Perlstein, "The Case Against Community: Bayard Rustin and the 1968 New York School Crisis," *Educational Foundations* (spring 1993): 45–65.

14. Clarence Taylor, *Knocking at Our Own Door,* 181–184; Back, "Up South in New York," 445–446; Podair, "Like Strangers," 90–91.

15. Brownsville Community Council, "Total Action Plan for 1967–1968," Owens Papers; Fantini, Magat, and Gittell, *Community Control and the Urban School,* 100–140.

16. "Total Action Plan for 1967–1968."

17. Fantini, Magat, and Gittell, *Community Control and the Urban School,* 106–107; Berube and Gittell, *Confrontation at Ocean Hill–Brownsville,* 24; Urofsky, *Why Teachers Strike,* 11–13; "Localities to Run New School Units," *New York Times,* 6 July 1967.

18. "A Plan for an Experimental School District, Ocean Hill–Brownsville," 1967, Papers of the Ford Foundation, New York, New York (hereinafter, "Ford Foundation Papers"), roll 2372; "Letter from Rhody McCoy to Mario Fantini," 22 August 1967, Ford Foundation Papers; Clarence Taylor, *Knocking at Our Own Door,* 192–193; Urofsky, *Why Teachers Strike,* 14; Berube and Gittell, *Confrontation at Ocean Hill–Brownsville,* 24–32; "McCoy Catalyst for Board's 19," *Daily News,* 13 September 1968.

19. "Memorandum" 14 February 1968, Ford Foundation Papers, roll 2372; New York City Commission on Human Rights, "Commission Report on Investigation of Demonstration District," 21 May 1968, AJCommittee Papers; Tim Parsons, "The Community School Movement," *Community Issues* 2, no. 6 (December 1970): Ford Foundation Papers, roll 2080.

20. "Memo from Rhody McCoy to All Heads of Schools in Ocean Hill Brownsville School Project," 19 September 1967, Ford Foundation Papers; Podair, "Like Strangers," 108–109, 122; Clarence Taylor, *Knocking at Our Own Door,* 194–195; interview with Father John Powis by Richard Broadman; Berube and Gittell, *Confrontation at Ocean Hill–Brownsville,* 24–32.

21. Fantini, Magat, and Gittell, *Community Control and the Urban School,* 160; Urofsky, *Why Teachers Strike,* 15.

22. Clarence Taylor, *Knocking at Our Own Door*, 195–197; Urofsky, *Why Teachers Strike*, 15; "Sam Wright Blasts McCoy in Raging School Hassle," *New York Amsterdam News*, 1 June 1968; "Classes Go On Despite District Woes," *New York Times*, 1 June 1968.

23. Urofsky, *Why Teachers Strike*, 15; Clarence Taylor, *Knocking at Our Own Door*, 145–147; "Positions of Ocean Hill–Brownsville Elected School Governing Board," AJ-Committee Papers, 17 September 1968; "Ocean Hill–Brownsville School District Fact Sheet," AJCommittee Papers, no date.

24. Urofsky, *Why Teachers Strike*, 16–17.

25. "Ocean Hill Boardsville Scene of Fights, Chaos," *New York Amsterdam News*, 5 October 1968; Henry Hampton and Steve Fayer, *Voices of Freedom: An Oral History of the Civil Rights Movement from the 1950s through the 1980s* (New York: Bantam, 1990), 498–499; Berube and Gittell, *Confrontation at Ocean Hill–Brownsville*, 170.

26. Berube and Gittell, *Confrontation at Ocean Hill–Brownsville*, 167; Urofsky, *Why Teachers Strike*, 22; Fantini, Magat, and Gittell, *Community Control and the Urban School*, 164.

27. Urofsky, *Why Teachers Strike*, 22; interview with Father John Powis by Richard Broadman, in possession of author; interview with Maurice Reid by Richard Broadman, in possession of author; interview with Paul Chandler by Richard Broadman, in possession of author.

28. Hampton and Fayer, *Voices of Freedom*, 175; Urofsky, *Why Teachers Strike*, 22.

29. "Brownsville Community Council, Inc. Supports the Governing Board of Ocean Hill–Brownsville District 100%," no date, Papers of the Brownsville Community Council, Brooklyn Collection, Brooklyn Public Library; "Letter from Arnold Bennett to Congressman Bert Podell," 28 October 1968, Celler Papers; "Letter from Milton Pincus to Congressman Emanuel Celler," 11 November 1968, Celler Papers.

30. "Letter from Arnold Bennett to Congressman Bert Podell"; "Letter from the Office of Economic Opportunity to Congressman Emanuel Celler," 15 November 1968, Celler Papers.

31. "Ocean Hill District: Will It Survive?" *New York Post*, 29 July 1969; "Board Likely to Scrap Ocean Hill," *New York Post*, 29 September 1969; Urofsky, *Why Teachers Strike*, 17; Clarence Taylor, *Knocking at Our Own Door*, 204–205; Podair, "Like Strangers," 190–193.

32. For the long-term impact of the crisis, see Albert Vorspan, "Blacks and Jews, in James Baldwin, ed., *Black Anti-Semitism and Jewish Racism* (New York: Richard Baron, 1969); Andrew Hacker, "Jewish Racism, Black Anti-Semitism," in Paul Berman, ed., *Blacks and Jews: Alliances and Arguments* (New York: Doubleday, 1994), 154–163; Johnathon Kaufman, *Broken Alliance: The Turbulent Times between Blacks and Jews in America* (New York: Simon and Schuster, 1995); Murray Friedman, *What Went Wrong?*

33. Podair, "Like Strangers," 11, 74, 87. See also Podair, "'White' Values, 'Black' Values."

34. "Ocean Hill Target for Black Militants," *New York Amsterdam News*, 22 March 1969; interview with Paul Chandler, 8 February 2000. On the rise of black nationalism, see Woodard, *A Nation within a Nation*.

Chapter 9

1. "Brownsville Erupts in Violence Over Huge Accumulations of Garbage," *New York Times*, 13 June 1970.

2. Ibid.; "A Neighborhood Picks up the Pieces," *New York Daily News*, 14 June 1970.

3. "A Neighborhood Picks up the Pieces"; "Brownsville Erupts in Violence over Huge Accumulations of Garbage."

4. "Promise Riot Area a New Broom," *New York Daily News*, 14 June 1970; "Refuse Still Deep in Brownsville," *New York Times*, 30 June 1970; Pete Hamill, "The Brownsville Troubles," *New York Post*, 15 June 1970.

5. "Disaster-Area Status Sought by Brownsville," *New York Daily News*, 7 October 1970.

6. "Looting and Clashes with Police Erupt in Brownsville," *New York Times*, 6 May 1971; "Firemen Say They'll Balk without Protection in Riots," *New York Times*, 7 May 1971; "Brownsville Back to Normal Despair," *New York Times*, 8 May 1971.

7. "State Leaders Invited to See 'Genocide' in Brownsville Area," *New York Times*, 8 May 1971; "The Brownsville Way of Life: Grinding Poverty and Squalor," *New York Times*, 9 May 1971; "Brownsville: All Fall Down," *New York Newsday*, 14 June 1971; "In Brownsville, Looting Is a Condition of Life," *New York Times*, 4 September 1971.

8. "Pitkin Avenue: Its Old Glory Hard to Discern Amid Blight," *New York Times*, 4 July 1977; "Poverty-Stricken Brownsville Has History of Despair," *New York Times*, 22 September 1974; "And a Man Who Knew It When," *New York Post*, 25 August 1972.

9. "Urban Renewal in Brownsville: The Management of Urban Renewal in Brownsville Area 15, 1960–1973," introduction to *New York State Study Commission for New York City* (New York: New York State Study Commission, 1973), City Planning Commission, "Focus on Brownsville," *Model Cities Newsletter*, 14 November 1970, Papers of Mayor John Lindsay, New York City Municipal Archives, New York, New York (hereinafter "Lindsay Papers").

10. Housing and Redevelopment Board, "News," 28 December 1966, Lindsay Papers; "Letter from Al Jurist, Chairman Earl W. Jimerson Co-op, to Congressman Emmanuel Celler," 3 October, 1962, Celler Papers.

11. "A Minister Spurs Housing in Brownsville," *New York Times*, 8 April 1973; "$16 Million Project Starts in Brownsville," *Daily News*, 21 June 1971.

12. City Planning Commission, *Plan for the City Of New York: Part II, Brooklyn* (New York: City Planning Commission, 1969), 48–52; Model Cities Committee, "Release," 19 June 1960; "Focus on Brownsville," *Model Cities Newsletter*, 14 November 1970; City Planning Commission, "Urban Renewal Fact Sheet," 3 May 1967; City Planning Commission, "Urban Renewal Plan," July 1968.

13. City Planning Commission, "City Planning News," 20 July 1970; *Plan for the City Of New York: Part II, Brooklyn*, 165.

14. "Urban Renewal in Brownsville," 2–3, 15–16.

15. Ibid., 15, 57; Flora Davidson, "City Policy and Housing Abandonment: A Case Study of New York City, 1965–1973" (Ph.D. diss., Columbia University, 1977), 102–104.

16. Frank Braconi, "In Re in Rem: Politics and Expediency in New York's Housing Policy," in Michael Schill, ed., *Housing and Community Development in New York City: Facing the Future* (Albany: SUNY Press, 1999), 93–119, 94–95.

17. "Ghetto Portrait: A Family in Brownsville," *New York Post*, 13–18 August 1973.

18. "Fire Fighting Trainees Teach Safety to Students," *New York Times*, 23 May 1971; "O'Hagen Assails Paroling 3 Guilty of Arson Fatal to 6," *New York Times*, 16 October 1974; "3 Are Found Dead in Brooklyn Fire," *New York Times*, 10 August 1971; "Arson Unit Arrests, 3 Boys," *New York Times*, 15 September 1977; "Woman Says She Set 2,000 Fires," *New York Times*, 1 August 1972; "Tells Cops She Set 2,500 Fires," *Daily News*, 1 August 1972; "Suspicious Fires Found to Have Patterns in City," *New York Times*, 12 November 1980; "Gang Leader Gets 15 Years in 6 Fire Deaths," *Daily News*, 22 March 1975.

19. "Braconi, "In Re in Rem," 101–102; Jacqueline Leavitt and Susan Saegert, "The Community Household: Responding to Housing Abandonment in New York City," *APA Journal* 54 (1988): 489–508; New York Department of Housing Preservation and Development, *The In Rem Housing Program* (1984); "1,000 Apartment Houses Seized as Tax Delinquent," *Daily News*, 23 January 1974; "City Seizes 600 More Buildings," *New York Post*, 23 January 1974.

20. "Statement of Community District Needs for Fiscal Year 1985," City Planning Commission, 280; New York Department of Housing Preservation and Development, *The In Rem Housing Program, First Annual Report*, 1979; New York Department of Housing Preservation and Development, *The In Rem Housing Program, Sixth Annual Report*, 1986; "City to Seize 7,500 Occupied Apartments in Brooklyn," *New York Times*, 13 April 1986.

21. Leavitt and Saegert, "The Community Household," 490; Braconi, "In Re in Rem," 105–106; *The In Rem Housing Program, First Annual Report;* "Tenant Group Eyes 6 Buildings, *Daily News*, 16 January 1975; "City Is Target of a Rent Strike," *Daily News*, 2 August 1974; "Brownsville Is Building with Hope," *Daily News*, 22 February 1976; "Scores Shiver as Boilers in Tenements Turn Cold," *Daily News*, 9 January 1973; "City Crisis Jeopardizes Housing, " *Daily News*, 12 September 1975; "Tenant Group Asks O.K. to Save Housing," *Daily News*, 12 March 1974; Ocean Hill–Brownsville Tenants Association, "History and Summary of Program 2000"; "Housing Group Lets Go of Management Role," *Daily News*, 8 February 1999.

22. "New Housing Is Host to Hope," *Daily News*, 24 March 1976; "New Look on Strauss Street," *Daily News*, 18 December 1977; "HDA Release," 29 January 1975; "Urban Renewal Lessons in Failure," *New York Times*, 25 May 1983.

23. Philip Thompson, "Public Housing in New York City," in Schill, ed., *Housing and Community Development in New York City*, 130–132; Brownsville Community Council, "Demands of Brownsville Public Housing Coordinating Council," 22 February 1972, Subject Files, Brooklyn Collection, Brooklyn Public Library.

24. Stern et al., *New York, 1960*, 924–925.

25. "City's Housing Administrator Proposes 'Planned Shrinkage' of Some Slums," *New York Times*, 3 February 1976.

26. Community Planning Board 16, Statistical Information, 1977, Subject Files Brooklyn Collection, Brooklyn Public Library, Brooklyn, New York; "Ghetto Portrait: A Family in Brownsville."

27. Wilson, *Truly Disadvantaged*, 39–40.

28. John Mollenkopf, *A Phoenix in the Ashes: The Rise and Fall of the Koch Coalition in New York City Politics* (Princeton: Princeton University Press, 1992), 47; John Kasarda, "Urban Change and Minority Opportunities," in Paul Peterson, ed., *The New Urban Reality* (Washington, D.C.: Brookings Institution, 1985), 44–47; Wilson, *Truly Disadvantaged*, 40–44. Roger Waldinger asserts that deindustrialization in New York City has had a less significant impact on blacks than it did in other cities for the simple reason that blacks never entered industrial occupations in large numbers. Because of discrimination, blacks were excluded from most of New York's factory jobs, and, as a result, they were not dislocated when these jobs were eliminated. Blacks, Waldinger argues, suffer high poverty rates not because they lost their jobs but because they never found stable employment to begin with. Since 1970, only a small percentage of blacks have entered working-class occupations such as the garment trades, low-skilled service positions, or construction, and blacks have been underrepresented in commercial operations. In both factory and commercial fields, Waldinger contends, whites have been replaced by new immigrants. Roger Waldinger, *Still the Promised City? African Americans and New Immigrants in Post-Industrial New York* (Cambridge: Harvard University Press, 1996), 6–12, 114, 206.

29. New York Police Department, "Crime Index," 1978.

30. "Crime in Projects Rose 30% Faster in Year," *New York Times*, 21 May 1975; "NYCHA News Release," May 1975, NYCHA Papers; Oscar Newman, *Defensible Space: Crime Prevention Through Urban Design* (New York: Collier, 1973), 39–49.

31. Interview with Maurice Reid, 9 February 2000; "Urban Renewal in Brownsville," 49. On the failure of black political mobilization to meet the needs of the poor, see Reed, *Stirrings in the Jug*.

32. "Anti-Antipoverty Election Is Blocked," *Daily News*, 20 July 1973; "Anti-Poverty Chiefs Assailed," *Daily News*, 25 September 1973; "Anti-Poverty Unit to Fight Ouster," *New York Times*, 16 September 1973; "City Plans to Oust BCC Despite Court Ruling," *New York Amsterdam News*, 29 September 1973; "The Anti-Poverty War, Brownsville vs. City," *New York Amsterdam News*, 10 November 1973; "Continuing Conflict in Brownsville," *New York Times*, 18 November 1973; "Community Aide Charges Corruption in Brownsville," *New York Times*, 29 November 1973.

33. "Ask Ouster and a Probe in School Board 23 Furor," *Daily News*, 13 October 197.

34. Connolly, *A Ghetto Grows in Brooklyn*, 218–220; "City's Tilden Plan Upheld by State," *New York Times*, 31 August 1973; "Mayor Resisting a Canarsie Stand," *New York Times*, 29 October 1972; "Canarsie: An Rx for Balance," *New York Post*, 21 November 1972; "Canarsie Parents Press Their Boycott of Schools," *New York Times*, 30 October 1972; "School Board Bids Canarsie Draft New Zoning Plan," *New York Times*, 2 November 1972.

35. "City Council Introduces a Bill Adding Six Seats," *New York Times*, 14 December 1972; "Sam Wright's Turf," *New York Times*, 14 April 1975; "Brooklyn Groups Rally Behind Project," *New York Times*, 23 January 1972; "200 Million Redevelopment Plan

for Brooklyn District 23," *New York Amsterdam News*, 18 September 1971; "Sam Wright Leaves Legacy of Black Clout," *New York Times*, 18 February 1998.

36. "2 Ex-State Senators Vie for Rep. Chisolm's Job," *New York Times*, 16 September 1982; "42nd District Suspicious of Claims Made by Politicians," *New York Newsday*, 29 January 1980.

37. "The American Underclass," *Time*, 29 August 1977, 14–15; Ken Auletta, *The Underclass* (New York: Random House, 1982); Charles Murray, *Losing Ground: American Social Policy, 1950–1980* (New York: Basic, 1984); Michael B. Katz, ed., *The Underclass Debate: Views from History*.

38. Timothy Ross, "The Impact of Community Organizing on East Brooklyn" (Ph.D. diss., University of Maryland, 1996); Samuel Freedman, *Upon This Rock*.

39. Zukin and Zwerman, "Housing for the Working Poor," 13–17; Samuel Freedman, *Upon This Rock*, 337.

40. "Nehemiah Marks Its Thousandth Low-Income House," *New York Times*, 29 September 1987; "City Agrees to Brooklyn Home Loans," *New York Times*, 28 July 1982; "Brooklyn Nails Down 1,000 New Homes," *New York Amsterdam News*, 3 November 1983; "City Gives Green Light to Build Up Housing in Brownsville," *Daily News*, 17 August 1982; "In Brownsville Churches Joining to Build Houses," *New York Times*, 1 August 1983.

41. "Nehemiah Plan: A Success But," *New York Times*, 22 September 1987; "Nehemiah Houses Are Homes," *Daily News*, 15 March 1998.

42. "From the Ground Up in East New York," *New York Times*, 4 April 1998; "Good Times Reflected in Home Buying Boom," *Daily News*, 28 May 1999.

43. Thompson, "Public Housing in New York City," 123; New York City Housing Authority, Project Data, January 1995.

Name	Year	Number of buildings/units	Population (estimated)
Rev. R. D. Brown	1985	2/200	216
Brownsville	1948	27/1,319	3,711
Marcus Garvey (A)	1975	3/318	909
Glenmore Plaza	1968	4/438	834
Howard	1955	10/814	2,189
Howard Ave (Twnhs)	1988	5/149	464
Howard–Park Place	1993	8/156	499
Hughes	1966	3/509	1,491
Low	1967	4/536	1,603
Prospect Plaza	1974	4/365	1,290
Ralph Avenue	1986	5/117	355
Tilden	1961	8/998	2,859
Van Dyke I	1955	22/1603	4,330
Van Dyke II	1964	1/112	129
Woodson	1970	2/407	423

Source: New York City Housing Authority Projects—Project Data, January 1, 1995.

44. Thompson, "Public Housing in New York City," 135.

45. Ibid., 138.

46. "Police Officer Fatally Shot in Brooklyn Housing Projects," *New York Times,* 14 April 1988; "Killings Crack Record," *Daily News,* 28 December 1988; "Living in Fear," *New York Newsday,* 24 October 1993; "Here Home Is Where the Horror Is," *Daily News,* 10 January 1988; "Mother Courage," *New York Magazine,* 6 December 1993; "Violence in the Ville," *New York Newsday,* 16 January 1994; "Almost 25% of Homicides in City in 1981 Tied to Drugs," *New York Times,* 19 March 1982.

47. Greg Donaldson, *The Ville: Cops and Kids in Urban America* (New York: Anchor Books, 1993), 56, 157; "Officers Arrested in Inquiry of 73rd Precinct," *New York Times,* 30 March 1994; Anna Quindlen, "Bad and Blue," *New York Times,* 3 October 1973.

48. For a discussion of New York City's crime decline, see "Symposium: Why Is Crime Decreasing?" *Journal of Criminal Law and Criminology* 88, no. 4 (summer 1998); "Crime Falls in Brooklyn North Precincts," *Daily News,* 8 July 1996; "Crime Is Down in Brownsville: A 73rd Precinct Project Plan Gets Results," *Daily News,* 6 October 1996; "Crime Statistics for 1999," *Daily News,* 10 February 2000.

49. Brownsville Community Development Corporation, "Description of the Brownsville CDC," 1999.

50. Ocean Hill–Brownsville Tenants Association, "History and Summary of Programs, 2000."

51. Ocean Hill–Brownsville Tenants Association, "History and Summary of Programs 2000"; "Peaceful Takeover," *New York Newsday,* 16 May 1992; "Abandoned Firehouse Is Occupied and Cleaned," *New York Times,* 16 May 1992; interview with Albion Liburd, director of operations, OHBTA, 23 March 2000; "Housing Group Lets Go of Management Role," *Daily News,* 8 February 1999.

52. Ross, "Impact of Community Organizing on East Brooklyn," passim; Samuel Freedman, *Upon This Rock,* passim.

53. Community Planning Board 16, "Introduction to Ocean Hill–Brownsville," 1998; "Clergymen Plan Massive 'Survival March' Through Brownsville," *New York Amsterdam News,* 26 November 1977; "Survival Rally in Brooklyn Free of Major Incidents," *New York Amsterdam News,* 22 November 1977; interview with Spurgeon Crayton, 24 November 1999.

54. Community Board 16, "Introduction to Ocean Hill–Brownsville," 1999; "Brownsville Community Center Gains," *New York Times,* 4 February 1973.

55. City Planning Commission, "Statement of Community Needs for Fiscal Year 1989, Community Board Number 16" (1989), 264–265; "Group Aims to Halt Construction of Brooklyn Juvenile Detention Center," *New York Amsterdam News,* 20 June 1992; "Kids Protest Jail Plan," *New York Newsday,* 17 June 1992; "New Jail Is for Youths but Neighborhood Feels Punished," *New York Times,* 3 May 1998; interview with Viola Greene, district manager, Community Board 16, 16 March 2000.

56. City Planning Commission, *Statement of Community Needs for Fiscal Year 1999* (New York: City Planning Commission, 1999), 294–295.

57. "Seeking a Change Where It All Began," *New York Times,* 20 December 1996; "District 23 Candidates Fight Apathy," *Daily News,* 6 May 1996; "Decentralization a Mixed Bag in New York City," *Daily News,* 31 December 1995; Lydia Segal, "The Pit-

falls of Political Decentralization and Proposals for Reform: The Case of New York City Public Schools," *Public Administration Review* 57 (March/April 1997): 141–149.

58. "Seeking a Change Where It All Began," *New York Times*, 20 December 1996; Jackie Robinson Center for Physical Culture, "Program Description," 1998.

59. "Seeking a Change Where It All Began," *New York Times*, 20 December 1996; "School Is Taken Over by Angry Parents in Protest," *New York Times*, 20 October 1993.

60. City Planning Commission, "Selected Education and Labor Force Characteristics, Brooklyn Community District 16," 1993.

61. "Shopping Spree: Pitkin Avenue/Manhattan Avenue," *New Brooklyn* (spring 1979): 40–43.

62. "Brownsville Pays a Small Price to Market Dreams," *Daily News*, 11 October 1994; Department of Business Services, "Pitkin Avenue BID Description," 2000; "A Report Criticizes Improvement Zones in New York City," *New York Times*, 8 November 1995; "Public Needs, Private Answers: Business Districts Gain, at Price of Accountability," *New York Times*, 20 November 1994.

63. "Real Estate: Brooklyn Industrial Complex," *New York Times*, 26 March 1986; Local Development Corporation of East New York, *The East Brooklyn Business to Business Directory*, 1999; "More Sites Spoken for in Industrial Park," *New York Times*, 13 December 1987.

Epilogue

1. Interview with Lenny Dryansky, by Richard Broadman, in possession of author.

2. Interview with Danny Culley, by Richard Broadman, in possession of author; Greg Donaldson, *The Ville*, 103–104.

3. On American mobility, see James M. Jasper, *Restless Nation: Starting Over in America* (Chicago: University of Chicago Press, 2000).

4. The literature on "community" in American society is voluminous. See, for example, Robert Bellah, *Habits of the Heart: Individualism and Commitment in American Life* (Berkeley: University of California Press, 1996); David W. Minar and Scott A. Greer, eds., *The Concept of Community: Readings with Interpretations* (Chicago: Aldine Publishing, 1969); Amitai Etzioni, *New Golden Rule: Community and Morality in a Democratic Society* (New York: Basic Books, 1996).

5. For a discussion of New York's urban renewal efforts in the first half of the century, see Max Page, *The Creative Destruction of Manhattan* (Chicago: University of Chicago Press, 1999), 69–110.

Index

Page numbers in *italics* refer to illustrations